Land and Lordship in
Early Modern Japan

Mark Ravina

# LAND AND LORDSHIP IN
# EARLY MODERN JAPAN

STANFORD UNIVERSITY PRESS
STANFORD, CALIFORNIA 1999

Stanford University Press
Stanford, California
© 1999 by the Board of Trustees of the
Leland Stanford Junior University
Printed in the United States of America

CIP data are at the end of the book

The costs of publishing this book have
been supported in part by an award from
the Hiromi Arisawa Memorial Fund
(named in honor of the renowned econo-
mist and the first chair of the Board of the
University of Tokyo Press) and financed
by the generosity of Japanese citizens
and Japanese corporations to recognize
excellence in scholarship on Japan.

*To Menachem Rosenbajm,*
*in loving memory*

# Acknowledgments

This study has its origins in a 1985 seminar paper for Peter Duus. I was then interested in the Freedom and Popular Rights Movement of the 1880s, particularly the movement's class composition. In that context I examined the class composition of Japan's first prefectural assemblies and found an intriguing pattern. In the southwest, *shizoku* (former samurai) dominated the assemblies, often with majorities of over 90 percent. In the Kantō and the Kinai, by contrast, *shizoku* representation was much lower, and the class composition of the assemblies was more in line with the class composition of the prefectures. In some cases voters sent only commoners to the assembly, and *shizoku* were actually underrepresented. These differences in class composition were clearly linked with Tokugawa patterns of rule. In the southwest, powerful domain governments dominated political life. In the Kantō and Kinai, by contrast, daimyo holdings were often fragmented, and critical administrative issues were handled by councils of wealthy and influential commoners. These Tokugawa class structures set precedents for the Meiji era. I also discerned a link between class demography in the general population and in the assembly. The *shizoku* tended to be heavily overrepresented in areas where they comprised a large proportion of the general population. In these areas there were not enough government posts, or government revenue, to keep samurai in the castle towns. Instead, they moved out to the countryside, where they displaced and competed with commoner farmers and merchants for political and economic power.

This book, however, is not about Meiji politics but about political economy in the Tokugawa era. The more I examined Meiji prefectural assemblies, the more I grew interested in the Tokugawa processes they reflected. Meiji politics appear in this study only as an epilogue, as a denouement to the Tokugawa era. This book is something quite different from what I planned nearly ten years ago, and my greatest intellectual debt is therefore to my dissertation adviser, Peter Duus. His encyclopedic knowledge of Japanese history allowed me to range back over a century from my original thesis question. Further, over many years, and despite periodic evidence to the contrary, he held steadfast to the conviction that given complete freedom I would nonetheless complete a coherent dissertation and publishable book. I hope this volume in some measure justifies his confidence. I also owe thanks to Harold Kahn and James Ketelaar, who pressed me to engage broader philosophical issues, and to Jeffrey Mass, who reminded me of the need to interrogate the seemingly obvious.

My understanding of Tokugawa politics has been shaped by both German historiography and the intriguing parallels between early modern German and early modern Japanese history. Although this is not a comparative history, I am convinced that early modern Japan is best studied when we abandon the notion that Japan is *sui generis*. For my understanding of German history, however shallow, I am indebted to three great historians of central Europe: Franklyn Ford of Harvard, who first taught me that Prussia was not Germany; James Sheehan of Stanford, who taught me to problematize the nation-state; and James Melton of Emory, who taught me the intricate politics of German historiography.

At Hitotsubashi University I benefited from seminars by Sasaki Junnosuke and Minami Ryōshin. Sections of this book rebut some of Sasaki's major theses, and this iconoclasm is due in no small part to Professor Sasaki himself, who seemed to enjoy my ideas more the less he agreed with them. I am grateful for Professor Sasaki's generosity with both his time and critical insight. Minami Ryōshin's seminar in economic history helped me put local history in a broader context. He and Makino Fumio also saved me from several pitfalls in applied econometrics. Saitō Osamu helped me with a variety of issues in demographic and economic history and endured presentations of my research in both Japanese and English. Sugano Noriko and Sakurai Katsumi were nominally my paleography tutors, but taught me how to interpret texts as well as how to decipher them.

This study would not have been possible without the help of local historians. Watanabe Fumio took the time to answer my many questions about Yonezawa, and Amano Masatoshi and Miyoshi Shōichirō shared with me their knowledge of the Tokushima. My greatest debt, however, is to the historians of Tsugaru. Hasegawa Seiichiro and Namikawa Kenji both helped me on numerous occasions with matters both practical and intellectual. I owe special thanks to Tazawa Tadashi, retired restauranteur, devoted amateur historian, and co-director of the Hirosaki paleography society. Mr. Tazawa made my instruction in *komonjō* his hobby and when my research funds were stretched thin, put me up in his study and fed me at his restaurant. Without him my research would have been markedly more difficult and infinitely less fun. Thanks also to Akaishi Reiko, formerly of the Hirosaki municipal library. Although it is hard to object to Hirosaki's new, climate-controlled archives and on-line catalog, I will always recall fondly how Ms. Akaishi could move effortlessly from children's books, to seventeenth-century manuscripts, to fishing magazines, all with equal aplomb and with only occasional reliance on such novelties as a card catalog. Progress indeed comes at a price.

I owe an immense debt to Conrad Totman, who read the entire manuscript on two occasions and individual sections many times more. Ronald Toby, Philip Brown, James Bartholomew, and William Hauser made numerous valuable suggestions for improvements. Rob Eskildsen listened carefully and critically to my most inchoate ideas, and Greg Pflugfelder forced me to clarify what I thought was already clear. Peter Aronson helped me with economic theory and economic history. I benefited greatly from the chance to present this research at the Princeton Japan Seminar, the Southeast Japan Seminar, and the Emory University James Allen Vann Seminar. Special thanks are due Marius Jansen, David Howell, and Sheldon Garon of Princeton for their specialists' insight and to Susan Socolow and

Michael Bellesiles of Emory for their comparative perspectives. David Lurie and Robert Hellyer helped me catch numerous gremlins. In the last stages of revision, my undergraduate students were among my most valuable critics, forcing me to abandon "dissertationese" and to engage the interested nonspecialist.

The research and writing of this study would not have been possible without the financial support of a number of institutions. A dissertation fellowship from the Japan Foundation allowed me to go to Japan in the first place and a grant from the Mabelle MacLeod Lewis Foundation allowed me to concentrate on writing once I returned. The Emory University Research Council supported a second trip to Japan and a semester's leave from teaching. The Northeast Asian Council of the Association for Asian Studies provided funds for a final, critical visit. Parts of this study appeared in different form in my article "State-building and Political Economy in Early-modern Japan" (1995). I gratefully acknowledge the permission of the *Journal of Asian Studies* to reproduce parts of that work here. Thanks also to Muriel Bell and Pamela MacFarland Holway of Stanford University Press for shepherding the manuscript through the lengthy publication process.

My parents, Oscar and Ruth, bit their tongues when I rejected both classical music and law school for graduate work in Japanese history and supported an endeavor they secretly suspected was a very bad idea. Their financial support in anxious moments was all the more valuable because it was so timely. My Japanese "parents," Ishikawa Quta and Yōko, kept me happy and healthy through their generosity, companionship, and good humor.

My wife, Kristin, knows enough about Japanese history to be an insightful reader, but has refused to become my editor. Indeed, she spent the past few years scrupulously avoiding my manuscript and has doggedly rejected the idea that her purpose in life is to help me write books. She has been steadfast in her conviction that writing a book provides no exemption from seeing movies, changing diapers, mopping floors, or playing ball with the kids. Without her this book would have been finished years ago, and my life would be much less happy and rich.

# Contents

*List of Tables and Figures*     xiii

*List of Maps*     xv

*List of Abbreviations*     xvii

*A Note to the Reader*     xix

Introduction     1

1    Land and Lordship: Ideology and Political Practice in Early Modern Japan     16

Assessing States, 23    Language and Land, 28    Language and Translation, 31    Language and Sovereignty, 34

2    The Nerves of the State: The Political Economy of Daimyo Rule     46

Sources of Revenue, 53    Demands for Expenditure, 61    Politics as Process, 69

3    Profit and Propriety: Political Economy in Yonezawa     71

Taxes and Monopsony in Early Yonezawa, 80    Fiscal Decline and Internecine Strife, 84    Uesugi Harunori and the Politics of Virtue, 87    Rebuilding a Moral Economy, 93    Fiscal Reconstruction and the Legitimation of Profit, 97    Labors of the Samurai, 103    Entrepreneurs and Laborers, 110    Success and Debacle, 113

4 Land and Labor: Political Economy in Hirosaki 115

Land Development in Early Hirosaki, 120 Hirosaki
Commercial Policy: The Hōreki Reforms, 122 A Return
to Origins: The Tenmei Famine and Samurai Resettlement,
128 Peculation and Pragmatism: Land Reclamation
Policy, 141 The Politics of Subversion: The Tenpō Famine
and Tsugaru Sōdō, 147 Bakumatsu Hirosaki, 152

5 Markets and Mercantilism: Political Economy
in Tokushima 154

Fiscal Policy in Early Tokushima, 161 Commercialization
and Popular Resistance, 164 Commercial Reforms and
Indigo Exports, 168 The Nobility of Treason and the
Treason of Nobility: The Fall of Hachisuka Shigeyoshi,
176 The Rise of Cartels, 180 The Tenpō Crisis in
Tokushima, 187 Millenarianism in Tokushima, 192

Conclusion 194

Appendix 213
Glossary 225
Notes 233
Bibliography 255
Index 271

# Tables and Figures

*Tables*

1. Hirosaki Stipend Reductions Under the Tenpō Reforms    151
A1. Data for Domains, 1869–71    216
A2. Data for Prefectures, 1869–74    221
A3. Domain to Prefecture Aggregation Scheme    222
A4. Regression Parameters for Domains    222
A5. Regression Parameters for Prefectures    223

*Figures*

1. Scatterplot of Output and Taxation for Domains (linear scale)    50
2. Scatterplot of Output and Taxation for Domains (logarithmic scale)    50
3. Scatterplot of Population Ratio and Taxation for Domains (linear scale)    51
4. Scatterplot of Population Ratio and Taxation for Domains (logarithmic scale)    51
5. Yonezawa Population and Sex Ratio    77
6. Yonezawa Population by Gender    78
7. Yonezawa Domain Revenue, 1791    79
8. Hirosaki Commoner Population    119

 9. Farm Wages and Rice Prices in Hirosaki                    129
10. Hirosaki Domain Expenditures, 1815                        146
11. Tokushima Commoner Population                             157
12. Land Reclamation in Myōzai district, Tokushima            162
13. Tokushima Indigo Cube Prices                              185
14. Tokushima Indigo Production                               186

# Maps

1. Boundaries of Yonezawa, Tokushima, and
   Hirosaki Domains 10
2. Towns, Villages, and Roads in Yonezawa 72
3. Changes in Uesugi Holdings, 1590–1868 74
4. Towns, Villages, and Roads in Hirosaki 116
5. Towns, Villages, and Roads in Tokushima 156
6. Tokushima Hōreki Indigo Protests 166
7. Tokushima Tenpō Protests 188

# Abbreviations

AKS    Aomori kenshi hensan iinkai, ed. *Aomori kenshi.* 8 vols. 1926.

GG    Yonezawa shishi hensan iinkai, ed. *Godaidai goshikimoku.* 6 vols. Yonezawa: Yonezawa shishi hensan iinkai, 1982–86.

HN    Aomori ken bunkazai hogo kyōkai, ed. *Hirayama nikki.* Tokyo: Kokusho kankōkai, 1963.

HP    Hanpō kenkyūkai, ed. *Hanpōshū.* 12 vols. Tokyo: Sōbun-sha, 1959–75.

HSS    Hirosaki shishi hensan iinkai, ed. *Hirosaki shishi.* Vol. 1, *Hansei hen.* Vol. 2, *Meiji-Taishō-Shōwa hen.* Hirosaki: Hirosaki shi, 1963–64.

IKNR    *Iwanami kōza Nihon rekishi.* 23 vols. (1962–64). Second ed., revised and enlarged, 26 vols. (1975–77). Tokyo: Iwanami.

NSST    Chihōshi kenkyū kyōgikai, ed. *Nihon sangyōshi taikei.* 8 vols. Tokyo: Tōkyō daigaku shuppankai, 1960–61.

NST    Ienaga Saburō, Inoue Mitsusada, Sagara Tōru, Nakamura Yoshihiko, Bitō Masahide, Maruyama Masao, and Yoshikawa Kōjirō, eds. *Nihon shisō taikei.* 67 vols. Tokyo: Iwanami shoten, 1970–82.

YKS    Yamagata ken, ed. *Yamagata kenshi.* 5 vols. Yamagata shi: Yamagata ken, 1982–87.

YKSS    Yamagata ken, ed. *Yamagata kenshi shiryōhen.* 21 vols. Tokyo: Gannandō shoten, 1960–81.

# A Note to the Reader

*Dates*

Prior to 1873 Japan used a lunar calendar with twelve months each of 29 or 30 days for a total year of about 354 days. Intercalary or "leap" months were used to keep this lunar calendar synchronous with the solar year. Following historiographic convention I have expressed lunar calendar dates in year/month/day format and have converted Japanese years, but not months or days, to the Gregorian calendar. Thus, the fifth day of the eleventh lunar month of the sixth year of the Hōreki era is rendered as 1756/11/5. Intercalary months are represented by the letter "i." Thus, 1756/11i/5 represents the fifth day of the eleventh intercalary (or twelfth) month of 1756. The Japanese year began "late," and the exact Gregorian date for the Japanese New Year varied between January 21 and February 19.

*Domain Names and Personal Names*

Early modern domains were commonly known by the names of their castle towns, the local government seats. Larger domains, however, often went by the names of their provinces. The Shimazu family's holdings in Satsuma province, for example, are known as Satsuma domain, rather than Kagoshima domain, the name of the castle town. Some names are irregular. The Mōri house's holdings in Nagato province, for example, are commonly known as Chōshū, a variant term for Nagato. Rather than artificially systematize domain names, I have followed convention and relied on the standard reference work *Hanshi sōran*, edited by Kodama Kōta and Kitajima Masamoto.

Japanese personal names are presented in the traditional fashion, family name followed by given name.

## Weights and Measures

### VOLUME

| | | | |
|---|---|---|---|
| 1 *gō* | | 0.18 liters | 0.38 pints |
| 1 *to* | 100 *gō* | 18.04 liters | 4.77 gallons |
| 1 *hyō* | 4 *to* | 72.16 liters | 19.06 gallons |
| | 4.5 *to* (in Yonezawa) | 81.18 liters | 21.45 gallons |
| 1 *koku* | 10 *to* | 180.39 liters | 47.66 gallons |
| 1 *ninbuchi* | 5 *gō* per day, or 1.8 *koku* per year | 319.30 liters | 84.35 gallons |

### LENGTH

| | | | |
|---|---|---|---|
| 1 *sun* | | 3.03 cm. | 1.19 inches |
| 1 *shaku* | 10 *sun* | 30.30 cm. | 0.99 feet |

### AREA

| | | | |
|---|---|---|---|
| 1 *bu* or *tsubo* | | 3.31 sq. meters | 3.95 sq. yds. |
| 1 *se* | 30 *bu* | 99.18 sq. meters | 118.64 sq. yds. |
| 1 *ninyaku* | 200 *bu* | 661.20 sq. meters | 790.93 sq. yds. |
| 1 *tan* | 10 *se* | 991.80 sq. meters | 0.25 acres |
| 1 *chō* | 10 *tan* | .992 hectares | 2.45 acres |

### WEIGHT

| | | | |
|---|---|---|---|
| 1 *fun* | | 0.37 grams | 0.013 ounces |
| 1 *momme* or *me* | 10 *fun* | 3.75 grams | 0.13 ounces |
| 1 *kan* | 1,000 *momme* or *me* | 3.75 kilograms | 8.27 lbs. |

Land and Lordship in
Early Modern Japan

# Introduction

In 1785 Uesugi Harunori, the daimyo of Yonezawa, marked the occasion of his retirement with a short epistle on statecraft. Written for his heir, Norihiro, it was intended as a father's advice on ruling the domain and sought to address the central questions of governance: how and why should daimyo rule?

The state (*kokka*) is inherited from one's ancestors and passed on to one's descendants: it should not be administered selfishly.

The people belong to the state: they should not be administered selfishly.

The lord exists for the sake of the state and the people: the state and the people do not exist for the sake of the lord.[1]

Uesugi Harunori's concise missive is arguably the best-known Japanese political document of the eighteenth century. Because Harunori was held up as a model of virtue in prewar Japanese textbooks, the epistle was widely disseminated among the general populace. To this day facsimiles of the original manuscript, now embellished by a portrait of its author, are available as souvenirs at the Uesugi shrine in Yonezawa. The document has also received sustained scholarly attention: it is cited in numerous studies of early modern political thought. Historians have commonly focused on the strong Mencian aspect of Harunori's notion of lordship. Although the lord did not rule at the behest of the people, he existed, nonetheless, to serve them. Harunori thus made peacetime civil administration the central task of warlord rule. By basing his legitimacy on the peace and prosperity of his subjects, Harunori presented the most enlightened face of Japanese enlightened despotism.[2]

As compelling as what Harunori included in his epistle is what he saw fit to exclude. His instructions make no mention of either the shogunate or the emperor. Harunori was scarcely unaware of the extent of shogunal power. As he wrote, his retainers and commoners were groaning under the burden of castle repairs mandated by the shogunate. For Harunori, however, the essence of statecraft was not serving the shogunate but honoring one's ancestors and providing for one's descendants by nurturing one's subjects. He was not challenging or defying the shogunate, and his epistle was not taken as an affront. Rather, he was conveying a simple fact of early modern politics: the shogunate was peripheral to broad areas of political practice.

Harunori's epistle also lacked any reference to warfare or combat. Although the Uesugi family was, by lineage, a warrior house, no member of it had seen combat since the early 1600s. Samurai still carried swords, but as marks of status, not signs of military preparedness. Eighteenth-century daimyo continued to rely on their sixteenth-century ancestors as a source of legitimacy, but they confronted a radically different political environment. For daimyo like Uesugi Harunori the focus of politics was not warfare or a struggle for national authority but government finance and political economy. Indeed, Harunori's glowing reputation as a ruler stemmed from his success in promoting sericulture and weaving in his domain. This concern with economic matters explains Harunori's failure to mention shogunal authority. He would not have thought to slight the shogunate's authority over diplomacy or foreign affairs, but such matters were of peripheral concern in eighteenth-century Yonezawa. His primary concerns, the moral and economic rejuvenation of his domain, were the areas where shogunal control and oversight were weakest.

Harunori's sense of independence from shogunal control was partly a product of his family's elite status. The Uesugi were among a small group of noble families known as the "eighteen country-holding houses" (*jūhachi kunimochi ke*). These houses were set apart by both their distinguished ancestry and the size of their holdings: a "country holder" ruled either an entire province or a contiguous parcel of comparable size. These daimyo enjoyed far greater freedom from shogunal control than did others of their class: the shogunate itself was reluctant to intervene in their internal affairs. Daimyo like Uesugi Harunori thus constituted a distinct minority of the country's 260-odd daimyo. It was the size of their holdings that made Harunori and his fellow "country holders" disproportionately important. The formal investitures of the "eighteen country holders" alone comprised one-third of the territory of Japan.[3] Below the official "country holders," we can discern a more amorphous category of powerful lords and great domains. These lords lacked the formal distinction of "country holder" but manifested many of the same qualities. They also ruled large, contiguous parcels and enjoyed special treatment from the shogunate. In their political rhetoric and economic policies, they struck an uneasy balance between their roles as shogunal vassals and as petty sovereigns.

Uesugi Harunori's epistle highlights the central question of this study: how did rulers in "country" domains justify and exercise their power? To answer it we must first locate daimyo power within the broader matrix of early modern politics. How was daimyo rule situated in relation to shogunal authority, imperial authority, and the political authority of the samurai estate? What was the ambit of daimyo authority within the early modern political order? Then we must explore the dialogic interaction between domain governments and their subject populations. Daimyo rule was shaped and defined by the actions of commoners. The ultimate end of most domain practices was to secure revenue from the subject population. A daimyo's political competence was thus defined by his ability to compel or induce popular compliance with government demands. The understanding that popular resistance was a powerful check on daimyo rule was implicit in Harunori's edict to rule in the interests of "the state and the people." The challenge for domain statesmen was to make the government's fiscal demands seem both tenable and legitimate.

These questions of political legitimacy and adaptation are not new. Indeed, the bibliography on Tokugawa politics and political

economy is both deep and broad. My interest here is in a striking la-
cuna in English-language scholarship. Research on Tokugawa politics has focused largely on the establishment of the Tokugawa order
in the seventeenth century and the collapse of that order in the
1850s and 1860s. By contrast, the intervening two centuries have
received relatively little attention. As Conrad Totman has observed,
"For a long time the eighteenth century was treated as the 'dead'
middle of the Tokugawa period, the poorly articulated time after the
system was established and before its disintegration became pronounced." As a result, "politics of the eighteenth century have received spotty treatment," with "the domains of the major daimyo"
forming one of the most notable oversights.[4] Virtually all American
studies of domain politics treat either the formation of the Tokugawa order or its demise. Albert Craig's *Chōshū in the Meiji Restoration*, for example, examines the role of Chōshū in toppling the
shogunate. Marius Jansen's studies of Tosa domain explore its foundations in the early seventeenth century and its anti-shogunal politics
in the later nineteenth century. John Hall's influential study of Okayama domain examines the region and its politics from prehistory
until 1700. James McClain's studies of Kaga focus on the construction of the domain castle town in the seventeenth century and Kaga
in the Meiji Restoration.[5] Regional politics in the intervening centuries have been examined only in broad surveys, such as Totman's
study of the Tokugawa shogunate and Bolitho's essay for the *Cambridge History of Japan*.[6] Domain politics of the mid-Tokugawa era
has been largely overlooked.

The sense that the mid-Tokugawa was a "dead" period stems in
part from the primacy in studies of domain politics written during
the 1960s and 1970s of two central topics, the formation of a new,
national order and the crisis that toppled it almost three centuries
later. These are topics of great moment, and their primacy in both
American and Japanese scholarship is natural. But in the context of
these questions, nothing much happened in the mid-Tokugawa era.
The national polity faced no massive internal or external disrup-
tions. There were no wars, no battles, and no abrupt changes in
structures of rule. The central political question for a lord like Uesugi
Harunori was not whether to support or oppose the shogunate in
battle or how to pacify a region torn by years of war but how to

manage the socioeconomic problems confronting his domain. My emphasis on these socioeconomic challenges leads to a markedly different paradigm from that of the classic American studies of the 1960s and 1970s. To employ a biographical metaphor, I am interested less in the birth and death of the core than with the midlife crises of the periphery.

My focus is on finances and taxation. My appreciation of the centrality of finances in Tokugawa politics is grounded in several observations. First, government finances reveal how daimyo rule was shaped by conflicting obligations. Daimyo needed to tax commoners in order to fulfill their financial obligations to their retainers. This demand for revenue was counterbalanced by popular resistance to taxation, as well as the daimyo's moral obligation to treat his commoners with "mercy" (*jihi*), "compassion" (*airen*), and "benevolence" (*jinkei*). It was the domain fisc, which channeled revenue from commoners to the daimyo and his retainers, that most directly reflected this tension, inasmuch as the daimyo's ability to please both his retainers and his commoners was ultimately constrained by the limits of his treasury. Second, finances point to the ambiguous boundaries of daimyo autonomy. The shogunate rarely challenged aspects of daimyo tax policy, treating such matters as local affairs. But daimyo financial concerns often provoked conflict with both the shogunate and other domains. When domain financial interests became enmeshed in interregional trade, daimyo found that their local interests cut across territorial boundaries. Finances were thus a local concern that could provoke national contestation and consequently point to what might be termed Tokugawa federalism: the coexistence of powerful regional regimes with a strong central government. Finally, unlike other variables, finances are statistically tractable and amenable to comparison across domains. Although quantitative measures such as per capita tax burden only partially reveal the impact of state demands, they do allow the construction of a general model relating taxation to demography and economic output. (I develop such a model in Chapter 2 and the Appendix.)

Tokugawa observers were well aware of the centrality of finances and taxation. In his famous essay *Seidan* (1727), Ogyū Sorai lamented how relations between samurai and commoner had degenerated into a simple struggle over resources. Since most samurai no longer lived in close contact with the commoners they ruled, the two parties knew each other largely as producers or consumers of government revenue. "The farmers know them as those who take away taxes [*nengu*], while they regard the farmers merely as those who pay taxes. The only sentiment that exists between them is, on the one hand, the desire to take taxes, and on the other, the determination to keep them from being taken."[7] For Sorai, this struggle represented the deterioration of samurai moral authority and pointed to the need for radical reform. My interest, however, is precisely in how this struggle defined early modern politics. How did samurai and commoners battle over resources? How was early modern politics shaped by their struggle? I call this set of issues and questions the political economy of daimyo rule.[8]

Two factors were central to the political economy of daimyo rule: demography and protoindustrialization. Commoners—farmers, artisans, merchants, or moneylenders—were the sole source of government revenue. Samurai, by contrast, were the major consumers. The expenses of the lord, and the stipends and emoluments of his retainers, accounted for the vast majority of domain income. Because government finance was so closely tied to class, it was closely linked with demography. For a given vassal band, the smaller the commoner population, the smaller the number of tax producers for each tax consumer. This led to a predictable correlation: domains with proportionally fewer commoners had comparatively higher taxes and faced severer competition over resources. Demography could thus ease or intensify the struggle between the classes. Cognizant of this relationship, daimyo and their retainers sought not only to adapt to demographic forces but to change them by promoting large commoner families and encouraging immigration from other domains.

Domains were concerned with demography because demography affected economic output. More commoners meant, all else being equal, more economic output and more government revenue. The complement to this strategy of increasing the number of commoners was increasing output per commoner. Here, too, we can discern a clear correlation: the more commoners produced per capita, the more the domain took. Domains could raise output per head by increasing factors of production, such as land, fertilizer, and tools. Such increases often coincided with population growth, since growing populations needed more land. But a stable population could produce more with increased acreage, fertilizer, and other capital inputs. This aspect of domain policy was reflected in the widespread land reclamation projects of the 1600s. Between 1598 and 1697 total arable land increased by nearly 40 percent, from roughly 18 million *koku* to over 25 million. Land reclamation was particularly extensive in less developed regions, such as the northeast and southwest.[9] Increased capital inputs and technologies such as double and triple cropping also served to raise both total output and per capita yield.

These methods of increasing output dominated seventeenth-century discourse on finances and political economy. The concept of producing more rice by using more people, land, and fertilizer was readily understood within the confines of Tokugawa agrarian discourse. But the rapid economic growth of the early Tokugawa era brought new issues to the fore. By the mid-eighteenth century, it was clear to most observers that manufactured products and cash crops were more lucrative than food grains or raw materials. Not only were expanding urban markets providing new demand for consumer goods, but the overproduction of food crops was also depressing the price of staples. This forced corresponding changes in domain strategies for increasing output. The seemingly straightforward strategies of producing more grain through greater application of land, labor, and capital were gradually eclipsed by strategies involving protoindustrialization: multistage systems of rural outwork producing commodities for distant markets.[10]

Protoindustrialization posed multilayered challenges to domain rule. First, geographic constraints on protoindustrial production, consumption, and distribution tended to entangle domains in complex, multiparty disputes over prices and market access. Because staples, such as rice and wheat, were produced throughout Japan, no single supplier could hope to affect prices. Protoindustrial products, by contrast, were often produced and consumed in circumscribed regions. Japanese indigo in the eighteenth century, for example, was produced largely in the Tokushima lowlands and consumed largely in the dyeing centers of Edo and Osaka. These market constraints made possible producer and consumer cartels. Protoindustrial production thus required that domains concern themselves with market intervention to an unprecedented degree. Not only could domains affect prices as producers, they also needed to prevent price manipulation by consumers. As domains sought to organize and sustain their own cartels, and to undermine hostile cartels, they found themselves in conflict with various domainal, shogunal, and merchant authorities.[11]

Protoindustrial production also brought to the fore issues of technology and quality. The ability of domains to exert monopoly or oligopoly control over commodities prices increased the appeal of protoindustrial production. To achieve this control domains did not hesitate to exploit monopolies that were more perceived than real. The ability of Tokushima to dominate the indigo market stemmed not from its complete monopoly on indigo production but from the consumer perception that Tokushima indigo was of distinct and superior quality. Tokushima indigo thus constituted a unique product for which standard indigo was only an imperfect substitute. The ability of Tokushima to affect supply and prices depended on the reputation of its indigo for quality. The prosperity of the domain thus came to hinge, indirectly, on the quality control of indigo exports. Similar forces were at work in Yonezawa, which was known for its distinctive linen-silk blend textiles. The domain sought not only to maintain quality standards but also to warn consumers about the danger of "counterfeit" Yonezawa weaving.

Protoindustrialization thus posed immense technical challenges for domains. Little in the warrior traditions of the sixteenth century prepared samurai for the demands of a consumer economy. But the intellectual challenges posed by protoindustrialization were still more profound. The legitimacy of the samurai class was grounded, in part, in their remove from commercial activity. Freed from the quotidian concerns of the market, samurai could reflect on the demands of selfless service and hone their moral faculties. This justified the samurai estate's monopoly on government offices. The rise of market intervention as a component of government service problematized this entire conception of samurai status. Ruling a highly commercial economy required an in-depth knowledge of, not a aloofness from, prices, profits, and markets. The effect of commerce on peasants was suspect as well. An influential, conservative strain of Tokugawa thought treated commercial production as morally pernicious and lauded the virtues of self-sufficient agriculture. The shogunate's Keian proclamation of 1649, for example, enjoined peasants from virtually all consumer activity. Peasants were not to wear cloth other than cotton, or to consume tea or sake. They were to eat barley rather than rice, and to produce their own farm and household tools. Although farmers were allowed to buy and sell grain for purposes of tax remission, they were warned of the evils of a "commercial mind." Instead, the edict lauded frugality, by which the authorities meant self-sufficiency.[12] Similar sentiments permeate domain tracts on political economy. Commercialization, argued conservatives, was morally corrupting and socially corrosive. It led to an increasing appetite for luxuries, undermined the spirit of frugality, and thus eroded the moral fabric of the domain.

Domains could, of course, adopt an extreme mercantilist approach toward consumer products, encouraging production for "export" while restricting the consumption of "imported" goods. But it was precisely the limits of self-sufficiency that drove peasants to pursue protoindustrial production. Although attempts to halt or roll back commercialization were not uncommon, such efforts rarely had lasting effects. This did not ease the plight of administrators who strove to shape protoindustrialization to the advantage of their domains. Such reforms proved not only difficult but politically dangerous because, as Bolitho has observed, any deviation from former practice could be treated by its opponents as a breach of faith.[13]

In this study I examine the political implications of demographic change and protoindustrial development through the history of three domains: Yonezawa, Tokushima, and Hirosaki. Because my interest was in the effects of change, I rejected the choice of a single "representative" domain. Instead I followed the observation that since variables need to vary, a broad range of values best reveals important patterns of association. I therefore selected three different sets of extreme values: Yonezawa, with a proportionally large samurai population and a commercial economy; Hirosaki, with a proportionally large samurai population and an underdeveloped economy; and Tokushima, with a proportionally small samurai population and a highly commercial economy. Politics in each of these domains reflected local socioeconomic conditions. In both Yonezawa and Hi-

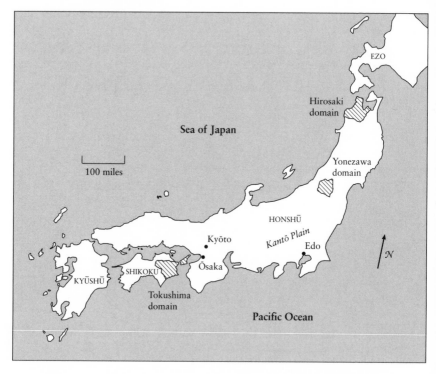

Map 1. Boundaries of Yonezawa, Tokushima, and Hirosaki Domains

rosaki, the burden of a large samurai class led the government to reevaluate radically the nature of samurai service. In Yonezawa, retainer households were encouraged to weave and sell cloth, openly violating traditional strictures against the pursuit of profit by samurai. In Hirosaki samurai were forcibly resettled on the land, where they were supposed to become a self-sufficient, rural gentry. In Tokushima, by contrast, the relatively large commoner population obviated the need for any such redefinition of samurai service.

Politics in Tokushima was shaped, instead, by commerce. The domain's heavy reliance on indigo exports made the government acutely aware of the power of the urban cartels that controlled fabric dyeing.[14] Combating the monopsony power of Edo and Osaka dye wholesalers became a major challenge for Tokushima administrators, leading ultimately to confrontations with the shogunate.

Further, protoindustrial production made the domain aware of commercial issues such as quality control. A drop in the quality of its indigo would undermine domain finances by reducing demand for the domain's premier export. The government thus became involved in distinctly non-martial activities, such as certifying the kind of sand used to pack indigo for shipment. Yonezawa engaged in similar enterprises. Concerned by the long-term implications of shoddy cloth, the domain took action to control the quality of Yonezawa textiles and thus insure continued demand for the domain's products. In Hirosaki, by contrast, protoindustrial activity was minimal: the domain's economy was based overwhelmingly on food grains. Hirosaki retainers thus approached economic development in far simpler terms. For most Hirosaki reformers and administrators, economic growth meant more rice.

By comparing these three distinct situations, I intend to show how the underlying forces of economic development and demographic change framed the challenges faced by Tokugawa statesmen. Demography and protoindustrialization did not determine political practice through some direct materialist linkage. But because they were the object of political strategies, they shaped both the magnitude and nature of the key political tensions.

The challenges of demographic change and protoindustrial development framed political debate in all domains. Great domains such as Yonezawa, Tokushima, and Hirosaki, however, produced a distinctive political discourse. Their size, contiguity, and ascriptive status combined to generate a level of political autonomy and authority markedly superior to that of the vast majority of daimyo holdings. First, their greater size allowed what might be called political economies of scale. Government monopolies, monopsonies, and product promotion offices were all more easily and effectively managed in large domains. Second, contiguous domains enjoyed corresponding spatial advantages. Because of geographic contiguity, the political borders of great domains commonly coincided with economic boundaries. Tokushima, for example, ruled the entire Yoshino river valley and its major port, the town of Tokushima. The entire process of indigo ball production, from cultivation to curing to shipping, occurred within the political purview of the Hachisuka, the domain's daimyo house. In smaller domains, by contrast, commercial processes commonly cut across domain borders, thus constraining the ability of any single governmental authority to control production.[15] Commerce thereby served to pierce and attenuate the boundaries of smaller domains but tended to strengthen economic integration in larger, contiguous domains.

The distinct political culture of great domains was reflected, in part, by the status system of early modern daimyo. In legal documents, such as the "Laws Governing the Military Houses" (*buke shohatto*) and the "Tokugawa House Edicts" (*gotōke reijō*), the shogunate explicitly described a class of "country-holding" daimyo with distinct powers and privileges. Roughly twenty of the largest and most established daimyo houses were distinguished by this elite designation.[16] The rank of "country holder" was linked both to the size of a lord's investiture and to the distinction of his lineage. As descendants of powerful sixteenth-century warlords, the Hachisuka of Tokushima and the Uesugi of Yonezawa were both ranked as "country holders." The Tsugaru of Hirosaki, by contrast, ruled one of the largest territories in the realm but lacked an ancestry sufficiently noble for "country holder" rank. By assiduously courting shogunal favor, however, the Tsugaru gradually garnered many attributes of "country holder" status. In 1808 their nominal investiture was increased to 100,000 *koku*, and they were then seated together with the Hachisuka and the Uesugi in the prestigious *ōhiroma* for shogunal audiences. In 1824 Tsugaru Nobuyuki, the eleventh Tsugaru daimyo, was granted fourth court rank (*shihin*), a further mark of a "country holder." Despite these promotions, the Tsugaru always remained a notch below the daimyo elite. Intriguingly, the Tsugaru's income (*gendaka*) was roughly double that of the Uesugi, although their nominal investiture (*hōdaka* or *omotedaka*) was smaller.[17] The two domains thus reveal the disjunction of practical and ascriptive hierarchies.

The lesser status of the Tsugaru had a discernible impact on domain political practice. Political discourse in Hirosaki was markedly less "nationalistic" than in Yonezawa and showed a lesser sense of the domain as an autonomous regime. We can delineate nonetheless a political culture and political language distinct to great domains such as Hirosaki, Tokushima, and Yonezawa. While lesser domains were commonly described as "territories" (*ryō*) or "holdings" (*ryōbun*), the seminal terms in great domains were "country" (*kuni*) and "state" (*kokka*).

The translation of *kuni* as "country" and of *kokka* as "state" violates historical convention. *Kokka*, in early modern Japanese, could refer to a variety of institutions ranging from ancient Chinese kingdoms, to the shogunate, to a large domain like Yonezawa. *Kuni* could mean entities as diverse as kingdoms, provinces, and domains. My insistence on translating *kuni* as "country" and *kokka* as "state" stems from my reading of texts, such as Harunori's epistle, that rely on the multiple meanings of *kokka*. In declaring that a lord serves the *kokka*, Harunori was making at least three coincident statements. In the narrowest sense, he was referring to the traditions of the Uesugi house. In this case, *kokka* means Yonezawa domain, the Uesugi patrimony. In a broader sense, Harunori was making a general, normative statement about Japanese political institutions: all lords, including the shogun, should serve their "states." In this case *kokka* means both the shogunate and various domains. Finally, by declaring that the lord exists for the sake of the people, Harunori was engaging classical Chinese texts such as the works of Mencius and the *Spring and Autumn Annals*. At this level, Harunori was making a broad philosophical statement about lordship and implicitly styling himself as a lord seeking to exemplify enlightened rule. In this sense *kokka* refers to all polities in which a lord determines the fate of his people. Yonezawa was thus grouped with the ancient Chinese Chou dynasty as a "state."

These multiple layers of meaning are effaced in conventional translations, but they are critical to understanding Tokugawa politics. Historians have traditionally rendered both *kuni* and *kokka* as "domain" when using these terms in the context of domain discourse. It is also common practice to render as "domain" the terms *ryō* (territory), *ryōbun* or *ryōchi* (holding), and *han* (domain or fief). Although entirely reasonable, such translations denude *kokka* of its multiple valences and thus conceal an important aspect of Tokugawa political discourse. Although *kokka* did not mean "state" in the modern sense of a fully sovereign political entity, the term set great daimyo apart from other lords. In describing their domains as "states," "country-holding" daimyo were establishing their unique position within the Tokugawa polity. Great domains rarely applied terms as subservient as "holding" (*ryōbun*) to themselves. Smaller daimyo, by contrast, rarely used terms as potent as *kokka*. Because conventional translations fail to convey how such terms marked distinctions among the daimyo, they obscure important aspects of daimyo ideology.

These differences in language are critical because they flag the distinct philosophy of rule of great domains. As Harunori's epistle reveals, the term "state" signaled a complex balance between independence and subservience. Although bound by ties of vassalage to the shogun, the daimyo of great domains simultaneously saw themselves as sovereign lords. This balance was a factor in the political practice of all domains. As Harold Bolitho has observed, even *fudai* daimyo, the lords who staffed the shogunate's administration, sometimes proved unwilling to subordinate local interests to shogunal interests. The terms "state" and "country," however, point to an ideology in which the domain was far more than an investiture. We can speak, instead, of "country" daimyo: great lords who defended local interests in grandiose terms, such as serving the "state," or succoring "the people."

My final criterion for examining Yonezawa, Tokushima, and Hirosaki was contrarian. I have chosen three domains that played little part in the Meiji Restoration. My goal here was to disentangle domain autonomy from the destruction of the shogunate. As Albert Craig observed over 35 years ago, domain autonomy or domain "nationalism" were necessary but not sufficient conditions for opposing the shogunate in the 1860s.[18] Indeed the domains that overthrew the shogunate (Satsuma, Chōshū, Tosa, and Saga) were all "country-holding" domains. But a majority of daimyo, great and small, were bystanders in the Restoration struggle. Yonezawa, Hirosaki, and Tokushima shared several key qualities with the great domains that toppled the shogunate. All three were large and geographically contiguous. All three were ruled by noble families that had distinguished themselves in sixteenth-century combat. All three were perduring political units: none of the three domains was moved or reduced by shogunal order after the 1660s. But unlike the "great southwestern domains" (*seinan yūhan*) that overthrew the shogunate, neither Yonezawa, nor Tokushima, nor Hirosaki opposed the shogunate in a sustained or important way. Hirosaki joined the imperial cause only after the defeat of the shogunate was clear. Tokushima acted with similar opportunism, committing forces only to battles already won. Yonezawa forces, ironically, opposed the imperial army, fearing the subjugation of the northeast by the southwest.

Thus I am not interested in why certain domains were able to attack and topple the shogunate. Rather I am interested in why dozens of similar domains did so little. The passivity of domains like Tokushima, Hirosaki, and Yonezawa points to a critical tension inherent in domain autonomy. Although large domains were autonomous in broad areas of civil affairs, this independence was predicated on the strength of the shogunate. Having ceded authority over diplomacy and foreign affairs to the shogun, the daimyo were dependent on his competence to defend the Tokugawa order. Like states in a federal union, daimyo were both fiercely protective of local autonomy and dependent on the union for their survival. Thus, although domains resented shogunal interference in their "domestic" affairs, they simultaneously needed a strong shogunate.

This tension and balance between central and local authority was a defining quality of the early modern order in Japan. This tension was also one of the first casualties of the Restoration. Beginning in early 1869, the new government systematically centralized authority over taxes, commerce, and samurai status. The national policies of the new state were an epitaph to domain autonomy: indeed, it was the destruction of the domains that made possible the centralized powers of the Meiji government. "Country" domains thus left a mixed legacy for modern Japan. We can find in domain politics the antecedents of such important Meiji policies as industrial promotion and samurai demobilization. But to enact those policies throughout Japan the Meiji regime required the destruction of the intricate web of overlapping sovereignties that defined the early modern polity. The task of writing Tokugawa political history is thus to understand domain politics, not merely as a precursor to the Meiji state, but as part of a world that the new regime systematically destroyed.

# 1

## Land and Lordship

*Ideology and Political Practice in Early Modern Japan*

> [Languages] determine the unique, often ambiguous tenor of human consciousness and make the relations of that consciousness to "reality" creative. . . . To a greater or lesser degree, every language offers its own reading of life.
> —George Steiner, *After Babel*

> Since the birth of humankind, where there have been things, there have been names. Names are, in origin, things affixed by common people, but this is so only for things with substance. Things that have no substance, in other words, things that cannot be seen by common people, are clarified and named by Sages.
> —Ogyū Sorai, *Benmei*

The political landscape of early modern Japan lacked anything resembling a modern state.[1] In the eighteenth century the shogunate, or *bakufu*, exerted direct control over some four million *koku* of land, roughly 15 percent of Japan.[2] Another 10 percent was entrusted to liege vassals (*hatamoto*), who staffed the shogunate's administration. The imperial family and various religious orders held roughly one-half million *koku*. The remaining three quarters of Japan was ruled by some 260 daimyo, whose domains ranged in size from 10,000 *koku* to over one million.

A political map of early modern Japan thus reveals an intricate patchwork of distinct governments, with broad areas of ambiguous and overlapping authority. Governmental control was at its most fragmented in the regions around Edo and Osaka: in the 1840s the five square *ri* (roughly 150 square miles) surrounding Osaka was governed by 165 different authorities. This checkerboard pattern of administration often led to coincident control over villages. After 1717, for example, several villages in the Kawasaki region were under multiple authorities. Twelve villages served two masters, either as both ecclesiastical lands of the Tokugawa house temple (Zōjōji) and liege vassal investiture (*hatamotoryō*), or as both direct shogunal holding (*tenryō*) and liege vassal investiture. Two villages were ruled, simultaneously, by all three authorities.[3]

Further from the Edo-Osaka corridor, political units tended to be larger and more contiguous: midsize domains such as Mito, Utsunomiya, Numata, and Fuchū traced a broad arc around Edo. At the periphery lay the massive, consolidated domains of great warlord houses like the Shimazu, the Mōri, the Yamauchi, and the Date. These territories encompassed resources in complete disproportion to their number. In the 1860s roughly one in twelve Japanese lived in the three largest domains: Kaga, Satsuma, or Chōshū.

This spatial fragmentation of authority was paralleled by a vertical division of political rights. The shogun was effectively the supreme political authority in Japan, but the title referred to a military appointment by the emperor. The daimyo were, in theory, invested vassals of the shogun, and their fiefs could be revoked for infractions of shogunal edicts. Within their domains, however, daimyo held formidable political power. The daimyo maintained independent standing armies, wrote their own legal codes, set and collected their own taxes, and controlled and policed their own borders. The shogunate maintained a monopoly on foreign policy, but the domains were entrusted with the management of their own domestic affairs.

The authority of the shogunate was, of course, an important part of the Tokugawa system. The *sankin kōtai*, or "alternate attendance system," for example, served as a constant reminder of the primacy of the Tokugawa house. Under *sankin kōtai*, daimyo were required to attend the shogun's court every calendar year and to leave their families in Edo, the shogun's capital.[4] The shogunate also regulated the personal conduct of daimyo and retained the right to oversee daimyo marriages and adoptions. But the authority of the shogunate focused on daimyo: it claimed only limited and indirect suzerainty over the commoner population of their domains. The shogunate never asserted a right to tax commoners outside its direct holdings. This resulted in a schism between the rights of the shogunate and its responsibilities: the shogunate claimed sole authority in issues such as foreign affairs, but it had financial authority over less than one-third of Japan.

Early modern daimyo were enmeshed in several coincident systems of hierarchy and classification. Daimyo were divided into three broad categories based on their ancestor's actions in the late 1500s. Daimyo who allied with Tokugawa Ieyasu, founder of the shogunate, early in his rise to power were designated *fudai*. Opponents, or more opportunistic allies of Ieyasu, were dubbed *tozama*, literally "outsider" daimyo. Daimyo related to the Tokugawa house, but who were not in the main shogunal line, were designated *kamon*, or collateral daimyo.[5] Daimyo were also distinguished by court rank (*kan'i*), which designated their eligibility for positions in the emperor's administration. *Kan'i* were based on the administrative grades of the ancient Nara and Heian courts and were originally modeled on rankings in the T'ang dynasty Chinese bureaucracy. Although court ranks had lost all practical meaning by the Tokugawa era, high court rank served as a mark of prestige in a status-conscious society. Daimyo were also ranked by their seating assignment for shogunal audiences. The daimyo were seated in seven separate chambers. Seats in the three most prestigious chambers were reserved for daimyo with large holdings or familial ties to the shogunate.[6]

A critical determinant of a daimyo's standing was the size of his investiture. Daimyo were commonly defined as shogunal vassals with investitures of 10,000 *koku* or more. The largest domain, Kaga, was thus over 100 times larger than the smallest daimyo holding. Because of this range in size, smaller daimyo resembled minor shogunal retainers, such as liege vassals, more than they did great lords. Liege vassals were shogunal administrators but, like daimyo, were empowered to invest their own armed vassals, to set and collect their own taxes, to issue their own legal codes, and to employ these to arrest and punish their subjects. In shogunal law the promotion from liege vassal to daimyo entailed only one new power: daimyo, unlike liege vassals, could sentence their subjects to death. The principal distinction between liege vassals and *fudai* daimyo was the size of their holdings: with rare exception, liege vassals fell below the 10,000 *koku* threshold for daimyo status.[7]

At the opposite end of the spectrum lay "country-holding" daimyo or "country" lords, the most powerful and autonomous lords of the realm. These lords enjoyed extensive de facto and de jure independence from the shogunate, and their domains functioned as quasistates within the broader Tokugawa state system. The "country-holding" daimyo were a loosely defined group. Although the shogunate employed the term "country lord" in its official decrees, it never offered a definitive list of "country lords." Instead, historians have relied on sources such as Kikuchi Yamon's *Zanshū ryūei hikan*, an account of political custom and ritual compiled in the mid-eighteenth century.

The *Zanshū ryūei hikan* lists ten daimyo as *honkunimochi*, or "true country holders": the Maeda of Kaga, the Shimazu of Satsuma, the Mōri of Chōshū, the Ikeda of Tottori, the Hachisuka of Tokushima, the Kuroda of Fukuoka, the Asano of Hiroshima, the Ikeda of Okayama, the Yamauchi of Tosa, and the Sō of Tsushima. These daimyo ruled at least an entire province. Another eight daimyo were described as *taishin kunomichi*, or "great country holders": the Date of Sendai, the Hosokawa of Kumamoto, the Nabeshima of Saga, the Tōdō of Tsu, the Arima of Kurume, the Satake of Akita, the Uesugi of Yonezawa, and the Yanagisawa of Kōriyama. These lords had large holdings, but none of them governed an entire province. Combined, these two groups were the "eighteen country holders." All these houses save the Yanagisawa were "outsider" (*tozama*) families. Only the Yangisawa were vassal (*fudai*) daimyo. Although *fudai* houses maintained a monopoly on important shogunal offices, they were accorded less importance as independent lords.

The *Zanshū ryūei hikan* also lists in a separate "country holder" category two collateral (*kamon*) houses: the Matsudaira of Fukui and the Matsudaira of Matsue.[8] The lower threshold for "country holders" seems to have been 100,000 *koku*: the Sō of Tsushima were given a putative investiture of 100,000 *koku*, although their true holdings were only 2,000 *koku*. Later accounts of "country holders" are similar. The *Buke kakureishiki*, published in 1836, also lists twenty "country holders," but omits the Sō of Tsushima and the Yanagisawa of Kōriyama. Instead, it lists the Matsudaira of Fukui and the Matsudaira of Matsue among the "eighteen country holders." The Nanbu of Morioka and the Matsudaira of Tsuyama are also listed as "country holders," but in a separate category.[9]

The *Zanshū ryūei hikan* describes three additional lords as "quasi country lords" (*junkokushu*) or "country-holding quality" (*kunimochi nami*): the Date of Uwajima, the Tachibana of Yanagawa, and the Niwa of Nihonmatsu. The Tachibana and Niwa were considered "country holders" only after they had been promoted to fourth court rank (*shihin*). Court rank was a necessary element of "quasi country lord" status. Lords such as the Matsura of Hirado and the Sakai of Obama ruled entire provinces but were not ranked among the "country holders." The Tsugaru of Hirosaki are not mentioned in any category of "country holder," but their promotion to fourth rank and 100,000 *koku* status came decades after the compilation of the *Zanshū ryūei hikan*. Moreover, by the 1700s the status of "country holder" had become a matter of precedent. It was, of course, possible to be promoted to "country holder." The inclusion of the Nanbu as "country holders" in the *Buke kakureishiki* was probably related to their service fighting the Russians in Hokkaidō. While the Tsugaru were also rewarded, they were still insufficiently prestigious to merit "country holder" status.[10]

The autonomy of "country-holding" daimyo was a function of both shogunal policy and the objective characteristics of their holdings. The shogunate officially gave "country-holding" daimyo broad discretion in civil affairs. In a 1633 edict on lawsuits, the shogunate decreed that "in the case of country holders, complaints from retainers, townsmen, or farmers should be dealt with in accordance with the wishes of that lord." Personal ties between the shogun and "country lords" were also *sui generis*. As Date Yoshimura (1680–1751), the fifth daimyo of Sendai, observed, the shogun treated "country-holding" daimyo "utterly unlike the vassal (*fudai*) daimyo: not quite as vassals and not quite as guests."[11] In virtually all areas of public life, "country" lords were given special perquisites denied most other lords. The gates to their Edo mansions were more formidable and impressive. Their alternate attendance processions were more regal.[12]

The special status of "country" lords in the Tokugawa order was reflected in their near total exemption from the shogunal sanctions of attainder (*kaieki*) and transfer (*tenpō*). Only once after 1700 did the shogunate move or reduce the holdings of a "country" lord. In 1866 the shogunate sought to reduce Mōri holdings by 100,000 *koku* as a punishment for their attack on the Forbidden Gate. But this reflects ambiguously on shogunal power, since the shogunate collapsed before the reduction took effect. This exemption from shogunal sanction can be linked with other factors. The shogunate focused its sanctions of attainder and transfer disproportionately on small, *fudai* domains. Roughly half of all daimyo were *fudai*, but after 1700, roughly 75 percent of all attainders and 90 percent of all transfers were directed against *fudai*. Only twice after 1650 did the shogunate move, seize, or reduce the holdings of a large *tozama* domain. The first incident was the reduction of Uesugi holdings in 1664 after the second daimyo died without an heir. The second was the Forbidden Gate reprisal of 1866. In the later Tokugawa era, large *tozama* daimyo could avoid shogunal sanction by planning their succession and avoiding outright rebellion.[13]

The autonomy of "country" daimyo was thus partially a perquisite of elite status. "Country" lords lived more like sovereigns than like vassals, and this was reflected in their political consciousness and practice. But the distinctive political culture of the great domains was supported by socioeconomic forces as well. The contiguity of "country" domains shaped political practice and political economy. In smaller domains, trade and commerce tended to weaken daimyo control. As Kären Wigen has observed in her study of Shinano, "Commercial ventures followed their own spatial logic, which was not that of the Tokugawa feudal settlement; economic regions coexisted with political regions, but did not conform to them."[14] Protoindustrialization therefore led to an ablation of political boundaries as "castle-town merchants pressed monopoly claims against their rural counterparts, and domains likewise sought to tax intermediate processing that occurred beyond their boundaries."[15] As economic practices crossed domain boundaries, so did the attendant political dissent. From the late 1700s on, peasant protest in the

Kantō and the Kinai was guided increasingly by regional concerns that crossed domain boundaries.[16]

In "country" domains, by contrast, economic and political boundaries tended to coincide. Tokushima, for example, constituted a coherent economic region. The cultivation of indigo leaves and the chopping, curing, and drying involved in making dye cubes were all conducted within its borders. This supported both the domain's sense of economic sovereignty and the commoners' sense that a single political entity governed their livelihoods. Similarly, in Yonezawa, the domain actively sought to keep all stages of sericulture, from silkworm breeding to weaving, within the domain. The development of "Yonezawa cloth" (*Yonezawa ori*) meant that sericulturalists, spinners, weavers, and the state shared a sense of Yonezawa as a discrete economic entity.

The impact of size on political economy appears in the different rates at which large and small domains introduced state commodity agencies (*kokusan kaijo*). By 1830 more than three-quarters of domains 100,000 *koku* or larger were running either domain monopolies or maintaining general economic development offices. Fewer than a quarter of the smaller domains maintained such agencies.[17]

Because of economic integration in large domains, economic activity and the related legal and political disputes were principally between subjects of the same domain, or between the domain and "foreign" traders. This reinforced the sense of "country" domains as "states." When commoners in large domains contested economic policies, they cited the daimyo's obligations to succor his "people," the commoners of the domain. Protoindustrialization and commercialization thus tended to reinforce political boundaries in great domains and weaken them in smaller investitures.

In Tokushima and Yonezawa the forces of ascriptive status, geography, and economics coincided in support of domain autonomy. Both domains were large, stable, and contiguous, and both ruling families were "country holders." The Tsugaru of Hirosaki, by contrast, lacked the imprimatur of "country lord." Hirosaki was contiguous, stable, and nearly twice as populous as Yonezawa, but its political autonomy was not supported by special shogunal dispensation. Hirosaki politics was thus characterized by a combination of the independence of a great domain and the subservience of a smaller holding. The samurai of Hirosaki sought both to serve their local "state" and "country" and, simultaneously, to curry favor with the shogunate.

## Assessing States

The politics of great domains reflected the internal tensions of the Tokugawa order. In the spheres of diplomacy and general public order, the shogunate claimed the powers of a centralized state. But in matters of taxation and broad areas of civil law, the shogunate was more the leader of a porous, federal union. This unbalanced portfolio of powers and responsibilities means that assessments of the strength and legitimacy of the shogunate vary with our understanding of state power. James White, for example, has argued that the shogunate constituted a state. Drawing on a reading of Max Weber, he noted that the shogunate maintained a monopoly on the use of physical force within Japan. The shogunate was not, White concedes, a modern state, but it prohibited daimyo from using force among themselves, while retaining for itself the right to use force against daimyo. The shogunate, moreover, steadily expanded its coercive authority over the people under daimyo rule. Following the Tenma Rebellion of 1764, which involved not only Tokugawa holdings but also liege vassal and daimyo lands, the shogunate sent investigators through the entire area. They arrested at will and ultimately sentenced several hundred commoners and officials for various offenses. The shogunate took similar action after the Kamo Rebellion of 1836.[18]

Ronald Toby, focusing on foreign policy, came to a similar assessment of Tokugawa strength. The shogunate's monopoly on foreign affairs established its legitimacy as the supreme government of Japan. As Toby puts it, "The ability autonomously to manipulate foreign states and foreign monarchs in the formative years of the dynasty served both to assure the physical security of the Japanese homeland and to prevent the subversion of the state from abroad, on the one hand, and to legitimate the new Tokugawa order, on the other." The shogunate's ostentatious reception of envoys from Korea and the Ryukyus served to enhance its legitimacy both internationally and domestically.[19]

We might contrast these approaches to statecraft with a fiscal approach. As Joseph Schumpeter argues, the modern state arose from the increased need of governments for revenue. "Taxes not only helped to create the state. They helped to form it. The tax system was the organ of development which entailed the other organs." For Schumpeter, the modern state emerged when "common exigencies," such as war, allowed princes to assert a right to tax superior to traditional, feudal privileges. Taxation then became the central link between state and society:

The fiscal history of a people is above all an essential part of its general history. An enormous influence on the fate of nations emanates from the economic bleeding which the needs of the state necessitates and from the use to which its results are put. . . . The spirit of a people, its cultural level, its social structure, the deeds its policy may prepare—all this and more is written in its fiscal history, stripped of all phrases.[20]

Schumpeter's argument that culture is a function of fiscal policy is hyperbolic, but his analysis rightly stresses taxation as a central link between state and society. Yet by this criterion the shogunate was a state in only one-third of Japan. In the remaining two-thirds, the shogun served as the leader of a confederation of daimyo, who retained for themselves the key power of taxation.

The shogunate thus sits uneasily among these single-power definitions of state. This tension becomes more apparent when we employ more expansive and robust definitions of "state." Charles Tilly, for example, while conceding the difficulty in finding widely accepted criteria for "stateness," denotes five areas as essential to state-building: the organization of armed forces, taxation, policing, control over the food supply, and the formation of technical personnel.[21] Joel Migdal delineates similar criteria in a more theoretical form. The essential aspects of a state, he argues, are the capability to penetrate society, regulate social relationships, extract resources, and appropriate or use resources.[22]

Within these more expansive definitions of the state, the shogunate's power and authority seem dangerously unbalanced. In the Tenma and Kamo rebellions, for example, the shogunate prosecuted peasant rebels in the territory of other lords in the Kantō. By White's criteria of "monopoly of coercion" this action suggests sovereignty over the region. Yet the shogunate did not claim the right to tax the area it policed, nor did it reduce or change the holdings of the lords whose domains were involved in the uprisings. In Migdal's terms the shogunate sought to increase its regulative responsibility but not its extractive capability. The shogunate's actions thus increased its obligations, but not its power. This mismatch of capability and responsibility proved a decisive factor in its demise. When confronted by the imperialist powers in the 1850s and 1860s, the shogunate found itself responsible for defending all of Japan, but with direct control over less than one-third of the country's resources. The "weakness" of the shogunate thus lay less in its lack of power than in its strange mismatch of power and responsibility. Yet this same imbalance had served shogunal interests for nearly two centuries. As long as foreign affairs remained peaceful, the shogunate's monopoly on diplomacy gave it stature superior to all domestic rivals.

The shogun's lack of full, central authority was paralleled by an absence of absolute sovereignty. The very title *shōgun*, for example, did not designate a position of supreme authority, but a military appointment confirmed by the emperor. Although the title implied broader civil authority in addition to military command, it lost much of its luster with the collapse of the Ashikaga shogunate in the fifteenth century. The formidable power of the Tokugawa house stemmed largely from its ability to claim that it had created peace and order after decades of chaos. In the early seventeenth century, at the peak of Tokugawa power, political analysts implied that the imperial house had lost heaven's mandate and the right to rule. The shogunate thus ruled in lieu of the emperor, rather than at his behest. But such claims were made largely in private documents. In public, even shogunal apologists were loath to assert shogunal supremacy over the emperor. Shogunal ideologues such as Arai Haku-seki argued for a hegemonic shogunate by ignoring the emperor rather than denying him. By the late eighteenth century, however, the shogunate was commonly seen as subject to imperial authority. In 1788, Matsudaira Sadanobu, then serving as shogunal regent, explicitly described the shogun as an imperial servant.[23]

Some historians have treated the term *kōgi*, or "public authority," as evidence of supreme shogunal authority. This is problematic. In the Warring States period, *kōgi* was a term commonly applied to domain governments headed by daimyo, but in the seventeenth century it came increasingly to refer to the shogunate. Some daimyo described themselves as servants of the *kōgi*, suggesting that their authority was based on shogunal assent.[24] But the term *kōgi* was not reserved for the shogunate. Even in the late eighteenth century, *kōgi* could refer to either the shogunate or a domain. The shogunate was sometimes distinguished by the term the "large *kōgi*" (*daikōgi*), but the meaning of *kōgi* is often clear only in context.[25] As Mary Elizabeth Berry has argued, *kōgi* is a "chameleon term that masks as often as it mirrors meaning." Even the translation of *kōgi* as "public authority," she argues, suggests a distinction between the public and private realms that was foreign to early modern thought.[26]

The shogunate's formidable authority stemmed less from any single title than from a concatenation of multiple systems of legitimacy. The shogunate drew legitimacy from the imperial house through a series of offices: minister of the right (*udaijin*), rector of the Junna and Shōgaku colleges (*Junna Shōgaku ryōin bettō*), captain of the left imperial guards (*sa konoe no daishō*), and inspector of the left imperial stables (*sa meryō no gogen*).[27] As Herman Ooms has noted, the shogunate also enhanced its legitimacy by refusing imperial appointments, thereby increasing the independence of those it accepted. Each shogun was also head of the Tokugawa house, the most powerful warlord house in the land. Through imperial assent and creative genealogy, the Tokugawa shoguns were further dubbed heads of the Minamoto lineage, the first warlord house to claim the title *shōgun*. Tokugawa Ieyasu, the first Tokugawa shogun, was posthumously refigured as Tōshōgū, a Shintō deity. A memorial shrine, spectacular in both architecture and setting, was built in Nikkō to burnish Ieyasu's image. Ieyasu's status as a Shintō deity also gave him elevated status in certain schools of Buddhism, where Shintō deities were viewed as alternative manifestations of *bodhisattva*. The shogunate was thus legitimized not by absolute authority within a single statist ideology but by commanding authority within multiple ideologies: neo-Confucianism, Shintoism, Buddhism, the emperor system, and the traditions of warrior rule were all brought to bear in defense of shogunal power. This gave the shogunate considerable power, but also bound it to the political institutions with which it shared political legitimacy. The shogunate thus existed in ideological interdependence with both the imperial house and rival warlords.[28]

Historians have long recognized that the Tokugawa order was a composite of multiple sites of authority. The term "bakuhan order" (*bakuhan taisei*), commonly used in both Japanese and English, reflects this awareness. First put forth by Itō Tasaburō and Nakamura Kichiji in the late 1940s, the term refers to the Tokugawa polity as a union of the shogunate (*bakufu*) and the domains (*han*). A later variant, "*bakuhan* state" (*bakuhan kokka*), reflects the sense that the early order established comprehensive national control over key socioeconomic practices. Both "*bakuhan* system" and "*bakuhan* state" have become the common terms in American historiography for the early modern order in Japan.[29]

Despite the widespread acceptance of these terms, I employ in this study a revisionist term, "compound state." As originally developed by Mizubayashi Takeshi, "compound state" highlights the status of large domains as small states within a broader state system. As Mizubayashi puts it, "The compound state order was created through the combination of the small states of the Tokugawa domain, which encompassed the *fudai* daimyo and the *hatamoto*, and the domains of the country-holding *tozama* daimyo, who were descendants of Warring States daimyo." Mizubayashi thus foregrounds the distinct status of country-holding daimyo within the early modern order.[30]

I find the term "compound state" appealing for several additional reasons. First, it aptly reflects the composite legitimacy of the early modern order. Tokugawa ideology was syncretic in two senses. It fused multiple ideologies and religions (Shintō, Buddhist, and neo-Confucian) in support of multiple forms of authority. The shogunate held the coincident, and eventually competing, roles of independent suzerain, imperial servant, and guarantor of daimyo privilege. The shogunate was thus not supported by a single statist ideology but by several ideological traditions. This greatly complicated government reform. When, for example, the shogunate sought to replace its liege vassals with a conscript army in the late 1860s, it was acting appropriately as a recipient of heaven's mandate but irresponsibly as a feudal lord. These reforms thus strengthened the shogunate's position as an absolutist regime but cast doubt on its reliability as a party to a feudal compact and as a guarantor of the rights of the liege vassals. Because of its compound legitimacy, the shogunate was simultaneously undermined and strengthened. Daimyo faced similar challenges. The details of similar struggles between alternative sources of legitimacy within domains are a theme of the three case studies developed here. The notion of a compound state helps us explore these competing forms and bases of political legitimacy.

Second, "compound state" allows us to avoid the term *han*, a component of terms such as "*bakuhan* state." Although sometimes treated as an historical expression, the term *han* was never used in shogunal investitures or official documents. Prior to the Meiji Restoration, *han* was an informal, literary term. It was used largely for its resonances with classical texts such as the *Book of Odes*, where it referred to military investitures granted by the Chinese emperor during the Chou dynasty.[31] The term *han* carried demeaning connotations, and in the eighteenth century, the scholar Arai Hakuseki, who sought to recast the shogun as a Chinese-style monarch, referred to daimyo holdings as *han* to diminish their authority relative to the shogunate. In the nineteenth century, imperial loyalists used the term to emphasize the subordination of daimyo to the emperor. It was in this sense of submission to the emperor that *han* was first used in an official context: in 1868 the Meiji government referred to all daimyo holdings as *han* as part of its reorganization of Japanese territory. In the strictest sense, *han* existed for only three years, between the Meiji Restoration and the implementation of the prefectural system in 1871. The term *han* thus reflects how advocates of a strong shogunate or imperial authority understood daimyo authority and, in doing so, effaces how daimyo, particularly "country-holding" daimyo, viewed their own domains.

### Language and Land

Early modern daimyo used a variety of terms to refer to their investitures. The records of small domains commonly refer to the "holding" (*ryōbun* or *ryōchi*) of the ruling family. In large domains, however, the most common term was *kuni*, or "country." Officials spoke of the traditions of their "country," the prosperity of their "country," and the well-being of their "countrymen" (*kokumin*). From a modern perspective this language is problematic because terms such as *kuni* could refer to a variety of political bodies: provinces, domains, or countries in the modern sense. The flexible and contingent meaning of *kuni* is revealed in the house records of the Motoki family, wealthy Tokushima landowners. Writing of Western ships in the 1840s, a Motoki referred to "warships of foreign countries." In such contexts, the family's allegiance was to the country of Japan, or *Nipponkoku*, led by the shogun (*shōgunsama* or *kokuō*). In most other contexts, however, the term "country" meant domain. In reporting the panic after Ōshio Heihachirō's failed rebellion, the Motoki wrote, "The dead are too many to number, and as a result of the disturbance the daimyo each tend to their own Edo residences, and the daimyo of neighboring countries race back to their castles."[32] The Motoki commonly associated the person of the daimyo with the country of Tokushima, referring to the daimyo as *okunisama*, or "lord of the country." Often the final honorific *sama* was elided, and the country served as a synecdoche for the lord. When Hachisuka Nariaki, who was without heir, adopted a child from the Tokugawa house, the Motoki recorded that "the country has adopted a young lord of the shogun."

Finally, the Motoki used *kuni* to indicate the provinces of the ancient imperial state, the *ritsuryō kokka*. These provinces had functioned as administrative units in the seventh and eighth centuries, but had little political meaning by the early modern era. This usage of *kuni* was most common in the context of the Kantō region, which was controlled by hundreds of small domains. The Motoki tended to distinguish between foreign countries and domestic "countries" through modifiers. Hence, other provinces or domains were "various countries" (*shokoku*), while Russia and European countries were "foreign countries" (*ikoku*). Yet even this distinction was far from consistent. During the Tenpō crisis of the 1830s, the Motoki wrote angrily of daimyo who would not allow ships of "foreign countries" to dock. The price of rice was therefore rising, despite bountiful harvests in "other countries" of Japan.[33]

Terms such as *kokka* had similar multiple meanings. In modern Japanese, *kokka* refers to a centralized state, but in the Tokugawa era *kokka* could signify either the shogunate or a domain. Tokugawa Japanese also carried over from ancient Chinese the sense of *kokka* as a kingdom, such as the kingdoms of the legendary sage-kings Yao and Shun. In much Tokugawa writing, *kokka*, literally the "house of the country," referred to the ruling family of a domain or, by extension, the ruling family and its retainers. The term thus lacked the sense of absolute sovereignty that characterizes the modern notion of a state. But *kokka* could designate an abstract political institution. In 1622, for example, the daimyo of Fukuoka, Kuroda Nagamasa, warned his heir to choose his successor wisely. Do not entrust the *kokka*, he cautioned, to someone who is immoral, willful, or who fails to heed his advisers. Such conduct would result in "divine punishment" (*tenbatsu*) and loss of the domain. The key to managing the domain lay in recognizing that it was not the daimyo's property, but something entrusted to him. A good ruler thus brought "peace to the people and farmers" and avoided self-indulgence.[34] This notion that the daimyo serves the *kokka* is echoed in Uesugi Harunori's statement that "the lord exists for the sake of the state and the people: the state and the people do not exist for the sake of the lord." This conception of the *kokka* embodies both a modern conception of the state as an abstract political entity and a less rarified notion of the state as the patrimony of the ruler. The notion that a daimyo inherits a "state" suggests that a *kokka* was little more than an investiture to be carefully managed for one's descendants. But the argument that the lord exists for the state is reminiscent of Frederick the Great's claim that the monarch is the first servant of the state. Because this conception of a *kokka* did not involve supreme political authority, Nagamasa and Harunori could describe their realms as "states" without denying that they were invested by the shogun. In Tokugawa writing, Japan thus consisted of "states" within a "state."

Most intriguing is Tokugawa usage of the term *kokumin*, literally "people of the country." After the Meiji Restoration, *kokumin* was used as a Japanese equivalent for "nation." Prior to the 1860s, however, *kokumin* could be used to refer to the people of a particular domain as well as to all the people of Japan. It could mean nothing more than "commoners," but it was often used to stress the obligation of the state to its subjects. In describing the failure of fiat money, the *Takaokaki*, an eighteenth-century account of Hirosaki politics, noted that "the *kokumin* were impoverished" and "driven to riot." When the daimyo learned of this he dismissed the responsible officials in order to "bring peace to the *kokumin*."[35] In some instances, *kokumin* could include samurai. In 1833, during the Tenpō famine, the government of Yonezawa referred to *kokumin* when justifying emergency rationing:

> Given the recent series of exceptionally poor harvests, his lordship has been pained by the prospect that his country will not have enough food for next year. Although there are both noble and base among the four estates [peasants, samurai, artisans, and merchants], the *kokumin* are one and indivisible. Accordingly, [his lordship] thinks of the entire country as one family and orders that even those who have ample rice should eat rice gruel, sending their surplus to those who do not have enough.[36]

Although the *kokumin* of Yonezawa were not a "nation," they were obviously understood to share a common interest and purpose, even across class lines. Luke Roberts's translation of *kokumin* as "countrymen" captures much of this sense of solidarity.[37] When constructed as a *kokumin*, the people of Yonezawa were loyal first and foremost to their fellow countrymen, irrespective of class.[38]

## Language and Translation

The polysemy of political discourse complicates the translation of Tokugawa texts. "Languages differ," as Roman Jakobson observed, "essentially in what they *must* convey and not in what they *may* convey."[39] There is no word in modern English that can capture the multiple meanings of *kuni*: "country" captures the sense of cultural commonality, "domain" the sense of political authority, and "province" the sense of geographic contiguity. Because our modern political vocabulary seeks to clarify sovereignty, formal translation tends to specify what the original Japanese has left unspoken. In much Tokugawa writing, a single meaning of *kuni* or *kokka* is clear in context. Much as speakers of modern American English do not confusedly wonder if the State Department represents the state of Kentucky, so Tokugawa-era Japanese could commonly distinguish between the "country" of Mutsu (a province) and the "country" of Ch'ing China (a kingdom).

Much of the rhetoric of country domains, however, hinged on the polysemy of *kuni* and *kokka*. The writings of Nyūi Mitsugi, for example, operate on several levels. Nyūi was both an important administrator in mid-eighteenth-century Hirosaki and a respected neo-Confucian philosopher. His essay the "Way of Merchant Profit" (*Shōka ridō*) can thus be read both as an abstract discussion of political economy and as a defense of Nyūi's policies, particularly his Hōreki reforms of the 1750s. These multiple meanings were made possible by the multiple meanings of *kuni* and *kokka*. When Nyūi wrote that "great merchants bring prosperity to the realm [*tenka*] and serve the interests of the state [*kokka no yō o tsūzuru*]," he was writing about both the "state" of Hirosaki and "states" in general. If we translate *kokka* as "kingdom" we can capture how Nyūi was engaging the Chinese classics on a seminal question in political economy: is a merchant's profit justified? At this level, Nyūi was responding to the writings of Mencius, Chuang Tzu, and Chu Hsi. If we translate *kokka* as "domain," however, we can foreground Nyūi as an active administrator, defending a particular vision of the merchants' role in 1750s Hirosaki. Nyūi's reforms were indeed directed toward insuring that Hirosaki merchants acted as "great merchants" and served "state" interests. My decision to render *kokka* as "state" stems from my reluctance to choose between these alternatives. Indeed, Nyūi's ability to signify both ancient Chinese kingdoms and his own domains with the term *kokka* is itself a salient aspect of political discourse in country domains. An adequate translation of Nyūi's thought thus hinges on capturing this simultaneity—this coincidence of "states."[40]

Although word-for-word translations of Tokugawa political discourse can sound quixotic and contradictory, contemporary English-language accounts of Japan employed a language as foreign as early modern Japanese. François Caron's widely read account of Japan, first published in 1645–46, describes a "country" ruled by an "Emperor," by which Caron meant the shogun Tokugawa Iemitsu. But the country was subdivided into "Countreys" ruled by the various "Kings, Princes, Dukes and Lords." The "Emperor" had formidable power over these nobles and could "banish or punish with death, at pleasure, his offending Kings and Lords, and . . . give away their Commands and Treasures to those he fancies more deserving than they."[41] Yet for Caron, the subservience of the daimyo to the shogun did not make them any less "kings."

Caron's political language was typical of early modern European political discourse. Into the eighteenth century Englishmen conflated countries and counties, speaking, for example, of the "country" of Lancashire. In central Europe, the supremacy of the nation-state, and the corresponding vocabulary, emerged still later. As late as the 1790s, Prussia was referred to as both a "state" and an amalgamation of "Prussian states." Similarly, the Holy Roman Empire could be defined, in 1786, as a "state [*Staatkörper*] made up of many small, particular states." In 1833 Metternich observed that Prussia was emerging as a "state within the state in the fullest sense of the term." The central concept in traditional central Europe was not the state but the *Land*. *Länder* were territorial units with distinct institutions, laws, and customs. Like *kuni*, *Land* implied political authority, but not sovereignty: "A *Land* asserted its identity but not its primacy." *Länder* were thus porous political units, and they could be penetrated by outside elements, such as the Catholic Church or the Holy Roman Empire. While neither the terms *country* of seventeenth-century English nor *Land* of eighteenth-century German are precise equivalents of the *kuni* of Tokugawa Japanese, all three convey the polysemantic ambiguity of early modern politics.[42]

By contrast, it is difficult to translate Tokugawa political texts into modern Japanese: the language of Tokugawa politics did not outlive the Tokugawa political order. In 1868/6 the *dajōkan* (council of state) designated three kinds of internal division for Japan: *ken*, *fu*, and *han*. *Ken* and *fu* were ancient Japanese terms for provincial units of the imperial state. The new *ken* and *fu* were created by aggregating Tokugawa house lands, liege vassal holdings, and small domains. Larger daimyo holdings were designated *han*. Under the pretext of restoring seventh- and eighth-century political institutions, the Meiji government eliminated the word *kuni* as a term for domain. Implicitly, Japan became the only effective country/*kuni*, the Meiji state the sole state/*kokka*, and the Japanese people the only true nation/*kokumin*. The introduction of distinct terms for prefecture, domain, and state was thus part of the construction of the modern state itself.

The polysemy of early modern Japanese has two important implications. First, the parallels between early modern Japanese and early modern European political discourse suggest that the "states within states" phenomenon was a political formation common to Europe and Japan, not some dysfunction of the state-building process unique to Japan. Second, the polysemy of Tokugawa discourse makes clarity in translation a problematic virtue. However vexing the ambiguities of "country," to translate *kuni* as a province, a domain, or a country, depending on context, is to translate Tokugawa thought into modern, post-Restoration thought. Although the result is increased clarity, this is a dubious virtue, since this lack of clarity was a salient aspect of Tokugawa political texts. In clarifying Tokugawa political language we run the risk of obscuring the complexities of the early modern political order. More seriously, the interjection of such "clarity" antedates the transformation of political language that accompanied the Meiji Restoration and treats the nation-state as an ontologically privileged institution, existing even in a world that had no words to describe it. That large domains called themselves "states" does not, of course, mean that they were states in the modern sense. But to translate *kokka* as state only when it refers to the shogunate is, in effect, to impose a modern theory of sovereignty on Tokugawa thought. The danger here is that we will find evidence of state-building because we have put it there through our process of translation.

## Language and Sovereignty

A close examination of early modern political language suggests a need to reexamine the bases of daimyo authority. Daimyo and their retainers employed a broad battery of arguments and rhetorical strategies to defend their interests. At root, these various arguments can be traced to three coincident sources of legitimacy: feudal authority, patrimonial authority, and suzerain authority.

Feudal authority was once seen as the primary source of legitimacy in the Tokugawa polity; hence George Sansom's characterization of the early modern order as "centralized feudalism."[43] I use "feudalism" here in a limited sense to refer to the personal compact between lord and vassal. The feudal bond was created when a vassal swore loyal service to a superior lord in return for an investiture.

Feudal authority was thus quasi-contractual. As Kitajima Masamoto has observed, the lord-vassal relationship was mediated by the exchange of land, and the retainer's sense of obligation to his lord was contingent on this exchange. This contractual aspect of the feudal bond was balanced by the Tokugawa-era emphasis on absolute loyalty and honor. Retainers who did not manifest unswerving loyalty and devotion were unworthy of their lord's protection. Samurai who did not defend their honor were similarly unworthy of service to their lord. This tension between the contractual and absolute aspect of the feudal bond was a persistent tension in Tokugawa thought.[44]

Feudal authority touched all samurai. Daimyo were invested by the shogun, and their authority over their domains stemmed partly from shogunal authority. Daimyo, in turn, invested their own samurai and demanded oaths of loyalty. These ties of vassalage also linked daimyo to the emperor, who, in theory, designated the shogun. Most daimyo oaths were simple vows of loyalty, based on the three-article oath originally demanded by Ieyasu. When Tsugaru Nobuaki of Hirosaki swore fidelity to the new shogun Ienari in 1787, he vowed to obey strictly all shogunal laws, to keep his house from wickedness, and to serve his lord with diligence. Failure to fulfill this oath warranted "all the divine retribution of Bonten [Skt. Brahmā], Taishaku [Skt. Shakra devānām Indra], the Four Heavenly Kings, and the gods of the 60 provinces of Japan, especially the *gongen* of Izu and Hakone, the *daimyōjin* of Mishima, the bodhisattva Hachiman, and Tenman Jizai Tenjin and their disciples."[45] Nobuaki signed his oath in blood before the assembled shogunal elders (*rōjū*). Daimyo demanded similar oaths from their high retainers. The domain elders (*karō*) of Takasaki domain, for example, assembled in the castle and swore in blood to obey all laws and edicts of the *kōgi*, to serve their lord above all others and in all things, and to carry out all his instructions without question or demur. The closing oath before the gods was identical to that demanded of daimyo by the shogun.[46]

The feudal bond between daimyo and shogun both created and conveyed authority. The ritual of blood oaths can be seen as reproducing authority as well as representing it: in drawing their own blood to proclaim their obedience, daimyo helped to create the authority they served. Similarly, the invocation of a wide panoply of deities gave the feudal bond a weight greater than the de facto military might of either party. Having enhanced shogunal authority, daimyo then had their holdings legitimized by it. The investitures of each daimyo house were confirmed by a vermilion seal on a certificate of investiture, which specified the location and extent of the holding.

The salient characteristic of feudal authority was its personal nature. It bound a single vassal to a single lord, not one institution to another.[47] Accordingly, feudal authority did not give the shogunate suzerainty over commoners outside its own holdings. The shogun was the daimyo's lord, not the lord of the daimyo's commoners. The feudal character of the shogun-daimyo bond is revealed in the original "Laws Governing the Military Houses" of 1615. The laws delineated acceptable daimyo conduct and established the authority of the shogunate in several key areas. Daimyo were not to arrange marriages without shogunal approval, enter into private alliances, or make modifications to their castles. Daimyo were also instructed on the rule of their domains, but these passages were largely hortatory. The thirteenth and final article, for example, instructed "country lords" [kokushu] to "select officials with a capacity for public administration [seimu]." While this edict suggested some shogunal oversight of domain affairs, it also confirmed the right of lords to select their own officials.[48]

As guarantor of the daimyo holding, the shogun reserved the authority to reduce or seize the investiture of a daimyo who violated these edicts. But because feudal authority focused on personal ties, feudal sanctions were directed predominantly toward personal conduct. During the first half-century of Tokugawa rule, the shogunate reduced or eliminated the investitures of scores of daimyo. Between 1600 and 1650 the shogunate seized over twelve million koku in over 130 incidents of attainder. The most common cause for seizure was the death of the daimyo: this accounted for nearly half of all attainders before 1650. Death dissolved the feudal bond, and the shogun could legitimately reject a daimyo's designated heir. Such seizures made heritability conditional, even for large, established daimyo. The other focus of attainders was the daimyo's conduct toward the shogun. Roughly one-third of attainders resulted from rudeness, "madness," tardiness in attending the shogun, or similar personal actions by the daimyo. Attainder was rarely used to punish a daimyo for incompetent rule or for violations of administrative procedures. Philip Brown has calculated that administrative issues accounted for a maximum of 12 percent of attainders between 1601 and 1760. A stricter definition of administrative failure would put the rate as low as 3 percent.[49] Feudal authority thus required loyalty, propriety, and general competence, rather than any strict adherence to an administrative code.

The feudal principle that death dissolved the bond between lord and vassal was counterbalanced by the patrimonial principle that investitures were heritable. Within the framework of patrimonial authority, an investiture was part of a family's patrimony and was transmitted from patriarch to patriarch across generations. Thus, while feudal authority linked two individuals until death, patrimonial authority made the feudal link a bond between houses across generations. Patrimonial authority was rooted in the *ie*, or Japanese family system. The *ie* system was characterized by what social scientists have termed "stem-linearity" or "stem succession." The head of an *ie* could be succeeded only by a single heir, either natural or adopted. Even when a family had more than one heir, the headship of the *ie* was not partible: the lesser inheritor established a separate, "branch" *ie*. Unlike a specific household, an *ie* was understood to exist as a singular, corporate unit across time. The task of each generation was successfully to sustain the *ie* and then cede it to the following generation. Although much of the solidarity of an *ie* stemmed from kinship ties, the survival of the *ie* was more important than kinship. Succession through adoption rarely diminished the legitimacy of an *ie*.[50]

Mizubayashi Takeshi has developed an important discussion of the political implications of the *ie* system. He argues that the decentralization of the Tokugawa order was rooted in the strength of the *ie*, not the weakness of central power. The most important political manifestation of the *ie* was the warrior household, wherein the warrior's investiture, with its attendant rights and privileges, was the family patrimony. The body politic consisted of a hierarchy of warrior *ie*: the shogun invested daimyo, who in turn subinfeudated vassals. Although the autonomy of these warrior *ie* was drastically reduced during the seventeenth century, the shogunate continued to honor the financial and legal autonomy of the daimyo. Indeed, it was the daimyo who were most effective in redefining their vassals as subordinate members of their own *ie* rather than independent *ie* heads. Thus, despite the supremacy of the shogunal house, shogunal power was constantly mediated through the authority of other daimyo *ie*. The notion of the *ie* is particularly important because it can be linked readily with other terms of Tokugawa political language: a "state" (*kokka*) is the *ie* of a *kuni* (country). This sense of *kokka* is thus semantically and logically linked with Mizubayashi's notion of a "compound state" (*fukugō kokka*), wherein the large daimyo domains existed as small countries (*shōkoku*).

The concept of *ie*, Mizubayashi observes, permeated early modern Japanese society, governing the management of farmer and merchant households, as well as religious orders. In True Pure Land Buddhism, for example, the headship of a temple was commonly treated as the patrimony of an *ie*. The eldest son succeeded his father as head priest, whereas younger sons held lesser positions in the temple complex. There are thus distinct parallels between the *ie* and the idea of *Herrschaft* in early modern Europe. Much as the concept of *Herrschaft*, or lordship, served to bind different *Länder* together in an imperial union, *ie*, linked through ties of vassalage, constituted a compound state. More broadly, *Herrschaft*, like *ie*, legitimized authority across class lines. Both concepts served to substantiate the authority of the father in a peasant household as well as the legal autonomy of a noble house.[51]

The vassal household held a potentially contradictory position with the daimyo's *ie*. The rights and privileges of each warrior house constituted an *ie* and were thus legitimized by patrimonial authority. This principle allowed retainers to resist reforms, such as the standardization of tax collection or limits on corvée, that challenged their established perquisites. The autonomy of vassal *ie*, however, could be challenged by subsuming vassal houses within the daimyo house. This process reconstructed the vassal *ie* as a subordinate unit of the daimyo *ie* and made the survival of the daimyo house the paramount concern for both lord and vassal. Because the head of an *ie* could direct family members in the broader interest of the *ie*, the daimyo, as patriarch to his vassals, could bind them to rules of conduct and strip them of traditional autonomy.[52] Patrimonial authority thus encompassed a tension between independent vassal *ie*, bound to their lord by a feudal pledge, and subsumed vassal *ie*, bound to their lord as members of his house.

Kasaya Kazuhiko has taken this tension as a defining quality of early modern politics. According to Kasaya, the early modern era was characterized not by the diminution of independent, patrimonial rights but by their transformation. In the Warring States era, samurai had broad, independent authority over their holdings. Their patrimonial authority (which Kasaya calls their *mochibun*, or holding) gave them broad latitude in defending their interests: to increase or defend their territory, they could declare war, conclude peace, and arrange alliances. In the early modern structure these powers were eliminated. Daimyo stripped their vassals of their rights to independent military action and made them subordinate to daimyo law. The shogunate exercised similar authority over daimyo. Kasaya insists, however, that we also look at what retainers gained when these autonomous powers were lost. As agents in a daimyo's government, retainers gained the power to affect the decisions of a larger political structure. Instead of raising an army to advance their interests, powerful warrior families could use their hereditary positions in the domain government regularly and systematically to influence policy. Kasaya notes how in early modern politics, dictatorial lords were vastly outnumbered by consultative lords: daimyo and shoguns who relied on the counsel of their retainers. Daimyo were rarely autocratic, he argues, because early modern politics was based on patrimonial authority. Daimyo respected the patrimonial rights of their vassals by consulting with them on major issues. The pervasiveness of consultative decision-making and the scarcity of daimyo autocracy reflect the continued power of subordinate warriors.[53]

The subsumption of a samurai's patrimony into the broader daimyo *ie* had a transformative effect on political practice. Because a warrior's *ie* was only as vital as the broader state structure of which it was a part, the preservation of patrimony became enmeshed with loyal service to the state. Effective service as a domain official became a part of defending and increasing one's patrimony. Kasaya has thus pointed to a "bureaucratic" tendency in the patrimonial system. If a lord acted against the best interest of his house or challenged the administrative traditions of the domain, a retainer could legitimately oppose him. Loyalty to the institution of the daimyo "house" took precedence over personal loyalty to the daimyo.

This aspect of Tokugawa tradition should not be overstated. Tokugawa-era administrative structures were not Weberian bureaucracies. Even when tightly bound by government regulations, samurai administrators were as concerned with rank and status as with the exercise of instrumental rationality. Further, administrative positions were heritable, thus making early modern administrative structures more *Gemeinschaft* than *Gesellschaft*. But Kasaya's notion of bureaucracy points to another essential tension within patrimonial authority: vassals owed service both to their own "houses" and to the "house" of their lord.[54]

Feudal and patrimonial authority coexisted with a third source of daimyo authority, which I call suzerain authority: the autonomy of country daimyo in civil affairs. Suzerain authority had its roots in the independent political authority of Warring States–era daimyo. *Sengoku daimyō* based their rule on their ability to bring tranquility and order to their holdings. They brought peace to their realms by stopping feuds among their retainers and repelling invaders. This, in turn, justified their expanded authority over commoners: *sengoku daimyō* claimed independent fiscal authority, conducted cadastral surveys, and regulated commerce and currency. Such daimyo described themselves as *kōgi* based on their ability to bring peace to the lands they ruled (*ando*) and to succor the people (*kokumin*) of their states (*kokka*).[55]

The early Tokugawa shoguns greatly restricted the ambit of daimyo autonomy, but the traditions of daimyo suzerainty remained an important part of the early modern political system. In the rhetoric of the great domains, the daimyo were lords invested by heaven with "countries" and obligated to succor their "people." The investiture was itself evidence of the lord's virtue, but it also demanded virtuous and sage conduct. From the mid-seventeenth century, suzerain authority drew largely on neo-Confucian conceptions of rulership. Daimyo were thus expected to manifest *jinsei*, or "benevolent rule." The concept of *jinsei* called for a wise and virtuous ruler dedicated to the promotion of the people's welfare. Like much of Tokugawa thought, the concept of suzerain authority was syncretic and also incorporated Buddhist elements. Daimyo were expected to treat their subjects with "compassion" or "mercy," thus manifesting Buddhist virtues.[56] Suzerain authority assumed an equivalence of daimyo and shogun. Both were lords entrusted by a higher power with the responsibility to bring peace and prosperity to their people. "The realm [*tenka*] is the realm of heaven, not the realm of any one man," wrote Sakai Tadayuki, daimyo of Obama. "Hence even what is held by the shogun, much less what is held by the lords, is held in trust."[57]

A critical issue was the role of the shogun in conveying this "heavenly mandate" to the daimyo: was the shogun an independent agent or merely a middleman? Ikeda Mitsumasa, the daimyo of Okayama, saw the shogunate as an autonomous authority. "The shogun," he observed, "receives his authority over the people of Japan as a trust from heaven. The daimyo receives authority over the people as a trust from the shogun. The daimyo's councillors and retainers should aid the daimyo in bringing peace and harmony to the people." In 1657, he reminded his district magistrates of the threat of shogunal intervention: "If we rule carelessly, and govern so that there are people who are starving and cold or so that parts of the province are depopulated, then we shall not escape confiscation of the domain by his majesty."[58] Although Ikeda clearly subordinated himself to the shogun, he was not a disinterested observer. He held advisory privileges with the shogun Iemitsu and was related to the Tokugawa house: his mother had been adopted by the shogun Hidetada and his wife was a niece of Iemitsu.[59] Daimyo without such strong links with the shogunate were less inclined to subordinate themselves to shogunal intercession. Kuroda Nagamasa, for example, had been a Tokugawa ally at the battle of Sekigahara and praised the shogun in his will as a leader peerless in both war and peace. Nagamasa, however, did not mention the shogun when instructing his heirs on managing the domain. Instead, his instructions implied that the daimyo was responsible largely to heaven. "If your descendants should carry on our spirit, strictly obeying the law, practicing frugality and prudence, ruling the people with humanity and virtue, perfecting government [*seidō o tadashiku*] and keeping the customs of our house gallant and upright, all the world [*tenka*] will hear of the humanity and virtue of our house and will submit [to our rule] in great numbers." A failure to rule in this fashion would result in "heaven's punishment" and the loss of the "state" and "country."[60] In a similar fashion, Tōdō Takatora, daimyo of Tsu, wrote, "As our precious country is something entrusted to us, we cannot be negligent in any way." Takatora skillfully left unanswered the question of who or what had entrusted Tsu to the Tōdō.[61]

In ignoring the role of the shogunate, apologists for daimyo authority were adopting a strategy parallel to that of shogunal apologists. In his essays on shogunal legitimacy, for example, Arai Hakuseki did not denigrate the emperor. Instead, he noted that Tokugawa Ieyasu had brought peace to Japan after a period of chaos and had received heaven's mandate. Hakuseki implied that the imperial house had lost heaven's mandate through incompetence and thus could not be superior to the shogunate. Hakuseki thus cast the shogunate as Japan's supreme ruler without directly challenging the emperor system. In a similar vein, apologists for daimyo authority did not deny that heaven's mandate passed through the shogunate. Yet, in neglecting to explore this process, they made the shogunate's role incidental rather than critical.[62]

Defenders of daimyo autonomy were careful not to attack the shogunate, much as Hakuseki was loath to attack the emperor directly. Yet a close reading of domain laws suggests that daimyo and their advisers had reservations about the ambit of shogunal authority. In the early 1600s, for example, Yonezawa repeatedly ordered retainers accompanying the daimyo to Edo strictly to obey shogunal laws.[63] Apparently, Yonezawa legal authorities thought that shogunal laws applied outside Yonezawa. But the situation inside Yonezawa remained less clear. There is no edict in the collected domain laws that explicitly commands retainers to obey shogunal laws when in Yonezawa. Instead, the orders to retainers in Yonezawa enjoin them from publicly criticizing shogunal edicts.[64] The difference here is telling. Outside Yonezawa the shogunate was both powerful and legitimate. Inside Yonezawa, however, the domain recognized the shogunate's power more than its legitimacy. Thus, the domain prohibited open disregard for the shogunate, rather than disregard itself. Although the domain often relayed shogunal orders, it explicitly interposed itself between the shogun and its retainers.[65] By implication, shogunal orders did not apply unless the daimyo conveyed them to his people.

Suzerain, patrimonial, and feudal authority often served as complementary rather than oppositional doctrines. The most effective daimyo brought all three forms of authority to bear on political challenges. Uesugi Harunori, for example, defined himself as both a servant of his patrimony and a feudal lord. In 1769, when the shogunate ordered Harunori to repair the Western enceinte of Edo castle (Nishinomaru), he appeared, head bowed, before his retainers to justify yet another reduction in their meager stipends.

At present the state is in dire financial straits. Thus, as the people and the noble house of Uesugi are approaching ruin, it is a time for utmost loyalty and for the strength of hundreds of thousands of people to be applied to restoring our noble house. In principle there can be no lord where there are no people, and reflecting upon this I humbly ask for your loyal service to our family name. . . . I in no way ask loyal service to the single man before you, but ask you to consider the great kindness that you have received from generations past. With lord and vassal bringing to bear a resolution to die, and with all exhausting their spirits and supporting our family name, we will receive the strength of 100,000 people and the Western enceinte [repairs] will be completed with ease.

As in his epistle to Norihiro, Harunori emphasized service to the "state" over service to the lord. Retainers were bound to support the domain because their ancestors had received benefits from Harunori's (adopted) ancestors. This obligation was a patrimonial transformation of a quasi-contractual feudal tie: the original feudal bond between lord and vassal now linked their descendants as well. But Harunori also appealed to a broader sense of state and subject. Since the fortunes of the Uesugi house (*oie, gomyōji*) and the people were linked, Harunori saw himself, his retainers, and his commoners, the "100,000 people," united in serving the Uesugi house. Harunori thus depicted himself not as a lord reducing his vassals' income but as fellow servant of the "state" of Yonezawa.[66]

At the same time, Harunori's rhetoric renewed the feudal bond. By appearing directly before his retainers and speaking of their shared goal, Harunori invoked the personal tie between lord and vassal. By disavowing any personal claim to his retainers' allegiance, Harunori made himself all the more worthy of such allegiance. Indeed, his reference to "lord and vassal bringing to bear a resolution to die" invokes the imagery of warfare for a budgetary problem.

While developing the institutional, patrimonial authority of the Ue-sugi house, Harunori also made full use of his personal claim as a warlord on the allegiance of his samurai. Takenomata Masatsuna, who helped shape Harunori's public persona, described this aspect of Harunori as the "lord of compassion" (*nasake no nushi*), in contrast to a "lord of obligation" (*on no nushi*). Although Harunori relied on the obligation of vassals to repay their stipends through loyal service, he also cultivated a sentiment wherein a sense of duty "permeated the bodies and filled the hearts of vassals so that they gave their lives for their lord." Takenomata observed that unlike daimyo who ruled through intimidation and thus alienated their retainers, Harunori was able to inspire his retainers and subjects to serve the domain.[67]

Ideally, suzerain, patrimonial, and feudal authority all reinforced a daimyo's obligations to the shogun. Feudal authority emphasized the daimyo's obligation to serve the shogun loyally. Patrimonial authority stressed the lord's obligation to safeguard the domain as his family's patrimony. Suzerain authority emphasized a lord's obligation to bring peace and prosperity to his people through a mastery of civil affairs. Sound and sage rule often fulfilled all these obligations. A lord whose domain was peaceful and prosperous was both a worthy recipient of heaven's mandate and a diligent custodian of his family's patrimony. Unless he displayed a contempt for shogunal regulation, he was also a loyal retainer. When a lord's obligations to "heaven" and the shogun coincided, a daimyo who brought peace and prosperity to his realm was also serving his lord, the shogun.

The situation was more complicated when shogunal authority was seen as injurious to the domain. In such cases retainers understood suzerain authority as justifying opposition to shogunal control. When the shogunate ordered Tokushima to disband an indigo trading center in 1767, the domain elected to oppose the decision. In light of the shogunate's power, however, the domain did not appeal the decision but feigned compliance while covertly continuing the existing policy under a new name. This tactic was justified by the de facto weakness of the shogunate and the de jure authority of the daimyo. "Although the shogunate [*kōgi*] has issued a ruling, they have not investigated the details of the situation," wrote a key

Tokushima retainer, "and it would be difficult for the shogunate to investigate all the districts of our state [*gokokka*]." As an economic matter, moreover, the issue was legitimately beyond shogunal authority: "Because this is a matter for the lord of our country," wrote the retainer, "I believe that the shogunate's decision can be taken lightly."[68]

Tensions between suzerain, patrimonial, and feudal authority also played out within domains. While feudal ties demanded absolute loyalty to one's lord, suzerain and patrimonial authority demanded obedience to the "state," a more abstract entity. Retainers could thus challenge their daimyo based on the traditions of the daimyo's house or the needs of the "people." In extreme circumstances, retainers forced their daimyo to retire in favor of a more satisfactory heir. In each of the three domains to be examined, retainers drove their daimyo into retirement after prolonged disputes over domain policy. Such disputes commonly hinged on the opposition of feudal, patrimonial, and suzerain obligations. Reformers in Yonezawa, for example, challenged the daimyo Uesugi Shigesada based on his failure to succor his subjects. Shigesada yielded to pressure and retired in favor of his heir, Uesugi Harunori.[69]

Early modern politics thus involved both multiple sites of power and multiple sources of legitimacy. Domain administrators engaged issues of political economy in a complex web of conflicting ideologies and interests. The challenges of demography and commercialization often cut across multiple spheres of interest and authority. Reduced stipends, for example, served the interests of the "state" but not the patrimonial interests of the retainer. A dissolute daimyo could command the personal, feudal loyalty of his retainers, but not their loyalty to the "state," since his actions undermined the patrimony of his own house and those of his retainers. For domain statesmen, the key to politics lay in confronting the challenges of a changing political economy without precipitating the overt collision of interests and authorities. The most heated and volatile conflicts emerged when this proved impossible. Then the plural ideologies of Tokugawa rule supported a pluralism of dissent.

# 2

## The Nerves of the State

*The Political Economy of Daimyo Rule*

> Financial means are the nerves of the state.
> —Jean Bodin

Feudal, patrimonial, and suzerain authority formed the structural framework of political action in the early modern era. Empowered by this syncretic authority, domains intervened actively and aggressively in the daily lives of their subjects. Domains sought to restrict the religious practices of their subjects, legislate their sexuality, control their access to and use of technology, monitor their language and literature, and regulate their footwear and hair styles.

The essential bond between state and subject was economic: all domains taxed commoners to support samurai. Indeed, the authority to extract surplus from commoners was a defining quality of warrior patrimony, and hence a defining quality of the daimyo domain. This economic interaction often proved the impetus for broader interventions into peasant life. Indeed, domains became concerned with commoner behavior whenever it affected the ability or willingness of commoners to remit taxes. Daimyo concerns over the immorality of infanticide, for example, were at least partly grounded in its perceived threat to the size of the tax-paying population. Bookshelves, tile roofs, cotton undergarments, and other "luxuries" were condemned or forbidden as "indulgent" because they consumed income that might have gone to the government.

Because taking from peasants to support samurai constituted one of the key functions of early modern government, politics was driven by the clash between two sets of interests. As Ogyū Sorai lamented, farmers knew their government only as something that took away taxes, while samurai thought of peasants largely as a source of income. Much of early modern statecraft involved balancing these conflicting goals: samurai demands for income versus commoner opposition to taxation. The daimyo and his elite retainers made formal policy, of course, but policy was ultimately determined by the need to balance samurai and commoner interests.

Although nominally powerless, peasants exerted considerable sway over domain policy. Because the rhetoric of daimyo rule required lords to manifest "mercy" and "benevolence," peasants could oppose taxation through suzerain authority.[1] Under suzerain authority, legitimate rule required benevolence. The ultimate popular check on revenue extraction was, of course, rebellion, but determined farmers could force domains to change economic policy without resorting to violent confrontation. In 1760, for example, Yonezawa announced plans to extend its monopsony on flax to the Hōjō district, a region that had traditionally been exempted. The affected farmers blocked the plan. Over 350 farmers signed a petition opposing the monopsony, threatening to destroy the crop rather than sell it to the domain at a loss: "We request that by his lordship's benevolence we might continue as farmers [*hyakushō uchitsuzuki*], but if this is not granted we will dig up [our] flax by the roots."[2] The government canceled the plan. The specter of popular opposition was often as effective as the actual event. Arguing against a series of proposed levies, a Tokushima retainer cited the threat of peasant resistance: "[These reforms] will definitely be painful to those below. . . . [B]ecause they are unlikely to submit, I am extremely concerned that there may even be conspiratorial actions."[3]

Although peasant rebellion did not shake the foundations of daimyo rule, it did intimidate samurai administrators. The officials held responsible for a disturbance were often stripped of office, rank, and stipend. The impact of peasant protest was magnified by the factionalism of domain politics. Samurai officeholders could assume that rivals, eager to advance their own careers, would portray even small disturbances as evidence of dereliction of duty. This fear made peasant protest an ever present factor in determining government policy.

Less forceful checks on the domain's power included what James Scott has termed the "weapons of the weak": dissembling, evasion, and fraud.[4] Domains often worked with antiquated cadastral surveys, which neglected vast areas of reclaimed and improved land. Domains were also unable to rid their tax systems of corruption, and tax surveys designed to compensate for harvest shortfalls (*kemi*) became a ready opportunity for tax evasion. A 1785 decree from the Hirosaki domain elders (*karō*) to the district magistrates (*kōri bugyō*) reflected this dilemma:

> Two years ago there was a great harvest failure, and last autumn it was ordered that the intendants [*daikan*] conduct a tax-abatement survey, but have our subjects responded to our compassion? Although the reduction of taxes for crop losses is done entirely for the sake of the farmers, last year was extremely disadvantageous for the treasury. . . . This year things have been worrisome since the spring, [but] there is great variation in harvest conditions. Although appeals have, of course, increased since the recent typhoon, we have heard reports that do not ring true. Accordingly, if the tax-remission survey is not conducted with the utmost care and precision, it will inflict a loss on the treasury.[5]

The elders, of course, protested too much: tax abatements were often necessary to insure the survival of poorer farmers. The machinations of village officials nevertheless meant that most domains were unable to offer essential tax relief without creating attendant opportunities for fraud.

Samurai demands on peasants were based on both patrimonial and feudal authority. An invested retainer's income was his patrimony, and he thus had the right either to secure it from the peasantry or to receive its equivalent in compensation from his lord. Warrior claims on usufruct were also supported by feudal bonds. A retainer's investiture was granted in return for loyal service, and this exchange carried contractual overtones. If a lord failed to provide a loyal retainer with the usufruct of his fief, then the lord stood in violation of an implicit trust. These reciprocal commitments of obedience and usufruct legitimized a daimyo's "country" as well as a foot soldier's daily allowance.

Because samurai controlled the machinery of government, their demands for income were commonly expressed in the form of higher taxes. The lower levels of the samurai estate, however, were capable of considerable violence in pursuit of their interests. In 1755, for example, several Yonezawa samurai responded to years of stipend cuts by leading a band of peasants in revolt. The rebels attacked merchants they suspected of hoarding rice and distributed it among the mob. Hirosaki faced widespread samurai lawlessness when it sought to resettle samurai in the countryside and cut their stipends. Rather than farm, as the domain had hoped, the retainers coerced food and labor from local commoners: samurai lawlessness forced the cancellation of the project. Elite retainers were more circumspect in their opposition but equally protective of their privileges. Daimyo who challenged the perquisites and income of the domain elite were likely to find themselves forced into retirement and replaced with a more pliant heir.

Both commoner and samurai resistance had a quantitative dimension. All else being equal, samurai were most satisfied with larger stipends and commoners with lower taxes. A critical component of early modern statecraft lay in finding a quantitative balance between these two forces. In essence, domain administrators sought to find the combination of taxes and stipends that produced the least destabilizing mix of opposition. The equilibrium point between taxes and stipends was affected by two key socioeconomic forces. First, taxes tended to rise with economic output per commoner. Domains, not surprisingly, took more as their commoners produced more. We might think of increases in commoner output as increases in the supply of taxes. Second, taxes rose as the number of retainers per commoner increased. As the numbers of retainers rose, so did the level of taxation needed to maintain even minimal stipends. Increases in the number of retainers thus increased the demand for taxes. These processes are shown graphically in Figures 1 through 4. These graphs compare taxes, output, and demography in 237 domains using data compiled by the Meiji government. Two clear patterns emerge. First, domains with more productive commoners collected more in revenue per commoner. Second, domains with more retainers per commoner collected more in revenue per commoner.

Ideally we would run cross-sectional correlations for earlier decades and time-series analyses of individual domains across time, but the Tokugawa-era data are too fragmentary to support these

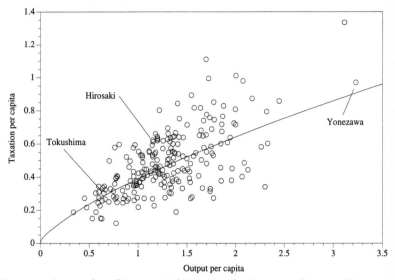

Figure 1. Scatterplot of Output and Taxation for Domains (linear scale)

NOTE: Output and taxation are in *koku*. For regression analysis and data sources, see the Appendix.

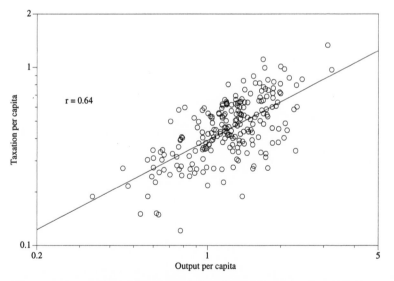

Figure 2. Scatterplot of Output and Taxation for Domains (logarithmic scale)

NOTE: Output and taxation are in *koku*. For regression analysis and data sources, see the Appendix.

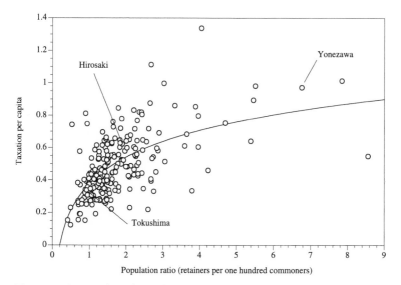

Figure 3. Scatterplot of Population Ratio and Taxation for Domains (linear scale)

NOTE: Taxation is in *koku*. For regression analysis and data sources, see the Appendix.

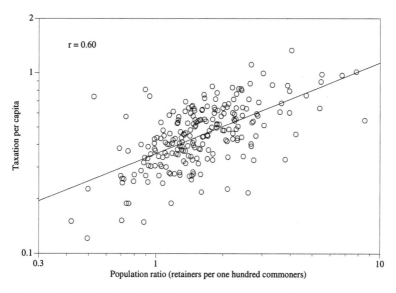

Figure 4. Scatterplot of Population Ratio and Taxation for Domains (logarithmic scale)

NOTE: Taxation is in *koku*. For regression analysis and data sources, see the Appendix.

calculations. Qualitative data, however, suggest that the correlations shown in Figures 1 through 4 did not suddenly appear in the 1860s. These correlations were a structural component of early modern political economy and existed in the seventeenth and eighteenth centuries. Further, these correlations held not only between domains but within domains over time. Officials in Yonezawa and Hirosaki, for example, were acutely aware that proportionally large retainer populations mandated high taxes. Administrators in Tokushima were interested in indigo prices because they affected the ability of commoners to remit taxes.

The correlations between output, demography, and taxation were axes of political and ideological conflict. Increases in commoner output, for example, were usually related to either protoindustrialization or commercialization. This meant that more profitable economic activities were also more directly tied to regional or national markets. Increases in economic output thus presented domains with increased revenue opportunities, but they also required that domains adapt to market forces. Increased demographic pressure also had a political and ideological aspect: the burden of a large samurai class prompted administrators in both Yonezawa and Hirosaki to reexamine the nature of samurai service. When faced with a choice between exorbitant taxes and meager stipends, domains were compelled to legitimize reductions in samurai emoluments. In response, Yonezawa portrayed samurai by-employments as opportunities for samurai to serve the "state," while Hirosaki represented samurai resettlement as a program of spiritual rejuvenation. Both programs, of course, served to reduce samurai demands on the domain fisc by promoting outside sources of income.

These policies also highlight the dialectic interaction between socioeconomic forces and domain policy. In Yonezawa and Hirosaki policy was shaped by the onerous burden of a large samurai class. But demography was not purely an objective phenomenon. When Yonezawa declared that retainer by-employments were not shameful but laudable, it made samurai more like commoners. What made retainers different from commoners was politics, not biology. Domain policy was thus both a cause and a result of socioeconomic forces.

## Sources of Revenue

An analysis of the interplay between the resistance of commoners and demands of the samurai requires a discussion of domain income. Agricultural sources dominated the revenue of Tokugawa domains. The largest single source of revenue was usually *nengu*, or tribute, a kind of agricultural tax levied on the annual harvest. Even in regions with highly developed commercial and nonagricultural sectors, direct levies on commodity production rarely exceeded income from *nengu*. Although historians sometimes speak of a *nengu* "rate," the proportion of crop taken as tax often varied both among and within villages. In 1639, for example, Yonezawa standardized the tax rate at 48 percent in four districts and at 41 percent in the remaining two. This standardization, however, did not involve setting the rate in each village at either 48 percent or 41 percent but adjusting the rates so that the district averages corresponded to the correct percentage. This practice of adjusting rates was called *narashimen*, literally "average rate." The domain abandoned the system in 1655, in part because arbitrary rate adjustments proved onerous to farmers.[6] As a result, the tax rate varied widely by village. An 1827 survey of the rural economy recorded statutory rates ranging from a low of 6 percent in the tiny village of Toinozawa and a high of 55.9 percent in Kuwayama: the domain-wide weighted average was 27.1 percent.[7] Such variations were not uncommon. In Tokushima, for example, the most common tax rate was 40 percent, but records for Higai village show various parcels taxed at nine different rates ranging from 18 to 80 percent. The 40 percent rate was common but in no way uniform.[8]

Even statutory tax rates are a poor guide to the actual tax burden. Tax payments commonly involved converting rice into specie, or lesser food grains into rice. By skewing these conversion rates, a domain could raise taxes indirectly. The inaccuracy of cadastral surveys complicates the issue even further. Accurate land records were expensive to maintain, and the peasantry had a clear interest in obstructing any attempts to update them. As a result, tax officials often worked with surveys that they knew to be seriously inaccurate.[9]

Distribution of the village's tax burden among the village families was handled by the headman (*shōya*) or other village officials.

*Nengu* was collected under two different systems, commonly known as the *kemi* system and the *jōmen* system. Under the *kemi* system every village was subject to annual assessment by a government official. The *jōmen* system used fixed assessments, subject to reevaluation every five to ten years. The system allowed, however, for the investigation of requests for tax reduction due to poor harvests. The *kemi* system was widespread in the early Tokugawa era but was replaced by the *jōmen* system in many domains during the late seventeenth and early eighteenth centuries.[10]

Japanese historians have taken the transition from the *kemi* to the *jōmen* system as a major development in early modern political economy. Because it extracted all grain that might result from increased yields, the *kemi* system has been seen as a powerful disincentive to increasing farm productivity. The annual assessments required under the *kemi* system were also associated with a high level of corruption and extortion by local tax assessors. By contrast, under the *jōmen* system assessments were made less frequently, the administration of the system was more centralized, and peasants were allowed to keep a greater proportion of any increase. Both Marxist and neoclassical economic historians have treated the introduction of the *jōmen* system as a turning point in Tokugawa political economy, although for differing reasons. Neoclassicists stress how fixed assessments provided an incentive to increase yields and hence led to economic growth. Marxists, on the other hand, see the abolition of the *kemi* system as the first in a series of failed domain policies. They argue that the *jōmen* system was intended to maintain the small peasant class by reducing the tax burden, but instead it furthered commercialization and led to the appearance of wealthy peasant landlords and landless laborers.[11]

The theoretical foundations of these arguments are clear, but in practice the *kemi* and *jōmen* systems were far less distinct than either theory suggests. Even domains that never formally abandoned the *kemi* system often neglected to conduct annual surveys. Hirosaki, for example, formally maintained the *kemi* system but conducted reassessments only after poor harvests.[12] Because even the *jōmen* system allowed for reductions in light of crises, the Hirosaki *kemi* system provided the same incentives to increase yields as the *jōmen* system. In practice both the *kemi* and *jōmen* systems used fixed assessments because most domains neglected to conduct surveys according to schedule.

Apart from *nengu*, the Tokugawa tax system was one of bewildering complexity. During the tax reform of the 1870s, the Meiji government recorded some 2,000 different forms of levy. Agricultural taxes other than *nengu* were often known generically as *komononari*, but more specific names were used with little consistency from region to region. For analytical purposes these taxes can be grouped into three categories: taxes on usufruct, taxes on by-employments, and corvée.

Taxes on usufruct were levied on such common resources as forests, woodlands, rivers, and oceans. Because the use of these resources was difficult to monitor, usufruct taxes tended to be levied by household. Charges on by-employments, ranging from fishing to moneylending, were levied either as flat charges or as percentage taxes. Corvée levies varied from onerous to trivial. Villages near the national highway system were subject to a corvée called *sukegō*, which required villagers to provide porters for *sankin kōtai* travel. In most of Japan, however, the corvée burden was incidental, save for occasional labor drafts linked to specific construction or riparian projects.[13]

As economic development increased the availability of wage labor, domains began to convert corvée levies into payments in cash or grain. The development of market networks provided a similar incentive to convert levies on usufruct and by-employments into cash. Such levies often became indistinguishable from surcharges on *nengu*. In the early 1600s, for example, Yonezawa levied both corvée and a usufruct fee for gathering firewood on farm households, but these were later combined into a single charge of fifteen copper *mon* per household. In 1657, the domain decreed that land yielding 32 *koku* in taxes (*mononari*) would be equated with one household. This reform effectively changed the firewood levy and corvée from separate taxes to a simple cash surcharge on the *nengu* payments.[14]

The traditional *nengu* system, which assessed only grain yield, was not designed to tax complex commercial networks, and commercialization has often been seen as inimical to the Tokugawa order. In much Japanese historical writing, domain financial problems stemmed from the inability of the domains to adapt to a peasant

commodity economy. Historians like Sasaki Junnosuke and Yamaguchi Keiji have argued that domains were predicated on a natural
economy that centered on the production of food grains by small
independent farmers (*shōnō keiei*). As the focus of economic activity
shifted from food production for a local market to commodity production for a national market, domains became dependent on merchant intermediaries for revenue. This undermined government control. Commercialization also served to polarize the farmers into
wealthy landlords and tenants, undermining the domains' agricultural base.[15] For Horie Hideichi, it was a "fundamental economic
law" that "the development of a peasant commodity economy by
small independent cultivators [*honbyakushō keiei*] intensified the
fundamental contradictions of the economic structure of the Tokugawa *bakuhan* system."[16]

Other scholars have emphasized the different rates at which early
modern domains were able to adapt to commercialization. In his influential study *Meiji ishin*, for example, Tōyama Shigeki argued that
the ability to harness the energies of peasant commodity production
was the deciding factor in the struggle between the *bakufu* and the
great southwestern domains of Satsuma and Chōshū.[17] The most
visible aspect of this adaptation to commerce was the development
of domain-sanctioned guilds (*kabunakama*) or commodity agencies
(*kokusan kaijo* or *sanbutsu kaijo*). Such agencies emerged throughout Japan in the latter 1700s and 1800s.[18]

This emphasis on commerce is not without foundation. While the
Marxian emphasis on the growing misery of the peasantry is empir-
ically questionable, the market economy did increase peasant vulnerability. The agricultural wage laborers of the nineteenth century
did enjoy higher incomes than their serf-like predecessors (*nago* and
*genin*) of the seventeenth century. But by custom, the seventeenth-
century landlord shielded his workers from the most ruinous effects
of harvest failures or market crises. The nineteenth-century em-
ployer extended no such protection to his wage laborers. The va-
garies of the market tended to polarize the village into borrowers
and lenders, or landlords and tenants, thus dissolving village solidarity.[19] Peasant protest changed accordingly. Rather than submit a
petition under the leadership of their village headman, peasants began to attack their headmen and to protest government policy in in-

creasingly violent and direct fashion. This transformed peasant protest from a manageable, almost homeostatic, check on domain policy to a destabilizing threat.[20]

These broader social effects of the market economy troubled many late Tokugawa thinkers deeply. For domain administrators, however, the more imminent problem was adapting domain finances to this changing economy. Domains struggled continually to adapt their tax systems to commercial products and activities. Yonezawa domain revised its cadastral surveys to record a wide range of commercial products, including lacquer trees, flax, chrysanthemums, and silk. The government then either taxed or established monopsony control over these products. Peasants were required to sell set volumes of flax to the domain at prices below market value. The system was formally a domain purchasing agency, although the domain often did not pay for flax in cash but in credit against other *nengu* obligations.[21]

The direct taxation of commodities, however, proved far more complex than the taxation of food grains. A silent constraint on the taxation of commercial products was the ability of commoners to stop producing what the domain taxed. As the expansion of markets allowed farmers to grow crops for cash and buy what they did not grow, farmers became interested in crops for their market value, not their usefulness in daily life. Since taxes reduced profit margins, taxation reduced the incentive to grow a given crop. This phenomenon was not a major concern under the *nengu* system. *Nengu* was a tax on the productive capacity of the land, a factor for which there was no ready substitute.[22] But while farmers could not avoid *nengu* they could easily avoid taxes on any particular commercial crop by switching to another. This meant that, from the domain's perspective, the market economy had a pronounced tendency to flee taxation.

It was here that traditional economic thought proved least effective. Yonezawa's monopsony on lacquer, for example, served to shrink the lacquer crop, because farmers sought more profitable alternatives. The more directly a domain taxed production, the more it confronted the ability of commoners to change economic activity or, more technically, the price elasticity of supply. Faced with the volatility of commercial production, domains sought to compel commoners to plant designated crops. In Yonezawa the domain mandated the cultivation of lacquer trees and penalized peasants for up-rooting them.[23]

The weakness of such coercive policies was the enormous cost of enforcement. The commoners of Yonezawa challenged the domain's orders to plant lacquer trees not through insurrection but by building "seedlings" from twigs to deceive inspectors. Such resistance through subterfuge proved effective precisely because it was so difficult and costly to police. Resistance to taxation did not need to be overwhelming, only expensive, in order to force the domain to reconsider its policies.

Domains that effectively taxed market activities commonly did so by recognizing this critical difference between subsistence farming and market-oriented production. Tokushima, for example, raised revenue by providing loans to indigo farmers, but offered a rate lower than traditional lenders in order to encourage indigo cultivation. Yonezawa successfully promoted sericulture in the 1800s by providing mulberry seedlings free of charge and exempting the crop from taxation. The resulting increase in productivity allowed the beleaguered population to meet their existing tax obligations. What unified these strategies was less an acceptance of the market as a legitimate principle of economic organization than a recognition that coercing economic activity was prohibitively expensive. As the Yonezawa reformer Nozoki Yoshimasa, observed, "It is inevitable, given human nature, that people will not do something unless they envy their neighbor's profit and thus pursue it of their own accord [*mizukara susumu*]."[24]

It is important to note that domains did not need to tax commercial farming or protoindustrial activity in order to benefit from it. An example of such indirect dependence on commodity production is Tokushima's indigo policy. By the late Tokugawa era, indigo constituted roughly 20 percent of Tokushima's agricultural production, and the manufacture of indigo cubes was a major local industry. Although Tokushima levied taxes on the sale of indigo leaves and balls, the domain's direct tax receipts from indigo were minimal. But because farmers were paying *nengu* with income from indigo, the government was effectively supported by indigo production. Once the domain realized its dependence on indigo, it began to intervene to support indigo prices and promote indigo production.

The most direct forms of control over commercial production were domain monopoly and monopsony agencies. Domains could restrict the sale of key commodities and become either the sole buyer or seller within the domain. While such agencies could be extremely profitable, monopoly systems also entailed formidable potential for mismanagement. A principal difficulty was securing the revenue with which to buy the commodities. Some domains granted tax exemptions instead of paying for goods, in effect "buying" the goods with tax credits. But these exemptions meant a drop in revenue. Since domains often turned to monopoly systems in times of fiscal crisis, this was an arduous option.

Domains could also secure capital through merchant houses: the merchant would monopsonize the product with private capital and forward a portion of the monopsony proceeds to the domain. Lack of capital was but one reason to ally with powerful merchants. Even when domains could successfully monopsonize a product domestically, they frequently needed established merchant houses to market the goods outside the domain. In Yonezawa such pressures led the domain to entrust its flax monopsony to a prominent Kyoto merchant, Nishimura Kyūzaemon.[25] Other domains relied on merchant guilds (*ton'ya* or *kabunakama*). Rather than tax production and distribution directly, the domain conferred monopsony rights on a guild and then taxed the guild. Such monopoly agencies were a common means of taxing commodities in the latter Tokugawa era.[26]

An alternative means of raising capital was through domain currency: using fiat money to purchase goods. Given their political authority, domains could require producers to accept currency in lieu of specie. As the currency began to circulate, however, the ability of the government to insure the acceptance of its notes decreased. While domains such as Himeji and Fukuoka controlled the volume of currency in order to avoid just such a crisis of confidence, other domains often flooded the market with worthless paper.[27] Akita, for example, began to issue domain currency in 1755 as part of an ambitious scheme to monopsonize rice. The government, unfortunately, overissued the currency, and its value deteriorated rapidly. Although the domain could compel some acceptance of the currency within its borders, non-domain merchants insisted on being paid in convertible currency. The Akita system collapsed in 1757, when a group of tea merchants from Mino appealed to the *bakufu* to demand the conversion of the notes. The currency scandal was not only an economic debacle but also a grave political humiliation for the domain: the advisers who had supported the currency issue were executed, ordered to commit *seppuku*, or banished.[28]

If managed properly, fiat money was a valuable fiscal tool. Tokushima, for example, used paper money to supplement a shortage of specie in the domain beginning in the 1680s. Because the domain accepted its own currency as legal tender for tax payments, the currency circulated fairly smoothly even when the domain could not guarantee convertibility.[29] Most domains, however, could not manage currency issues over the long term. When domains printed currency to cover their immediate revenue shortfalls, and thus ignored the economy's demand for money, they commonly overissued the currency and caused severe inflation. Intriguingly, currencies associated with monopoly agencies were usually more stable than general issues.[30] Fukuoka successfully managed a currency linked to its wax monopsony but was unable to maintain the value of an independent currency known as *kitte*. The currency depreciated so severely that, according to one account, commoners used the certificates to wipe their noses.[31]

Domains could also supplement tax revenue through contributions from merchant houses or wealthy farmers. Commoners would give money to the domain in exchange for various titles or perquisites of samurai rank. In the case of wealthy families, such contributions could be considerable. A well-known example is the relationship between the Honma family and Shōnai domain. The Honma house was a Shōnai merchant family that emerged in the 1700s as the largest landlord and most powerful financier in Shōnai. The family's contributions to the Shōnai fisc were enormous. From 1843 to 1873, the Honma donated 225,560 *ryō* and neglected to collect 203,172 *ryō* in loans. Total contributions were 428,732 *ryō*, roughly equal in value to an annual harvest in Shōnai. The Honma were rewarded correspondingly. The government conferred full samurai status on the head of the main house and routinely solicited the advice of the Honma in important matters of fiscal policy.[32]

Yet the Honma were atypically wealthy, and most domains could not rely on steady contributions from one merchant household. In the absence of such gifts, securing contributions from merchant households tended to degenerate into the sale of ranks. Some domains issued price lists detailing the costs of various attributes of samurai status. Such strategies were widely viewed as demeaning to samurai, since they implicitly valued wealth over both nobility and loyalty. The sale of status often provoked acrimonious responses. When Mori Heiemon of Yonezawa sought to secure loans by flattering wealthy merchants with investitures, he provoked a conflict with the domain elite that resulted in his assassination.[33]

When domains could not solicit "gifts," their final option was interest-bearing loans. Domains commonly borrowed from major merchant houses in Edo and Osaka, sometimes using future revenue as collateral. Interest rates varied depending both on the creditworthiness of the government and on personal ties between the domain and the lender. Irrespective of the interest rate, loans were not a practical means of supplementing consistent revenue shortfalls. Loans could provide a temporary revenue supplement or be used to capitalize important ventures, but the dangers of accumulating an unmanageable debt were not lost on domain administrators. Beyond the burden of interest payments, a domain that became heavily dependent on loans lost control of its fiscal policy. Kumamoto was generating deficits of 70,000 to 80,000 *koku* per annum throughout the 1750s until its financier, Osaka merchant Kōnoike Zen'emon, refused to support the domain further. The domain was functionally insolvent until credit was secured from another merchant house.[34] Budget problems in Sendai in the 1790s led the government to cede much of its fiscal authority to the Yamagata merchant house.[35] To avoid such situations, domains sometimes unilaterally rescheduled or abrogated their credit obligations. During the Tenpō reforms Chōshū and Fukuoka defaulted entirely, while Satsuma agreed to repay its debt, but without interest and over 250 years.[36]

## Demands for Expenditure

Domains taxed commoners to cover government expenditures. The major expense for most Tokugawa daimyo was the maintenance of their vassal bands. Stipends were, in theory, investitures that retainers received in return for fealty to their lord. All retainers thus shared a link to the means of production. Samurai income, however, was extremely unequally distributed. The elite in many domains received stipends in excess of 10,000 *koku* annually, equal to the investiture of a small daimyo, while lower vassals often subsisted on less than ten *koku*. This gross disparity in income was a constant source of tension within the samurai class. Lower samurai were well aware that they lived on less than did the servants of the domain elite.[37] It was difficult for reformers to justify a more equal distribution of income, because to do so would challenge the tradition of patrimonial authority that legitimized the stipends of all members of the samurai class.

Because most important government offices were reserved for samurai, stipends were, in part, government salaries. Samurai not only served as police, soldiers, and tax collectors but also administered and maintained granaries, ports, and roads. But the supply of samurai often exceeded the demand. In many domains, large numbers of samurai were unemployed or underemployed. In some cases, several retainers held the same office concurrently and served in rotation.

Retainers were supported under two types of investiture: landed fiefs and non-landed fiefs. Non-landed fiefs were known as *kuramai chigyō* (stipended fiefs), *kuramai* (stipends), or *hōroku* (salary). With non-landed fiefs, grain was taken from farmers, sent to a central treasury, and disbursed to retainers residing in the castle town. Such stipends were measured in rice, but retainers were often paid in a combination of rice, lesser grains, specie, and domain currency. A stipend paid largely in rice was generally a sign of prestige, while payment in cash was associated with menial status. Retainers who received their stipends in grain converted a suitable proportion to cash through authorized castle-town merchants. In theory, the claim to a *kuramai* stipend constituted an investiture, but the system of payments resembled that of a salary.[38]

Vassals with landed fiefs (*jikata chigyō*, or simply *chigyō*) maintained greater control over their holdings. These retainers often resided in the countryside and exerted direct legal and economic control over the peasantry. They determined the size and schedule of tax payments and were allowed to demand labor services from the peasants on their fiefs. Rather than receive a salary in rice, convert it to cash, and hire servants, a retainer with a landed fief would demand corvée services of his peasants. Even when landed vassals lived in the castle town, they received tax payments directly from the peasants or village headman on their fief.

Landed fiefs commonly have been taken as a legacy of the medieval period, while stipends are understood as the typical investiture of the early modern era. Most domains are assumed to have shifted from *jikata chigyō* to *kuramai/hōroku* and assembled their vassal bands in the castle town in the seventeenth century. Where *jikata chigyō* survived, historians have treated them as a vestigial institution wherein the fiefholder's rights were sharply curtailed. The abolition of landed fiefs and the assembling of retainers in the castle town is understood as essential to the development of early modern political economy because it altered relations not only between lord and vassal but also between vassal and peasant.[39] A good summary of this interpretation is given by Stephen Vlastos:

> The most important [feature] for understanding the political economy of Tokugawa feudalism . . . was the absolute separation of the samurai and peasant classes, enforced in both Bakufu territory and private fiefs. . . . All samurai retainers were required to live in castle towns, where they subsisted on stipends drawn from the lord's storehouse. This arrangement eliminated subinfeudation and the last vestiges of the manorial (*shōen*) economy of the medieval (*chūsei*) period, and gave rise to new bureaucratic procedures of exploitation. Unable to command peasants' labor directly in agricultural production, the Tokugawa seigneurial class derived its revenue from land rents assessed on villages.[40]

In *Kōzaha* thought, the principal Japanese Marxist interpretation, this separation of warrior and peasant (*heinō bunri*) is seen as a major contradiction within the Tokugawa system. The abolition of landed fiefs allowed daimyo to centralize control over their domains, but since retainers were now salaried urban consumers, *heinō bunri* led to the commercialization of both peasant production and samurai consumption. It is argued that this commercialization of the farm economy led to the development of landless wage laborers and, ultimately, to the appearance of the semi-proletarianized peasants who constituted the revolutionary forces that destroyed the *bakuhan* system. The foundation of the Tokugawa system thus produced the seeds of its own destruction, and the internal contradictions of Japanese feudalism parallel the fundamental contradictions of capitalist economic development.[41]

Although the link between *heinō bunri* and commercialization is persuasive, the contention that landed fiefs were a vanishing, medieval institution is misleading. A study frequently cited in support of this thesis is Kanai Madoka's analysis of *Dokai kōshūki*, a peerage register of some 240 lords compiled in 1690. While the register is concerned primarily with the finer points of court rank and genealogy, it also describes how the daimyo administered their domains, including whether they supported their retainers through landed fiefs or stipends. According to the register, over 80 percent of the domains in Japan had shifted to stipends by the late seventeenth century.[42]

Such an analysis ignores the skewed distribution of land and population among domains. The domains that maintained landed fiefs were in fact the largest, including Kaga, Chōshū, Satsuma, Kumamoto, and Fukuoka. Of the ten largest domains, nine maintained landed fiefs. The choice of fief system seems to have been closely linked to the size of the domain: all domains over 500,000 *koku* maintained landed fiefs, whereas virtually all below 50,000 *koku* abandoned them. In this context, the number of domains that adopted stipends rather than landed fiefs is an unreliable indicator of the importance of the institution. *Dokai kōshūki* gives the size of the domain in *omotedaka*, a formal measure that only indirectly reflects the actual productivity of the domain. Guarded estimates suggest, however, that although less than 20 percent of domains maintained landed fiefs in the late seventeenth century, these domains comprised roughly half the territory of Japan.[43]

Hirosaki, Tokushima, and Yonezawa all maintained landed fiefs in some form throughout the Tokugawa era. The rights attendant upon a landed fief varied with the domain. In Tokushima landed vassals retained extensive rights over their fiefs throughout the Tokugawa era. In the seventeenth century landed fiefholders were obliged to prepare soldiers for military emergencies. Landed vassals selected peasants from their fiefs and drilled them as their personal foot soldiers, arming them with long or short swords at their discretion. Peasants were subject to a wide variety of other corvée services, and retainers whose duties took them to Edo or Osaka brought peasants with them as servants (*hōkōnin*). Such services were gradually converted to cash payments over the seventeenth and eighteenth centuries, but the daimyo always recognized the legal immunity of landed fiefs. Such fiefs were specifically exempted from domain cadastral surveys, and peasants on landed fiefs needed the authorization of the vassal for transactions involving the sale or pawning of land. Since most landed fiefholders were high-ranking, powerful retainers, these rights became an important perquisite of elite status.[44]

The most powerful landed vassals in Tokushima were the Inada, whose holdings exceeded 14,000 *koku*. In the early seventeenth century, the Hachisuka charged the Inada with the defense of two castles, one in Sumoto on the island of Awaji and the second in Waki in western Tokushima. To support their services, the Inada were granted large fiefs (each over 7,000 *koku*) near both castles. The power of the Inada was enhanced by their rank in the Hachisuka retainer band. As vassals of *karō* rank, the Inada were one of a handful of families entitled to hold the post of domain executor (*shiokiyaku*), the most powerful administrative position in the land. The foreign crisis of the mid-nineteenth century led to an increase in the autonomous prerogatives of the Inada, such as subinfeudation. To manage the defense of Sumoto castle, the Inada invested large numbers of vassals. The vassal band based in Sumoto grew from under 70 in the early 1800s, to 501 in 1832, and 1,311 in 1842. Acutely aware of the foreign threat, Inada vassals emerged as enthusiastic imperial loyalists. Although Tokushima remained cautiously neutral until the defeat of shogunate forces, Inada vassals fought independently as loyalists.[45]

In Yonezawa landed fiefs remained into the nineteenth century, but the rights of landed fiefholders were strictly regulated. The tribute that landed vassals could levy was fixed by decree in 1683, and retainers were directed to bring delinquent taxpayers to the intendant's office, a thinly veiled restriction on the vassal's independent juridical rights. Fiefholders remained entitled to a variety of payments in kind, including sugar, rope, and straw, but these tax rates were set by the government as well.

In Yonezawa the major difference between landed fiefs and non-landed fiefs was administrative. Tax revenues from stipended fiefs (*kuramai chigyō*) went from the peasant to the village headman (*ki-moiri*), through the local intendant's office (*daikansho*), and into the daimyo's treasury. With landed fiefs, the revenue went from the peasant through the village headman and to the retainer. Such landed fiefs represent what Japanese scholars call "skeletonized" landed fiefs: since the domain usurped most rights attendant on a landed fief, the fiefs were *jikata chigyō* in name only.[46]

The prominence of landed fiefs was closely linked with fiscal pressures on the domain. Under a stipend system, the daimyo had full legal and fiscal control over his domain, but he assumed direct responsibility for the livelihood of his retainers. With landed fiefs, a daimyo ceded legal and fiscal authority over territory to his vassals but accordingly relieved himself of direct responsibility for their support. In theory, rural samurai could live on less than urban samurai: living expenses were lower in the countryside, and retainers could supplement their income through farming or by-employments. Accordingly, rural samurai (*gōshi*) remained common in regions with many retainers per commoner. These retainers continued to support themselves though farming, by-employments, and direct control over peasant villages. The domains best known for their large *gōshi* populations (Satsuma, Tosa, Chōshū, Wakayama, Sendai, and Yonezawa) were all domains with large numbers of retainers per commoner.

Since landed fiefs could legitimately be smaller than other investitures, a domain could restore its finances by shifting from stipends to landed fiefs or by having landed vassals reside in the countryside. Chōshū employed such a policy throughout the latter Tokugawa period. Although the domain did not force vassals to resettle on their fiefs, it allowed poorer retainers to live on their fiefs until their finances recuperated. Rural residence was designed to be temporary. Retainers were to stay on their fiefs only until they had repaid their debts. By the 1840s, however, roughly a third of the vassal band was living in the countryside for this reason.[47]

In Hirosaki, the government used landed fiefs both to reduce expenditures and to increase revenue. Landed fiefs were central to the reclamation of land in the 1600s. Retainers who reclaimed farmland were allowed to keep 40 percent as their fief with the remainder going to the domain treasury. In the 1680s the domain began converting landed fiefs to stipends, but the tradition of landed vassals remained an important precedent for Hirosaki administrators. In the wake of the Tenmei famine, the domain forcibly resettled vassals in farm villages as a means of curtailing its financial obligations. Proponents of the undertaking, which proved extremely unpopular, cited seventeenth-century precedent.

The prevalence and importance of landed fiefs into the nineteenth century belies any notion that landed fiefs or landed samurai were a medieval vestige. The choice between landed fiefs and stipends was not a choice between medieval and early modern institutions but a balancing of rights and obligations. The choice between the two institutions involved the patrimonial authority of the retainer versus the patrimonial and suzerain authority of the lord. Suzerain authority gave the lord the right to define samurai compensation in the best interest of the "country." As a supreme lord, the daimyo laid claim to all the domain's tax rice and also assumed the full fiscal obligation of supporting its retainers. This transition from land to salary can also be understood as the subsumption of retainer patrimony within the daimyo's patrimony. The retainers thus lost some of their landed rights but gained increased protection under the powerful patrimonial authority of the lord. For this reason, retainers sometimes actively requested that their fiefs be converted into stipends.

Beyond stipends, the largest fiscal burden in most domains was the household expenses of the daimyo. Under *sankin kōtai* the daimyo was required to maintain two residences, one in his castle town and one in Edo. Because the lord's family remained in Edo even when the daimyo returned to the domain, both residences were staffed with a full complement of cooks, attendants, and servants. The common practice was for daimyo to live alternately in Edo and in their domains, and the annual journey between residences was extremely costly. Daimyo were carried in palanquins along strictly specified routes, accompanied by a large retinue.

The level of consumption in Edo was driven in large part by the elite culture that developed under *sankin kōtai*. The rivalry among daimyo that had formerly led to warfare now generated extravagant building projects and lavish entertaining. Expensive banquets and gifts became an essential part of court politics. Such expenditures consumed an enormous proportion of domain revenue.[48]

The consumption of the daimyo was inextricably linked to that of his closest advisers and counselors. Since a house elder (karō) could not live more ostentatiously than his lord, the administrative elite in each domain depended on the daimyo's extravagance to justify their own. Such powerful retainers often used their influence with the daimyo to oppose proposed reductions in the lord's expenses. Some lower-ranking retainers, such as attachés (koshō) or attendants (osobayaku or kinju), were similarly dependent on the lord's standard of living and could wield considerable power through their intimate knowledge of castle affairs. Finally, concubines subsisted on the daimyo's largesse, and their physical proximity to the daimyo gave them formidable influence. Reformers attempting to reduce their lord's expenses thus confronted opposition from a powerful and potentially dangerous coalition of interests.

Because the conspicuous consumption of the daimyo house was encouraged by such an entrenched and powerful lobby, daimyo expenditures often remained high even during fiscal crises. The fiscal histories of Hirosaki, Tokushima, and Yonezawa reflect the difficulty of enforcing daimyo frugality. All three domains had dedicated reformist daimyo who sharply reduced their personal expenses and cut both the power and income of high-ranking retainers: Uesugi Harunori of Yonezawa, Hachisuka Shigeyoshi of Tokushima, and Tsugaru Yukitsugu of Hirosaki. All three daimyo were outsiders, however, who became daimyo through adoption. Our knowledge of the private lives of daimyo comes largely from two types of sources: official government records, which omit the details of scandal and intrigue, and the memoirs of retainers, which either excoriate or beatify. Given these biases, conclusions about adopted daimyo must remain tentative.

Conjecture suggests that much of the flattery and cajoling of court retainers was lost on daimyo who entered the castle as adults. As younger sons, adopted daimyo were accustomed to far less extravagance than heirs apparent. Rather than accept daimyo extravagance, they may well have learned to resent it as an inequity of birth order. Finally, since primogeniture had worked against them, adopted daimyo were unlikely to be bound by traditional hierarchies. Adopted daimyo were quick to ally with ambitious lower retainers against privileged families. Their administrators were thus notable for their ability rather than their genealogy, suggesting a shift from aristocracy toward bureaucracy. The potential radicalism of younger sons was noted long ago by T. C. Smith, who suggested that primogeniture led younger sons to anti-establishment activities, including the Restoration movement.[49] Adopted daimyo, however, were far less iconoclastic in general statecraft than in their disregard for traditional hierarchies. Although they favored meritocracy and reform, they did so only within the existing social framework.

Retainer stipends and the personal expenses of the daimyo consumed most of government revenue. What little remained was usually spent on debt service or administrative expenses. Prudent statecraft demanded that a domain maintain grain and cash reserves for use in time of famine. Port facilities and riparian works required maintenance, as did government offices. A domain could reduce these expenses only by endangering its infrastructure and productive capacity. Finally, domains were subject to the occasional demands of the *bakufu*. Such levies could be ruinous. In 1753, for example, the shogunate ordered Yonezawa to repair and rebuild Kan'eiji, the *bakufu* temple at Ueno. The project cost the domain several years of revenue. In Hirosaki, the domain was required to maintain coastal fortifications against invasion after the appearance of Russian warships in the 1790s. As a proportion of long-term expenditure, however, the cost of *bakufu* demands was small. *Bakufu* levies were onerous less because the absolute cost of the services was high than because the demand was sudden and unexpected.

## Politics as Process

By the late 1600s, the struggle to balance government income and expenses had come to dominate domain politics. Although domains varied widely in their solvency, the challenges of a changing economy and the temptations of an emerging consumer culture made government debt a virtually universal problem. We can say less, however, about how domains addressed fiscal strain. Domains taxed their commoners and paid their retainers in a bewildering variety of forms. I stress this diversity of political practices not out of a sense of antiquarianism or particularism. Instead, I find this multiplicity of political economic practices to be a distinguishing feature of the

Japanese compound state. The Meiji reforms of the early 1870s eliminated this need to qualify endlessly statements about taxation and samurai remuneration. Tax assessment and collection were standardized nationwide and taxes paid into a national treasury. The government converted stipends into bonds based on nationally applicable formulas. These nationally defined practices mark the rise of the nation-state, with its ability to speak as the sole sovereign of the Japanese people. It is precisely the lack of such tidy structures and practices, however, that points to the coincident and multiple sovereignties of the early modern state. Perhaps the most striking difference between the Meiji village and the Tokugawa village is how much more readily we can generalize about the former.

In describing the political economy of the compound state, I have thus sought to emphasize process as much as policy. My concern, in other words, is not only with the specific policies domains developed but also with how and when these practices emerged and were deployed. What Hirosaki, Yonezawa, and Tokushima shared were not solutions but problems. The attempt in Hirosaki to turn samurai into self-sufficient farmers and the Yonezawa program of samurai weaving are largely opposite strategies. The commonality lies in the underlying ideological and socioeconomic conditions under which the policies were produced. The leaders of both Hirosaki and Yonezawa were bound by feudal and patrimonial ties to support their invested retainers. Both domains sought, however, to transform the samurai class because, within the logic of the compound state, they could not abandon it. The disparate solutions chosen in Yonezawa, Tokushima, and Hirosaki reflect the autonomy enjoyed by great domains. The critical similarity between these three domains thus lies not in their specific policies but in the problems they perceived and the ideological boundaries of their shared discourse.

# 3

## Profit and Propriety

*Political Economy in Yonezawa*

> It is inevitable, given human nature, that people will
> not do something unless they envy their neighbor's
> profit and thus pursue it of their own accord.
> —Nozoki Yoshimasa

Yonezawa domain lay roughly halfway between Edo and the
northern tip of Honshū, in an area now known as Okitama county,
Yamagata prefecture. Okitama is a small landlocked basin surrounded by the Mutsu, Azuma, Iide, and Asahi mountains. The cli-
mate of the region is forbidding: winters are among the coldest in
Japan, and winds from the Sea of Japan strike the Iide and Asahi
mountains to produce heavy snowfalls. Snow cover is common from
November through April. Summer temperatures are hot and humid,
and the seasonal temperature variation in Okitama is among the
widest in Japan. In the Tokugawa era, the area suffered from poor,
thin topsoil and difficult irrigation, leading to generally low yields
for staple crops such as rice. The economic development of the region was further impeded by poor transportation. The castle town
of Yonezawa was connected only indirectly to the national highway
system by a series of small roads linking it to the Ushū highway.
The other trade route to the market centers of the Kantō and Kinai
was the Mogami river, which flows northwest to the Sea of Japan.
The upper reaches of the river, however, were unnavigable and for
most of the seventeenth century products had to be transported
overland to Funamachi in Yamagata domain and transferred to
river ships. A major riparian project in 1694–95 cleared several

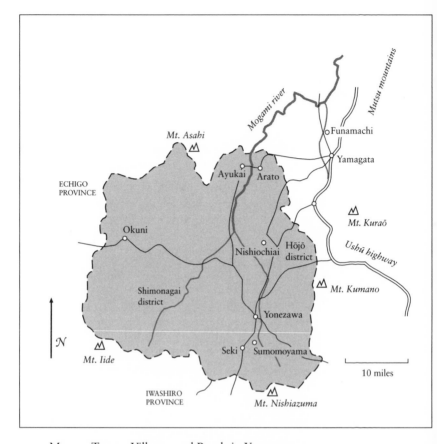

Map 2.  Towns, Villages, and Roads in Yonezawa

SOURCE: Adapted from *Kadokawa Nihon chimei daijiten*, 6: 1300.

dangerous passages north of Arato. This opened the upper reaches of the Mogami to smaller ships, but the best river ports still lay outside the domain.[1]

The Uesugi family, which ruled Yonezawa throughout the Tokugawa era, was among the great losers in the Tokugawa settlement. In 1598 the Uesugi controlled a domain of over one million *koku* in the Aizu-Wakamatsu region, but the family was among the foremost opponents of Tokugawa rule. Uesugi Kagekatsu's threatened attack on Tokugawa Ieyasu in early 1600 precipitated the battle of

Sekigahara later that year. After routing his opponents, Tokugawa Ieyasu singled out the Uesugi for particularly harsh treatment. Not only had the clan opposed the Tokugawa, but their domain lay within striking distance of the Tokugawa capital of Edo. In 1600 Ieyasu cut Uesugi holdings by three-quarters, and the following year the family was moved from Wakamatsu to a 300,000 *koku* domain in the provinces of Mutsu and Dewa.[2]

Uesugi holdings were threatened again on 1664/5i/1 when Uesugi Tsunakatsu, the second daimyo, died without an heir. Although the shogunate had begun to allow deathbed adoptions in 1651, Tsunakatsu had died suddenly of a perforated ulcer, leaving no time for his advisers to find a suitable successor. Without a legal heir, the domain was open to attainder by the shogunate, and as enemies of the Tokugawa the Uesugi expected the worst. In 1664/6/5, after an intensive lobbying effort by Uesugi allies, the shogunate recognized Tsunakatsu's postmortem adoption of his nephew, Tsunanori, but the *bakufu* demanded the return of half the domain. The domain lost its land in Mutsu and was reduced to a 150,000 *koku* holding in Okitama. In two generations the Uesugi's holdings had shrunk by almost 90 percent.[3]

The attainder of Uesugi holdings in the seventeenth century resulted in enormous demographic pressure in Yonezawa. In 1692 nearly one-quarter of the population of Yonezawa was samurai.[4] In 1872 the Yonezawa population ratio was 6.77: 100 commoners supported nearly 7 invested samurai households. This ratio was 3.58 times higher than in Hirosaki and 6.39 times higher than in Tokushima.[5] For the Uesugi, autonomy in domestic affairs thus meant the freedom to choose from among several unpleasant fiscal alternatives. To reduce expenditures the domain could either reduce the number of retainers or the size of their stipends. To increase revenue, the domain could either increase per capita revenue extraction or increase the number of commoners. In its move from Aizu to Yonezawa, the domain sought to maintain the integrity of the vassal band, reducing investitures rather than dismissing retainers. After the death of Tsunakatsu, however, this strategy could no longer be sustained: samurai could not endure stipend cuts of 90 percent. Between 1647 and 1670 the domain had relieved over 1,400 retainers, decreasing the vassal band by about one-quarter.

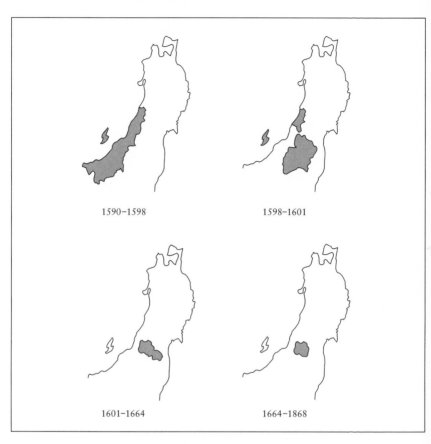

Map 3.  Changes in Uesugi Holdings, 1590–1868
SOURCE:  Redrawn from Hanseishi kenkyūkai, ed., *Hansei seiristushi*, p. 300.

The government, however, could not blithely discharge devoted re-tainers. Feudal and patrimonial authority required that the lord maintain his vassals' fiefs and stipends. The domain therefore acted against its weakest retainers: the majority of samurai dismissed were low-ranking soldiers with unstable tenures.[6]

Despite these drastic measures the domain's expenses continued to outpace its revenues, and in 1702 the government resorted to "borrowing" one-quarter of retainer stipends. The reductions were accompanied by austerity measures. Retainers and their families were ordered to wear only cotton clothing for daily wear. The domain forbade lavish weddings, funerals, and memorial services: meals at weddings were limited to "one soup, three greens, and three glasses of sake."[7] In 1704, because of a *bakufu* requisition, the domain "borrowed" one-half of stipends. In 1719 the government, crippled by deficits, withheld stipends from retainers with "ample" funds until the following year. A premium of 15 percent per annum was promised. The domain's huge stipend liabilities continued to outpace revenue, and as the government's debt grew, merchant houses began to question the government's creditworthiness. In 1721 the domain publicly confessed its inability to secure credit: "Treasury shortfalls have continued . . . and this year we were able to borrow less than half as much as in previous years in Osaka and neighboring countries. With no one from whom to borrow, we are without recourse and, with the possibilities of retrenchment exhausted, there seems no way to sustain the treasury."[8] The domain was again compelled to reduce stipends, and from this point stipend "borrowing" became a regular part of domain finances. In 1733 the domain again borrowed one-half of retainer stipends, and in 1750 this became standard.[9]

Although the domain continued to use the euphemism "borrow," the loans came to resemble permanent cuts. The domain intermittently repaid borrowed stipends, but this was the exception rather than the norm. Between 1750 and 1828 the domain made no payments on "borrowed" stipends. The cumulative effect of these cuts on retainer income was enormous. According to a 1791 budget, the domain spent only 19,482 *koku* on over 4,000 *kuramai* stipends, or less than 5 *koku* per retainer. Lower retainers, unable to survive on their investitures, turned to by-employments, particularly such crafts as weaving. Samurai craftsmen, often treated as a symbol of the decline of the Tokugawa system in the *bakumatsu* era, were common in Yonezawa from the early 1700s. Domain edicts paint a grim picture of samurai life. Retainers were reminded not to sell their swords, not to abandon their posts, and not to commit infanticide.[10]

Despite radical reductions in stipends, Yonezawa was still faced with enormous expenses and resorted to an inordinately high rate of surplus extraction. Peasants were subject not only to *nengu* but to as many as three forms of corvée or cash equivalents, usufruct fees on forests, mountains, and rivers, and taxes on *sanshō* pepper, walnuts, cotton, chrysanthemum petals, flax, lacquer, wax, and charcoal. The government used exchange-rate manipulation and monopsony systems to extract more revenue. Yonezawa mandated that farmers pay taxes half in kind and half in copper coin, the "half rice, half copper" (*hankoku han'ei*) system. By manipulating the exchange rate of copper and rice the domain could raise the tax rate indirectly. In 1655, for example, the domain effectively raised taxes 20 percent by changing the exchange rate from 100 copper *mon* per 0.6 *koku* to 100 copper *mon* per 0.5 *koku*.[11] Finally, government monopsonies on products such as flax functioned as onerous indirect taxes. By the mid-1700s local officials estimated that the domain was taking close to 70 percent of farm production.[12]

As the rate of per capita revenue extraction rose, the tax system grew more openly coercive. Local tax officials reportedly seized farmers behind in tax payments, bound them, and threw them naked into cold water. Large numbers froze to death. From the Kyōhō era (1716–35) peasants who failed to make tax payments were subject to *kamadome*, or enjoined from harvesting their crop until taxes were paid. The domain also seized household goods, farm tools, housing, and manure in lieu of taxes.[13] These draconian tactics might have increased revenue had farmers been concealing a surplus. The Yonezawa tax system, however, had reduced the farm population to subsistence, and the increasing brutality of tax collection led thousands of commoners to flee the domain. The Yonezawa tax system made agriculture so uneconomical that vast areas of farmland lay idle for want of farmers. By the mid-eighteenth century, the depopulation of the countryside and punitive taxation had made farmland nearly worthless. According to *Kangendan*, a critique of domain policy written in 1790:

By the mid-1760s [*Meiwa no hajimari*] there was utterly no profit in farmland, and those samurai and townspeople who held land either sold it for a pittance [*suteuri*] or gave it away for free. Land no one would take was given away together with money.[14]

The depopulation of the countryside can be documented using the government's annual census. Between 1700 and 1760 the total population fell from 128,696 to 99,369, a drop of over 20 percent (see

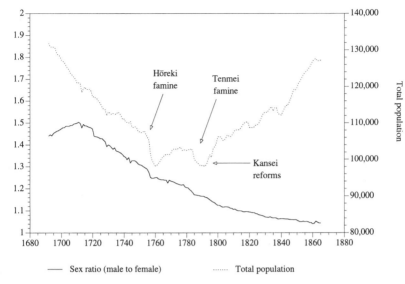

Figure 5. Yonezawa Population and Sex Ratio

SOURCE: Yoshida, *Okitama*, pp. 112–18.

Figures 5 and 6).[15] Although poor weather caused population loss in the surrounding region as well, Yonezawa's decrease was exacerbated by government policy: between 1721 and 1786 the population of the Uzen-Ugo region (excluding Yonezawa) fell by 8.3 percent but the population of Yonezawa fell by over 15.3 percent.[16] As contemporary observers noted, the domain's tax policies drove farmers to seek better conditions in neighboring domains. The population of Yonezawa reached its nadir in 1792, dropping to 99,085 persons.

The domain's fiscal problems worsened as its population decreased. By 1771 depopulation had left vast areas of land abandoned, and tax defaults produced a revenue shortfall of 25 percent.[17] The shortfalls were covered through borrowing: according to a budget compiled in 1791, the domain's outstanding loans totaled over 310,000 *ryō*. This debt was equal to nearly seven years of normal revenue. The domain was spending over 37 percent of its income on debt service despite an interest moratorium on 200,000 *ryō* in loans. Worse, the domain continued to accumulate debt: in 1791 alone expenses exceeded revenues by 18,538 *ryō*, or 41 per-

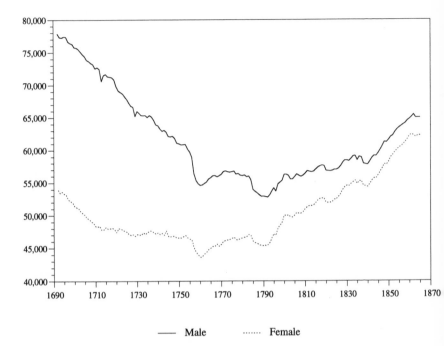

Figure 6. Yonezawa Population by Gender
SOURCE: Yoshida, *Okitama*, pp. 112–18.

cent. Most grievous, the domain's "income" included massive stipend "borrowing." In 1791 Yonezawa "borrowed" 11,028 *koku* and 2665 *ryō* from its retainers. This amounted to over 18 percent of the domain's revenue (see Figure 7). Without stipend "borrowing" the domains's expenses would have exceeded its income by 26,582 *ryō*, or over 72 percent.[18]

Depopulation was a major cause of Yonezawa's fiscal distress, and repopulation was central to its recovery. The steady increase in population that began in the 1790s was part of a broader regional trend, but it also reflected substantial changes in Yonezawa government policy. The Kansei reforms of the 1790s, directed by Nozoki Yoshimasa, focused on increasing population through an easing of the tax burden, the promotion of rural industry, and financial incentives for early marriage and large families. Particularly intriguing is the increase in the female population. The sex ratio in eighteenth-

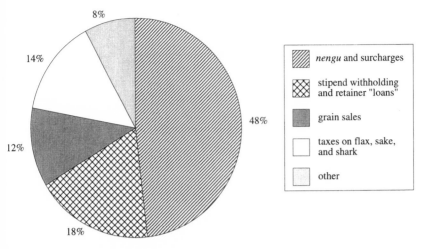

Figure 7. Yonezawa Domain Revenue, 1791
SOURCE: Yoshida, *Okitama*, pp. 171–75.

century Yonezawa was over 1.5 males per female, suggesting both sex-selective infanticide and the underreporting of female births. The Kansei reforms produced a steady growth in the reported female population (see Figure 6). Cash payments to farm families with infants proved an effective incentive both to report female births and to rear female infants. The reforms produced clear and sustained results: from 1790 to 1860, the population of Yonezawa grew at roughly 0.3 percent per year, reversing the losses of the eighteenth century. Because the domain was encouraging sericulture and land reclamation, population growth meant economic growth. This increase in taxable production in turn eased the domain's fiscal dilemma. In 1823, after decades of crisis, the villagers of Yonezawa remitted their taxes in full.[19] Although improved climatological conditions produced population growth in the surrounding Uzen-Ugo region as well, Yonezawa was distinct in its ability to withstand the disastrous harvests of the Tenpō famine (1833–36). The relative prosperity of Yonezawa and the careful management of its supply of reserve grain allowed the domain to weather the crisis without a pronounced drop in population.

In both Yonezawa and Hirosaki, population was a critical determinant of government policy, yet the histories of the two domains point to different aspects of the interrelation of demography and fiscal stability. In Hirosaki fluctuations in population were largely exogenously determined. Flooding, and the resultant harvest failures, sparked massive population drops during the Tenmei and Tenpō periods. Domain policy was largely reactive, namely, directed toward repopulating a countryside devastated by natural disasters. In Yonezawa, by contrast, depopulation was caused by factors both political and natural. Yonezawa's population loss was exacerbated by oppressive taxation policies, which encouraged emigration and flight, further raising demographic pressure. The links between demographic and fiscal policy were thus endogenous and interdependent. This made Yonezawa administrators acutely aware of the limits of government power. The ability of commoners to leave Yonezawa proved a constant reminder of the tenacity of popular resistance.

A pivotal issue in Yonezawa statecraft was the efficacy of government power. For much of the eighteenth and nineteenth centuries, administrators differed less in their visions of an ideal society than in their understanding of how the domain could serve to realize such a society. Prior to the 1790s, statecraft was undermined largely by overestimations of the government's ability to coerce economic action. Prior to the Kansei reforms, Yonezawa statesmen consistently associated increased revenue with increased domain control. The economic decline of the 1700s, catalyzed by the Tenmei famine, forced administrators to reconsider these assumptions. In a break with domain tradition, the Kansei reformers acknowledged that policies that did not appeal to the economic interests of farmers would provoke sustained resistance. Prudent statecraft thus required that the government recognize the inevitability, if not the legitimacy, of popular resistance.

## Taxes and Monopsony in Early Yonezawa

Yonezawa's two major cash crops in the early Tokugawa era were flax and lacquer trees. Lacquer trees were cultivated both for their fruit, which was used to make wax, and for their sap, which was processed into lacquer. The trees, which could grow in relatively poor soil, served as an important cash crop for Yonezawa farmers, and cultivation spread rapidly in the early 1600s. The domain began taxing lacquer trees in 1649, using a rate of 350 copper *me* per 100 trees and 320 *me* per *kan* of wax. In 1656 the tax rate was roughly doubled: 800 *me* for 100 good-quality trees, 600 *me* for medium-quality, 400 *me* for poor-quality. The government also claimed 5 *gō* of sap per 100 trees.[20]

In the late 1680s the domain began to intensify its control over lacquer production, and by 1689 the government had established a full monopsony. From 1690 on farmers were to pay between 0.6 and 1.0 *koku* in wax fruit per 100 trees, the higher rate levied on more productive villages. Any surplus was to be sold to the domain at 5.3 or 5.7 silver *me* per bushel (*hyō*). The collection of lacquer sap was also changed to one cup (*ippai*) per 200 trees, resulting in a tax increase of several hundred percent. If farmers could not provide wax or sap in kind, then the domain demanded cash equivalents.[21]

The new tax system helped to transform lacquer trees from a highly profitable cash crop to an economic liability. The cultivation of lacquer trees was labor intensive. The trees required shade during the summer, frost protection during the winter, and frequent applications of manure. Trees commonly did not produce fruit until their tenth year. The tax and monopsony system cut so deeply into the profit margin on lacquer trees that farmers found it more economical to uproot their trees than to pay taxes on them. As observed in *Kangendan*, "The farmers hate lacquer trees, and drain them of sap so they will not grow. . . . [W]hatever the government officials do under the present system [*Meireki ooaratame*], because of the taxes the farmers pay, lacquer is like a pestilence on the people."[22] Despite edicts banning the destruction of lacquer trees, lacquer cultivation steadily declined, from over 260,000 trees in 1689 to some 190,000 in 1772.[23]

Yonezawa flax policy was similarly ill-conceived. The origins of flax cultivation in Yonezawa are unknown, but the crop has been grown in the Echigo region since antiquity. According to *Mura kagami*, a survey of village conditions completed in 1598, flax cultivation was concentrated in the Shimonagai district of western Yonezawa. In 1638 the Uesugi first recorded flax cultivation for tax purposes as part of a cadastral survey.[24] Land planted in flax was registered as top-quality dry field and taxed like other upland fields.

In 1651, however, the domain registered flax fields separately as part of a government monopsony system: farmers were ordered to sell flax to the government at fixed prices. For a one *tan* field (0.245 acres) of good quality, a farmer had to sell roughly eight *kan*, about 70 pounds, of flax to the domain monopsony office.[25] It is difficult to compare the government price with the market price because monopsony flax was subdivided into two types, which were purchased at different prices, and commodity prices rose rapidly in the eighteenth century. Rough calculations suggest, however, that by the 1780s the domain monopsony price was less than one-quarter of the market price. The government, moreover, did not pay farmers in specie when it purchased flax, but instead calculated a deduction from *nengu* payments or paid in tax vouchers. Thus, although the system was technically a monopsony, farmers perceived it as merely another tax.[26]

The inherent flaw in the monopsony system was that it emphasized the revenue requirements of the government but ignored the productive capacity of the populace. The system, for example, did not allow tax exemptions for crop failures. Commoners who could not grow the required volume of flax either had to purchase it for payment in kind or pay a cash equivalent. As the revenue base of the domain shrank, the domain began to manipulate this aspect of the monopsony system for maximum return, demanding payment in kind when flax prices were high and payment in cash when prices were low. Faced with such a tax burden commoners resorted to abandoning their fields, and unclaimed land (*teamarichi*) in flax-growing areas abounded. By the 1790s as much as 20 percent of registered flax fields had been abandoned.[27]

The flax monopsony system, like many Tokugawa tax systems, was also ill-suited to economic change. Because the monopsony system was based on seventeenth-century cadastral surveys, it applied only to the Shimonagai district, which pioneered the cultivation of flax in Yonezawa. The district was to provide 530 bundles (*da*) of monopsony flax annually, a volume fixed in 1657 and not changed until the reforms of the 1780s.[28] Flax not claimed by the monopsony, however, could be sold independently, although the government restricted the number of flax buyers. Initially the domain granted monopsony rights to Nishimura Kyūzaemon, a powerful Kyoto merchant. In the 1690s, however, Nishimura fell out of favor, in part because of the failure of a project he had advocated and supervised, the widening of the Mogami river near Arato. When the project ran severely over budget, the government stripped Nishimura of his monopsony rights and instead authorized 33 rural merchants to purchase flax.[29]

Although the domain taxed flax sales at two gold *bu* per bundle, the market price remained high, and the cultivation of non-monopsony flax flourished. This trend was most evident in the Hōjō area, a group of roughly 40 villages north of Yonezawa castle. The area was not responsible for monopsony flax, and flax cultivation expanded accordingly. By the 1750s flax cultivation in the Hōjō region had come to the attention of administrators, and in 1760 the government announced plans to extend the monopsony system to the area. The plan drew a quick and impassioned response. In 1760/6 over 350 farmers, led by the headman (*kimoiri*) of Nishiochiai village, signed a petition opposing the monopsony. Their language was both defiant and submissive: "We request that by his lordship's benevolence we might continue as farmers [*hyakushō uchitsuzuki*], but if this is not granted we will dig up [our] flax by the roots." In Miyauchi village over 600 farmers gathered at the local shrine and staged a boisterous demonstration. The government, overwhelmed by the depth of popular opposition, rescinded its orders and dismissed, demoted, and banished from the castle town the administrators who had advocated extending the monopsony. The protest leaders were assessed heavy fines.[30]

The Yonezawa flax monopsony was in many ways a model of maladministration. Outdated and inequitable, the system taxed flax producers into desertion, thus both reducing government revenue and oppressing the population. In seeking to raise revenue through an extension of the monopsony, the domain demonstrated its inability to confront determined popular resistance. The flax protests of 1760 thus mark a low point in Yonezawa's political fortunes. Those fortunes reached their nadir three years later, when a cabal of high-ranking retainers assassinated Mori Heiemon, the daimyo's adviser, plunging the domain into political chaos.

## Fiscal Decline and Internecine Strife

The administration of Mori Heiemon was remarkable more for its spectacular demise than for its policies. A victim of victors' history, Mori has been portrayed as the archetypal villainous adviser. Mori's policies, however, were little different from mainstream reform efforts. The murderous resentment that felled Mori stemmed less from his politics than from his relations with the domain elite.

Mori had risen to prominence rapidly from exceedingly humble origins. In 1748 he held a stipend of just over six *koku* as a member of a battalion of foot soldiers (*yoitagumi*).[31] By 1754 he was chamberlain (*osobayaku*) to the daimyo, Uesugi Shigesada, and by 1756 he had risen to lead secretary (*koshō gashira*) with a stipend of 250 *koku*. As lead secretary, Mori controlled the machinery of the inner court. He engineered the dismissal of officials nominally his superiors, gradually eroding the influence of the domain's elite families. By 1760, Mori had appointed allies to key posts in the administration and emerged as the most powerful official in Yonezawa.[32]

Once in power, Mori employed traditional policies to stem the domain's fiscal deterioration. Citing the impending collapse of the "country" and "public authority" (*kōgi*), he instituted broad reforms in the domain's system of tax collection and rural control. Farmers were allowed to pay taxes on soy beans, rice cakes, and vegetable oil in cash rather than in kind, converting the taxes at market prices. Mori allowed *nengu* payments to be divided into three monthly installments and reorganized tax districts to streamline collection. To curb corruption and abuse of office by domain administrators, he reorganized the machinery of local control. Of particular concern were the intendants (*daikan*), whose hereditary claim on office weakened their responsibility to the government. The daikan were notorious for abusing the peasantry through high-interest loans and simple extortion. In 1760 Mori established vice-intendants (*fukudaikan*), who were to monitor the intendants' conduct. The intendants and vice-intendants were both put under the authority of a new agency, the office of rural affairs (*gundaisho*).[33]

Mori also relied on wealthy merchants, offering status in exchange for financing. Although it was common practice to offer the right to a surname or sword in return for loans, Mori began granting lenders sizable and prestigious investitures. The Terashima and Igarashi families, the domain's largest local creditors, were both given investitures comparable to those of elite retainers. In 1754 the Terashima were granted a landed fief of 130 *koku*. In 1750 the Igarashi family had their landed fief increased from 50 to 100 *koku*. Moneylenders thus held stipends larger than those of nine out of ten retainers. Mori treated prominent merchants from outside the domain, such as the Mitani from Edo, with the deference due high cabinet officials, consulting them on major fiscal matters. These policies were a patent affront to the domain elite, who felt themselves challenged, both in status and authority, by traders and parvenus.[34]

Mori's administration was threatened by a series of political and natural disasters. In 1753 the *bakufu* ordered Yonezawa to perform repairs and construct a gate at the shogunate's Kan'eiji temple in Ueno. The total cost of the project came to nearly 100,000 *ryō*, or roughly two years' revenue. The burden of the shogunal levy was exacerbated by the domain's credit history. Yonezawa was already deeply in debt, and creditors were reluctant to extend further financing. In 1755, the chancellors of the exchequer reported that "the lord's reputation is poor" [*oie hyōban ashiki*] and the domain was therefore being refused loans "both here and in other countries." The domain was able to borrow less than 20,000 *ryō* and turned to stipend "borrowing" and new taxes to provide the rest. In 1754/3, Mori announced a poll tax. Retainers, foot soldiers (*ashigaru*), and property owners (*hantō*) were to pay fifteen *mon* per month, while tenants and landless farmers (*genin*, *nago*, and *mizunomi*) were to pay ten *mon*.[35]

During this financial crisis the domain was struck by natural disasters. From 1755/6/23 to 7/7 floods destroyed 6,735 acres and led to tax losses of 37,780 *koku*. The price of one *hyō* of rice soared to 1.730 *kan*, nearly doubling in a few months. On 1755/8/13 the government ordered that rice be sold at 1.5 *kan*, but farm villages stopped sending rice completely, and the shortages worsened. Hearing reports of hoarding, the government ordered inspectors to search the homes of merchants, but only 197 *koku* of rice was discovered. The domain began distributing rice from its treasury, but this proved inadequate, given the magnitude of the famine.[36]

The harvest shortfalls continued, and in 1757/5 and 1757/6 Yone-zawa was struck by torrential rains that broke major riparian works and flooded the castle town. Flooding damaged or destoyed thousands of homes and inundated tens of thousands of acres of cropland. The countryside was devastated, and by 1760 the population of Yonezawa had fallen under 100,000, a 7 percent drop in only five years.[37]

The extreme privation suffered by communers and samurai alike led to an alarming deterioration of public order. On 1755/9/10 a small group of low-ranking retainers entered the castle town, leading five or six hundred peasants from Seki and Sumomoyama villages. The retainers led the farmers in a series of attacks on brewers and merchants suspected of hoarding and price gouging. The protesters broke into storehouses, seizing and distributing rice. The riot was motivated as much by hunger as by anger at gouging. Hearing of the protests, two merchants greeted the peasants with rice gruel. The protesters ate and disbanded. The riots revealed the depths of the domain's fiscal crisis. Lower retainers had been reduced to such poverty that they allied with the peasantry against the government. The domain punished the samurai severely. Four samurai were executed by decapitation or crucifixion. The others were stripped of their investitures or imprisoned. The peasants, by contrast, were merely fined.[38] The rebellion, moreover, was but an extreme example of a general deterioration in samurai morale. In both the castle town and Edo, retainers were failing to report for duty and failing to conduct domain business. Seemingly friendly social gatherings were degenerating into violence.[39]

Squeezed between the commoners and the lower-ranking samurai, Mori sought new sources of revenue. In 1757 he moved against the rights of landed fiefs, which were held largely by elite retainers. Farmers on landed fiefs had traditionally paid taxes to local tax officials (*yokome*), who then forwarded the taxes to the fiefholder. To increase government revenue, Mori ordered that taxes from landed fiefs be paid into the domain treasury.[40] Fiefholders were instead paid in vouchers, which they could exchange for rice at authorized castle-town merchants. The details of the voucher system are unclear, but the result is not. Like many Tokugawa currencies, the vouchers were overissued and depreciated rapidly. By 1758 the vouchers were worth only one-eighth of their face value. Mori's vouchers thus amounted to progressive stipend reductions. Mori had, in effect, sought to balance the domain's budget by penalizing its wealthiest retainers rather than its poorest. This strategy, however, amounted to an attack on the patrimonial authority of landed fiefholders. Mori denied them the usufruct of their fiefs, emoluments they had inherited from their fathers. By challenging their patrimony, Mori earned the enmity of the most powerful families in the domain.[41]

The domain elite appealed to the daimyo Shigesada to dismiss Mori, but without success. Mori was insulated from their charges in part because he and his allies indulged the daimyo's extravagances. Unable to unseat Mori through persuasion, the domain elite launched a palace coup. On 1763/2/8, four senior officials, Chisaka Tsushima, Imogawa Masanori, Irobe Tsuneyoshi, and Takenomata Masatsuna, confronted Mori with a list of charges and stabbed him to death. For official purposes, Mori was said to have committed suicide to atone for his crimes. In their memorial to the daimyo, the assassins criticized Mori for his cavalier, despotic, and willful (*jiyū*) use of power, a thinly veiled reference to Mori's preference for the advice of merchants and his disregard for the domain elite.[42]

## Uesugi Harunori and the Politics of Virtue

Officials such as Takenomata had hoped that the assassination of Mori would begin an era of extensive reform. To their chagrin, Shigesada remained unwilling to curtail his personal expenses: Mori had fed, but not caused, the daimyo's taste for luxurious clothes, food, and appointments. Shigesada's self-indulgences were not only costly in their own right but also stood to undermine any attempts to demand further sacrifices from domain samurai. In light of the daimyo's intransigence, the reform faction began to focus on his heir, Uesugi Harunori.[43]

Born the second son of Akizuki Tanemi, the daimyo of Takanabe, Harunori entered the Uesugi house in 1760 at age nine. His adoption was prompted by the Uesugi's need for an heir: Uesugi Shigesada had fathered three daughters but no sons. From his childhood, Harunori had garnered a reputation as an avid learner, but his suitability as an heir was also enhanced by his bloodline. Harunori's maternal grandmother was the daughter of the fifth daimyo, Uesugi Tsunanori: Harunori's mother was thus Shigesada's cousin.[44]

Given their dissatisfaction with Shigesada and the domain's deteriorating finances, reformers sought to accelerate Harunori's succession. Beginning in 1763 a group of retainers known as the Seigasha began to press Shigesada to retire. The Seigasha were a small but powerful network. Takenomata, the nominal leader of the Seigasha, was *shissei bugyō* (supreme magistrate), the highest-ranking official in Yonezawa. Seigasha members included Nozoki Yoshimasa, the daimyo's secretary (*koshō*); Shiga Sukeyoshi, the daimyo's chamberlain (*osobayaku*); and Warashina Shōhaku, Shigesada's physician and an instructor in the domain academy. With supporters throughout the domain administration, the Seigasha were able to apply consistent pressure on Shigesada.

Over the next four years the reform faction waged a dogged campaign to force Shigesada into retirement. The domain *karō* threatened to resign en masse, rather than preside over the demise of the domain. They enlisted Shigesada's in-laws, the Tokugawa of Owari, and asked the *karō* of Owari to pressure Shigesada to resign. In some dangerous brinksmanship, Takenomata recommended that Shigesada return the domain to the shogunate rather than drive it to ruin and cause further suffering among the people. Virtually besieged by critics, Shigesada yielded. In 1767 he left the castle for an elegant retirement villa, and Harunori, at age seventeen, succeeded as the daimyo of Yonezawa.[45]

Led by the Seigasha, Harunori rapidly embarked on a series of reforms. In stark contrast with Shigesada, Harunori embraced strict reductions in his own expenses. In 1767/9 the government announced a program of radical retrenchment: the daimyo's *sankin kōtai* retinue was reduced, unused residences and offices closed, and the exchange of gifts prohibited. Palace officials were ordered to wear cotton garments, and meals were to be limited to "one soup, one green." The reformers also cut ties with the merchants houses favored by Mori and dismissed merchants like the Terashima from their advisory positions.[46]

In 1772 special inspectors were dispatched to rural villages to monitor peasant conduct and reduce theft, gambling, and indolence. The system of rural offices was reorganized to reduce corruption.

Later reforms included several programs directed at rural reconstruction. In 1773 and 1774, thousands of samurai, including members of elite regiments, were sent to the countryside to work on land
reclamation, bridge repairs, and riparian projects.[47]

The reforms precipitated a split between the Seigasha and their
erstwhile allies in elite (*fudai*) families. The domain elite was particularly incensed by the austerity program, not only because it was
formulated without their advice or consent, but also because it curtailed the luxuries appropriate to retainers of their station. Conflict
between the reform faction and the *fudai* came to a head in 1773/6
when seven elite families, led by Suda Mitsutake and Imogawa
Masanori, presented the daimyo with a petition criticizing his conduct. The daimyo, they claimed, had let Takenomata and a clique
of mid-ranking officials monopolize power. Although Harunori's intentions were commendable, his youth and inexperience had led him
to pursue unsound policies. The reforms, they argued, were de-
stroying politics and society: old policies had served the "national
polity" (*kokutai*) in eight matters out of ten while the new policies
were pernicious in nine out of ten. The *fudai* asked that they again
be allowed to advise the daimyo, and that Takenomata and his
clique be dismissed. Harunori responded by ordering Imogawa and
Suda to commit ritual suicide (*seppuku*) and placing the other petitioners under house arrest. Although Harunori pardoned the seven
petitioners in 1775/7, the purges left Takenomata and his allies
firmly in control of the domain.[48]

Takenomata's victory over the *fudai* reflected the extensive influence of the Seigasha network. The coordinated efforts of Nozoki
and Takenomata were particularly potent. Nozoki's position as secretary gave him extensive, unofficial influence over Harunori, while
Takenomata held the formal reigns of government. Harunori's support for the Seigasha was also rooted in a shared political vision.
Harunori, Takenomata, Nozoki, and Warashina Shōhaku were all
followers of the philosopher Hosoi Heishū (1728–1801).

Harunori first encountered Hosoi in 1764, when Hosoi lectured
at the Yonezawa mansion in Edo at the invitation of Warashina
Shōhaku. Shigesada and Harunori were sufficiently impressed to re-
tain Hosoi as a regular lecturer. In 1771 Harunori invited Hosoi to
Yonezawa, where he lectured widely and attracted an influential

group of students. In the wake of the great Edo fire of 1772, Hosoi hurriedly returned to his Edo academy. He returned again to Yonezawa in 1776 for six months, during which time he helped revive the domain academy, the Kōjōkan.[49] Although Hosoi spent less than two years in Yonezawa, he had a profound influence on Yonezawa statecraft. In his memoir, *Kokuseidan* (Discourse on national politics), Takenomata described Hosoi as a sage whose wisdom helped save the domain "at a time when the unlettered maladministration of the senior ministers [*rōshin*] was violating the Way of Governing [*onseiji no dō*] and gradually leading the state to ruin."[50]

In his philosophy, Hosoi was a scholar of the Eclectic school (*Setchūha*) of neo-Confucianism, which, as its name implies, was a loose, syncretic movement. Like many intellectual movements of the latter Tokugawa era, the Eclectic school was strongly influenced by Ogyū Sorai, and several figures in the movement, such as Inoue Kinga and Katayama Kenzan, were originally students of the Sorai school. The Eclectic school has received little scholarly attention, perhaps because most historians have shared Maruyama Masao's view that "eclecticism is eclecticism and implies little creativity, so they contributed very little that was theoretically new."[51]

From Maruyama's perspective, because Sorai had advocated a *Gesellschaft* logic of politics, the Eclectic school was indeed a step backward. Although the movement concurred with Sorai's separation of politics and cosmology, it ignored his emphasis on the historical determination of political action, focusing instead on the abstraction of political virtue from classical texts. Hosoi, like Inoue Kinga and Katayama Kenzan, reincorporated elements of Sung-Ming Confucianism that Sorai had repudiated. Hosoi, for example, explicitly rejected Sorai's notion that the Way (*dō*) was historically determined. "What sages create are rites," he wrote; "as for the Way being made by sages, I believe that this is not so." "The Way," he declared, "is a heavenly natural order [*tenchi shizen no dō*], not something made by man."[52]

For Hosoi, political principles could not be discerned from cosmological observation, but proper political practice was nonetheless naturally determined and immutable. The salient question, therefore, was how to discern this immutable Way. Hosoi, ironically, agreed with Sorai that heaven could not be known, and since Hosoi saw the Way of Governing as naturally determined, politics itself became something unknowable. Hosoi concluded that the heavenly natural order was indeed impenetrable, but not to sages, and this knowledge of the Way empowered their authority. The purpose of a sage, therefore, was to return civilization to its natural state, a heavenly determined order known only to the initiate. Because only a true sage could properly discern the Way, Hosoi's vision of politics was infused with a transcendental or quasi-religious theory of authority. The power of a sage to discern the Way, moreover, justified and required absolute obedience.[53]

Hosoi's influence can be discerned in several areas of Yonezawa statecraft. First and foremost, Hosoi's philosophy lent gravity to patrimonial and suzerain authority. In his earliest lectures to Harunori, Hosoi portrayed the daimyo as a servant of heaven. A virtuous lord "does not forget for an instant that if despite his noble status, he does not reject luxury; if despite the wealth of his land, he does not reject lavishness; and if he does not serve as parent of his people [*banmin no fubo*], he will have erred in his office of servant of heaven and will have violated the filial piety that an heir owes his ancestors."[54] Wise rule was thus mandated by both patrimonial authority (filial piety) and suzerain authority (service to heaven). These themes were echoed in an oath Harunori took at Shironoko shrine soon after succeeding Shigesada: "For years the state has fallen into decadence and the people have suffered. In light of this, I will conduct myself with great frugality and pray that I might serve to restore [*chūkō*] them to prosperity. Should I be negligent in my resolve, may all the punishments of the gods befall me." Harunori's oath portrayed him as subordinate to the domain and the people. In employing terms such as "serve" (*tsukamatsuri*), he humbled himself before the goal of a Yonezawa restoration. More seriously, Harunori made negligence in serving his house and subjects a cause for divine retribution.[55]

Second, Hosoi's notion of loyal service contributed to the beatification of Harunori. Because the Way was unchanging, and the authority of a ruler-sage devolved from his ability to perceive the Way, legitimate rulers did not approve flawed policies. If a ruler were not infallible, virtuous conduct by a vassal required that this be concealed. Further, since a lord served as the moral template for his land, revealing his moral lapses would spread decadence among the people. Hosoi thus argued that "in serving his lord, a retainer conceals the lord's faults and lauds his virtues so that those who observe him are moved with admiration."[56]

The depiction of Uesugi Harunori as a perfect and virtuous sage was thus essential to Hosoi's model of proper governance. Although retainers in all domains sought to glorify their daimyo, Hosoi Heishū's philosophy made the promotion of Harunori's virtue and wisdom a special priority. There is, accordingly, a large hagiographic tradition that depicts Harunori as a man of boundless virtue. Toward the end of the Tokugawa era Harunori was celebrated as a benevolent and wise lord (meikun) whose virtue and erudition had saved Yonezawa from certain ruin. In the Meiji era, popular biographies invoked Harunori to instill the virtues of loyalty and frugality, a practice adopted by the government in 1904 with the inclusion of Harunori as a moral exemplar in school textbooks.[57]

This tradition is reflected in Robert Bellah's discussion of Harunori, based on an account by Murdoch.

Entering his fief for the first time as a young man, he found direst poverty and misery in all quarters. With the aid of his adviser, the Confucian scholar Hosoi Heishū (1728–1801), he soon mapped out a policy to restore prosperity to his fief. One of his first acts was to cut the salaries of the samurai in half and his household expenses to a fifth those of the former lord. He wore only cotton garments and ate the simplest of food. He adopted as his fundamental maxims "To have no waste places in his domains," and "To have no idlers among his people."

As for positive policies, he undertook an extensive policy of land reclamation, which involved turning his samurai into farmers; he introduced mulberry trees and established a thriving silk industry; he required every family to plant a certain number of lacquer trees and established this industry as well.

As a result of these policies, "Yonezawa became one of the most prosperous fiefs in Japan."[58] Postwar scholarship has treated Harunori more critically, and most historians now treat him as an influential lord, but not a direct, or infallible, ruler. For Yonezawa retainers, however, the laudatory depiction of their lord was a part of loyal service.

Finally, Hosoi's influence can be discerned in policies directed at moral rejuvenation. Proper government, wrote Hosoi, lay in "educating the hearts of the people" and "beautifying their customs."[59] Hosoi's moral vision, however, was essentially a conservative idealization of Tokugawa society. His rejection of historicism and embrace of metaphysics produced a staunch moral conservatism. Rectitude and frugality became virtues of transcendental importance because moral lassitude could invoke heavenly retribution. Indeed it was incumbent on the daimyo to "educate and nurture" the people so that they too might manifest traditional virtues.[60]

Hosoi's emphasis on "educating" the people and his belief in the need for absolute obedience were reflected in a 1769/10 directive, which made gambling a capital crime. Such strict laws were balanced by exhortations to morality. The domain dispatched teachers to rural areas, hoping to instill the virtues of diligence and honesty in the common people. These teachers also served as inspectors, reporting abuses by landed fiefholders to higher authorities.[61] Hosoi himself participated in this process of enlightenment, touring the countryside to lecture in the villages. This emphasis on moral rectitude was the most troubling aspect of Hosoi's legacy. Although his disciples tried diligently to legislate popular morality, the populace proved remarkably resistant to the government's "nurturing." The domain succeeded in economic development only after it sought to enrich the commoners rather than enlighten them.

## Rebuilding a Moral Economy

Takenomata confronted the deterioration of Yonezawa's finances with an eclectic series of programs designed to promote new crops and industries. The underlying principle was to enhance the ability of Yonezawa commoners to pay taxes by enhancing the value of their labor. In 1776 Takenomata invited a weaving teacher to Yonezawa and sponsored a small textile factory. In 1778 he began a small cattle ranch, and in 1779 he established a ceramics workshop in Hanazawa village. He also promoted the manufacture of fans, ink, inkstones, and indigo, and the cultivation of Japanese pears.[62] Takenomata's principal concern, however, was lacquer tree cultivation. In 1776 he announced a program to plant three million trees in Yonezawa, one million each of lacquer, mulberry, and paper

mulberry (*kōzo*). The trees were provided free of charge, and cultivators were paid twenty copper *mon* for each seedling that reached
one *shaku* (approx. one foot). Takenomata foresaw enormous profits when the trees reached maturity: 19,157 *ryō* from lacquer trees,
7,407 *ryō* from mulberry, and 5,555 *ryō* from paper mulberry. Although Takenomata sought to plant one million of each type of tree,
he was most interested in lacquer, presumably because it seemed the
most profitable. Takenomata envisioned lacquer trees almost every-
where. Farmers were to plant 640,000 trees, 30 per household. An
additional 75,000 trees were to be planted by retainers, 15,000 at
temples and shrines, and 5,000 by townsmen. The lacquer trees were
exempted from taxes but were subject to the domain monopsony on
wax. Although Takenomata's plan of 1,000,000 trees proved too
ambitious, his memoir reports that nearly 740,000 lacquer trees
were planted. More objective sources report nearly 250,000 trees.[63]

Takenomata's choice of lacquer was unfortunate, because the
crop was rapidly losing its market. Lacquer fruit faced increasing
competition from wax fruit (*hazerō*), grown in the southwest. Both
*hazerō* and lacquer fruit were sources of candle wax, and by the
mid-eighteenth century, wax fruit was more economical. Yonezawa
wax production fell accordingly, from 10,800 *kan* in 1747 to 4,128
*kan* in 1794. By the mid-nineteenth century, the price disparity was
so large that even Yonezawa candlemakers began using imported
*hazerō* rather than the domestic product. Despite these problems
with lacquer fruit, lacquer tree sap remained valuable for use in lacquerware. But lacquer cultivation for sap and cultivation for fruit
were different projects. Trees could be tapped for sap years before
they bore fruit, and tapping impeded the production of fruit. Further, the lacquer tree is dioeceous; only female trees produce fruit,
while male trees were preferable for lacquer sap.

Because Takenomata's program emphasized lacquer fruit while
the market demanded lacquer sap, his subsidies had pronounced
unanticipated consequences. Under the domain monopsony system,
the profit margin on lacquer fruit was minimal, and farmers had
little incentive to maintain their trees. Because farmers grew the
tree for sap rather than wax, however, they tapped their trees dry
as soon as they topped one *shaku* and were eligible for the twenty
*mon* subsidy. The government soon noticed the phenomenon of

"dried trees," plants dead from over-tapping and useless for fruit production.[64]

The domain repeatedly issued edicts to stop the destruction of the trees. Takenomata's original plan imposed a penalty of twenty copper *mon* for killing trees through over-tapping, but this was insufficient to prevent the problem. In 1779 the government informed retainers that they would have to repay the subsidies for any trees tapped dry. A further warning involved fraud: those using fake trees would have to plant five trees for each fraudulent tree.[65] In 1794, farmers were prohibited from tapping trees bearing fruit. Illegal tapping was punishable by a fine of twenty silver *me*. In 1798 the domain restricting tapping to the portion of the tree above 1.8 *shaku* (1.8 feet). In 1809 tapping was limited to the first 60 days after the autumnal equinox.[66] Despite these measures, Takenomata's trees began to disappear. A 1790 survey of twelve villages in the Shimonagai region revealed that roughly 30 percent of Takenomata's lacquer trees had disappeared by 1790. In some villages the losses were as high as 60 percent. An 1808 government report noted 130,000 trees missing.[67]

Although Takenomata's emphasis on wax production was, in part, simply misadventure, it highlights the problems of Hosoi's enlightened despotism. Takenomata's approach was grounded in the assumption that the "state" was responsible not merely for ruling the people but for enlightening them. In his 1772 essay *Nōka rikkyō*, Takenomata observes that "we are birthed by our parents, but we are nurtured by our lord." Because the domain is parent to all the people, farmers should remember their "obligation to the country" (*kokuon*) and "love their lord as their father and mother."[68] This paternalistic appreciation of the domain made economic development a central goal of statecraft. It also, however, gave popular resistance the air of childish obstinance. Describing popular resistance to lacquer cultivation, Takenomata wrote, "Because of their greed, the people [*tami*] do cunning things such as planting lacquer trees without roots, or putting sticks in the ground which look like plants." Others "grow defiant, and resentment mounts day by day." Takenomata thus read opposition to growing lacquer trees as evidence that farmers did not understand the profitability of lacquer: "Although farmers are certainly not blind to profit," he wrote, "they do not see profits which lie ten years hence." This was all the more reason for senior ministers, as "the parents of the people" (*tami no fubo*), to educate the populace. Takenomata's classicism here undermined his broader political goals: although he did not disavow empiricism, Takenomata's understanding of farming was rooted more in classical texts than in observation. In his essay *Kokuseidan*, Takenomata cites Mencius when discussing mulberry cultivation, the *Analects* when discussing sericulture, and the *Great Learning (Daigaku)* when discussing lacquer. In the context of Hosoi's philosophy, these references to classical texts were appropriate. "If [we] deviate from the teachings of the sages," wrote Takenomata, "then we cannot follow the Way." This understanding of the sages, unfortunately, led the domain to promote aggressively a crop with little economic value.[69]

To his credit, Takenomata saw economic development as central to fiscal recovery and recognized that Yonezawa's farmers were already overtaxed. Takenomata, indeed, sought to distinguish his policies from the existing government lacquer program: he had local officials assure farmers in writing that lacquer trees planted under the "million tree" program would never be counted as "tax trees" (*yakuki*) and taxed under the old lacquer system. But if Takenomata's "million tree" program did not impoverish the peasantry, it did little to promote long-term growth or fiscal recovery. Takenomata's original plan, to use funds from the wax monopsony to repay "borrowed" samurai stipends, was tragically overoptimistic.[70]

Takenomata's inability to reverse the domain's decline weakened his grasp on power. He was ultimately unseated in 1782/10 because of personal indiscretions. According to the charges made against him, he had monopolized political power, ignored the advice of responsible retainers, and used public funds for personal expenses. Further, he had indulged in drinking and revelry, even on the day of mourning for Uesugi Kenshin, the great sixteenth-century warlord. He was forced into retirement, although his heir was allowed to inherit his full stipend.[71]

Takenomata was succeeded by Shiga Sukeyoshi, a member of the Seigasha who had come to oppose his former ally. Shiga was almost immediately confronted by the Tenmei crisis of 1783–86. Unseasonable cold and rain in 1783 reduced Yonezawa's harvest by nearly

50 percent, and crop losses in 1786 approached 35 percent. Similar devastation was prevalent throughout the northeast and led to a surge in the price of rice: in Yonezawa prices rose nearly 130 percent between 1783/8 and 1784/5. Between 1783 and 1787 over 4,000 people died or fled, and the population, which had begun to recover from the Hōreki famine of the 1750s, fell again below 100,000. Those farmers who survived and remained in the domain faced long-term financial devastation. The domain distributed rice from its relief granaries and purchased rice outside the domain, but farmers were still forced to pawn farm tools and household items to buy food.[72]

Shiga proved adept at handling the short-term crisis of the famine, but he failed to confront the more serious questions of rural poverty and chronic budget shortfalls. He rescheduled the domain's debt and found new creditors, no mean feat given the domain's dismal fiscal state. But his policies were essentially negative: he increased stipend borrowing and cut expenses by curtailing horseback riding, cutting staff, and eliminating Takenomata's economic development programs. Since his reforms lacked a coherent plan, retainers saw Shiga's retrenchment policies as mere privation. His contemporaries linked his policies with low-level government corruption and general moral decay: attendance at the domain academy decreased, retainers sold their names to merchant houses, and drinking and carousing were rampant. Whether such phenomena increased under Shiga is less important than his inability to propose coherent solutions. Shiga's rule proved short-lived: as the immediate effects of the Tenmei famine waned, the government turned to more substantive reform.[73]

## Fiscal Reconstruction and the Legitimation of Profit

Nozoki Yoshimasa emerged from retirement in 1791 and rose within a year to the post of *bugyō* with a stipend of 1,000 *koku*. His reforms, which were an explicit repudiation of nearly two centuries of policy, reversed the domain's population decline and restored its fiscal solvency. Nozoki was originally a close ally of Takenomata, and he resigned his position as head secretary (*koshō gashira*) in 1783, a year after Takenomata's dismissal. Nozoki, like

Takenomata, was a disciple of Hosoi Heishū, and this shared intellectual orientation supported their political alliance.[74]

In his eight years out of office, Nozoki had begun a reconsidera-
tion of Hosoi's thought. In his 1789 essay *Seigo* (Comments on politics), Nozoki repudiated much of traditional statecraft, but he remained within the ambit of Tokugawa neo-Confucianism. Like
many contemporaries, Nozoki viewed commoners as ignorant and
prone to vice. Government resources, however, were inadequate to
confront these problems directly. An attempt to disseminate the Way
throughout the realm, Nozoki argued, would result in a tyrannical,
oppressive regime. Nozoki thus criticized Takenomata's and Hosoi's
policies as counterproductive. Although well-intentioned, their attempts to educate the populace were overly idealistic and did not
account for commoners' stubbornness or deceitfulness. In seeking
to bring peace to the people,

> The state often forbids the people things which are profitable, and compels
> them to do things which are unprofitable. If, however, everyone had a full
> knowledge of the Way and the wisdom of a gentleman, government would,
> in principle, be unnecessary. . . . It is, however, impossible to bring wisdom
> to each and every household in the land, and if the people know only bits
> and pieces of the Way, they become wise in trickery. They are concerned
> only with their own profit and do not know that the profit and peace they
> enjoy are encompassed by the polity which rules over them. Thus, if an in-
> struction leads to inconvenience or a prohibition causes them harm, they
> will criticize the government, upsetting the hearts of those in neighboring
> villages and ultimately impeding public peace [*anmin*]. Therefore, people
> should be taught to be filial to their father and respectful to their lord even
> if they do not know why.

It was a mistake, Nozoki concluded, to suffer the common people to
read books, to lecture to them, and to explain to them the Way.
What the common people should learn through books and lectures
is that if the state forbids them things that are profitable and com-
pels them to do things that are unprofitable, it is for the common
peace.[75]

Given the limited ability of the domain to effect changes in popular morals, it was essential for government to overlook the majority
of popular vices and to allow the people to reform themselves. The

key to statecraft was thus leniency and tolerance, rule through persuasion rather than edict. A government seeking to have farmers separate rice from chaff would do well to invoke the image of a winnowing fan in an ode rather than order its use. The populace would then naturally begin separating grain from chaff.[76]

By 1792 this line of thought had led Nozoki to reevaluate completely the link between economy and morality. Nozoki still inveighed against frivolity and luxury, the perennial concerns of traditional reformers. But he was now critical of treating morality as a primary cause of economic decline. In *Jujin kengi* (Recommendations on population cultivation, 1792) he employed a physiological metaphor to trace popular distress to demographic problems:

If we diagnose the ailments [of the countryside], we find that since the price of rice is low, there are places where people do not farm. Further, we should also note that customs in clothing, food, and housing have gradually become luxurious. Some villages suffer under incompetent village officials, and some regions suffer from frequent droughts. Some people are by nature lazy or weak, corrupted by wine and women or run wild with gambling. . . . If we treat each of these symptoms individually it will come to naught. Although we should consider blending different medicines so as efficaciously to restore health, in the end, the central ailment is that there are not enough people in relation to the land. Compared with the other symptoms, this is extremely difficult to treat.[77]

Because Nozoki saw immorality as a secondary issue, he dismissed attempts to enlighten the populace. Breaking with Hosoi and Takenomata, who saw greed as pernicious, Nozoki saw envy as inevitable and potentially useful. In *Jukiku kengi narabi shūhyō* (Recommendations on farming with public comments, 1792) he proposed that cotton be promoted through market incentives: "It is inevitable, given human nature [*ninjō*], that people will not do something unless they envy their neighbor's profit and thus pursue it of their own accord [*mizukara susumu*]." Although Nozoki thought textiles would be extremely lucrative, he rejected any mandatory or coercive policy. If commoners were forced to weave, he argued, they would weave poorly and produce shoddy cloth. The key to sound policy was not to overcome this resistance through coercion, but to use the peasants' desire for profit. The government, he wrote, should patronize villages that grew cotton, buying the product for official use. Other villages, seeing their neighbors' profit, would begin producing cotton.[78]

Nozoki thus saw little value in monopsony systems. He suggested, indirectly, that the entire flax monopsony be abandoned: "[Farmers] have despised the state purchase of flax [*kaiage*] from the outset, and because of this popular sentiment, no matter what price is paid, I do not think such purchases will succeed." The people, he argued, preferred to use the flax themselves, weaving at home. As to lacquer, Nozoki thought the monopsony system amounted to "poisoning the people."[79]

In contrast to Takenomata's dirigiste policies, Nozoki suggested a need to tolerate the chaos that stemmed from unregulated production:

If we liberalize [*jiyū*] the planting of mulberry, some undesired crops will be planted, but even if some seedlings are planted carelessly, the number of mulberry trees will increase. If there are many mulberry trees, then the price of mulberry leaves will fall. If the price of mulberry leaves is low, those raising silkworms will naturally [*onozukaru*] increase in number. If there are many people raising silkworms, our exports will naturally increase, women workers will naturally benefit, the four estates will profit [*shimin no ri*], whereupon national prosperity [*kokueki*] will be achieved.[80]

This aspect of Nozoki's thought is strongly suggestive of economic liberalism. Indeed, his use of the term *jiyū* to mean "freedom" or "liberty" rather than "wantonness" resembles progressive Meiji discourse more than the Yonezawa tradition in which he worked.

Nozoki was concerned less with freedom, however, than with tyranny. Nozoki opposed coercive economic programs not because they violated the liberty of commoners, but because they led to tyrannical rule. Nozoki, like Hosoi, felt that commoners were generally stupid, but paramount in his politics was the fear that any attempt to change basic human inclinations or to "enlighten" the populace would result in "tyranny as fierce as a wild tiger." Nozoki thus embraced the virtues of leniency and tolerance. "If one is lenient," he argued, "the masses will come." Central to good government, he claimed, were simple, patient policies that accepted rather than challenged human nature (*ninjō*).[81] There is thus a tension in Nozoki's thought between stern moral conservatism and economism. Despite his beliefs that vice often stemmed from privation and that government was ill-equipped to change entrenched commoner mores, Nozoki embarked on a campaign to eliminate prostitution. On the central issue of economic development, however, Nozoki was consistent. The government could not command the people, only guide them.

Nozoki's approach to government policy was unprecedented and was resisted by more traditional retainers. The rebuttals to Nozoki's position paper reflect open dissension, with one respondent characterizing Nozoki's opinion as absurd (*fusetsu*). Nozoki, indeed, appears to have had little success in dismantling such established institutions as the lacquer and flax monopsonies. The struggle over the flax monopsony outlasted Nozoki himself. After his death in 1803, his son and successor, Nozoki Masamochi, continued to oppose the monopsony, achieving a modicum of liberalization in 1807. Flax and lacquer, however, were industries in decline. Lacquer was unable to compete with wax fruit, and the demand for flax was shrinking as cotton replaced linen as the popular fabric. The importance of Nozoki's reforms thus lay elsewhere, in sericulture and rural reconstruction.[82]

The focus of Nozoki's reforms lay in reversing the domain's population decline. Recognizing that the domain had been taxing its people into desertion, Nozoki declared a tax moratorium. For five years, from 1791 to 1795, the government ceased collection of back taxes. After 1795 arrears were collected, but amortized over 30 years. Collection of domain-financed loans (*haishaku maigin*) was suspended for seven years, and repayment was to be rescheduled over 50 years. In 1796, however, the government simply forgave all outstanding debts. Nozoki recognized that family size was determined largely by economic factors and thus began awarding premiums for large families. Beginning in 1792/11 families with five or more children under fifteen years old were to receive a stipend of *ichinin buchi* (roughly 1.8 *koku*) until the youngest child was five. On the birth of the fifth child under fifteen, the domain awarded the family three bolts of white cotton cloth. To allow poor farmers and younger sons to marry, Nozoki established special incentives: newlyweds were given building materials, title to fallow or abandoned land, and a three-year tax exemption.[83]

To combat abortion and infanticide, Nozoki turned to both regulation and incentives. Village officials were directed to register all pregnancies and insure that farmers did not "send back" infants. But Nozoki saw infanticide as a product of privation, not as a moral failing:

Although regulations [banning infanticide] have been issued repeatedly for years, old evils are slow to pass and it has been reported that there are those who send back [kaeshiyari] infants. Although in principle there should be no one willing to harm a child, practically, there are those who, due to strained circumstances [funyōi], practice this evil custom.

The government promised to pay indigent families up to one *ryō* to make child rearing economically viable. The government urged relatives and neighbors of pregnant women to insure that they registered to receive the subsidy.[84]

The promotion of rural industries was also based on incentives rather than directives. In 1792 the government established twelve mulberry farms throughout the domain. The farms purchased mulberry seedlings at above market price to attract the interest of farmers. Farmers wishing to raise mulberry were given seedlings free of charge and provided with loans to finance land clearing and reclamation. Farmers could borrow up to 1.8 *kan* per *tan* up to 5.4 *kan*. After a three-year grace period, the loans were repaid at 0.7 percent interest per month. Land newly planted to mulberry was exempted from *nengu* for three years. To help farmers with other aspects of sericulture, the domain published a "Handbook of Sericulture" (*Yōsan tebiki*). The guide, which included advice on mulberry cultivation, cocoon shelling, and the manufacture of silkworm egg cards, was available to farmers upon request.[85] In keeping with Nozoki's emphasis on the counterproductive effects of heavy taxation, the domain avoided heavy taxes on mulberry, thread, and textiles. Mulberry cultivation grew in part at the expense of lacquer, as farmers planted mulberry trees to enjoy the exemption from *nengu*.[86]

Because the domain did not tax or monopsonize sericulture, aggregate data are scanty. Surviving evidence suggests, however, that the promotion of sericulture was an immense success. An 1827 rural survey reported domain-wide revenue from sericulture as 42,321 *ryō*, or nearly three *ryō* per farm household. Sericulture production was equal in value to nearly one-half the domain tax burden of roughly 80,000 *koku.* Qualitative observations describe an increasingly affluent countryside. According to *Ushi no yogore,* the journal of a rural doctor, "While formerly houses had dirt foundations and not a single house had a stone foundation, within 50 years houses have grown extravagant, and now, in the second year of Bunsei [1819], there is not a single house with an earth foundation." This sense of rural prosperity is confirmed, indirectly, by government edicts. In 1826 the domain banned farmers from building luxurious homes with amenities such as writing alcoves (*shoin*), bookshelves, transoms, and *shōji* doors, luxuries inconceivable in previous decades. The domain did not try to justify these restrictions through economic necessity, but argued, rather, that such indulgences were contrary to heaven's design and were injurious to the *kokutai.*[87]

This increasing prosperity corresponded to a rise in recorded population. Population growth began in 1796, soon after Nozoki's reforms, and continued uninterrupted until the Tenpō famine of the 1840s. Female infanticide seems to have all but disappeared: the female population grew faster than the male population, and by 1860 the sex ratio had fallen to 1.04 males to females. This change in the sex ratio was further supported by the spread of sericulture, spinning, and weaving, industries that increased the value of women's labor. Because Nozoki's policies encouraged the accurate reporting of births, some "population growth" may have been a result of better reporting, especially of girls. The sustained rise in both male and female populations, however, in tandem with reports of improved rural conditions, suggests a real increase. This combination of improving rural conditions, and a growing population was reflected in tax returns. In 1822, after roughly a century of shortfall, the farmers of Yonezawa were able to remit their *nengu* obligations in full.[88]

## Labors of the Samurai

Population growth and increasing rural productivity helped Yonezawa back to solvency. Yet even with a growing commoner population, the domain still faced one of the highest ratios of retainer to commoner in Japan. The tax rates necessary to provide adequate stipends for all Yonezawa retainers would have weighed heavily on the most productive commoners. Nozoki's complement to rural reconstruction was the promotion of samurai by-employments. By providing its retainers additional income, the domain was able to support the samurai estate without taxing the peasantry into destitution and desertion.

Samurai by-employments began in the late 1600s as a result of steady decreases in retainer income. According to *Kangendan*, retainers engaged in a variety of pursuits, working as pawnbrokers, potters, vegetable farmers, and weavers. Warashina Ritsutada, the author of *Kangendan*, revealed a fear of samurai industry typical of conservative Yonezawa statesmen. "The duty [*yakugi*] of farmers, artisans, and merchants is purposefully to seek profit [*ri o tsunori*]," but this made it impossible for them to have "loyal hearts" (*chūgi no kokoro*). As samurai became increasingly concerned with worldly advancement and rewards (*risshin shusse*), they risked losing their "samurai ethos." Citing Mencius, Warashina noted that the pursuit of duty (*gi*) and the pursuit of profit (*ri*) were mutually exclusive. Warashina thus feared a national crisis if poverty continued to force samurai into by-employments.[89]

Although Yonezawa statesmen found samurai industry unsettling, they understood that the inability of the domain to pay adequate stipends made by-employments inevitable. This led to somewhat contradictory policies. Takenomata, for example, hoped to use the revenue from lacquer trees to pay retainers their full stipends and end samurai by-employments. In the interim, however, Takenomata established a government office to teach weaving to samurai women. The office had a staff of nine and employed an expert weaver from Echigo, but had only six or seven students at a time.[90]

The large-scale promotion of samurai by-employments came during the administration of Nozoki Yoshimasa. Under Nozoki's rule, weaving became a commonplace in samurai households. By-employments were part of a broader program to make retainers less dependent on government support. Nozoki also advocated rural resettlement for non-stipended relatives in retainer families. Younger sons, brothers, uncles, and nephews were encouraged to take up farming along with their wives and children. The government provided land and housing, loaned the settlers food, and granted three years of tax amnesty. The government assured samurai that farming would not diminish their status but bring them honor, and it pledged to observe all perquisites of samurai status for farming samurai. Farming, the government insisted, was nothing shameful: "Farmers, second after samurai [in the social order], are not base and there is nothing shameful about agriculture."[91]

In a similar fashion, Nozoki sought to remove the stigma associated with sericulture and weaving. In a 1797 edict encouraging retainers to grow mulberry and raise silkworms, the domain announced that ladies-in-waiting at Yonezawa castle were engaged in sericulture. Retainers of all ranks were thus to follow suit.[92] Weaving by elite women was given a high profile when Harunori used homespun fabric as gifts.[93]

Samurai weaving has commonly been identified with women, and the contemporary observers saw the industriousness of Yonezawa samurai wives as the wellspring of the domain's economic health. Little in the Kansei-era (1798–1800) promotion of weaving, however, was directed strictly at samurai women. While the domain saw weaving as a traditionally female activity, it valorized weaving before a general audience. In a 1792 edict addressed to the "four estates," the domain cited women weavers as examples of service to the "state":

Painfully aware of the decline of the people, his lordship wishes both high and low to exert themselves in these crafts. By working in sericulture and weaving, women fulfill the needs of his lordship [for cloth]. Men too should earnestly promote national prosperity [*kokueki*] by engaging in their occupations and should above all seek to promote our national commodities. Those who wish to contribute to the national prosperity through the production of local products should apply to our national commodity office.[94]

Later edicts regarding samurai weaving were commonly gender neutral.[95] In the government-sponsored sericulture manual, *Yōsan tebiki*, gender is mentioned only in reference to silk larvae.[96] Whether or not retainers physically sat at a loom, weaving was a household enterprise, and they engaged in commerce when they bought thread and sold finished cloth. The domain thus issued edicts instructing merchants to treat their samurai clients with appropriate respect, allowing them to use side entrances when selling cloth.[97]

Under Nozoki's program, samurai weavers commonly worked through a putting-out system. Weavers received 500 *me* (about four pounds) of thread from a cloth wholesaler (*ton'ya*), returned 400 *me* (about 3.25 pounds) of cloth, and received a standardized wage. Although weavers could own their own looms, they often borrowed them from wholesalers. The putting-out system remained loosely organized until 1807, when the domain ordered weavers to take thread only from authorized thread brokers (*nakagai*). The new regulations were designed to stop the use of weak or cheap thread, which produced a poor-quality cloth. Enforcement of the *nakagai* system proved difficult, and retainers continued to buy thread independently in farm villages.[98]

Quality control emerged as the most intractable aspect of commodity regulation. Although Nozoki was loath to restrict production or trade, shoddy cloth threatened to destroy the market for Yonezawa's textile exports. When quality problems began to hamper export plans, Nozoki feared that the nascent textile industry would collapse entirely.[99] The domain thus sought to balance free-market access with regulations on quality. The result was a patchwork of cartel agreements subject to frequent renegotiation.

Government intervention in textiles was originally intended to expand market avenues, not restrict them. Because of the region's poor transportation networks, Yonezawa weavers often had difficulty selling their product outside the domain. To insure a steady demand for cloth, in 1793 Nozoki ordered the domain commodity office (*kokusansho*) to begin purchasing cloth and entrusted Mitani Sankurō, an Edo merchant, with marketing Yonezawa textiles. The domain's ties with the Mitani were long-standing: in 1725 they had been entrusted with marketing Yonezawa wax in Edo, and by 1767 they had provided Yonezawa with nearly 20,000 *ryō* in credit.[100] The commodity office was not a monopsony agency. Mitani was directed to pay market prices for cloth, and the government allowed producers to sell independently in Edo or through contacts in the domain's Edo residences. The goal of the office was to provide market opportunities rather than to restrict them.[101]

The following year, however, the domain made Mitani the sole authorized textile purchaser. The domain was reportedly concerned with product quality. To undercut their competitors' prices, Yonezawa weavers were using cheap thread and producing shoddy fabric. The domain recognized that the value of its exports would drop if Yonezawa became known for poor-quality cloth. Under a monopsony arrangement, Mitani could insure that no substandard textiles were sold. Unfortunately, the new monopsony arrangement suited neither party. Mitani was distressed by the poor quality of Yonezawa cloth, and the domain was disappointed by his inability to market the domain's production. The domain sought help from Shimaya Sajirō, an Edo clothing merchant, but Shimaya was similarly unable to handle the volume of Yonezawa textiles.[102]

In 1796 the domain abandoned monopsony, acknowledging that Shimaya alone could not handle the domain's exports. Weavers were again allowed to sell independently (*katte shidai*) to buyers throughout Japan. Samurai weavers were further allowed to send their textiles to the domain's three Edo residences. The domain remained concerned with quality, and it exhorted weavers not to injure Yonezawa's reputation in pursuit of excessive profits. Quality weaving, the government declared, was "an eternal blessing and a source of national prosperity [*kokueki*]," and weavers should make every effort to produce high-quality fabric.[103]

This tension between restricted and free trade became a central theme of Yonezawa economic policy. Agreements with cartels or central purchasing agencies gave the domain control over the quality of its exports and insured that all producers would have access to major markets. But the restrictions of commodity agencies and cartels antagonized producers with standing marketing arrangements. As the sericulture industry expanded and matured, these issues grew more intricate. The domain's initial monopsony arrangement with Mitani covered all textiles. As textile production and sericulture diversified, merchants came to specialize in specific varieties of cloth. By the 1850s the domain had authorized specialized cartels such as the *ito ton'ya*, which dealt in raw silk thread, and the *tsumugi ton'ya* to deal in silk pongee. Within each specialized market the domain attempted to balance the demand for free-market access with the need for quality control. In each case the domain moved freely from cartels to commodity agencies to unrestricted trade.

The authorization of *ton'ya* often came after failed attempts to control quality without market restraints. The institution of a monopsony cartel for silk pongee in 1827, for example, came after repeated edicts relating to cloth quality. In 1822 the domain prohibited the use of dyes that artificially increased the weight of thread and fabric. In 1824 the domain again warned against dye additives that increased fabric weight. The additives produced a cloth that looked adequate when sold but spotted during the rainy season. The domain further inveighed against lightweight and weak cloth. Such substandard products, the government observed, "led to a decline in the country's product [*kokusan*]." These exhortations had limited effect. Two years later, the domain authorized a three-member cartel for silk pongee. The purpose of the new arrangement was to stop the spread of "counterfeit" (*nisemono*) silk pongee.[104]

Because the justification for cartels was closely tied to quality control, merchants strove to maintain the reputation of Yonezawa cloth. In 1854, for example, the cloth cartel began putting printed notices in the cloth they sold. The notice informed the buyers that Yonezawa cloth was esteemed throughout Japan and that the *ton'ya* carefully checked its cloth for gloss, color, and soilage. Buyers were advised to look for the cartel's stamp of approval on all cloth and to contact the *ton'ya* with questions about the authenticity of their cloth.[105]

The domain's exhortations against slipshod or "counterfeit" products drew on both the language of commerce and the language of loyalty. In 1799 the domain declared that sloppy textiles were a "stain on samurai [honor]."[106] Unfortunately, "disgraceful" commodities were lucrative: cloth doctored with starch and additives was cheaper to make but sold at the same price as the genuine article. The domain thus began linking individual actions with a greater common good. In 1796 the domain contrasted the short-term profits of shoddy cloth with the "endless blessing and national prosperity" of carefully crafted fabric. If weavers were led astray by immediate gain, then "excessive profit will, in the end, become a loss for each and everyone."[107] The domain thus inveighed against profiteering without condemning profit. Moral exhortations on production continued, but they assumed a "nationalist" tone. In 1806 the domain declared that "when the small profits from each house are combined, they amount to great national prosperity [*kokueki*]. By engaging in sericulture one can accomplish the objective of repaying one's debt to one's country [*kokuon*]."[108] An important trope in such edicts was the "country's" reputation. In 1801, for example, the domain warned that the use of poor-quality thread would cause "disgrace throughout the country."[109] Elsewhere the domain warned against "sullying the country's name."[110] By the Tenpō era the domain commonly used the term *kokujoku* (national disgrace) to describe poor-quality textiles. This linkage of national honor with commerce reflected the transformation of the lord-vassal bond. As by-employments grew in importance as a source of samurai income, the bond between lord and vassal became more managerial than feudal. A "national disgrace" was thus an action that impugned the health of Yonezawa textiles, the joint economic interest of the daimyo and his retainers.

In this way, the promotion of sericulture was grounded in suzerain authority. Without this form of legitimacy, the regime could not have asked retainers to discard their patrimonial privileges and engage in sericulture. In styling the domain as the defender of the "nation" (*kokumin*), however, Nozoki transformed the notion of samurai service. The issue became not how retainers had served in generations past but how they could best serve the daimyo in his capacity as guardian of the "nation" and "national prosperity." Nozoki's reconceptualization of the domain was supported by his masterful use of symbols. The image of the daimyo's harem busily weaving cloth for his robes undermined the argument that sericulture was unbecoming to a samurai. In *Ushi no yogore*, Nagao Ushio observed that seeing sericulture in the daimyo's castle had popularized it among retainers and led to great prosperity.[111] Having made weaving a form of service, Nozoki could demand that retainers serve with customary honor and valor. Retainers who produced poor cloth were not defending their patrimony but failing to repay their obligations to their country (*kokuon*) and thus disgracing, rather than honoring, their ancestors.

This use of "national" honor and obligation to transform the definition of the samurai estate recalls Ernest Gellner's conception of nationalism. For Gellner, cultural homogeneity is not a source of nationalism but its result. "Nationalism is not what it seems, and above all it is not what it seems to itself. The cultures it claims to defend and revive are often its own inventions, or are modified out of all recognition." National culture, he argues, stems from the objective need of industrial societies for "mutually substitutable atomized individuals" both as bureaucrats and as workers.[112] The common culture of a modern nation-state is created when an industrial society allocates offices and resources based on function rather than status. Ironically, this Weberian functionalism obliterates subnational distinctions by creating a new national culture, complete with new parochialisms.

Yonezawa's samurai weavers suggest Gellner's nationalism writ small. The promotion of samurai weaving was part of the promotion of a "national" culture of weaving and sericulture in which all Yonezawa subjects could participate. In asserting that "his lordship wishes both high and low to exert themselves in these crafts . . . [and] above all seek to promote our national commodities," the regime impelled both samurai and peasant toward protoindustrial production.[113] Government declarations that service to the "state" and samurai honor were linked to the quality and value of economic output reflect the objective, economic emphasis of the nation-state. Two major caveats apply: Yonezawa weaving was not an industrial enterprise, and Yonezawa was a domain with suzerain autonomy, not a nation. But the mobilization of Yonezawa samurai in sericulture and weaving anticipated the Meiji government's promotion of commercial and industrial enterprises for samurai (*shizoku jūsan*) a century later. In both cases, governments redefined the samurai estate by appealing to the broader economic needs of the "nation."

### Entrepreneurs and Laborers

The public promotion of retainer by-employments transformed the lives of Yonezawa samurai. Detailed knowledge of retainer sericulture comes from the journal of Minamoto Toshinaru, a minor official. Minamoto worked with four other retainers in a small government office in Ayukai village, in northern Yonezawa. The office was entrusted with border defense, disaster relief, and the suppression of protests and disturbances. Minamoto's major duty, however, was clerical, making final copies of documents for submission to central agencies, such as the office of the exchequer (*kanjōyaku*). Minamoto's diary suggests that his duties left him ample time for other activities: in 1833, he appeared in the office only 187 days. We do not know Minamoto's stipend, but much of his income seems to have come from by-employments. He grew, for personal consumption, Japanese radish (*daikon*), burdock, carrots, soy beans, red beans (*azuki*), black-eyed peas, and chestnuts. For market he grew mulberry and flax and raised silkworms.[114]

Despite his menial stature in the hierarchy of retainers, Minamoto's business interests were formidable. From 1833 to 1847, he planted over 500 mulberry trees to provide for his silkworms. When the yield from his own trees was insufficient, Minamoto purchased mulberry leaves at a market in Arato. While Minamoto and his family (a wife and son) did much farm work themselves, during the peak season Minamoto hired day laborers. In the fifth month, when the silkworms required near constant feeding, Minamoto hired as many as twelve people to feed mulberry leaves to the worms. The standard wage was 25 copper *mon* per *kan* (8.27 lbs.) of mulberry leaves, or roughly 440 *mon* per day. Minamoto also hired as many as ten workers to shell the silk cocoons and other day laborers to spin the combed cocoons into thread. Once the silk had been spun into thread, Minamoto sold the finished product to local merchants. Minamoto's records show dealings with at least eight different buyers, most of them from Arato. Minamoto's business appears to have prospered, buoyed by rising silk prices. Despite wide short-term fluctuations, the price of silk thread rose steadily against both mulberry (a major factor of silk production) and staple crops, such as rice.[115]

The local government office (*yakusho*) made allowances for Minamoto's by-employments. During the summer months, when sericulture demanded his full attention, Minamoto did not appear at work for months at a stretch, or he went to the office only when urgent business demanded his services. Several other retainers, including the office head, were engaged in sericulture or farming as well, and the office seems to have run on a skeleton staff in the summer. The *yakusho* made up shortfalls in its operating expenses by borrowing from the same merchants who provided credit to Minamoto.[116]

Yonezawa's tradition of retainer by-employments foreshadowed the Meiji reforms and helped ease the transition to the new regime. According to a constabulary report filed in 1883:

Most Yonezawa retainers reside in Yonezawa. Stipends were low under *han* rule so they became involved in sericulture and the manufacture of silk thread and learned to support themselves [lit. "live off nature"]. Even now they pursue these occupations, and there are few who are without property [*musan*].[117]

Ironically, Yonezawa's meager stipends in the Tokugawa era increased the ability of retainers to adapt to the new order. For many Yonezawa retainers, the demise of the Tokugawa order provided new economic opportunities. When stipends were converted into bonds in 1876, retainers could afford to purchase the looms that they had rented from the weavers' cartel. The bond issue coincided with a period of great difficulty for the *ton'ya*, whose customary marketing and patronage systems were collapsing. The putting-out system of the *bakumatsu* era was thus rapidly transformed into a network of small independent weavers.[118]

The economic success of the Yonezawa retainers stemmed less from the infusion of capital provided by stipend reform than from experience with capital. In neighboring Shōnai *han*, retainers were unable to profit from a similar bond issue. Comparing Shōnai to Yonezawa, the constabulary report noted:

Most Ōzumi [Shōnai] retainers live in Tsuruoka. Under *han* rule stipends were generous so they are lazy and idle and even if they receive stipend bonds they live off the interest, unable to find other livelihood. In response to the recent rise in prices some suddenly sold their bonds and began businesses, but these were complete failures and they found themselves in worse straits than before.[119]

Although the Yonezawa textile industry generally served to supplement stipends, it produced at least one samurai industrialist, Machida Hachinosuke. Machida originally held a stipend of less than two *koku*, but he rose to become one of the major textile producers in Yonezawa. His singular achievement was the development in the early 1800s of *sukiaya*, a type of silk crepe popular for use in men's summer waistcoats (*haori*). Hachinosuke was succeeded by his son, Toyomasa, and grandson Toyokatsu, who were equally adept in business. By 1829, Toyomasa was purchasing nearly 1,900 ryō of silk thread and selling 2,600 ryō of cloth annually. Toyokatsu is said to have brought total assets to 30,000 ryō and made the family the richest retainer house in Yonezawa. As entrepreneurial samurai, the Machida occupied an ambiguous position in Yonezawa society. Hachinosuke fulfilled his duties as a retainer until his last days, handling affairs as varied as auditing public-works projects and settling peasant disputes. But the Machida also acted as wealthy merchants, supplying the domain with relief grain during the Tenpō crisis. Samurai by-employments thus left a complex legacy in Yonezawa. Entrepreneurs like Minamoto and Machida learned to be major capitalists. Most of their fellow samurai learned to be laborers or petite bourgeoisie.[120]

## Success and Debacle

The expansion of sericulture and textiles in Yonezawa proceeded for a half century with a remarkable lack of dissension. In the 1830s, however, fissures began to emerge between spinners and weavers. The source of conflict was the appearance of opposing price trends for silk thread and finished fabric. The price of thread rose gradually in the early 1800s and began to soar after 1858 because of European and American demand for Japanese silk. But Yonezawa fabric prices saw no such rise. Instead, Yonezawa weavers began to face increased competition, as weavers in other regions copied the most popular styles of Yonezawa fabric. By the 1830s these "price scissors" had begun to produce thread shortages in Yonezawa. When the shortages worsened, the domain moved to protect Yonezawa weavers, and in 1859 the domain prohibited the export of thread. The edict seems to have slowed the outflow of thread, but it led indirectly to a surge in the export of silkworm egg cards. Yonezawa textile production, meanwhile, contracted sharply as political turbulence led to a fall in the demand for luxurious fabrics. This price scissors crisis had ominous social implications, since it divided the domain along class lines. Weaving was largely a samurai by-employment, while raw silk was produced mostly by commoners. The domain was thus forced to choose between protecting its retainers or its taxpayers.

Despite these difficulties, contemporary observers regarded nineteenth-century Yonezawa as a model of competent statecraft. The domain's response to the Tenpō famine, for example, stood in sharp contrast to that of governments nearby. In the shogunal territory of Shibahashi, for example, the famine caused havoc. By late 1834, the territory, which encompassed 69 villages, had lost 1,405 people to starvation. Over 200 houses stood empty.[121] In Yonezawa, however, the domain relied on rice from its emergency granaries and imposed strict regulations on private supplies. The crisis battered the domain's finances and exhausted its relief supplies, but it caused no rash of deaths or desertions. An 1834 edict imposing strict rice rationing declared, "Because everyone, for the sake of the country [kakoku] has stretched grain by eating gruel, the people have survived with no starvation and his lordship's joy is unconfined."[122]

The great irony of Yonezawa history is that despite this transformation in domestic politics, Yonezawa's fortunes in diplomacy changed little. In the Restoration struggle of 1868, Yonezawa emerged as a leader in the Ōuetsu reppan dōmei, the ill-fated alliance of northeastern domains that opposed imperial forces. Uesugi Narinori, the last daimyo of Yonezawa and most unlikely of Tokugawa allies, led his troops against imperial forces in defense of neighboring Shōnai domain. The domain of Yonezawa ended much as it began, on the losing side of a great battle.

# 4

## Land and Labor

*Political Economy in Hirosaki*

> Settling samurai in the countryside is an essential part
> of feudalism—it is an institution of the sages.
> —Mōnai Giō

Hirosaki domain lay in western Mutsu province at the north-ernmost tip of Honshū, an area now known as western Aomori prefecture. In the Tokugawa era, as today, agriculture and commerce centered on the Tsugaru plain, which runs along the Iwaki river from Hirosaki city to the Sea of Japan. The castle town was linked to several regional ports: Jūsan, Fukaura, Ajigasawa, and Aomori. All but Aomori face the Sea of Japan and thus favor trade along the "western" route (*nishimawari*) to Osaka and Kyoto instead of the "eastern" (*higashimawari*) route to Edo. The castle town was also a stop on the Ushū highway, the major overland route in the north-east. Summers are short and winters long and cold on the Tsugaru plain. Like other regions facing the Sea of Japan, Hirosaki sees more rain than areas at the same latitude facing the Pacific. Northern winds striking the Ōu mountain range often produce rain or snow in western Aomori and clear days to the east. Hirosaki, however, is comparatively well protected from the *yamase*, a cold summer wind that can cause frost damage east of the Ōu mountains. The region is thus relatively well-suited to irrigated rice agriculture, which local inhabitants have pursued since at least the third century.[1]

The origins of the house of Tsugaru, which came to power in the region during the late sixteenth century, are a matter of contention.

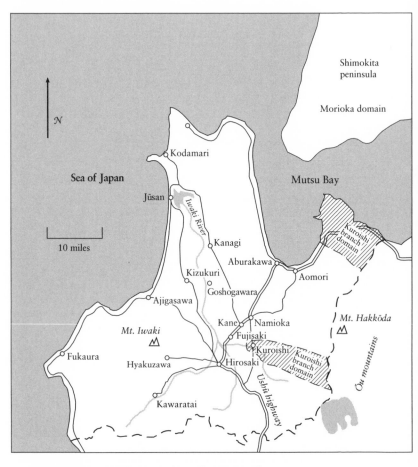

Map 4.  Towns, Villages, and Roads in Hirosaki
SOURCE: Adapted from *Kadokawa Nihon chimei daijiten*, 2: 1450–51.

According to Tsugaru records, the line was founded by Tsugaru Tamenobu, a nephew of Ōura Tamenori, lord of Ōura castle. In 1567, Tamenobu married Tamenori's daughter and became heir to the Ōura line. A distant descendant of the Fujiwara, the illustrious court nobles, Tamenobu claimed ancient precedents for his authority over the Tsugaru plain and waged a determined campaign to wrest control from the Nanbu, a rival daimyo house. Between 1571 and

1585 Tamenobu drove the Nanbu from critical castles in Ishikawa, Daikōji, and Aburakawa. By 1585 Nanbu vassals were defecting to Tsugaru ranks. In 1589 Tamenobu allied himself with Toyotomi Hideyoshi, the rising hegemon, and the following year he was awarded the surname Tsugaru and invested with the three districts of the Tsugaru plain.

Not surprisingly, Nanbu records tell a different story. In the Nanbu account, Tamenobu was born into the Kuji house, a minor branch of the Nanbu line. He left the family because of discord with his older brother and allied himself with the Ōura, thus betraying his original patrons. Nanbu records concede Tamenobu's cunning, but unlike Tsugaru records they do not laud his courage or military skill. The Nanbu claimed, for example, that Tamenobu took Ishikawa castle not through superior strategy but by poisoning its lord.[2] Whatever Tamenobu's origins, his political acumen is beyond question. Quick to ingratiate himself with Hideyoshi and then Tokugawa Ieyasu, he easily faced down Nanbu allegations about his traitorous past.

In 1600, Ieyasu bestowed on Tamenobu a formal investiture (*omotedaka*) of 47,000 *koku*. Ieyasu's successors increased this to 70,000 *koku* in 1805 and to 100,000 *koku* in 1808. The status of the Tsugaru daimyo changed accordingly. Beginning in 1808 the shogun received them in the *ōhiroma*, rather than the less prestigious *yanaginoma*. In 1820, Tsugaru Yasuchika was awarded the court rank of chamberlain (*jijū*), the highest rank commonly given to *tozama* lords.[3] These changes in formal investiture and court rank were, of course, only loosely correlated with actual Tsugaru territory. Land reclamation increased Tsugaru holdings by several fold in the seventeenth century; by 1700 the domain's real holdings totaled nearly 300,000 *koku*. These changes, however, were not reflected in the domain's *omotedaka*. The shogunate increased the Tsugaru's formal investiture largely as a reward for their service against the Russians in Hokkaidō. This disparity between the domain's large holdings and its rather unimpressive formal investiture was reflected in its policies. Hirosaki statesmen acted in many ways like those of "country" domains: they assumed that their land was autonomous in a broad range of sociopolitical issues. Both samurai and commoners regularly referred to Hirosaki as their "country," although it had never been a province under the *ritsu-ryō* system. "Kuni" thus meant "country" solely in terms of Tsugaru dominion. But the rhetoric of Hirosaki politics was pointedly less "nationalist" than that of either Yonezawa or Tokushima. Although administrators assumed that Hirosaki affairs were "politics" writ small, they appealed far less to suzerain authority than did their counterparts in Yonezawa or Tokushima. Although the logic of suzerain authority was often implicit in Hirosaki policy, the terms *kokka* and *kokumin* appeared comparatively rarely. The domain's laws also reveal a deference to the shogunate not found in the laws of either Tokushima or Yonezawa. In the seventeenth century the domain repeatedly ordered its retainers, without qualification, "strictly to obey the laws of the shogun."[4] The Tsugaru thus lay on the boundary between the broad autonomy of true "country-holding" daimyo and the more constrained powers of ordinary landed nobles.

Throughout the Tokugawa era, the house of Tsugaru maintained its vassal band on a proportionally small peasant population. According to early Meiji data, Hirosaki supported 4,338 retainers on a commoner population of 229,006. Demographic pressure in Hirosaki, the number of retainer stipends per 100 commoners, was just under two (1.89). Demographic pressure was thus far lower than in Yonezawa (6.77) but higher than in Tokushima (1.06). What makes demography central to an understanding of Hirosaki's political economy, however, is not the magnitude of its demographic ratio but the degree to which this ratio varied. The Tenmei famine of the 1780s and the Tenpō famine of the 1830s were felt throughout Japan, but in Hirosaki the effects were particularly grim and severe. The domain suffered massive depopulation because of peasant starvation and flight (see Figure 8). Such wide fluctuations in the commoner population made the Tsugaru regime acutely aware of the relationship between a large commoner tax base and stable finances. Over the Tokugawa era the government engaged in a variety of schemes to increase its farm population, including resettling samurai as farmworkers and inviting immigrants from other regions. The problems of maintaining a stable agricultural population were central to Hirosaki statecraft and political practice.

The economic underdevelopment of northeastern Japan reinforced the Tsugaru regime's concern with increasing Hirosaki's farm

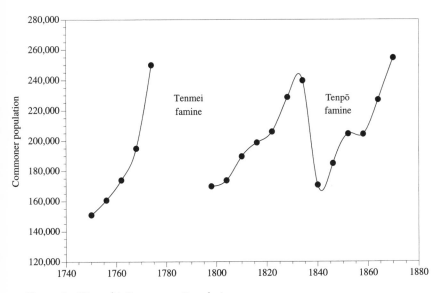

Figure 8.  Hirosaki Commoner Population

SOURCE: Hirosaki daigaku kokushi kenkyūkai, ed., *Tsugaru shi jiten*, pp. 115–21.
NOTE: Tsugaru did not conduct population surveys in 1780, 1786, and 1792.

population. Although Hirosaki produced a variety of goods for domestic consumption, its exports were limited to food grains and
lumber: to cite a contemporary expression, "The country produces
rice and only rice" [onkuni no bussan wa kome yori hoka ni kore
naki].[5] In 1815 taxes on crafts and industries other than sake
amounted to less than 1 percent of the domain's income.[6] Even in
the early Meiji era, the economy centered on food grains. In 1877,
almost 80 percent of the agricultural production of Mutsu province
was rice.[7] Since commodity production was relatively underdeveloped, the domain could not rely on commercial taxes or monopolies
to stabilize government finances, and domain officials concentrated
their efforts on increasing grain production. Hirosaki did not neglect commercial production entirely. The domain consistently encouraged the cultivation of lacquer trees and promoted the production of *Tsugaru nuri*, a distinctive local lacquerware. But the revenue generated by such undertakings was small.[8]

The burden of Hirosaki's attempts at fiscal stabilization thus fell
on increasing the agricultural population and food grain produc-

tion. To this end, Hirosaki pursued land development (*shinden kaihatsu*) on a scale unparalleled in Tokugawa Japan. Although many domains, particularly those in Tōhoku and Kyūshū, encouraged the development of arable land, none was as dependent on revenue from newly opened land as Hirosaki. In 1600 the domain's formal investiture consisted of 133 villages producing 47,000 *koku*. A cadastral survey in 1872, by contrast, recorded 836 villages yielding 340,000 *koku*. The domain's arable land increased by 623 percent and the number of villages by 528 percent.[9] In addition to general land development, the domain also undertook reclamation projects in response to crop failures and famines. After the Tenmei famine, for example, the government invited immigration from neighboring domains to settle abandoned land.

The distinguishing feature of Hirosaki fiscal policy was the role of samurai labor in land development and reclamation. The government actively encouraged samurai to open and reclaim land, and Tsugaru samurai were responsible for vast increases in the domain's total agricultural production. The involvement of samurai in agriculture served government finances in two ways. When land cleared or cultivated by samurai was registered as *kurachi* (lit. "treasury land"), the tax yield would enter the domain treasury, thus increasing revenue. Alternately, if the land was registered as the personal fief of the retainer (*chigyō*), the tax yield served to supplement the retainer's stipend. This indirectly relieved the government of the financial burden of retainer stipends. This fiscal strategy reached a peak in the wake of the Tenmei famine when the government undertook a policy called *dochaku*, the forced resettlement of thousands of retainers to farm villages. Resettled samurai were to clear land, grow crops, and pay the same land taxes as farmers. The need to increase grain production and revenue thus drove Hirosaki to challenge the very distinction between samurai and peasant.

## Land Development in Early Hirosaki

Hirosaki administrators of the later Tokugawa era were deeply influenced by two precedents: the early success of government-promoted land development, and the failure of government-controlled commerce. Hirosaki encouraged land development from the early seventeenth century, and tax rolls grew rapidly during the first century of Tokugawa rule. Between 1600 and 1687 domain tax rolls (*kokudaka*) increased by 453 percent and the number of villages increased by 377 percent.[10]

Hirosaki managed such enormous increases in arable land largely through small-scale land development projects undertaken by retainers, rural samurai (*gōshi*), masterless samurai (*rōnin*), and commoners. Capital was provided primarily by the developer, and reclamation was encouraged by a policy of tax exemptions. The domain exempted reclaimed land from *nengu*, corvée, and other service obligations for from five to seven years, and developers were allowed to claim a portion of the developed land as their landed fief, or *chigyō*. Fiefs thus granted in return for land development were known as *kochigyō*, literally "little fiefs."[11]

Because a diverse range of people received *kochigyō* during the early 1600s, generalizations about "little fiefs" must be made with caution. There are, for example, cases of both high-ranking wealthy retainers and commoners holding "little fiefs." According to scholarly consensus, the most common *kochigyō* holder was a low-ranking, low-income retainer.[12] Most "little fief" holders, moreover, were enfeoffed as retainers, not as farmers with tax-exempt holdings. A 1670 edict, for example, noted that "a great number of 'little fief' holders have been declared foot soldiers [*ashigaru*]."[13]

Whatever the details of the *kochigyō* system, its effect on the countryside is clear: large numbers of retainers settled in rural Hirosaki. A 1684 land register from Kanaki village lists about 105 homes, 62 of which were held by landed vassals, 40 of whom were described as "hand-working samurai" (*tezukuri kyūnin*), retainers who actively worked the land. The distribution of property suggests that these families dominated village life: 78 percent of the paddy land and 86 percent of the dry field was held directly by samurai as landed fief (*kyūchi*). A similar situation obtained in Motomachi village, where samurai owned 21 of 40 homes and controlled 76 percent of the land.[14]

The massive samurai presence described in these village registers undoubtedly raised the total agricultural productivity and increased government revenue. The program, however, was not without cost. By encouraging the independent development of land by samurai, the domain increased the authority of its retainers at the expense of its own centralized control. The *kochigyō* system thus ran in opposition to the policy of transforming vassals from financially independent, rural warriors to a centralized and salaried staff of soldiers and administrators. The *kochigyō* system was also more costly than alternative means of land development. In the strictest sense, of course, the *kochigyō* system gave the domain something for nothing: the domain made no initial outlay of capital and increased its tax base of arable land. But the *kochigyō* system was not as attractive as its alternatives. Under the *kochigyō* system only 60 percent of the new land was subject to taxation, since the remainder became fief. By contrast, when the government developed land through forced drafts of farm labor, the initial cost was minimal and the domain could then tax the entire annual yield.[15]

Such considerations underlay the policy changes taken in the 1680s. In 1685 the domain began to convert landed stipends (*jikata chigyō* and *kochigyō*) into salaried stipends (*kuramai* or *kirimai*) and to assemble retainers in the castle town.[16] At roughly the same time, the domain began a program of centrally directed land development using peasant labor.[17] While significant, this shift from fiefs to stipends did not represent a rejection of fiefs. Indeed, the domain returned to landed fiefs from 1712 to 1774.[18] Fiefs remained important because they enabled the domain to shift the burden of tax collection from its treasury to its retainers. But fiefs also took on moral implications. As officials became concerned with the deleterious effects of luxuries and urban life on samurai, they came to see the rural samurai of the 1600s as models of self-reliance and vigor. Enhanced by the rhetoric of tradition, rural fiefs became Hirosaki's means of addressing both fiscal and social crises.

## Hirosaki Commercial Policy: The Hōreki Reforms

The land reclamation projects of the 1600s increased Hirosaki's income several fold. Nonetheless, by the early 1700s the domain was plagued by chronic budget deficits. In Hirosaki, as in other domains, the deficits stemmed largely from costs related to the alternate attendance system and the daimyo's Edo mansion. These problems were exacerbated by several severe famines and numerous harvest shortfalls. The Genroku famine of 1695 killed some 30,000 people and forced the domain to borrow from the shogunate and cut stipends by half. Repeated shortfalls in 1711, 1720, 1728–29, and 1740 gradually depleted domain coffers and forced the domain to "borrow" from retainer stipends. In 1750, after three years of flooding, the domain again cut stipends by half. The cumulative effect of these events was enormous. By 1754 the domain owed over 300,000 *ryō* to various merchants, and its debt exceeded twice its annual tax revenue.[19]

Hirosaki's first reform movement was led by Nyūi Mitsugi (1712–92), an iconoclastic political theorist and official. Born into a low-ranking family, Nyūi rose to power through his close friendship with the domain elder, Tsugaru Mondo. From his initial post as apprentice page (*hōkō minarai*) in 1735, he rose to head of the castle kitchen staff (*zenban*) in 1744, valet (*konandoyaku*) in 1745, personal secretary (*kinju koshō*) in 1749, and then magistrate of the exchequer (*kanjō bugyō*) in 1753. With a close ally among the domain elders, Nyūi dominated domain politics from 1753 to 1758.[20]

Despite his humble career path, Nyūi was a philosopher of considerable range and achievement. Heavily influenced by Yamaga Sokō, Ogyū Sorai, and Dazai Shundai, Nyūi rejected Chu Hsi learning and sought to return to the original writing of the ancient Chinese sages. Like Sokō, he was deeply concerned with the practical questions of statecraft (*keisei saimin*) and dismissed Chu Hsi metaphysics as pointless abstraction. Like Dazai Shundai, he was deeply concerned with the workings of the commercial economy and finances. Nyūi also shared with Shundai and Kaiho Seiryō an interest in the Taoist thought of Lao-tzu and Chuang-tzu.[21]

Central to Nyūi's thought was the idea of "utility" (*yō*). Everything exists, he argued, to fulfill a particular purpose. For people, "utility" determines their social function. "All living things possessing some form [*katachi*], including human beings, must perform some useful [*yō*] function in accordance with their particular form. . . . From the day one is born, one must exert one's whole body and mind in the service of people and things in order to be of use [*yō*] to the realm [*tenka*]." In the case of objects, "utility" determines their value. "Well water is valuable only because it is able to give people life. People do not value water for itself, but only to the extent that it is beneficial to their lives. . . . Pure water, if it is not used, may be less valuable than dirty water that is put to use."[22]

For Nyūi, well water was the ideal commodity. Because, he claimed, it is drawn only when needed, there is never a surplus of well water. Further, because people can draw water according to their need, there is never a shortage. Because water appears only when needed, supply and demand are always in balance. Thus, no one covets well water, nor does anyone seek to economize and use less water. Further, no one trades in well water, and there are no waterlenders or waterbrokers. Under rule by sages, all things, including grain, gold, and silver, would flow like well water, and people would know neither want nor greed. The goal of government, Nyūi argued, was to make man-made products function like water, a natural, heaven-made product.[23] It is noteworthy that Nyūi's idealization of well water was predicated on ready and equal access to wells. Nyūi's philosophy thus assumed something closer to the idealized well-field system of ancient China than to the complex irrigation systems of Hirosaki.

In Nyūi's philosophy merchants served an important but limited function. It was both right and proper for merchants to exploit spatial price differences. The "Way of the merchant" was to buy products in one region and sell them in another, keeping the price differential as profit. The ideal merchant house would use a fixed price scheme, buying for a set price in western Japan and selling for a set price in eastern Japan. In doing so, a merchant would be working in harmony with the Way by restoring equilibrium (*kin/hitoshii* or *chū*).[24] But Nyūi had no tolerance for temporal price differences. Price speculating, he argued, was injurious not only to the "state" but to merchants themselves. Since no one could forecast prices, a merchant house seeking to profit through speculation ultimately would come to ruin. Nyūi thus distinguished between "great" and "petty" merchants. A "great" merchant

transports rice, gold, and valuables through the realm [*tenka*], trading by buying cheaply and selling dearly and thus profiting through these imbalances. These accumulated profits are his investiture, and this garnering of profit is his Way and his method. By guarding this way and keeping to this method, he will never lose his principal, he will never gain and then lose. . . . [He] does not covet profit from others, knows much about loss and thinks little about gain, knows much about great profits and thinks little about petty profits. On a large scale he enriches the state and on a small scale he helps the poor, lends without collecting, sells for little and buys for much, and maximizes his house's shares [*kabu*] without losing its principal. This is the great Way of merchants.

Petty merchants, by contrast, were a despicable lot. Obsessed with fleeting profits, they acted against the interest of both the state and their fellow subjects.[25]

For Nyūi, trade was legitimate only to the degree to which it served the state, and he thus favored far-reaching restrictions on commerce. With the support of Tsugaru Mondo and Mōnai Ariemon, the daimyo's steward (*yōnin*), Nyūi sought to bend merchants to his vision of the merchant Way. Beginning in 1753 Nyūi imposed a broad range of restrictions on merchants. He ordered merchants to pay licensing fees (*unjō*) and appointed government "assistants" to merchant organizations to insure their cooperation with domain projects. To enforce frugality, he banned all merchants, save pawnbrokers and brewers, from operating in the countryside. Particular emphasis was placed on stopping the sale of "luxury" fabrics, such as cotton and silk. In keeping with Nyūi's emphasis on "utility," merchants were required to use their store names as family names. In order to gain control over rice shipments, Nyūi issued "rice bills" (*kome kitte*), essentially promissory notes for rice backed by the domain. The notes served as a means of refinancing the domain debt: in exchange for gold and silver, the domain gave Osaka merchants paper, which it promised to convert into rice within three years. Nyūi also pursued more traditional reform plans. He renegotiated the domain's debt, deferring some payments indefinitely and others for three years. He promoted local exports such as horses, sulfur, and cinnabar.[26]

The reforms were largely successful, and in 1755 the domain was able briefly to stop "borrowing" stipends. Nyūi's policy of exporting promissory notes instead of rice proved especially fortuitous. In 1755 unseasonably cold weather caused severe harvest shortfalls throughout northeastern Japan. In Hirosaki, the harvest fell by almost 80 percent. Because Nyūi had restricted grain exports, the domain had large stores of rice for famine relief. Nyūi's increased control over merchants also helped to bring private stores of grain under government control. Although neighboring domains reported extensive disease and starvation, in Hirosaki the death toll was minimal: contemporaries marveled at the absence of beggars and refugees. Impressed by their achievement, the daimyo commended both Nyūi and Mōnai. Nyūi was selected for particular praise: he was given the unique position of general overseer (*motoshi*) and became the dominant figure in domain politics.[27]

In the wake of the 1755 harvest failure, Nyūi moved toward more radical reforms. In part, he was emboldened by his success in handling the harvest crisis, but he also faced financial pressures. The "rice bills" he had issued were coming due, and the domain treasury and relief granaries had been depleted by the famine. Beginning in 1756 Nyūi moved to establish complete control over commerce. He issued a rationing coupon, called *hyōfu*, to replace specie within the domain. Retainers were paid in *hyōfu*, and merchants were ordered to accept it as legal tender. *Hyōfu* were designed to increase the government's store of specie. The government paid for goods and services with *hyōfu* and forced merchants to accept them in exchange for precious metals. The domain also supplanted all private financial services. Nyūi declared void all samurai debt owed to merchants within the domain and assumed responsibility for debt owed to merchants in other domains. Nyūi also instituted a distribution bureau (*unsōyaku*) to redistribute merchant property. Merchants were barred from trading in more than one kind of goods and were ordered to report their total assets and stock to the government. The domain purchased the goods with ration coupons and redistributed them to other merchants. In short, Nyūi's reforms established complete government dominance over finance and commerce. Kojima Yasunori has aptly dubbed these efforts a "feudal command economy."[28]

Within Nyūi's philosophy, his efforts were not anti-commercial, only an attempt to guide merchants toward their "true" Way and away from the path of "petty" traders. In practice, the impact of his policies on local merchants was devastating. The notebook of the Sakaiya merchant house describes Nyūi's reforms as a reign of terror:

In the eighth month of 1756 we compiled a list of [our] money, merchandise, pawned goods, land, ships, and loans, etc., and offered it to the Hirosaki survey office [*inzūyakusho*]. Later, we delivered cash to them. All of the remainder was delivered to stores according to their orders. They quickly took charge of the pawned goods, later giving us *hyōfu* in exchange. In the eighth and ninth months of last year, we took charge of a wool and cotton business. However, the merchandise was taken by the government [*yakusho*]. We received *hyōfu* for the silver and estimated value of the merchandise and gave it to the *yakusho*. We obeyed the orders of the government in all things: we handed one store over to two clerks, Yanagitamura Kansaemon and Obamaya Kyūbei. We head out daily to their offices in Kotobukiyama and Tsubakiyama, but they will not let us again engage in sales. . . . Though there is simply no way to stop the ruin of the family fortune, more fearsome still is the threat of government censure, and there is no peace, awake or asleep, day or night.[29]

The broader result of Nyūi's policies was widespread confusion and economic stagnation. Most serious was the complete failure of *hyōfu*, which failed to earn popular acceptance as currency and were viewed with great suspicion. In 1756/12 the government reissued *hyōfu*: the old issue was redeemable at the rate of 75 to one, a depreciation of 98 percent in three months. This corresponds to an annual inflation rate of over three billion percent. The government's policy of debt repudiation also made merchants outside the domain wary of doing business in Hirosaki, which led to a shortage of consumer goods and then staples. By the summer of 1757, shoppers were lining up in the early morning hoping to buy whatever meager supplies were available. This combination of shortages and hyperinflation sparked widespread discontent. Graffiti described *hyōfu* as worthless, and the diary of a rural doctor reported, "*Hyōfu* have caused retainers and city folk ten times the suffering of a crop failure."[30]

By mid-1757 the failure of Nyūi's policies was impossible to ignore, and Nyūi began to lose his hold on the administration. In 1757/6 the domain abandoned *hyōfu* and arrested for financial improprieties Ashibane Jirōsaburō and Ashibane Chōjūrō, the merchant father and son who had managed the coupons for Nyūi. In the following weeks the domain arrested dozens of merchants associated with the distribution bureau. In 1758/3 Nyūi himself was dismissed and confined to quarters (*chikkyo*). Although Nyūi was pardoned in 1778, the Hōreki reforms were over.[31]

Nyūi's policies highlight the limits of domain economic intervention. Even a relatively underdeveloped domain like Hirosaki was dependent on merchants for essential commercial and financial services. Government economic interventions thus could not be sustained without support from major merchants. Although Nyūi had relied on the Ashibane family, this produced its own dilemma. By giving the Ashibane the power to issue currency and redistribute assets, Nyūi created the opportunity for massive corruption and peculation. Whether the Ashibane defrauded Hirosaki is all but irrelevant: the suspicion of impropriety was sufficient to raise doubts about *hyōfu* and drive down their value. The failure of the Hōreki reforms lay in Nyūi's assessment of government power. In aiming to supplant commerce with government directives, Nyūi vastly overestimated the capacity of the domain to constrain and shape popular actions. The ensuing debacle was a powerful negative precedent for Hirosaki statesmen. Although later reformers shared Nyūi's distaste for commerce, none sought to supplant urban commerce. Rather, officials turned to the countryside as a means of restoring an unsullied, uncommercial society.

## A Return to Origins: The Tenmei Famine and Samurai Resettlement

The Tenmei famine of the 1780s proved the gravest crisis in Hirosaki history and provoked the most striking government reactions. The famine, a result of continued unseasonable weather, caused over a million deaths throughout Japan. Hirosaki was struck with particular severity. Heavy rains, flooding, and unseasonable cold reduced the 1782 rice crop to one-half its usual size. Continued cold wind and rain destroyed most of the 1783 harvest as well. In 1783/12 the government borrowed 10,000 *ryō* from the *bakufu* for disaster relief, but this was insufficient: peasants were reduced to eating grass, horses, and cats. Unseasonably cold weather continued into the winter of 1783–84, leading to widespread deaths from frost, and in early 1784 the domain was struck by an epidemic. Between 1783/9 and 1784/6 over 80,000 people reportedly died, approximately one-third of the population of 250,000.[32]

The severity of the Tenmei crop failures forced the domain to pro-

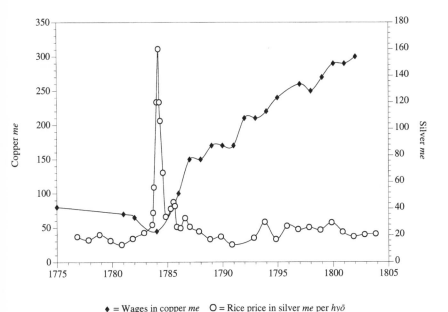

◆ = Wages in copper *me*    O = Rice price in silver *me* per *hyō*

Figure 9. Farm Wages and Rice Prices in Hirosaki
SOURCE: *Hirayama nikki* (HN), pp. 370–604 *passim*.

vide extensive tax relief. According to the tax relief survey (*kemi*) of 1783/9, 25 of the 27 tax districts had rice crop losses of 80 percent or more, and seven districts were granted full tax relief because of complete crop failure. Without tax revenue, however, the government could not continue its traditional level of expenditure. The domain was forced to make radical cuts in samurai stipends: all stipends were reduced to four *gō* of rice per day with supplementary monthly payments of 170 copper *me*.[33]

The famine also devastated the long-term prospects for the economy. As food shortages led to starvation and flight, the rural economy began to suffer a severe labor shortage. Population surveys are lacking for the critical years of 1780, 1786, and 1792, but we can infer the effects of the famine through the wages of farm laborers (*kariko*) (see Figure 9).[34] Initially, farm wages dipped slightly as laborers searched more desperately for work. After 1784, however, wages rose steadily because landlords were unable to find workers.

Between 1784 and 1803 wages rose 500 percent, while rice prices remained comparatively stable, an indication of the tremendous shortage of rural labor caused by starvation and flight.

By mid-1784 it was apparent to many officials that the severity of the famine required concerted government intervention. At the depth of the crisis, however, the seventh daimyo, Tsugaru Nobuyasu, died, leaving leadership of the domain to his 22-year-old heir, Nobuharu. This change in leadership afforded the opportunity for a radical break in policy. A particularly dramatic proposal came from Mōnai Giō, the heir of Nyūi's ally, Mōnai Ariemon.

Mōnai claimed that the magnitude of the Tenmei famine demanded an urgent samurai resettlement program. In the past year, by his estimates, some 150,000 people had died of famine or resultant disease, thereby decimating the countryside. In fields where twenty people had worked, there were now five or six, weak from hunger and struggling with shortages of seed and draft animals. Under these circumstances, he argued, it would be twenty years before the peasantry could remit taxes at the traditional level. The alternative was to resettle retainers, along with their wives and servants, in the countryside. With this additional workforce of over 20,000 people, most fallow land might be recovered in six or seven years and the financial health of the domain restored.[35]

Mōnai justified samurai resettlement by arguing that it was not a new policy but an old one that had been practiced as late as the reign of the fourth daimyo, Tsugaru Nobumasa. The ancestors of the domain's noblest families, not only lower retainers, had served their lord while residing in the countryside. High-ranking vassals had lived in small rural castles, while lower vassals for the most part commuted (*kayoi tsutome*) from their rural homes. Mōnai explicitly cited *kochigyō* as a precedent for promoting land reclamation through the granting of fiefs, although his understanding of *kochigyō* was somewhat simplified. *Kochigyō*, he explained, were farmers who cleared over 30 *koku* of land and were thus rewarded with stipends of 30 *hyō* and invested as foot soldiers (*ashigaru*). Those who opened over 100 *koku* were invested as full retainers (*kyūnin*). The descendants of *kochigyō* holders, he claimed, still served in the Hirosaki vassal band as castle guards (*rusui*). For Mōnai, this was clear evidence that the policy of assembling retainers in the castle town was a flawed policy, contrary to both Hirosaki tradition and the principles of good government. The true tradition of feudalism (*hōken*), by contrast, was to be found in the works of the sages, most notably Ogyū Sorai's *Seidan* and *Kenroku*.[36]

Mōnai's petition presents samurai resettlement as something of a panacea for the domain's moral and political problems. Samurai resettlement, he claimed, had six virtues: it would encourage military preparedness; restore the simple habits of the past; promote rural prosperity; return commoners to their proper occupations; interdict roving bands of hoodlums (*akutō*); and improve mountain and river management.[37]

Mōnai detailed these virtues individually, but central to his entire argument was a belief in the transformative power of rural life. If samurai were resettled, he claimed, they would grow interested in farming and, seeking to make their fields fertile, plant trees and collect varnish. In the slack time between spring and fall, they would hunt with guns and bows, becoming skillful and strong. Their wives and children would raise silkworms and plow the fields. The cumulative effect would be not only a restoration of the samurai class to its former rugged glory, but a transformation of class relations:

> Such people would understand the sentiments of the lower classes, know the suffering of the three estates, and be well acquainted with farming and geography. Thus, if appointed as administrators, they would not oppress the people, but apply themselves ceaselessly to farming and the martial arts. Unconcerned with luxury and pomp, they would naturally [*mizukara*] grow simple and ingenuous. Thus, even when dealing with their farmers and servants, they would show benevolence and justice and [the farmers and servants] would effortlessly come to know the Way of Heaven.[38]

To support these grand claims, Mōnai cited the writings of Ogyū Sorai, one of the period's most influential scholars. Mōnai was particularly interested in Sorai's treatise *Seidan*, a policy recommendation submitted by Sorai to the shogun Yoshimune in 1727. The scope of *Seidan* is extremely broad, but Mōnai was concerned solely with Sorai's proposal to return retainers to their fiefs as a means of restoring their economic and physical health. Urban life, thought Sorai, had led the warrior class to grow soft. They had grown accustomed to luxuries they could ill afford and had lost their physical strength and martial skills. Still more grave, however, was how urban residence had poisoned class relations:

> At present they [samurai] live in Edo and have neither familiarity with nor feelings of obligation toward the people of their distant fiefs. The farmers know them as those who take away taxes [*nengu*], while they regard the farmers merely as those who pay *nengu*. The only sentiment that exists between them is, on the one hand, the desire to take *nengu*, and on the other, the determination to keep them from being taken, and there are samurai who treat their farmers with great cruelty.

The solution to this, thought Sorai, was resettlement:

> If they [samurai] lived on their lands and grew used to seeing and speaking with their farmers, they would naturally come to feel love and compassion for them, and it is human nature [*ninjō*] that no one in these circumstances would treat their farmers with the sort of cruelty seen today. The settlement of the warrior class on the land would have these virtues and would be extremely beneficial.[39]

Both Sorai and Mōnai considered samurai resettlement essential to any comprehensive program of government reform, but Sorai's *Seidan* and Mōnai's recommendations were philosophically distinct. Unlike Mōnai, Sorai did not see samurai resettlement as a cure for all social and political ills: his advocacy of *dochaku* was based on his understanding of specific socioeconomic problems. Mōnai, by contrast, drew on a romantic, pastoral vision. Samurai resettlement would, by returning warriors to their "roots," resurrect an uncorrupted past. For Mōnai, the precedent of *dochaku* was indisputable evidence of its validity and efficacy. Mōnai's reference to Sorai may also, in some part, have been disingenuous. The daimyo's principal tutor in Edo had been Uzami Shinsui, a disciple of Sorai and editor of Sorai's work.[40] Mōnai's references to *Seidan* and *Kenroku* may thus have been in part intended to win the daimyo's favor by citing a philosopher to whom the daimyo was undoubtedly partial.

Mōnai's proposals treated the domain as an autonomous government dedicated to the independent realization of wise rule. His goal was not the better implementation of shogunal edicts or directives, but the achievement of *fukoku kyōhei*, "national prosperity and strong defense." In drawing on recommendations presented to the shogunate, Mōnai implicitly ranked Hirosaki and the *bakufu* as parallel rather than hierarchical regimes. Mōnai's reliance on *Seidan*, moreover, coincided with the shogunate's repudiation of Sorai's writings. In 1790 the shogunate deemed Sorai's writings heterodox and proscribed them as instructional texts for the shogunal academy. This decision had no palpable effect on the debate over resettlement in Hirosaki. Yet, when compared with Nozoki's policies in Yonezawa, Mōnai's efforts to reform the samurai class seem almost timid. Rather than assert that a samurai's role was to serve his domain, even as a farmer, Mōnai sought to ground his argument in precedent. The precedent of farmer-samurai was important precisely because it would bring peace and prosperity to the people of Hirosaki. But propriety, for Mōnai, was insufficient reason to support so radical a change in the social order. Rather than challenge the patrimonial perquisites of Hirosaki retainers in the name of a greater good, Mōnai argued that these perquisites were a distortion of true "feudalism" and called for a return to tradition. Unlike Nozoki, Mōnai found reasons of the "nation" insufficient grounds to challenge entrenched traditions.

The reaction to Mōnai's proposal was cautious. Mōnai submitted his memorial on 1784/9/30. Three months later the domain issued a decree encouraging voluntary resettlement in the "national interest." It is clear, however, that Mōnai's proposals were the subject of fierce dissension. The daimyo himself seems to have been partial to Mōnai's plan but was put off by its radical bent. A vocal faction meanwhile argued that resettlement would be "a betrayal of the laws of our [daimyo's] ancestors." The result was a tentative plan, which provided an allowance and one year's relief from service for those retainers voluntarily resettling to reclaim fallow land. Settlers, however, were to pay taxes the year following resettlement.[41]

These terms appear to have attracted few if any volunteers. The policy, moreover, had a haphazard look: no provisions were made for housing resettled retainers, and important details, such as the size of reclamation allowances, were left vague. Similar edicts were issued on 1789/10/1 and 1790/10/1, also to little effect. What is clear, however, is that the domain understood samurai resettlement as a means of augmenting peasant labor with samurai labor. The 1790 edict described a shortage of agricultural labor and ordered that samurai avoid hiring farmers or servants but instead assemble their relatives, especially second and third sons, and resettle as an extended family.[42]

These repeated announcements of a voluntary resettlement program suggest a stalemate between those supporting resettlement and those opposed. This deadlock was broken early in 1791 when the upper level of the administration was purged. Thirteen officials rose to power following this upheaval, but power soon coalesced around a smaller group of reform-minded administrators known as the "group of seven." Two of this group, Akaishi Yasuemon and Kikuchi Kanji, were outspoken advocates of resettlement.[43]

Like Mōnai seven years earlier, Akaishi and Kikuchi had great expectations for samurai resettlement. In their opinion paper and their audiences with the daimyo, they argued that resettlement would serve to revive the manly warrior virtues of the past and put an end to needless extravagance. Unlike Mōnai, however, Akaishi and Kikuchi depicted resettlement largely as a means of solving the domain's budget problems. As samurai began to farm and the number of idlers decreased, they argued, the domain's assets would naturally increase. The details of their proposal reveal a direct relationship between resettlement and fiscal solvency: retainers were to be resettled on fiefs one-half the size of their investitures. Their program also contained a distinct class bias. Retainers with investitures above 250 *koku* were exempted from resettlement.[44]

Although they now led the ruling faction, Akaishi and Kikuchi proceeded with caution. They continued to promote resettlement as "voluntary," but their desire to force retainers out of the castle town was clear. In order to receive a house in the countryside, retainers had to surrender their homes in Hirosaki. These homes were then dismantled for use in new construction.[45] Reaction among the retainers to this new policy was mixed. A small number resettled and successfully reclaimed land, but most seem to have avoided resettling entirely. Even so, resettlement caused problems for the regime: a 1793/2 directive to the district magistrate (*kōri bugyō*) complained that retainers were ignoring domain orders and settling wherever they wished. The magistrate was to see that retainers obeyed the decisions of the responsible intendant.[46]

In the fall of 1793 the reform faction achieved a decisive majority, and the government abandoned all pretense of voluntarism and ordered retainers to leave the castle town.[47] The government made a token offer to hear requests for extensions, but it appears to have granted none. Since most retainers inclined to resettle had already done so, the domain's decision was met with consternation and anger. The government was unyielding. To demonstrate its resolve, the domain began dismantling vast tracts of samurai housing, some 46.6 acres (19 *chō*) in 1793/10.[48] The government immediately began reforming social regulations as well: a 1793/10/1 edict changed the domain's marriage laws to allow retainers and peasants to marry.[49]

The domain's resettlement program produced a flood of decrees regulating samurai income, tax obligations, employment, housing, transportation, dress, and custom. The administration of the program was further complicated by distinctions among the retainers: regulations were different for retainers holding salaried fiefs (*kirimai*) and those holding landed fiefs (*chigyō*), for retainers with the rank of *omemi* or above and those below, for those with stipends above 200 *koku* and those with stipends below 40 *hyō* 3 *ninbuchi* (about 22 *koku*). Additional distinctions were drawn according to when the retainers settled, where they settled, and the importance of their offices. Overall, the series of decrees is somewhat confusing, and some decrees openly contradict others.[50] Reports of wild rumors among the retainers suggest that the domain was unable to manage an undertaking of such complexity and size.[51]

Despite contradictory edicts, we can reconstruct the broad outlines of the resettlement program. The policy was aimed largely at the broad middle stratum of retainers: samurai with stipends above 200 *koku* or below 40 *hyō* 3 *ninbuchi*) were exempt from *dochaku*.[52] There were initially different policies for landed and stipended retainers. The domain assumed that stipended retainers (*kirimaitori*) were reclaiming land. These retainers were to choose a village in consultation with local authorities and begin developing a parcel. They would then receive an allowance of 6 *tō* (0.6 *koku*) of rice per *tan* of land and were granted an exemption from *nengu* for the first year. If they declined the allowance, the exemption was extended by one year. Once the exemption had expired, the land was subject to taxation much like peasant holdings. While they developed land they were paid one-quarter their initial stipend. This policy appears to have encountered problems from the outset. The government repeatedly reprimanded samurai for having peasants reclaim land while presumably claiming the allowance for themselves.

Stipended retainers were treated somewhat differently. Although all retainers had been paid out of the treasury since 1773, landed fiefs were still associated with a given village or villages. *Chigyōtori* retainers were to return to the villages that constituted their putative fiefs. If a landed holder's fief was fragmented, the domain would substitute less scattered or more desirable parcels. When their fiefs contained fallow land, landed vassals received special allowances similar to those for stipended retainers.[53]

While the final resettlement program did not cut investitures in half, as Akaishi and Kikuchi had initially proposed, *dochaku* let the domain shift the tax burden of fallow land onto its retainers. The domain structured resettlement in order to force most retainers to work in reclamation. Many landed retainers were given parcels that were largely fallow. The first edict, issued on 1792/8/21, promised *chigyōtori* retainers replacement parcels if their fiefs were entirely wasteland. But a 1794 decree was less lenient. Retainers who suffered a drop in income because their fiefs were largely fallow were directed to appeal, but were to remain in the designated village while the government considered action.[54] Thus, even when the domain claimed only to be changing the form of payment, it was actually forcing retainers to reclaim land. Where retainers reclaimed land, samurai became, in essence, agricultural workers. Once their tax exemptions expired, samurai holdings contributed directly to the treasury.

The importance of resettlement is that it expressed this policy of austerity and forced labor in the language of social reconstruction. The bond between lord and vassal, while not contractual in the modern sense, involved mutual obligations. Severe stipend reductions were a failure on the part of the daimyo to reward his retainers' loyal service. While excusable in the short run, continued stipend reductions constituted a unilateral abrogation of the bond between lord and vassal: the lord continued to demand the services of his vassals but refused to provide them with the usufruct of their fiefs. Samurai resettlement recast this dilemma as a return to the original, unsullied lord-vassal bond. The reduction of samurai stipends through resettlement was not an abrogation of the daimyo's responsibility to his vassals but a rectification of the lord-vassal bond and of society in general.

This philosophical elegance was lost on most Hirosaki retainers. Since voluntary resettlement programs had been offered since 1784, those retainers who had not resettled by 1793 had little interest in farming, much less in the subtler virtues of rural life. The immediate reaction of most Hirosaki vassals seems to have been panic. Rumors and graffiti reported that a stone-throwing mob had attacked Akaishi's residence and that assassins were pursuing Kikuchi.[55] On 1793/10/11 the government thought it necessary to issue an edict threatening to punish those who spread "wild rumors" about the *dochaku* program.[56]

In the countryside the *dochaku* program quickly became a source of tension between samurai and the landlord class. Rural landlords, accustomed to their role as local authorities, took poorly to the official perception that they were merely prosperous peasants. The family diary of the Hirayama house, a wealthy and powerful landlord family in the Goshogawara area, reports: "The authority of the rural resident [*zaitaku*] samurai is formidable, and their [manner] is severe. We have been ordered to dismount before the houses of rural resident samurai and avert our eyes from high-ranking retainers [*omemi ijō*]. They have become extremely haughty."[57]

A prime example of the tensions caused by resettlement is the murder of Hara Shōhachi in 1794. Shōhachi, the uncle of Hara Shōuemon, a village official and *gōshi*, was murdered by Kudō Genpachi, a resettled retainer and scribe. The incident, recorded in considerable detail in the Hirayama diary, was precipitated when Shōhachi came across Genpachi engaged in a violent marital dispute. Shōhachi, who as the relative of a local official considered himself a figure of some authority, sought to intervene, but this led to a confrontation between the two men. The encounter grew violent, and Shōhachi, although reportedly a man of some martial skill, found his hoe no match for Genpachi's sword. Genpachi struck him dead. Wild with rage, Genpachi then strode into the street, his sword dripping blood, and stormed about, terrifying the villagers, who secured their doors and windows. A group of villagers, directed by a village official, chased Genpachi and attempted unsuccessfully to tie him up. Genpachi was finally apprehended through subterfuge when another rural retainer, Tsuchiya Magotarō, lured him into Hara Shōuemon's house with a request that he write something. Once inside, Genpachi was seized and bound by the crowd. He was taken back to his home, a guard was posted, and the authorities notified.[58]

The murder of Hara Shōhachi reveals the deep animosity that developed between resettled samurai and the rural elite. It is an ironic comment on Mōnai's vision of *dochaku* as a means of promoting harmony between samurai and commoners. The murder, moreover, presented the administration with a delicate legal problem. By the tradition of *kiritsute gomen*, by murdering Shōhachi, Genpachi was merely exercising his privilege to cut down commoners who acted in an untoward manner. But the domain's decision to allow marriages between retainers and commoners would seem to have undermined this tradition, unless the government were willing to extend *kiritsute gomen* to in-laws. If the domain ruled that Genpachi's actions were proper, however, it would weaken the authority and prestige of the commoner elite, who were essential to rural administration. The domain's system of revenue extraction depended entirely on the cooperation of commoner village officials. Unless samurai could readily assume these functions, the authority of the domain would continue to rest on the authority of its commoner agents in the village, the landlord strata. The political authority of the daimyo, however, rested on the ascriptive status of the warrior class and was thus intertwined with a tradition of privileges that included a general superiority to commoners. This conflict between the privileges of the two elites was, to some degree, inherent in the Tokugawa system. With the majority of samurai living in the cities, however, this tension remained a latent, largely invisible issue. The forcible resettlement of samurai made the depth of this tension impossible to ignore.

The domain sought to resolve this situation by punishing all parties involved. After a careful investigation in which authorities exhumed the body of Shōhachi and interrogated both Genpachi and Shōuemon, the government ruled that Genpachi had acted properly in killing Shōhachi. Genpachi, however, was not without guilt, for while the murder of Shōhachi was justifiable, terrifying the other villagers was not. Genpachi was demoted from the middle rank of *yoriki* to the menial rank of *rusui shihai*. Tsuchiya, who had helped restrain Genpachi by luring him into Shōuemon's house, was demoted for reasons not recorded. Both men fell ill and did not live out the year. Shōuemon was punished for having acted improperly in tying up Genpachi. He was stripped of *gōshi* status and was punished by *tojime*: the shutters (*amado*) of his house were nailed shut, forcing him to abandon his home until it was reopened by the authorities. The remarkable cruelty of the domain's decision highlights the failings of the resettlement program.[59]

Although the hostility between landlords and samurai was particularly explosive, *dochaku* exacerbated tension between samurai and common peasants as well. The Hirayama diary reports that corvée levies by the director of land development (*kaihatsuyaku*) and by resettled samurai were economically disastrous for most farmers.[60] This is confirmed by edicts that repeatedly ordered retainers to stop burdening peasants with illegal and onerous levies. Another edict reprimands samurai for failing to reclaim or cultivate land and for seizing *nengu* from the peasantry, thereby making it impossible for them to remit their taxes.[61] By 1796 the situation had grown so serious that peasants were openly ignoring the orders of samurai, and the government found it necessary to revise and reissue its regulations governing levies by resident samurai.[62] Peasants appear to have ignored domain orders with increasing frequency: when the domain abandoned *dochaku* in 1798, it also declared a general amnesty, pardoning all prisoners save murderers and lunatics (*ranshin kyōki*).[63]

Resettlement thus antagonized all parties concerned: retainers, landlords, and peasants. In 1798, after five years of growing opposition, the policy was abandoned. On 1798/5/23 a new ruling faction abolished *dochaku* and ordered all retainers to return to Hirosaki. The new faction wasted no time in cleaning house. Makino Sajirō, the *karō* who had supported Akaishi and Kikuchi, was forced to retire, while Akaishi and Kikuchi were removed from office for misconduct and placed under house arrest.[64] Akaishi was subjected to particular abuse. He was accused of subverting justice with wickedness and falsely citing the interests of the "country" to justify a policy of oppressive taxation. Although such behavior warranted stricter punishment, the daimyo, in his mercy, merely stripped Akaishi of his office and sentenced him to *chikkyo*, confinement to one room in his quarters. Akaishi's son Konojirō was allowed to succeed his father as a retainer, but at the menial rank of *rusui shihai* and with a stipend worth about 3 percent of Akaishi's. Kikuchi and two other officials, Sasamori Kodayū and Yoshikawa Jinzaemon, were cited separately but given similar punishments.[65]

This purge of domain officials brought Hirosaki's *dochaku* program to a close, but the radical experiment left a complex legacy for Hirosaki political economy. Although most retainers had proved themselves completely unsuitable for rural life, a small minority found *dochaku* a useful means of supporting second and third sons, children who would not inherit their father's stipend. Enough retainers either wished to remain on the land or wished their second and third sons to do so that the government saw the need to regulate the matter. In 1803/4 the domain again permitted retainers and their sons to return to farming. The government, however, had no wish to revive *dochaku* and made this clear. Samurai could return to farming if they wished, but they were to register with the village headmen as farmers (*hyakushō meimoku*), not as samurai.[66]

The failure of resettlement in Hirosaki stands in sharp contrast to the success of samurai by-employments in Yonezawa. Resettlement, of course, was a less appealing option than by-employments. Resettlement compelled retainers to relocate, abandon their posts in the castle town, and undertake the arduous labors of farming. But resettlement was also undermined by the chasm between Mōnai's utopian vision and the government's edicts. Nothing in the government's resettlement orders instilled in Hirosaki retainers the sense that they were participants in a restoration of a glorious past. Instead, in the hands of Akaishi and Kikuchi, resettlement became an elaborate means to reduce the stipends of less powerful retainers. Significantly, Akaishi and Kikuchi exempted retainers with stipends over 200 *koku* from resettlement, thus sacrificing to political expediency Mōnai's vision of a broad community of rural farmer-warriors. The failure of *dochaku* also points to the limits of suzerain authority in Hirosaki. Mōnai's goal of *fukoku kyōhei* stemmed from the belief that Hirosaki, as a "country," could effectively transform its social structure without aid, sanction, or assistance from the shogunate. But the rhetoric of "state" and "nation," which figured so prominently in Yonezawa, was lacking in Hirosaki. Although the domain referred sporadically to "national interests" (*kokueki*), the government never articulated why the daimyo's authority should so overwhelm the patrimonial interest of Hirosaki retainers. The goal of resettlement thus exceeded both the domain's ideological and its coercive capacities. Without a coherent and explicit focus on the "state" and "nation" the government could neither persuade nor compel its retainers to exchange their swords for plowshares.

## Peculation and Pragmatism: Land Reclamation Policy

Widespread dissatisfaction with the *dochaku* policy made it easy to depose the "group of seven." Drafting a new strategy to confront the domain's fiscal problems was another matter. Unlike the "group of seven," the new administration had no clear approach to the domain's continuing fiscal difficulties, and the government openly solicited suggestions on how to tackle the crisis. Ultimately, the domain employed peasant settlers to develop and reclaim land. Because many of the settlers were from other domains, the policy can be seen as the demographic complement to samurai resettlement. Instead of turning samurai into farmers, the domain simply recruited farmers from other domains. Hirosaki had pursued this policy on a small scale in the 1790s. After the failure of *dochaku*, however, it was pursued on a grand scale, with the aim of developing 50,000 *koku* of land. The central figure in this policy was an erstwhile samurai named Hirasawa San'emon.[67]

Hirasawa was born into a rural, low-ranking samurai household in 1748 and succeeded his father in 1770. He soon became involved in land development and reclamation and in 1775 was awarded with a stipend increase for the development of four villages in the Hirosu area. Records partial to Hirasawa claim that by 1794 he had developed an additional 15,984 *ninyaku* (over 2,600 acres) of land, an area yielding some 64,000 *koku* in annual tax revenue. For this accomplishment he was further promoted within the vassal band and undertook yet another reclamation project. Amid this great success, however, Hirasawa was allegedly slandered and punished with the loss of his samurai status.[68]

The Hirayama family records portray Hirasawa's accomplishments in quite a different light. An entry for 1792/3 records a commendation for Hirasawa bestowed in light of his development of

2,000 *ninyaku* (327 acres) of land. Hirayama Magojūrō and two other prominent local landlords were then assigned to work with Hirasawa on further development.[69] In Magojūrō's opinion, however, Hirasawa's reclamation procedures were extremely ill conceived. A Hirayama diary entry for early 1793 describes Hirasawa's efforts as follows:

This year Hirasawa San'emon of Yoshizumi village was once again appointed director of land development [*kaihatsuyaku*]. He is inviting people from the Akita area [to develop land]. They wander around to various village districts and are given horses as well as a full supply of food, farm tools, pots, pans, and buckets. What is more, [the domain] builds houses for them, levying the residents for lumber and reeds, and when they develop a field of their choice, it is tax exempt for one year. Such people who come from other parts are called "repatriates" [*kikokunin*]. Moreover, menial folk who have no land are sent to villages where large areas lie fallow. These idlers are said to have "relocated" [*iutsuri*], and they receive the same allowance [*teatekin*] as repatriates. Now, there are large tracts of land not on the tax rolls [*onden*] that survived the crop failure. Although not much land is developed by the repatriates or those who relocate, farmers use this opportunity to report their own land development and receive [the allowance of] six *to* of rice per *tan* of paddy. Land is also gradually being developed by rural samurai. This is how most land is developed.[70]

Hirasawa's land development efforts thus increased registered arable land less by reclaiming fallow land than by offering an incentive to register concealed holdings. More land appeared on the domain's tax rolls, but this had little to do with reclamation.

The Hirayama family was equally critical of Hirasawa's later efforts. Hirayama Magouemon, Magojūrō's father, was involved in a reclamation project the following year in which 8,000 *ninyaku* (1,307 acres) of land were cleared. Magojūrō was aghast at the staggering costs incurred by the project, sums that seemed completely out of proportion to the areas reclaimed. If development had been left to the natural increase of the population, he reasoned, such enormous outlays would not have been necessary.[71] Finally, the Hirayama records do not portray Hirasawa as a victim of slander but as an embezzler. According to an inquiry conducted by the domain censor (*metsuke*) in 1797, Hirasawa had repeatedly extorted or conspired to extort money and rice from villagers and conspired with villagers to transfer land titles illegally. As punishment, the domain stripped Hirasawa of his stipend, seized his house and personal assets, and banished him from the castle town.[72]

Despite his criminal record, Hirasawa managed a remarkable return to power. In 1802, while still exiled from the castle town and stripped of samurai status, Hirasawa composed a plan for land reclamation and presented it to the daimyo via an old ally, Takeuchi Jinsaemon. The daimyo was impressed sufficiently to grant Hirasawa a private audience. Hirasawa presented a massive reclamation plan aimed pointedly at the daimyo's pecuniary interests. Hirasawa proposed developing some 50,000 *koku* of land, 40,000 of which would go directly to the daimyo's privy purse (*konando*) and 10,000 to the branch house of Kuroishi Tsugaru, raising their status to that of daimyo. Since the daimyo, Tsugaru Yasuchika, had been adopted from the Kuroishi branch of the Tsugaru family by Tsugaru Nobuharu, Hirasawa's proposal was undoubtedly appealing. Cautioned by his previous failures, Hirasawa anticipated future attacks on his project. He recognized that the extensive corvée his proposal demanded would burden the peasantry, and accordingly he asked that the daimyo give him sufficient time to generate results before considering any such complaints. The daimyo was won over by Hirasawa's argument and appointed him magistrate of land development (*shinden bugyō*), restoring him to samurai status.[73]

Hirasawa was able to realize much of his proposal. Some accounts credit Hirasawa with developing over 38,000 *koku* between 1803 and the early 1820s.[74] An 1820 government audit reports increases of 19,206 *koku* between 1803 and 1810 and 28,996 *koku* between 1803 and 1820.[75] According to a fiscal survey compiled in 1817, the treasury received 7,250 *koku* under a special heading from the land development office (*shindenkata*) in 1815. Newly reclaimed land was producing roughly 5 percent of domain income. By 1816 this had increased to 10,000 *koku*, and a later gloss to the budget reports 13,000 *koku* for 1831.[76] The remaining tax rice went to the privy treasury: in 1822 the daimyo received 5,200 *koku* directly from the magistrate of land development (*shinden bugyō*).[77] Hirasawa's land was also used to promote the Kuroishi branch house. In 1809 Tsugaru Chikataru of Kuroishi was awarded a 6,000 *koku* fief, raising his total investiture to 10,000 *koku* and establishing him as a daimyo.

Hirasawa developed land at considerable cost. A detailed account exists for the reclamation of Tsukari swamp, a small marsh some twelve miles south of the castle town. On 1803/3/6 Hirasawa reported that 26 families had been resettled and 40 *chō* (98 acres) of land cleared at Tsukari. The families were of two types: *kikokunin* and *iutsurinin*. *Kikokunin*, although putatively "repatriates," were peasant settlers from outside the domain. *Iutsurinin*, or "migrants," were farmers from within the domain. In Tsukari, 12 of the 26 families were settlers, and the remaining 14 were "repatriates." It cost 312 copper *me* to construct housing for a settler family and 500 *me* for a family of "repatriates." Settler were paid 168 *me* per family for their labor services, and "repatriates" 156 *me*, so total expenses came to 14,800 *me*. The project also required 650 man-days of corvée labor, but these costs were deducted from the labor allowances paid to the settlers. Hirasawa specifies that he did not give the settlers tools or household supplies and that the standard allowances of six *to* per *tan* were paid only after careful scrutiny. Settlers were allowed three years' tax exemption, after which they were to pay a special reduced tax for three years.[78]

The cost of developing Tsukari swamp was roughly 200 *koku* for 40 *chō* of land. If this land was of average quality, the total yield would be about 400 *koku* and the tax yield, at the high rate of 60 percent, about 240 *koku*. Hirasawa's cash expenses were small, equivalent to only a few *koku* of rice, but the domain's rice allowance was equal to a year's tax yield. In addition, the government was providing three years of tax relief. The domain could not expect to see a return on its initial investment until sometime in the fifth year or after. If tax rates were lower, or if crops yields were less than average, returns would be delayed still longer.[79]

This combination of high initial cost and delayed returns seemed absurd to many Hirosaki officials: rather than the peasants struggling to pay the government, the government was struggling to pay the peasants. Initially Hirasawa's opponents merely questioned the practicality of his plan. While acknowledging that many Hirosaki "countrymen" (*kokumin*) had fled and were living in neighboring domains, they questioned whether these farmers could easily be repatriated.[80] But the financial burden of land development grew particularly striking after 1805 when the *bakufu* ordered the domain to contribute to the defense of Hokkaido. The most heated opposition to land reclamation came from neither the peasantry nor the rural elite, but from within the administration. While peasants were troubled by the additional corvée burden, land reclamation was most disturbing to retainers who resented Hirasawa's influence in domain affairs.

In 1807, Hirasawa was directly challenged by the magistrate of the exchequer (*kanjō bugyō*), who petitioned that reclamation be indefinitely postponed and Hirasawa and his associates dismissed. In the opinion of the magistrate, Hirasawa had run up expenses to an unforeseen and extreme degree. This was especially troubling in light of the massive expenses related to the domain's military obligations in Hokkaido and to *sankin kōtai*: given the present situation, there simply was no way to fund the land reclamation agency (*kaihatsukata*) for the next three or four years. More seriously, the magistrate challenged the general merit of Hirasawa's projects: although fallow land remained, most of it was difficult to irrigate or was of such poor quality that even if reclaimed it would yield little. As to newly cleared land, these projects were costly and had not produced the expected tax yield. Finally, the labor services demanded by Hirasawa imposed enormous burdens on the peasantry, a situation exacerbated by the continued shortage of farm labor. The magistrate thus proposed an indefinite reclamation moratorium: "I submit that time will not be lost if your lordship orders the resumption [of reclamation] at a later date when the number of farmers has increased and the undertaking has become more manageable."[81]

Despite this critical tone, the magistrate showed a marked deference to Hirasawa, suggesting that Hirasawa had indeed won the daimyo's favor. He proposed, for example, that Hirasawa be honored for his achievements. Elsewhere he remarked that "since they [Hirasawa and his assistants] have, indeed, served with diligence I fear your lordship will think [dismissing them] regrettable, but I believe there is no choice but to give priority to our inability to fund such expenditures." Despite the magistrate's measured tone and careful argument, Tsugaru Yasuchika refused to dismiss Hirasawa. The daimyo reportedly showed Hirasawa the complaints lodged against him, but then ceremoniously destroyed them.[82]

The debate over repatriation in Hirosaki reflected the ambiguity

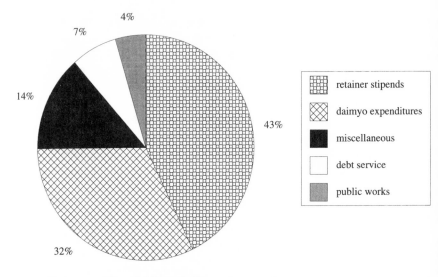

Figure 10. Hirosaki Domain Expenditures, 1815
SOURCE: Hirosaki shi shiritsu toshokan: "Tsugaru han zaisei hikae."

of the domain's status. It was not quite a "country" domain but much more than a simple investiture. Even Hirasawa's opponents described Hirosaki farmers as "countrymen" who should be "repatriated," suggesting a broad acceptance of Hirosaki's position as a "country." The determining factor in favor of repatriation, however, was not Hirasawa's appeal to reasons of state, but rather his appeal to the daimyo's own pecuniary interests: repatriation increased the daimyo's discretionary income. Hirasawa thus based his program not on suzerain authority but on a narrow definition of the daimyo's patrimony.

Because land reclamation was intimately connected with the daimyo's private interests, it had a mixed effect on the fiscal health of the domain. Overall, reclamation improved domain finances. In 1815 the domain ran a deficit of 17,270 *koku*, but this was because of a harvest shortfall. In an average year the domain would have met its expenses. The domain had large outstanding loans, at least 46,000 *ryō*, and total debt service was 10,906 *koku* in interest plus 800 *koku* in principal. Hirosaki's debt was manageable, however, in comparison with that of other domains. Domain debt was equivalent to one-half-year's income, and debt service, including payments on principal, was only 7 percent of total outlays.[83] But while Hirasawa's efforts contributed to this relative solvency, they also contributed to the domain's major fiscal burden: the personal expenses of the daimyo. By 1815 the personal expenses of Yasuchika and his courtiers consumed one-third of the general budget (see Figure 10).[84] Adding the daimyo's privy purse, the daimyo's personal expenses matched the stipend income of all his retainers. Although the domain could support such spending, Yasuchika's penchant for luxury set a precedent for his son and successor, Nobuyuki. When the the Tenpō crisis struck in the 1830s, Hirosaki retainers deposed their spendthrift daimyo in the interests of their "country."

## The Politics of Subversion: The Tenpō Famine and Tsugaru Sōdō

Like the Tenmei famine, the Tenpō crisis stemmed from natural disaster. From 1833 to 1836 the countryside was devastated by unseasonable cold and inundating rains that destroyed crops throughout Japan. In Hirosaki the government quickly recognized the potential for disaster and prohibited the export of rice in 1833/8, but the domain was ill prepared for the magnitude of the crisis.[85] Over the seven years from 1833 to 1839, the population of Hirosaki dropped by over 80,000 persons: some 47,000 fled the domain while the rest died of starvation.[86]

Like the Tenmei famine, the Tenpō battered the domain fisc. Harvest shortfalls sharply diminished the domain's revenues, and the loss of population meant long-term reductions in the domain's tax base. Amid this crisis the domain was riven by an exceptionally bitter factional dispute known historically as the *Tsugaru sōdō*. The conflict centered on the excessive expenses of the daimyo Nobuyuki. In 1839, after years of resisting retrenchment, Nobuyuki was forced into retirement by a faction of reformers and replaced by his adopted heir, Tsugaru Yukitsugu.

The *Tsugaru sōdō* had its origins in the social aspirations of Tsugaru Yasuchika. Yasuchika was concerned with raising his standing in Edo, and his aspirations were fulfilled by Kasahara Hachirobei, an ambitious retainer with formidable diplomatic skills. In 1820, after years of lavish, calculated entertaining and outright bribery, Kasahara engineered Yasuchika's promotion to court chamberlain (*jijū*), a prestigious but administratively meaningless post in the imperial administration. The following year Kasahara found a prestigious bride for Nobuyuki: Tayasu Kanehime, niece of the shogun Ienari. Kasahara's schemes proved a serious drain on the domain fisc. To pay for Nobuyuki's marriage, stipends were cut 20 percent in 1824 and again in 1826. The domain debt also rose sharply, from 300,000 *ryō* in 1825 to 500,000 *ryō* in 1830.[87]

These problems worsened under Nobuyuki, who succeeded his father in 1825. Nobuyuki was notoriously dissolute. His retainers referred to him disparagingly as "lord nighthawk" (*yotaka donosama*) for his passion for prostitutes, and his extravagance and carousing eventually became matters of "national" concern. In 1826/4, on his first *sankin kōtai* trip to Edo, Nobuyuki indulged in a nightlong debauch. He could not be awakened the following morning and his retinue, late for its scheduled departure, did not make its next stop by nightfall. Since maintenance of *sankin kōtai* protocol was a symbol of a daimyo's loyalty to the shogun, the matter was of grave import. Takakura Sagami, the ranking official on the *sankin kōtai* embassy, rebuked Nobuyuki but could not convince him of the gravity of the situation. As a final desperate reprimand to his lord, Takakura committed suicide.[88]

Appalled by Nobuyuki's irresponsible extravagance and its effects on the domain fisc, the magistrate of the exchequer, Ogasawara Ryōhachi, began to campaign for retrenchment and reform. His faction focused on overthrowing the *karō*, since Kasahara was widely regarded as indulging rather than restraining Nobuyuki's behavior. In 1830 the faction arranged to have Kasahara dismissed from office and placed under house arrest. His son, Kasahara Ōmi, was demoted. This action earned the reform faction a bitter enemy. Ōmi, convinced that his father had been unjustly punished, swore to "eat the livers" of his father's opponents.

With Kasahara removed, the reform faction moved to curtail Nobuyuki's expenditures with a traditional austerity program. Two of the daimyo's four Edo villas were closed and a variety of payments to the daimyo's privy fisc redirected to the general fisc. The reformers sought to make the court a model of frugality: the number of palace maids was cut and the size of the daimyo's stable reduced; lavish courtier clothing was replaced with simple garments.[89]

The reformers, however, gained control of the domain on the eve of the Tenpō famine, and the harvest failure of 1833 provided a ready means for Kasahara Ōmi to discredit the faction's austerity program. The reformers had also run afoul of Masue, the daimyo's favorite concubine. Masue had convinced Nobuyuki to build her a sumptuous private mansion in Edo, and the reform faction was appalled not only by the cost but by the threat of shogunal censure. The reformers had the unfinished mansion demolished and Masue restricted to the home domain. Sensing an opportunity, Ōmi ingratiated himself with Masue and used her to gain direct access to Nobuyuki. In a private meeting with the daimyo, Ōmi convinced him that the austerity program was nothing but disloyalty. In 1833/11, Ogasawara and the reform faction were themselves dismissed and placed under house arrest. Ōmi then engineered the "discovery" of a conspiracy to unseat Nobuyuki and replace him with Tsugaru Yukinori, daimyo of the branch domain of Kuroishi.[90] The conspiracy may well have been real: seven years later Nobuyuki adopted Yukinori (who then took the name Yukitsugu) and retired in his favor. But Ōmi's evidence seems too convenient, and it is possible that the conspiracy was real but the evidence fake. The purported plot nonetheless gave Ōmi the pretext to complete his vendetta. On 1833/12/26 he ordered the summary execution of Ogasawara and his two closest allies.[91]

Once in power Kasahara found that he had inherited the reform faction's problems. Worse, since he had opposed retrenchment, he was obliged to indulge both Nobuyuki and Masue. For two years Kasahara managed to entertain his lord with luxurious tours of the domain. The trips, described as "inspections," involved the company of hundreds of women, dancing girls, and ample sake. Kasahara funded these trips by borrowing against future harvests. This strategy was undermined in 1836 when eight ships carrying rice from Hirosaki sank in a storm. Desperate for revenue, Kasahara then sold grain previously promised to creditors. The domain's creditors were furious, and Kasahara was unable to secure further loans. In 1836/12 he was summoned back from Edo and stripped of his stipend.[92]

Nobuyuki remained in power until 1839, but his ability to rule had been deeply compromised. He had allowed the execution of several prominent domain officials and then dismissed their executioner. He had also antagonized the shogunate through his ostentation and violations of protocol. In early 1839 Nobuyuki adopted Tsugaru Yukitsugu, daimyo of the branch house of Kuroishi and three months Nobuyuki's senior. In 1839/5 Nobuyuki, officially claiming poor health, retired at age 40.[93] Nobuyuki's infirmities were political, not medical. He died 23 years later in 1862, only three years before his heir, Yukitsugu.[94]

Although Yukitsugu was of distinguished lineage, he had no blood tie to the Tsugaru house. He was selected for reasons other than pedigree: the new daimyo enacted the strict austerity program that Nobuyuki had resisted. In 1839/10 Yukitsugu issued a 30-point, five-year retrenchment plan. Beyond the standard exhortations to frugality in food and clothing, Yukitsugu made deep cuts in his own expenses. In his residence, damaged paper doors (*shōji*) and *tatami* mats were patched rather than replaced, unused rooms were closed, and heating charcoal rationed. The daimyo economized on candles, stationery, cookware, and New Year's decorations. The fiscal impact of such measures was twofold. First, since expenses of the daimyo and his court consumed over 30 percent of the budget, Yukitsugu's austerity itself amounted to serious fiscal reform. Further, as symbolic acts, the daimyo's frugalities allowed him to demand similar restraint from his retainers, thus paving the way for broader retrenchment.[95] The government thus cut retainer stipends, but through a progressive system in which the wealthiest retainers bore the greatest burden (see Table 1). Under a standard payment schedule, a retainer with a stipend of 1,500 *koku* received 100 times the income of a retainer with a stipend of 15 *koku*. Under the progressive stipend cuts of the Tenpō reforms, this income difference was drastically reduced, although nominal stipends were left unchanged. In 1841 a 1,500 *koku* stipend paid only 22 times as much as a 15 *koku* stipend.

In key areas Yukitsugu's reign in Hirosaki resembles Uesugi Yōzan's reign in Yonezawa. Both daimyo were brought into their domains by reformers seeking to stop the excesses of their lords. Both established themselves as models of frugality and thereby en-

TABLE 1
*Hirosaki Stipend Reductions Under the Tenpō Reforms*

| 1840 | | 1842 | |
|---|---|---|---|
| Nominal stipend in *koku* | Reduction in paid stipend | Nominal stipend in *koku* | Reduction in paid stipend |
| | | 1,500 | 54.2% |
| 1,000 | 78.0% | 1,000 | 48.3% |
| | | 500 | 44.4% |
| 300 | 72.0% | | |
| 200 | 71.0% | 200 | 40.2% |
| >100 | 58.0% | >100 | 36.1% |
| >50 | 48.0% | >50 | 32.3% |
| | | >10 | 11.2% |

SOURCE: *AKS*, 3: 80, 97.

hanced the legitimacy of stipend cuts. But there is nothing in Yuki-tsugu's reign to compare with Yōzan's broad reconstruction of the Yonezawa polity. Instead, the domain again looked back to its traditional methods of rural reconstruction.

The Tenpō famine left in its wake vast areas of fallow land: by one estimate over 23,243 acres (9,487 *chō*) of arable land had been abandoned. In 1839 the government received only 65,574 *koku* in *nengu*, less than one-half the expected yield.[96] Although the situation clearly called for land development, the domain could ill afford the level of investment required by reclamation schemes like Hirasawa's. Instead the domain granted title to those who cleared land at their own expense. This policy was then extended to samurai as well as commoners. On 1842/2/17 the government decreed:

This year landed samurai [*jitō*], of course, and even farmers, have been unable to work, and immeasurable areas of land have fallen fallow. As land abandoned in this way is not easily returned to arable land, orders were given last spring in rural areas that those clearing land of their own accord should be granted title in perpetuity, even if the land is in a different village or district. However, with regard to *jitō* landholdings, there are also many *jitō* in Hirosaki and [the] Kyūra [region], and these *jitō* should be informed of these orders as well. In Hirosaki, of course, and in Kyūra, persons menial and propertyless, as well as artisans and merchants interested in farming, should apply to the appropriate authorities as well and reclaim land of their own accord.[97]

This approach to land reclamation was grounded in precedent. While the forced resettlement of the Kansei era failed miserably, the small number of retainers who had resettled voluntarily after the Tenmei famine had reclaimed land with relative success. Confronted with a similar crisis after the Tenpō famine, Hirosaki returned to this precedent. It is unclear how many samurai, if any, attempted farming after the Tenpō famine. Response to the edict may well have been tepid, but the proclamation demonstrates again the introspection and consistency of Hirosaki policy. Faced with a crisis, Hirosaki administrators looked to their past for solutions.

## Bakumatsu Hirosaki

Little in Hirosaki during the *bakumatsu* era foreshadowed the great transformation of the Meiji era. After the Tenpō famine there are no reports of major peasant rebellions or millenarian movements, nor is there any evidence of increased discontent among retainers. Although relatively free from domestic strife, the domain was acutely aware of the foreign crisis. Perched at the northern tip of Honshū, Hirosaki was required by the shogunate to cooperate with neighboring domains in the defense of Hokkaido against Russia: by 1809 Hirosaki had over 400 troops dispatched to Matsumae. In return for these services the daimyo received a two-month reduction in his *sankin kōtai* sojourns. In 1822 the shogunate transferred the defense of Hokkaido to Matsumae domain, but Hirosaki was still required to maintain 100 troops for dispatch in emergencies. To defend its own coastline, the domain prepared naval fortifications, purchased hundreds of guns and cannon, and attempted small-scale arms manufacturing. As the cost of military modernization grew, the government began to shift the burden onto its retainers. In 1864 the domain ordered retainers with stipends over 100 *koku* to provide one gun for every 100 *koku* of income.[98]

Hirosaki was almost entirely divorced from the emerging struggle between the shogunate and the self-appointed defenders of the imperial court. The domain ultimately chose the victorious side, but for reasons unrelated to the ideology of the imperial cause. When forced to choose between the Satsuma-Chōshū alliance and the *bakufu* in 1868, the administration vacillated. In 1868/4, Hirosaki obeyed the orders of the new regime and dispatched 540 troops to Shōnai. Yet only two months later the government considered joining *Ōuetsu reppan dōmei*, the alliance of 33 domains that opposed what they saw as an invasion of the northeast by two southwestern domains. At a conference of high retainers on 1868/6/23, the prevailing response was in favor of the alliance. This decision was reversed two weeks later when the daimyo received a letter from the Konoe family, related to the Tsugaru house by marriage, urging them to support the imperial court.[99]

The triumph of the Meiji regime meant the end of Hirosaki as an independent domain, but this was apparent to no one in 1868. In a revealing turn of phrase, daimyo Tsugaru Yukitsugu assured the new government that his "country" would unfailingly serve the "imperial country."[100] For the moment, Hirosaki administrators could commend themselves on a great success. In return for breaking with the *Ōuetsu reppan dōmei*, Tsugaru Tsuguakira, the twelfth and last daimyo of Hirosaki, was given continued authority over his domain and jurisdiction over the defeated northeastern domains, including Sendai, Morioka, and Fukushima. The "country" of Hirosaki had survived. This had been the primary concern of two centuries of Hirosaki statesmen, and it was the primary concern of the last.

# 5

## Markets and Mercantilism

*Political Economy in Tokushima*

> Indigo is the premier product of the land and since
> ancient times it has greatly served national interests.
> —Tokushima government memorandum (1767)

Tokushima domain encompassed two "countries": Awa and
Awaji. Awa lay at the southeastern corner of the island of Shikoku,
across the Straits of Kii from Wakayama. Awaji, a small but strate-
gic island, lay in the straits, roughly midway between Awa and Wakayama. Awa, now Tokushima prefecture, has historically been divided into a northern and southern region. In the north the population was concentrated along the Yoshino river, which runs east,
framed by the Sanuki and Tsurugi mountain ranges. Tokushima, the
major city of the region, lies in the broad coastal plain formed by
the Yoshino river and its branches. The south was more mountainous and less developed, with its population scattered in small
coastal villages. These variations in terrain led to different regional
economies. In the north the economy was characterized by intensive
commercial agriculture, in the south by salt farming and fishing.[1]

The Hachisuka house ruled Tokushima domain throughout the
Tokugawa era. The family was first enfeoffed in Tokushima in 1585
with an *omotedaka* of 181,000 *koku*, but it was briefly displaced
when Toyotomi Hideyori seized their domain on the eve of the battle of Sekigahara. The reigning daimyo, Hachisuka Yoshishige, allied himself with the Tokugawa forces, and the fief was soon restored. Yoshishige sided again with the Tokugawa at the siege of

Osaka castle and was rewarded in 1615 with an increased investiture. The domain now encompassed all of Awa and Awaji provinces, for a total *omotedaka* of 250,000 *koku*.

Tokushima enjoyed relatively low demographic pressure, with only 1.06 retainer stipends per 100 commoners. In 1871 roughly twice as many commoners supported a single retainer family in Tokushima as in Hirosaki, and over six times as many as in Yonezawa. Demography was clearly reflected in revenue extraction: per capita revenue extraction in Tokushima was less than one-half that of either Hirosaki or Yonezawa. Like taxes, stipends also varied as demographics would suggest. The average stipend income in Tokushima was nearly seventeen *koku*, 20 percent more than in Hirosaki and nearly triple that of Yonezawa.[2]

The number of commoners per stipend in Tokushima increased steadily throughout the Tokugawa era. From 1721 to 1846, the population increased by 27 percent (see Figure 11). The total Japanese population, by comparison, was stable over the same period.[3] Most important, population growth was steady: unlike Yonezawa and Hirosaki, Tokushima never experienced severe depopulation. Given these demographic factors, Tokushima administrators had little incentive to change the domain's population parameters. Thus, unlike Hirosaki and Yonezawa, Tokushima did not try to attract immigrant peasants or increase peasant fertility, nor did the domain turn its retainers into farmers or craftsmen. The government, by contrast, enjoyed the luxury of being able to invest younger sons of retainers with their own stipends.[4] The thrust of Tokushima economic policy was managing commercial agriculture, but because the government's need for revenue per commoner was relatively low, there was little need to tax commercial agriculture directly. Tokushima fiscal policy was concerned instead with maintaining the quality and price of raw indigo and manufactured indigo cubes.

Tokushima farmers engaged in commercial agriculture from early in the Tokugawa era. This was partially a result of ready access to national commercial centers. The widespread protoindustrialization of the economy, however, did not begin until the early eighteenth century, when the development of the Osaka cotton textile industry led to increased demand for indigo. The lowlands of the Yoshino river valley, with its sandy soil and poor irrigation, was as well-

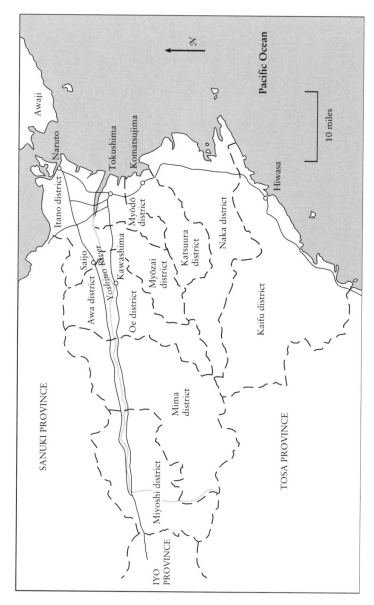

Map 5.  Towns, Villages, and Roads in Tokushima
SOURCE: Adapted from *Kadokawa Nihon chimei daijiten*, 36: 1062–63.

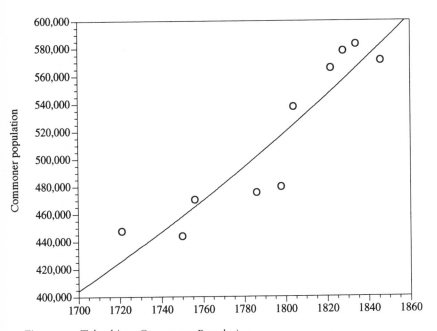

Figure 11. Tokushima Commoner Population
SOURCE: Sekiyama, *Kinsei Nihon no jinkō kōzō*, pp. 136–40.
NOTE: Population data are the sum of Awa and Awaji provinces.

suited to the cultivation of indigo as it was ill-suited to rice. Indigo cultivation began in the lower reaches of the Yoshino river, but by the mid-eighteenth century it had spread into western Tokushima: from 1650 to 1750 the acreage planted in indigo increased some tenfold.[5] In 1740, 237 of the 331 villages in northern Tokushima, over 70 percent, were growing indigo.[6] Many of these villages were highly specialized. In 1764, nearly 90 percent of the arable land in Takenose village was planted in indigo, roughly 7 percent in potatoes, and only 0.2 percent in rice.[7] By 1877, indigo constituted over 20 percent of Tokushima's total agricultural production. In the lowland districts of Myōdō, Oe, Itano, and Awa, it was over 30 percent. The importance of indigo to the general economy was still greater because the manufacture of indigo cubes from raw indigo was a major local industry.[8]

Indigo cultivation was less common in the mountainous regions of the south and west, but these areas were also drawn into broad commercial networks. Villages along the Pacific coast specialized in salt farming, while mountain villages in the west tended to specialize in tobacco. Salt was especially important. In 1877 total annual salt production was worth some ¥200,000, roughly one-half that of indigo. Over 60 percent of salt production was concentrated in the coastal district of Naka.[9] As a result of this high level of commercialization, rice was relatively unimportant to the Tokushima economy: in 1877 rice accounted for only 35 percent by value of the agricultural production of Awa province. Rice was thus only one-half as important to Awa as to Mutsu, the province containing Hirosaki.[10]

This quantitative difference in agricultural production led to two distinct approaches to political economy. As a commercial product, indigo demanded more intervention than rice or wheat. Since the production and consumption of rice were widespread, it was vulnerable to neither monopoly nor monopsony control. Further, the widespread cultivation of rice meant that a single domain's impact on the market price was small. A domain like Hirosaki could not withhold its rice supply in order to inflate the rice price. Under such circumstances domain revenue was approximately a linear function of rice production: increased rice production meant a proportional increase in government revenue. Control over markets was thus tangential to the Hirosaki fisc.

Both supply and demand for indigo, by contrast, were localized and subject to manipulation by cartels. Most indigo was purchased by wholesalers (ton'ya) in the textile centers of Edo and Osaka. These wholesalers then resold it to dyers. For much of the Tokugawa era, indigo wholesalers were members either of government-sanctioned guilds (nakama) or informal cartel organizations. During the eighteenth century the wholesalers used their oligopsony at the expense of Tokushima farmers (sakunin) and processors (aishi). The wholesalers forced down prices, charged special handling fees, and delayed payments.

The cartel was supported by the capital requirements of indigo cultivation and processing. Indigo needed fertilizer six times per season and was labor intensive at harvest. Indigo was also extremely sensitive to handling because the distinctive color of the dye results from a bacteriological process. If the leaves fermented too early or too late, the resultant dye was less desirable. Because harvested leaves withered rapidly, indigo needed to be harvested and chopped the same day, and workers chopped by lamplight to complete the task on time. The following morning the diced leaves were air-dried, sorted, and packed for processing or sale. Because the window for an ideal harvest was narrow, farmers commonly relied on wage labor to bring the crop in on time. Indigo processing also had large capital requirement. Processors mixed the indigo leaves with water, then fermented and pressed this mash for several months in special storehouses, carefully controlling temperature, pressure, and moisture. The cured mash was then pounded and cut into *aidama*, indigo balls or cubes. The curing processes required experienced craftsmen as well as laborers, since mistakes in curing decreased the quality and value of the finished dye cubes.[11]

Both indigo growing and processing were extremely profitable, but both required large and regular outlays of cash. Because of these high costs, farmers and processors commonly raised capital by borrowing against future production. Since small independent dyers could not provide credit, producers of necessity turned to Edo and Osaka wholesalers. The wholesalers then used this leverage to set arbitrarily low prices for the indigo harvest. The wholesalers thus used their control of capital markets to reinforce their oligopsony on indigo. This tactic was especially effective against ambitious farmers who sought to process their own indigo and who were therefore particularly inclined to borrow heavily.

Tokushima was in a unique position to combat the cartels. Tokushima was the largest indigo producer in Japan and also the most esteemed for quality. The oligopoly position of the domain could be used to challenge the oligopsony of the wholesalers. Attempts to defeat, undermine, or co-opt the wholesaler cartels were a major theme of Tokushima political economy after the 1760s. The fight against oligopsony led the domain to extensive economic intervention, including trust busting, the establishment of agricultural price supports, and the regulation and subsidization of agricultural and commercial banking. Like Yonezawa, the domain also sought to insure the quality of its exports by regulating production methods.

Because much of the domain's income from indigo was indirect it is difficult to estimate the contribution of indigo to the fisc. In the

1770s direct taxes of indigo cubes yielded only 552 silver *kan*, or roughly 5 percent of government income. Receipts in the late 1800s appear to have been still less.[12] Indigo, however, was far more important to the fisc than these figures suggest. From 1681 on, Tokushima farmers were allowed to pay *nengu* either in kind, in domain currency, or through a special form of voucher called *sashigami*. Tax payments listed as *nengu* were thus partially cash payments supported by revenue from indigo cultivation and processing. Although direct revenue from indigo was trivial, indirect revenue was probably comparable to indigo's importance in the overall economy. Because domain income was so dependent on indigo, the domain had a compelling interest in insuring the prosperity and stability of the indigo market.[13]

Because the domain's fiscal interest in indigo was indirect, government agencies were run to maximize its value, not the direct income it could generate for the government of the domain. In 1798, for example, Tokushima established a monopoly on sand from the beaches of Komatsujima. While some historians have focused on the revenue from the monopoly, its major fiscal purpose was indirect. Since the 1640s sand had been used in the manufacture of indigo cubes both as a preservative and to increase weight. Because indigo was sold by weight, dye cube manufacturers packed high proportions of sand into the cubes. Too much sand, however, produced a poor-color dye and diminished the reputation of the domain's product. Because sand increased the profit margin on indigo cubes, a market for sand developed. Sand from the beaches at Komatsujima could be added in large volumes without loss of quality, unlike sand from the Yoshino river. Sand merchants, however, mixed sand from different sources, and indigo cube manufacturers were thus unable to determine safe volumes of sand or to produce indigo cubes of consistent quality. The domain sand monopoly was intended to confront these problems by insuring a consistent supply of uncontaminated Komatsujima sand at reasonable prices. By insuring the quality of sand, the domain could protect the reputation of Tokushima indigo and domain revenue. This indirect fiscal contribution was far more important than the few hundred *koku* in income generated by the monopoly.[14]

## Fiscal Policy in Early Tokushima

In the early seventeenth century, Tokushima fiscal policy was remarkably similar to that of Hirosaki. Both domains emphasized land reclamation (*shinden kaihatsu*) as a means of increasing revenue. Tokushima, however, was more densely settled and developed than Hirosaki, and the potential for land reclamation was thus smaller. Once land reclamation reached its peak in the early 1600s, the government turned to commodities as a revenue source (see Figure 12). In 1625 the government began promoting the improvement of indigo processing techniques through an indigo division established within its lacquer tree office. Indigo growers were rewarded with an ad hoc system of incentives, including cash rewards for production, allowances (*teatekin*) for impoverished indigo growers, and special treatment in the payment of late taxes.[15] As early as 1673 the domain was involved in quality control: in response to complaints by Osaka jobbers (*nakagai*) the domain prohibited the use of earth as filler in the manufacture of indigo cubes.[16] The first recorded tax on indigo is a levy called *kuchigin*, begun in the late 1600s. Indigo leaves were taxed at 5 silver *fun* per *hyō* and indigo cubes at 9 *fun* per *hyō*.[17]

The spread of indigo production in the eighteenth century led to closer government intervention. Competition for the right to sell indigo outside the domain led to a dispute among Tokushima merchants. One faction, led by the merchants of Komatsujima, favored free and direct sales to dyers, while the other, composed of merchants from Miyajima and Tsurujima, favored selling to the Edo *ton'ya*. The underlying question was one that would dominate domain politics. Should Tokushima merchants work under cartels based in Edo and Osaka, or should they form a countercartel? The merchants of Komatsujima favored a Tokushima cartel. The merchants of Miyajima and Tsurujima, however, had long-standing dealings with the Edo cartel and opposed direct sales to dyers.[18]

Tokushima had little theoretical basis on which to adjudicate the dispute, and domain's rulings on this issue were erratic and contradictory. In 1702 Tokushima attempted to resolve the dispute by dividing the market: sales west of Sagami were to be free, while sales

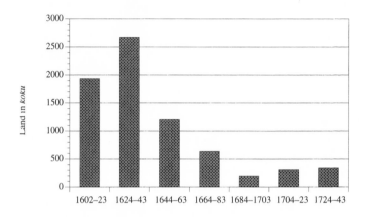

Figure 12.  Land Reclamation in Myōzai district, Tokushima

SOURCE: Ōtsuki, "Awa ni okeru hansei kaikaku," p. 133.

east of Sagami were to be made through the Edo *ton'ya*. In 1705 the domain reversed itself, allowing the unrestricted export of indigo. In 1707 the domain returned to its original ruling on dividing the market. In 1718, however, the Edo city magistrate (*machi bugyō*), in response to a suit by Edo dyers, abolished the *ton'ya* system and ordered direct sales to dyers. In 1724 the domain attempted to subvert this edict by designating two Edo merchants as official wholesalers and encouraging sales to this cartel. The cartel, however, used government support to levy transaction charges on its clients and delay payments. Indigo sellers met this challenge with passive resistance: they used assumed names to avoid the cartel and to ship their goods to Osaka and Hyōgo. The machinations of the Edo *ton'ya*, moreover, led to a general drop in indigo exports. The market grew depressed, and the number of indigo farmers began to drop. In 1731 the domain returned to unrestricted trade.[19]

The domain's vacillation on this issue was reflected in its lack of a language with which to discuss the costs and benefits of commerce. The domain based its decisions on precedent and vague notions of fairness and propriety. The 1705 edict allowing free trade was intended to insure appropriate trade (*sōgō shōbai*), that is, trade that would not impoverish merchants. The 1707 ruling returning to the *status quo ante* argued that the market should be divided equally (*byōdō no dōri*) so that both factions could continue trading with their existing customers. In the absence of any coherent concept of commerce, domain policy swung erratically between unregulated trade and oligopsony by the Edo *ton'ya*. The most salient feature of domain indigo policy was indifference: the 1705 edict stated that indigo trade should not inconvenience the government in any way.[20]

Tokushima's ambivalence toward the indigo trade was partially a result of the domain's small direct interest in indigo. As late as 1733 the government's direct fiscal interest in indigo was minimal, restricted to *kuchigin*. The spread of indigo cultivation, however, made the domain indirectly dependent on the crop: farmers used income from the sale of indigo to pay *nengu*. By 1731 the administration had come to consider indigo cultivation an important part of political economy. In explaining to the Edo city magistrate its decision to return to free trade, the domain argued that the depressed indigo market "has become a hindrance to retainers collecting *nengu*, has impeded state finances [*kokuyō no sawari*], and impoverished indigo processors, not to mention farmers."[21] Despite the domain's small direct interest in indigo, the crop had become essential to its fiscal policy.

The increased fiscal importance of indigo forced the domain to re-examine its indigo policy. Yet it attempted to intervene in the indigo trade before it had constructed a coherent commercial policy. The deregulation of the Kantō indigo market in 1731 had resulted in a surge in indigo cube production and depressed prices. "Indiscriminate trading in indigo cubes," declared the edict, had impoverished farmers and reduced the volume of silver entering the domain. Instead of returning to *ton'ya* oligopsony, however, in 1733 the domain established an indigo office (*aikata goyōjō*), which it authorized to buy and sell indigo in order to stabilize prices. The domain also levied a 4 percent indigo leaf sales tax: 2 percent was to be paid by the buyer and 2 percent by the seller, with 1 percent returned to the village to cover administrative costs. The following year, the domain levied an indirect indigo export tax: for each *hyō* of indigo cubes, merchants were required to change ten silver *me* into domain currency. This mandatory conversion raised revenue directly through a small conversion fee, and indirectly through seigniorage.[22]

The new tax system was followed by a series of decrees combating tax evasion. The government undertook a new rural survey to record both indigo cube production and the number of people engaged in it. Those selling indigo cubes were to maintain receipts for tax purposes. The domain appointed a specific censor (*metsuke*) to keep track of indigo cube producers and investigate smuggling.[23] The domain also sought to restrict the ability of farmers to market their own indigo cubes. In 1735 the government issued orders prohibiting farmers from entrusting indigo cubes to someone else or selling them under a different name. The edict was intended to curtail the "reckless" (*midara*) sale of indigo. In 1739 the domain began recording the names of all "foreign" indigo traders. Underlying these edicts was the suspicion that too many sellers, particularly farmers acting as sellers, led to "reckless" and potentially injurious trade. This shift toward restricting merchant activity culminated in 1754 when the domain established an indigo cube guild (*kabunakama*).[24]

## Commercialization and Popular Resistance

The indigo cube *kabunakama* of 1754 is known largely for the vigorous popular resistance it provoked. By the mid-1700s the manufacture and sale of indigo cubes had become essential to the Tokushima farm economy. Indigo was not only an important source of income, but also an avenue of social mobility for moderately successful farmers. The rural indigo cube merchants of the eighteenth century were largely former farmers who had moved from marketing their own crop into manufacturing and trade. The indigo cube *kabunakama*, by restricting the right to trade in indigo cubes, closed this avenue of social mobility and raised the specter of oligopsony price fixing.

Popular dissatisfaction with the *kabunakama* grew increasingly apparent in late 1756. In 1756/10 there were rumors that the farmers of Myōzai district were gathering at shrines and in the forest to discuss a protest petition. On 1756/11/16, before the government could confirm the rumor, the farmers staged a protest at the tutelary shrine of Takahara village and in a nearby forest. The headman and other leaders attempted to quiet the crowd, but the farmers would not settle down until they had stated their requests. The protesters gave a detailed description of their grievances and were gradually persuaded to disperse. This was reported to the district intendant (*gundai*), who ordered that, thereafter, protests should first be pacified and then reported to higher authorities. On 11/18, however, there came reports of a large protest at Oyakokengen shrine. The headman (*kumigashira shōya*) of Kunizane village hurried out and calmed the crowd. Only two days later, the farmers of a nearby village assembled at the local shrine and staged a protracted, rambunctious demonstration. When the village headman (*shōya*) realized that he could not disperse the demonstrators, he reported the disturbance to higher authorities. The headman of nearby Takabatake village was quickly dispatched to the scene. He accepted the farmers' petition and restored calm.[25]

The stream of protests continued unabated, with demonstrations almost daily. The protests spread upriver to Nishioe village in Oe district, downriver to Shibahara village in Myōdō district, and then across the Yoshino river to Fukita village and Kanyake village in Itano district. The protest movement now covered some 40 square miles in the heart of the Yoshino river valley, the most productive region in Tokushima. Rumors suggested that the movement was directed by four or five men who traveled from village to village, encouraging farmers to join the protests and threatening to destroy villages that did not.

These rumors proved sound. In the middle of 1756/11i, reports reached the government that an anonymous manifesto was being passed from temple to temple. The document read, in full:

Twenty-four years ago [1733] a 4 percent tax on indigo was levied, and in 1754 the indigo cube guild [*kabu*] was established. All indigo growers are therefore in great distress. This is, moreover, a poor harvest year and we can neither pay *nengu* nor provide for our parents, wives, children, or livestock. In accordance with the deliberation of all indigo growers, we shall meet on the 28th at Akui riverbed. When the growers of each village hear the sound of the bell and drum, they should all prepare straw raincoats, bamboo hats, and spears [*tsukubō*] and prepare to record their names and affix their village seal. This circular should be relayed to the temple at each village. Should you fail to relay this circular, we will attack and burn your temple.[26]

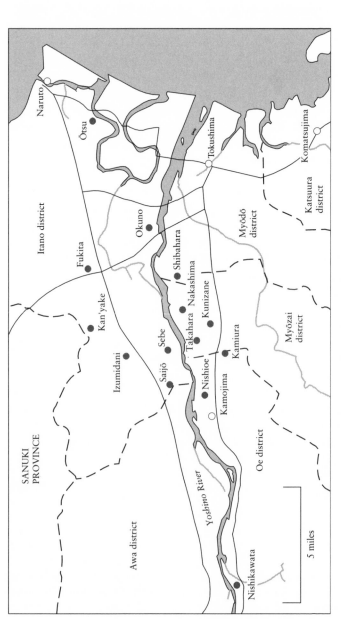

Map 6. Tokushima Hōreki Indigo Protests

SOURCE: Adapted from *Kadokawa Nihon chimei daijiten*, 36: 1062–63, with data from Miyoshi, *Awa no hyakushō ikki*, pp. 164–82.
NOTE: Shaded circles mark sites of protests or disturbances.

The manifesto not only provides ample evidence of determination and organization but also gives insight into the economic expectations of Tokushima farmers. It is clearly the work of relatively prosperous commercial farmers, not peasants: the circular treats livestock ownership as an activity comparable to providing for one's parents. Since it was written to rally popular support, we can assume that most farmers held livestock and shared this view. In less developed regions, such as Hirosaki, however, livestock ownership signified wealth, and such an appeal would have polarized rather than united the farm community.

In response to the petition, the government increased its surveillance of the region, but the domain's grip on public order remained tenuous. The authorities issued warnings not to participate in the protests and dispatched spies to suspect villages. These precautions proved inadequate, and disturbances were reported as far east as Ōtsu village and as far west as Nishikawata. On 11i/12 a *jōruri* performance in Kamiura village degenerated into chaos when rebels surrounded the audience and attempted to coerce them into joining their protest. The protest movement was crushed only when the government traced the petition to Takahara village, where demonstrations had begun the month before. The village leadership was arrested and tortured. On 1757/3/25 four officials (*goningumi*) and one farmer from Takahara village were crucified for seditious conduct.

The Gosha rebellion, named for the shrine erected in 1783 to commemorate the martyrs of the movement, forced the domain to reassess its approach to commercial agriculture and trade. The domain's initial reaction was muted. The government could not immediately comply with the farmers' demands without revealing the efficacy of protest. The domain thus took measures that could ameliorate rural conditions without appearing acquiescent to the protesters' demands. To improve the indigo market, officials under the magistrate of corvée (*fushin bugyō*) were dispatched to villages and purchased 10,000 *hyō* of indigo leaves.[27] In 1758 the domain made further patchwork reforms on the tax system, allowing annual rather than monthly payments of the indigo tax.[28] Finally, on 1760/8/7, the government complied with all the protesters' demands: the indigo office was abolished, and the 4 percent indigo tax was abandoned. The indigo cube guild was suspended, and the licensing fees were refunded. To compensate for lost revenue, the domain raised the indigo cube levy (*kuchigin*) by 30 percent.[29]

Although the 1760 reforms were largely a reaction to the Gosha rebellion, they mark the beginning of a new approach to political economy. The edict that abolished the indigo cube guild declared:

Indigo farmers are thus to do as they please [*katte yoroshiku*], and subjects may do as they wish in trade and all other matters. It is thus expected that villages that heretofore did not grow indigo or that, unable to sell indigo, stopped growing it will in light of this edict, plan to grow indigo again. . . . Indigo merchants are allowed to trade freely [*jiyū*], no indigo leaf transaction tax will be collected, and the indigo cube guild has been stopped. The indigo leaf harvest should therefore gradually increase.[30]

The assumptions underlying this edict are nearly opposite those of early indigo policy. The edict contains an implicit recognition of market forces: farmers grow indigo to sell it at a profit. Because the guild system decreased profits and market opportunities, villages stopped growing indigo. The domain recognized this causality as legitimate and sought to change policy accordingly: the new indigo system was designed to increase the indigo harvest through an open economy. Unrestricted trade was no longer seen as "reckless," but as salutary, and the economic interests of farmers were seen as consonant with those of the domain.

## Commercial Reforms and Indigo Exports

The abolition of the indigo cube cartel in 1760 foreshadowed the radical reforms of the Meiwa era (1764–71). Free trade, as Tokushima reformers were to discover, was more than the absence of government regulation. Because of their dependence on credit and the Osaka market, Tokushima farmers were vulnerable to the machinations of the Osaka indigo cartel. Using their oligopsony and financial power, the Osaka cartels used Tokushima's open trade policy to manipulate prices and exploit indigo farmers. A free-trade policy thus required government intervention to combat external cartel intervention.

Tokushima's approach to protecting a market economy was first articulated by Ogawa Yasozaemon, a wealthy indigo processor and headman (*kumigashira shōya*) of Takabatake village. Ogawa presented the government with a detailed opinion paper in 1766/2. He laid blame for the depressed indigo market on the Osaka cartel. Even under free trade, he observed, indigo growers were dependent on the Osaka *ton'ya*. Indigo growers might make their own indigo cubes and try to sell directly to dyers, "but if the payment is late, it becomes difficult [for the farmers] to pay taxes. Therefore, unavoidably, they dispatch [someone] to Osaka and survive by borrowing against future sales [*kawase*]." With the Tokushima grower thus committed to the cartel, the jobbers who purchased for the cartel could manipulate prices. "When [indigo farmers] offer the goods [against which they have borrowed], the *nakagai* stop buying until large quantities accumulate and the price falls." A similar oligopsony allowed the cartel to manipulate the market for finished indigo cubes. The situation, concluded Ogawa, was injurious to all parties:

The present dealings of the Osaka *ton'ya* and *nakagai* make it difficult for the indigo processors and even the indigo farmers of Awa to stay in business. The market for a valuable commodity, moreover, is depressed and the harvest continually grows smaller. This is not in the interests of the country. In the final analysis it impedes the payment of *nengu* and other taxes and is disconcerting to the general populace [*shita ittō*].[31]

In response to the machinations of the Osaka cartels, Ogawa argued for a radically new system of trade. Rather than allow Tokushima merchants to ship directly to Osaka, the indigo cube market would be relocated in Tokushima under the scrutiny of the domain:

Henceforth, [I would have your lordship order that] the shipment of indigo cubes to distant customers continue as presently practiced. As for trading in Osaka, the Osaka *nakagai* should be ordered to come to Awa and negotiate with Awa merchants at designated markets. If this is done it will be in our interests [*ontame*], the intemperate ploys of Osaka can be avoided, and traders will thus not have to pay various surcharges [*zokuyō*]. I believe, further, that the untimely low prices of Osaka will stop and, in particular, that prices will rise. In this regard, not only indigo processors and indigo growers, but city merchants and day laborers as well, will all profit [*ittō no jun*] and [such markets] will be of great value.

Ogawa believed that under such a system fair prices would occur naturally. "At this market," wrote Ogawa, "trade should be conducted in this manner: buyers and sellers must negotiate and receive the approval of an appointed assessor." Prices were thus to be determined by a market mechanism, with government intervention necessary to block the cartel. Ogawa's proposed market resembled less a traditional cartel arrangement than a stock market or commodity exchange in which the state intervenes not to fix prices but to prevent price fixing.

Because the power of the Osaka indigo cartel stemmed from its financial control over indigo producers and merchants, breaking the cartel required alternate sources of credit. Ogawa thus proposed that the domain supplant the Osaka wholesalers as the supplier of credit for the Tokushima indigo merchants. The Osaka cartel, for example, lent to Tokushima merchants at 2 percent per month: 1.3 percent interest and a 0.7 percent surcharge (*tokuyō*). If the domain replaced the cartel as creditor, it could provide credit at 1.2 percent, break the cartel's hold on Tokushima merchants, and still receive 43 *kan* in annual revenue.

By moving the market to Tokushima the domain also could stop Osaka *ton'ya* from levying various surcharges and instead charge these levies itself. The Osaka cartel charged Tokushima merchants a 4 percent surcharge called *kuchizeni* on indigo cube sales: this generated roughly 320 *kan* in annual income for the cartel. Ogawa calculated that the government could drop the surcharge to 3.5 percent and still receive 280 *kan* annually. In toto, Ogawa believed that the potential government revenue from merchant surcharges was 580 *kan*. To realize this revenue, however, the domain would have to provide 5,600 *kan* in credit to supplant merchant capital.[32]

Ogawa's proposal was a marked departure from traditional commercial policy, but it received a rapid and largely favorable response. In 1766/4 the proposals were made public for general evaluation. Because of the radical nature of the reforms and because the reforms were, in part, a response to popular discontent, the domain was especially concerned with popular acceptance. On 1766/4/9 the district magistrate (*kōri bugyō*) issued these orders to select village headmen:

The indigo processors and growers of the countryside should be informed of the purport [of the proposed reforms]. If thereupon you know of anything that might benefit his lordship or contribute to the prosperity [kutsurogi] of those below, report this without reservation in full detail.

Further, if an indigo processor or indigo grower knew of something in the reforms likely to cause "distress," this was to be reported to the village headman and related immediately to the district office (gunsho).[33]

After minor revisions the reforms were decreed on 1766/7/6. The new system banned entirely the export of indigo cubes to the merchants of Osaka. Shipments of stock on hand were allowed to the provinces of Yamashiro, Settsu, Harima, Izumi, Kawachi, Kii, and Awaji. Direct sales to dyers were allowed, but only to existing customers at levels regulated by and under the scrutiny of the indigo office. Credit (kawase) was offered at 1.2 percent per month rather than 2.0 percent as charged by the cartel. The domain established a free-market system with an anti-cartel mechanism like that proposed by Ogawa. Transactions required the approval of a government assessor, but the assessor himself did not fix prices. The government maintained existing levies on indigo cubes such as kuchigin but also added a new surcharge. As suggested by Ogawa, the domain replaced the 4 percent surcharge of the Osaka cartel with a 3.3 percent surcharge of its own.[34]

The domain officially notified the shogunate of its new policy on 1766/7/13 with a letter from Hachisuka Shigeyoshi to the senior counselor (rōjū) Matsudaira Takemoto. The daimyo argued that he was acting in the interests of indigo processors and growers, who had suffered from excessive surcharges and unfair trading practices. While the domain would still allow exports to ton'ya that were "properly prepared" (temawashi yoroshiku), other ton'ya would have to come to Tokushima to purchase indigo cubes. The daimyo was careful to balance his role as a vassal of the shogun with his status as lord of a "country." "It is our belief," he concluded, "that since this matter concerns a product of our country [kokusan], it does not involve your lordship's laws [osata], but because it is a change in custom we hereby notify your lordship."[35]

The new indigo policy prompted a protracted legal battle among the Tokushima government, the indigo wholesalers and jobbers, and the Osaka dyers guild. In 1766/9, roughly two months after the re-

forms were implemented, the 24 indigo wholesalers and jobbers delivered a petition opposing the Tokushima reforms to Magaribuchi
Kai, an Osaka city magistrate.[36] The new system, they claimed, was
blocking the shipment of indigo cubes to Osaka, causing them severe distress. The appeal involved roughly one-half the wholesalers
and jobbers: the 26 *ton'ya* and *nakagai* from Awa did not participate.[37] The domain contested the suit later that month, arguing that
the plaintiffs had been earning excessive profits and ruining farmers. In 1766/10 the Osaka city magistrate Udono Izumo launched
an inquiry and questioned Tokushima's Osaka chargé d'affaires (*ru-
suiyaku*) and its indigo cube inspectors (*aidama yokomeyaku*).[38] The
magistrate seems to have been inclined toward Tokushima, but on
1766/10/26 the Edo senior counselor (*rōjū*) rendered the Udono inquiry moot and requested a new investigation.[39]

The new inquiry was begun in early 1767. The Osaka magistrates
received new testimony from the plaintiffs and on 1767/2/19 summoned Tokushima's Osaka chargé d'affaires. Tokushima quickly
dispatched its indigo magistrate (*aikata bugyō*) to Osaka to respond
to the new investigation. The domain argued that its actions were
all justified by its need to protect indigo growers and traders. Assessors were required to insure that jobbers did not purchase "good
indigo for the [price] of poor indigo," and inspectors (*kimoiri*) were
needed to see that both parties agreed to the price. The indigo magistrate himself was appointed to insure that no one cornered the
market. The new credit system was to see that growers did not become victims of high-interest loans.[40]

The Osaka magistrates then summoned 43 indigo dyers and questioned them on the new trading system. The dyers' testimony was
influenced largely by their business dealings: the vast majority were
dependent on credit from indigo wholesalers and thus testified in
support of the plaintiffs. Fukushimaya Kichiuemon, a lone dissenter,
argued that the reforms had caused no problems at all. He was "rewarded" for his "honesty" by Tokushima with an annual salary of
twenty silver *mai*. The magistrates appear to have come to a decision in mid-1767, but the Edo *rōjū* again intervened and ordered a
further inquiry.[41]

These repeated interventions by Matsudaira Takemoto suggest a
schism between the Osaka administration and the Edo senior coun-

selor.[42] Takemoto, indeed, was known as strong-minded, if not obstinate. Impervious to gifts, flattery, and bribes, he is said to have so vexed the shogunal counselor Tanuma Okitsugu that the latter conspired to hasten his death by exhausting him on hunting expeditions.[43] On the issue of Tokushima's indigo center, Takemoto objected to the city magistrate's willingness to abandon precedent and to accept the trading center. On 1767/8/25, Takemoto summoned Tokushima's chargé d'affaires in Edo and conveyed the shogunate's decision. The terse edict quoted Tokushima's original letter of notification, but concluded: "The establishment of a market in Tokushima [*kunimoto*] is something new [*shinki no mono*]. Therefore, be informed that matters should continue as heretofore." The *rōjū* offered no justification for his decision, but the rationale was implicit in the language of the edict. Although Tokushima had called itself a "country," the edict referred to the "investiture" (*ryōbun*) of Tokushima.[44] As an investiture, rather than a "country," Tokushima had no authority to act independently, even in the interest of its people. The edict also alludes to the *buke shohatto*, which barred daimyo from undertaking "innovations" (*shingi*).[45] Matsudaira Takemoto's edict thus rested squarely on feudal authority: the shogun could prohibit the indigo market simply because it violated precedent.

The shogunate's edict dismayed the Tokushima administration. The domain requested a clarification of the decision and reiterated its original justification for the market. Since the indigo market addressed the problems of Tokushima indigo cube traders and farmers, they claimed, it was a matter of "national," meaning local, politics (*kokusei*). But the domain knew through back channels that Matsudaira Takemoto was unlikely to reverse his ruling. Resigned to a formal defeat, the administration planned to bypass through subterfuge what it could not overturn through legal appeal. The shogunate's refusal to acknowledge's Tokushima's rights as a country did not weaken Tokushima's resolve to defend those rights.[46]

In a letter dated 1767/9/10, Hasegawa Ōmi, a domain elder, detailed a strategy for feigning compliance with the shogunal decision while maintaining the Tokushima market. The domain would initially ship to Osaka all of its indigo cubes. The following year, however, it would ship 70 percent, then 50 percent, and then 30. By 1773 the domain would have effectively returned to its initial plan of forcing buyers to come to Tokushima. The strategy relied on the shogunate's poor knowledge of conditions in Tokushima: "Although the shogunate [*kōgi*] has issued a ruling, they have not investigated the details of the situation. . . . It would be difficult for the shogunate to investigate all of our own state [*gokokka*]." Because the domain could feign compliance in case of an official visit, it could effectively ignore the shogunal decision. "Because this is a matter for the lord of our country, I believe that the shogunate's decision can be taken lightly."[47] Hasegawa believed that the shogunate had exceeded its jurisdiction in banning the Tokushima market, but he did not advocate a direct legal challenge. Instead, he proposed that the domain test the shogunate's ability to enforce its decrees.

To feign compliance with the shogunate, the domain renamed the relevant agencies. In 1767/9i the name of the domain indigo office was changed from *aiba yakusho* to *aikata daikansho*, or indigo intendant's office. Indigo cubes were now collected as *nengu tsugi*, literally "after *nengu*," and sold to interested merchants. These name changes served to disguise the reforms as a traditional domestic policy. Because the collection of *nengu* was an accepted privilege of the domain, the *bakufu* could not question how Tokushima dealt with its *nengu* indigo. Intriguingly, *nengu tsugi* does not appear to have functioned anything like *nengu* and does not appear where it should in domain tax records. Furthermore, this covert trading system functioned much as Yasozaemon had originally proposed. Indigo sellers left their cubes at the indigo intendant's office for examination by merchants. Buyers were to examine the quality of the indigo and explain the quantity and price they wished to purchase to the assessor (*mekikiyaku*). The assessor would then report this price to the sellers. If the two parties agreed, a sale was complete. The new indigo agency also was designed to keep Tokushima producers from growing dependent on merchant credit. By custom, merchants could delay payment for 60 days while they shipped their purchases to market. To insure that the producers did not borrow from merchants to cover this lag, the domain offered tax deferrals and loans comparable to the value of the sale. The domain also provided recovery loans to growers whose indigo had gone bad while curing, as well as loans of fertilizer to growers who ran short of the needed capital to complete a growing season.[48]

The domain's assessment of the shogunate's response was substantively correct. The initial surge in shipments to Osaka gave the appearance of compliance, while the gradual reduction was largely unnoticed. For nearly two decades, Tokushima was able to regulate the indigo trade without provoking a response by the *bakufu*. By the late 1780s, however, the Osaka merchants recognized that their legal victory was a practical defeat. On 1788/8/25 a coalition of Osaka merchants appealed to the shogunate, arguing that Tokushima was monopolizing the indigo market and undermining their business. The Osaka city magistrate conducted an investigation and reported, in a letter disclosed surreptitiously to Tokushima officials, that Tokushima was violating the 1767 order to abolish its indigo market. The letter does not specifically mention *nengu* indigo, but it complains that Tokushima had licensed a three-member cartel that was stopping indigo cubes from leaving the domain and forcing *nakagai* to buy indigo cubes in Tokushima. A complaint lodged by the Edo dyers with the Edo city magistrate in 1789 refers to a Tokushima indigo center that was forcing up prices. Tokushima responded that no such market existed, but that *nengu* indigo cube buyers were purchasing indigo from farmers. Despite these equivocations, Tokushima's subterfuge could not be concealed from the sustained scrutiny of the shogunate. On 1790/3/13 the shogunate issued a decision banning Tokushima from restricting the indigo trade.[49]

The shogunate's order was a severe blow to the Tokushima indigo reforms. The domain stopped collecting "*nengu* indigo" through the indigo intendant's office and allowed brokers to purchase indigo directly from producers. The domain lost much of its ability to block the Osaka cartels. The edict was particularly effective because from 1789 to 1791 Tokushima was embroiled in a struggle between a clique of elite families and the young daimyo, Hachisuka Haruaki. The domain was thus unable to formulate a coherent response to the shogunate's new challenge.

The temporary victory of the *bakufu* did not blunt Tokushima's resolve to gain control over the indigo trade. Beginning in 1802 Tokushima again moved to check the power of the Osaka cartels, albeit with a different strategy. The indigo dispute thus reveals how shogunal power was constrained by the logic of suzerain authority.

In matters concerning the welfare of their "countries," domain officials were unwilling to submit to shogunal decisions. Instead, domains pursued, both openly and in secret, policies that contradicted shogunal directives.[50]

## The Nobility of Treason and the Treason of Nobility: The Fall of Hachisuka Shigeyoshi

The struggle between Tokushima and the shogunate over indigo reveals how Tokushima retainers could act as Tokushima "nationalists." When their own patrimonial perquisites were challenged, however, these officials proved equally willing to draw the shogunate into domain affairs. In 1769 the Tokushima *karō* engineered the remarkable feat of having the shogunate depose their daimyo. The Tokushima elite thus, simultaneously, ignored the shogunate in the name of the "state" of Tokushima and used the shogunate to challenge their own daimyo.

The struggle between the Tokushima *karō* and their daimyo, Hachisuka Shigeyoshi, had its roots in a series of reforms Shigeyoshi introduced in 1759/2. Shigeyoshi was by birth the fourth son of Satake Yoshimichi, the daimyo of Akita shinden. He was adopted into the Hachisuka house in 1754/6 when the ninth daimyo, Hachisuka Yoshihisa, fell severely ill, and he succeeded Yoshihisa later that year. In the wake of the 1756 indigo protests, Shigeyoshi sensed deep-seated problems in the domain's political hierarchy. In 1759, at age 22, the brash new lord confronted the domain elite with a radical reform of Tokushima's political structure.

Tokushima had lacked strong daimyo leadership since the early Tokugawa era, and by the mid-1700s political power had devolved to a tightly knit cabal of five families: the Inada, Kashima, Yamada, Hasegawa, and Ikeda. The families controlled the top posts in the domain, executor (*shiokiyaku*) and Edo executor, by virtue of hereditary rank. Only retainers with the rank of "house elder" (*karō*) could hold these offices, and only the five families were ranked as elders. This monopoly on power was accompanied by great wealth: in the 1750s the head of the Inada house, Inada Kurobei, held an investiture of 14,361 *koku*, equal to that of a small daimyo. The house elders had also allowed the domain to accumulate a debt of over 300,000 *ryō*.[51]

The next level of retainers, the *chūrō* or "middle elders," resented the control of the five *karō* houses over domain politics. These administrators saw the accession of Shigeyoshi as an opportunity to challenge the "house elders." They advised their lord to return to the tradition of direct daimyo rule. Their intention, presumably, was to serve as close advisers to a malleable daimyo.[52] Shigeyoshi, however, used the appeal of the *chūrō* to undertake a complete revision of the domain's administrative hierarchy. In 1759/2 Shigeyoshi announced the "rank and stipend reforms" (*yakuseki yakudaka*), which replaced the existing ten ranks with a system of three groups. Membership in a group reflected both hereditary rank and office. The first group consisted of retainers with the rank of elder and those with the posts of executor or Edo executor. The posts of executor, however, were no longer restricted to *karō*. Within the first group, moreover, an executor, irrespective of rank, would be seated above a *karō* without portfolio. The second group consisted of those of *chūrō* rank and those holding the offices of attendant (*kinjuyaku*) and magistrate of appeals (*saiso bugyō*), which were now opened to lower-ranking retainers. So that lower-ranking retainers could meet the stipend requirements for high office, Shigeyoshi established supplemental stipends called *tashidaka*, which were paid during their term.[53] By creating greater mobility within the domain administration, Shigeyoshi opened important offices to both talented officials and his own political allies.

Shigeyoshi's disregard for the *karō*'s control over domain policy challenged their patrimonial authority and drew an impassioned response. On 1759/2/27 Yamada Oribe Masatsune, head of the Yamada house, submitted a remonstrance to Shigeyoshi. The new system, he argued, was a grave mistake. It showed a lack of respect for one's ancestors and a lack of the humility becoming an adopted son. Further, argued Yamada, harmony was the key to successful administration: even if Shigeyoshi's policy had merit, it would fail if it provoked resistance among the retainers.[54]

Shigeyoshi responded aggressively. On 1759/3/1 he summoned the house elders, Kashima Kazusa, Kashima Bizen, Yamada Oribe, and

Ikeda Noboru, and, having seated them below lesser-ranking retainers, read his response to Yamada's remonstrance. Yamada, he argued, had failed as a house elder by obstinately defending the existing administrative system: rather than note the failings of previous daimyo, he had aided and abetted a faulty system. Further, Yamada had failed to understand Confucian principles. He had argued, based on the *Analects*, that "one does not change the way of one's father for three years," but he had failed to note that this did not apply in critical matters, nor had he demonstrated that a birth son and an adopted son have the same obligations. Finally Shigeyoshi accused Yamada of hypocrisy: Yamada had argued that harmony was essential to successful rule, but had the arrogance to accuse Shigeyoshi of unfilial conduct.[55]

Shigeyoshi had hoped to rally the *chūrō* against the *karō*, but his reforms threatened not only the *karō* monopoly on high offices but also the *chūrō* monopoly on middle offices. To galvanize the *chūrō* Shigeyoshi turned to brinksmanship. On 1759/3/2, claiming that his inability to achieve consensus reflected his unworthiness, Shigeyoshi offered to resign. His gambit succeeded. Shigeyoshi agreed to postpone implementation of the stipend reforms and the *chūrō* united behind him. He then dismissed Yamada Oribe from his post as executor and ordered him into isolation. Shigeyoshi faced one final challenge: a conspiracy by Yamada to draw in the *bakufu* and have Shigeyoshi replaced with Hachisuka Shigetaka, a grandson of the fifth daimyo, Hachisuka Tsunenori. Shigeyoshi managed to divide the *karō* and further consolidate his control over the domain. He then ordered Yamada to commit *seppuku* and sentenced two other *karō*, Hasegawa and Kashima, to confinement.[56]

His hold on the domain now secure, Shigeyoshi resolved to move decisively on reform: in 1761 he declared a seven-year retrenchment program. In stark contrast to common practice, Shigeyoshi reduced the investitures of high-ranking retainers while maintaining or increasing the stipends of poorer retainers. Shigeyoshi also challenged the immunity of landed fiefs, ordering a cadastral survey of *karō* Inada Kurobei's fief. Shigeyoshi insisted that this was not a reprisal against Inada but part of the standardization of stipends under the *yakuseki yakudaka* system. The daimyo further shocked the domain establishment by putting in prison retainers opposed to his reforms.

Shigeyoshi justified his actions by arguing that such persons had been stripped of rank for improper conduct and then sentenced to jail. Thus, samurai were not being imprisoned. Overall, Shigeyoshi showed little respect for rank and protocol. He ignored the *karō* and promoted officials of *chūrō* rank to high office.[57]

The domain elite was battered but not defeated. While Shigeyoshi challenged their perquisites at home, the domain elders were arranging their daimyo's ouster with shogunal officials. When Shigeyoshi arrived in Edo on 1769/10/22, he was presented by the *bakufu* with a four-count indictment of his conduct. The shogunate charged him with upsetting traditional domain regulations, beleaguering his subjects with ill-conceived policies, failing to consult with his elite retainers (*kachū fudai*), and indulging in selfish disportment at the expense of his retainers and subjects. Shigeyoshi defended his reforms but the *karō* clique prevailed: on the last day of 1769/10 Shigeyoshi was ordered into retirement for improper conduct. The retirement was a clear victory for the Tokushima old guard. Shigeyoshi was succeeded by his twelve-year-old son, Haruaki. True power thus returned now to the *karō* clique, led by Hasegawa.[58]

The forced retirement of Shigeyoshi suggests, at first, a victory for the *bakufu* and a defeat for domain autonomy. The shogunate cited how Shigeyoshi's failure to rule his country properly had harried the people (*kokusei torimidare, kokumin nangi ni oyobi*), suggesting that the shogunate could intervene in the interest of the subjects of Tokushima. Suzerain authority over the people of Tokushima thus lay with the shogunate, not the Hachisuka house. Yet this logic was tempered by the shogunate's insistence on maintaining the traditions of the Hachisuka house, implying that these precedents bound not only the daimyo but the shogunate as well. Indeed, Shigeyoshi was punished, in part, for reforms that violated Hachisuka tradition. Thus, even when it asserted suzerain authority, the shogunate continued to recognize the patrimonial authority of the Hachisuka house. Accordingly, the shogunate made no prescription for the future rule of Tokushima save an exhortation to return to precedent, nor did the shogunate assign any agents to supervise or direct Tokushima politics. The thrust of shogunal authority thus remained largely feudal: the shogunate exerted power over the rulers of Tokushima, but not Tokushima itself. The victory of the house elders lay in their ability to exploit this tension among feudal, patrimonial, and suzerain authority. Unable to unseat Shigeyoshi on their own, they successfully used the *bakufu* to depose him and install a pliable heir.

Despite their reliance on the shogunate, the *karō* were hardly shogunal allies. The domain elite was no more willing than Shigeyoshi to cede control over trade in indigo. It was the elders, led by Hasegawa, who conspired to feign compliance while effectively ignoring the shogunate. It is tempting to dismiss this apparent contradiction as opportunism: the *karō* deceived the shogunate in the name of their lord, and their lord in the name of the shogunate, as it suited their immediate interests. This opportunism, however, was grounded in the patrimonial authority of the *karō* houses. Hasegawa and his allies acted to defend Tokushima's economic interests because their patrimony as elite retainers depended on the vitality of the Tokushima economy. Yet they were equally willing to depose their lord when his reforms threatened their patrimonial claim on the domain's premier offices. The *karō* acted consistently, not as vassals, but as defenders of their patrimony. These concerns were reflected in the shogunate's indictment of Shigeyoshi. The shogunate found him unfit for rule because he broke with the tradition of consulting his elite retainers. The *karō* thus made the shogunate itself an instrument in the defense of their patrimony.

## The Rise of Cartels

When Shigeyoshi was deposed in 1769, he was succeeded by his twelve-year-old son, Haruaki, and control over the government reverted to the *karō* clique. Led now by Hasegawa Ōmi, the *karō* promptly reversed the reforms that threatened their economic interests. While Shigeyoshi had cut elite stipends to subsidize those of poorer retainers, the *karō* clique made flat cuts. One source describes cuts on the order of 50 to 60 percent, but domain fiscal records suggest smaller reductions.[59]

In general policy, the *karō* clique tended toward short-term solutions with problematic long-term implications. The administration retired some of its debt by demanding payments from local merchants. It also sold licenses to handle tobacco, cotton, and corvée, in essence subcontracting parts of the domain tax system to wealthy merchants. Further funds were raised by selling "relief rice" in the coastal districts, which were dependent on grain imports. These policies were critiqued as both injurious and dangerous. Ikeda Namie, a high-ranking retainer, warned that "[these reforms] will definitely be painful to those below. . . . Because they are unlikely to submit, I am extremely concerned that there may even be conspiratorial actions." The daimyo, Hachisuka Haruaki, wrote in his later years that the *karō* clique had "progressively exhausted the nation's strength."[60]

Despite these measures, the *karō* clique could not cover domain expenses. Having overturned Shigeyoshi's retrenchment policies, they allowed the domain debt to climb. In 1779 total indebtedness reached 17,159 silver *kan*, or 1.31 times the annual revenue. The clique was entirely unable to respond to the Tenmei crisis, which drove poorer farmers to abandon their land. In 1790 Hasegawa Ōmi and his faction were dismissed from power by Haruaki, who, having attained his majority, proved as strong-willed as Shigeyoshi. Like his father, Haruaki sought centralized control over the domain, which he described as a return to the tradition of Yoshishige, Tadateru, and Mitsutaka, the first three daimyo of Tokushima.[61]

The focus of Haruaki's reforms was agricultural policy, particularly the promotion of the domain's principal commercial crops: indigo and salt, as well as tobacco, sugar, paper, and tea. The center of this policy was control of the indigo cube market through control over indigo cube distribution. The Kansei reforms were thus directed toward the same goal as the Meiwa reforms: insuring high prices for indigo cubes. But in method Kansei policy was markedly different. Instead of breaking the Osaka cartel through free trade, Haruaki promoted the establishment of rival cartels.

The first major cartel of the Kansei reforms was a fertilizer *ton'ya* established in 1799: the domain appointed eighteen merchants as official fertilizer wholesalers. The establishment of the *ton'ya* was a reaction to price manipulation by merchants under the existing system of government-subsidized loans. Under the existing system, declared the government, "the conduct of the *ton'ya* and *nakagai* is displeasing and year after year the prices rise. Thus, rural [indigo] cultivators and small farmers are gravely troubled."[62]

The centerpiece of the Kansei reforms was the establishment of control over the national distribution system. In 1802, in response to a petition by Kantō merchants, the domain granted the merchants oligopsony privileges: indigo cubes sent to the Kantō were now to be sold only to 36 designated merchants. Under the direction of the Edo chargé d'affaires they were directed to set indigo cube prices.[63] In 1804, the domain established a parallel system in Osaka. The government authorized a four-member indigo cartel and appointed an indigo agent (aikata gakari) to supervise indigo shipments to Osaka.[64] The cartel's effect on prices was evident the following year. In 1805, despite a bumper crop of indigo leaves, the Osaka price of indigo cubes rose by 30 percent. The Osaka dyers retaliated quickly. On 1806/2/21, five members of the Osaka dyers' associations petitioned the Osaka city magistrate, charging that merchants trading in Awa indigo were hoarding indigo cubes and refusing to trade in indigo from regions other than Awa. Within the week representatives from the Osaka indigo merchants association and the tie-dyers association (shiboriya) had joined the suit.[65]

The Tokushima government confronted the lawsuits by tightening its regulations. In 1806/5 the domain enjoined non-Awa subjects from trading in Awa indigo without special authorization. The domain based its confrontational tactics on its assessment of the market. Awa accounted for nearly 70 percent of the indigo shipped to Osaka and had no rivals in quality. The domain thus sought to force the hand of its opponents. The excluded merchants protested and again petitioned the Osaka city magistrate. On 1806/7/29, the parties reached a rudimentary settlement: of the 101 indigo merchants, 80 would deal only in Awa indigo while 21 would deal solely in indigo from other regions. Key members of the non-Awa faction seem to have envisioned establishing a monopoly on non-Awa indigo.[66] Tokushima then moved to tighten its control. In 1806/8 the government ordered all indigo cubes shipped from Tokushima to Osaka to be sold to a licensed indigo ton'ya and prohibited direct sales to dyers or sales to other merchants. To insure compliance with these regulations, indigo merchants going to Osaka were required to receive authorization from the indigo intendant (aikata daikan), and merchants returning to Tokushima from Osaka were to receive authorization from the Osaka chargé d'affaires. Disputes within the Osaka cartel were to be settled by the Osaka chargé d'affaires. Finally, the domain issued regulations prohibiting the direct sale of indigo to the five provinces of the Kinai: Yamashiro, Yamato, Izumi, Settsu, and Kawachi.[67]

Although Tokushima's actions seem consistent with the 1806/7 settlement, non-Awa merchants were outraged. In an 1806/12 lawsuit they accused Awa of seeking to control the entire indigo market and of stopping supplies of non-Awa indigo from reaching Osaka. The regulations of 1806/8, they argued, were a "new system" (shinki no shihō) and violated the out-of-court settlement. By citing the "newness" of Tokushima's efforts, the plaintiffs sought to link the 1806 reforms with the Tokushima indigo market of 1766.[68]

The lawsuit confronted the Osaka city magistrates with two opposing principles. Shogunal respect for precedent argued against recognizing Tokushima's "new system." Tokushima, however, could appeal to the shogunate's preference for out-of-court settlements in commercial disputes. The parties had reached an initial settlement, and the dispute was the type of suit the shogunate preferred not to hear: litigation eventually involved two dyers associations, three factions of merchants, and intricate commercial issues. A distaste for this sort of complex commercial litigation ultimately swung the case in Tokushima's favor. The Osaka magistrates repeatedly summoned the parties and demanded that they reach a negotiated settlement. This served Tokushima's purposes perfectly. With its dominant position in the indigo market, the domain could dominate any trade system based on "compromise" among merchant groups. In 1807/9 the plaintiff's case collapsed when the magistrates refused to overturn the 1806/7 agreement.[69]

Buoyed by this success, the domain moved to have all Awa indigo sent to Edo or Osaka shipped directly to its government warehouses. This strategy would give the domain exacting control over distribution. In a 1813/7/18 letter to the Edo senior counselor Makino Tadakiyo, the daimyo of Tokushima described the domain's actions as a conservative attempt to maintain the status quo. The daimyo observed that improprieties by various indigo merchants had caused problems for Tokushima indigo growers. In response, the domain had begun to register the names and addresses of indigo merchants to insure that they conducted themselves properly. This action had provoked lawsuits from various indigo merchants, so the government sought an out-of-court settlement. The merchants and the domain indigo office agreed that merchants should not trade in both Awa and non-Awa indigo. Although this agreement had helped the daimyo bring peace to his people (*kokumin mo ando*), it was increasingly being ignored by unscrupulous traders. The lord feared for his people (*kokumin*) and had thus been forced to take the more drastic action of demanding that indigo be shipped to the Osaka warehouse. This, the daimyo insisted, was strictly according to precedent: there was no precedent for mixing Awa and non-Awa indigo, and there were precedents for domains establishing strict controls over their exports. Any claim that the domain's policy was "new," the daimyo argued, was deceptive. Tokushima policies, the government argued, were firmly grounded in precedent.[70] The domain's strategy was again successful. By styling itself as a defender of precedent and compromise, the domain cast its opponents as litigious and impatient with the status quo. After consultation with the Osaka city magistrates, the shogunate authorized the reforms.[71]

Over the following years Tokushima gradually extended this monopoly system to the rest of Japan. In 1810 the domain established a guild (*kabunakama*) in Ise and Owari, in 1816 in Kyoto, and in 1830 in seven provinces including Aki, Iyo, Sanuki, Echigo, and Hizen. In 1831 the domain authorized an additional 21 guilds. Tokushima's government-controlled distribution system now covered most of Japan, stretching from Mutsu in the far northeast to Tsushima in the southwest.[72] The effect on prices was marked: in the 1810s indigo prices rose by 20 percent (see Figures 13 and 14).[73]

In the 1830s the cartel system came under increasing pressure from non-Awa suppliers. The success of the cartel in raising prices had, paradoxically, increased the incentive for traders from other regions to improve the quality of their indigo. As early as 1813 Tokushima had warned its indigo cube makers of industrial espionage. Some day laborers, the domain warned, were actually spies working for indigo cube makers in other regions.[74] The domain's efforts to stop the spread of indigo technology were insufficient, and by the 1820s the rising volume and quality of non-Awa indigo threatened the efficacy of the cartel system.[75] If merchants could profit by trading in non-Awa indigo, there was little reason to submit to the cartel's regulations. Facing this challenge, the domain

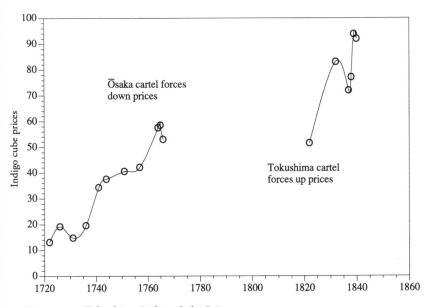

Figure 13. Tokushima Indigo Cube Prices

SOURCE: Nishino, *Awa ai enkakushi*, pp. 358–59.
NOTE: Prices are for the Osaka market in silver *me* per bushel of low-grade cubes. One bushel weighed 20 *kan*, or about 165 lbs.

elected to bend rather than break. In 1830 the domain began to allow Edo cartel members to trade in non-Awa indigo as well. Although the change broke with precedent, the cartel members were required to obey cartel policy on prices for non-Awa indigo and to maintain the ban on mixing Awa indigo with dye from other regions.[76] The cartel thus retained its essential powers. The reform is significant because it belies Tokushima's early defense of the cartel system. In the early 1800s the domain had argued that trading in both Awa and non-Awa indigo was inherently injurious to the domain's economy. The 1830s reform made it clear that the domain would tolerate such trade so long as it did not undermine the domain's control over indigo prices. The government's essential goal was to maintain high prices for its major export. In this modified fashion, the cartel system survived into the 1860s. When the shogunate ordered the dismantling of *kabunakama* in 1842 as part of the Tenpō reforms, Tokushima used back channels to negotiate an ex-

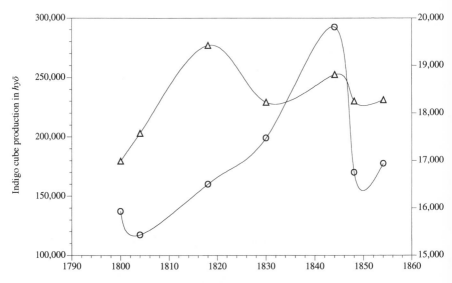

Figure 14. Tokushima Indigo Production

SOURCE: Yamada, Iinuma, and Oka, eds., *Nihon nōsho zenshū*, 30: 365.

emption. Although the cartel faced repeated challenges from other suppliers, only the volatile market conditions of the 1860s broke its grip on prices.[77]

Although the cartel system appears to be a stark departure from the free-trade policies of the Meiwa era, there is an underlying consistency between the two. Both policies sought to maintain high prices for indigo by breaking the control of the Osaka cartels over Tokushima indigo producers. The Meiwa reforms were largely defensive: the domain did not seek to dissolve the cartels but to undermine their ability to set oligopsony prices. The mechanism for these reforms, an open market in Tokushima, clashed directly with *bakufu* policy. The cartel system, by contrast, was more traditional but more aggressive. The domain sought not merely to defend its producers against oligopsony pricing but also to establish its own network of cartels. The underlying common thread was the establishment of economic institutions that maintained high prices for the products of Tokushima. Regulated auctions and cartels were different means to this end.

## The Tenpō Crisis in Tokushima

The unseasonable cold and rains of 1833–37, which caused wide-spread famine in Hirosaki, were comparatively benign in Toku-shima. Contemporary sources recount serious economic dislocation but not starvation. As an austerity measure in 1834, the domain or-dered its subjects to eat rice gruel once a day. Such austerity would have been an indulgence in either Hirosaki or Yonezawa. When the domain ordered the cessation of sake production, it cited rice prices, not absolute shortages.[78] The impact of the Tenpō crisis was severe nonetheless. The diary of the Motoki family, wealthy landowners from Takahara village in Myōzai district, reports adverse weather and soaring prices: rice rose from 100 gold *me* per *koku* in 1836/1 to 250 *me* in 1837/6. Heavy rains killed rice and cotton, while in-digo appeared too early in the season and rotted. Equally serious was the depression of central markets. The rise in cotton prices led to a slowdown of the Osaka textile industry, which in turn de-pressed the demand for indigo.[79]

For laborers and poorer farmers, however, the surge in the rice price meant privation. An 1837/10 entry in the Motoki diary reads:

Throughout the country [*kuni*] people are suffering and incidents verging on rebellion [*sōdō ikki gamashiki koto*] have occurred in some villages. Thus, wealthier people distribute rations of wheat in the villages. In Taka-hara village, for approximately 200 people twenty *koku* of wheat was col-lected and distributed.[80]

The poor were more incensed at the cunning of fellow villagers than at the domain. According to the diary of the Shikichiya family, a merchant house from Hirata village in Mima district:

Various prices continue to rise and thus farmers from here and there wander about, sometimes acting rebellious [*ikki gamashiki koto*]. This, however, is not directed at his lordship [*mikami*]. Rather, there is talk of people break-ing into the houses of wealthy folk who have bought up stores of rice.[81]

The Shikichiya blamed the rice shortages on other domains:

I hear that other countries [*shokoku*] have strictly curtailed the export of grain to anywhere in Japan [*Nihon hitomaru*]. In particular, we have not received so much as a cup of grain from Sanuki.[82]

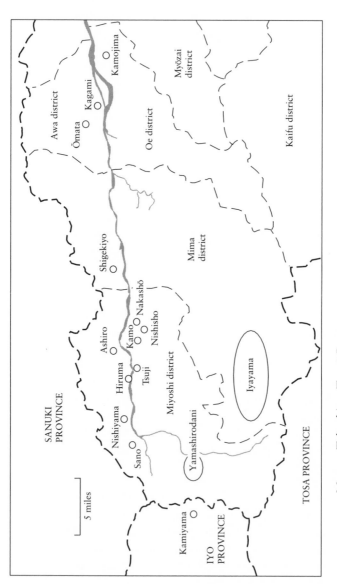

Map 7. Tokushima Tenpō Protests

SOURCE: Adapted from *Kadokawa Nihon chimei daijiten*, 36: 136–37, 717–19, and 1062–63, with data from Miyoshi, *Awa no byakushō ikki*, pp. 68–82. NOTE: The villages of Yamashirodani and Iyayama were composed of many scattered hamlets, and village boundaries are approximate.

The dislocations of the Tenpō famine declined as rice prices returned to normal in 1838. Nor were there any major popular rebellions, perhaps because the fear of rebellion, evident in the diaries cited above, drove wealthy farmers and merchants to undertake relief.

Ironically, the major rebellions in Tokushima of the Tenpō era were ignited not by famine or privation but by government reforms. In 1838 the domain instituted a system requiring permits for tobacco exports to neighboring domains. Local officials used these permits as an opportunity for graft, charging excessive fees for the licenses. Resentment of the permit system added to long-standing grievances over the manipulation of *sashigami*, a type of domain scrip. Since *sashigami* were used to pay taxes, demand was seasonal: the currency appreciated in the fall when the annual harvest tax was due, and depreciated thereafter. This provided a ready opportunity for landowners and merchants to profit through moneychanging, particularly in western Tokushima, near the domain border, where speculators could take advantage of price fluctuations in neighboring domains.[83]

Opposition to the permits erupted on the evening of 1841/12/4, when 631 farmers from Yamashirodani village in Miyoshi district fled (*chōsan*) across the border to Imabari domain. When the farmers reached Imabari, they took refuge in Anrakuji temple in the town of Kamiyama. The village officials of Kamiyama, while sympathetic to the protesters' plight, were unnerved by the prospect of feeding and housing 631 refugees and sought to arrange the repatriation of the farmers. Tokushima dispatched two commoner officials, Inoue Kiyoemon and Shimada Kamesaemon, to negotiate with the officials of Kamiyama. The petitioners presented a long list of grievances involving not only *sashigami* and tobacco but also regulations on paper mulberry, lacquer, cattle feed, bamboo, and lumber. Eager to defuse the situation, the government moved quickly to grant peasant demands. On 1842/1/20 the domain agreed to appoint new officials for tobacco licensing, to allow the payment of taxes in either *sashigami* or in kind, and to control the manipulation of exchange rates. On other matters, such as the sale of paper mulberry, the government promised careful consideration. The farmers then returned to their village, and the protest was resolved without further incident.[84]

Although the Yamashirodani protest was resolved without arrests or violence, it galvanized farmers across the Tokushima highlands. Throughout 1842/1 farmers attacked and destroyed the houses of village officials. Roughly a dozen such "smashings" (*uchikowashi*) have been documented: most involved local notables accused of peculation. In Shigekiyo village in Mima district, for example, the villagers destroyed the home of a headman who had not distributed the relief rice he had received from the domain. Although the protests subsided within the month, they reflected a serious collapse of public order: in several attacks the farmers used guns, hatchets, and sickles against their purported local leaders. In some areas the protests resembled large-scale insurrections. In Iyayama village in Mima, for example, some 600 farmers, over 200 armed with guns, attacked both their headmen and several local samurai, destroyed their houses, and then fled over the border to Tosa.[85]

Historians have interpreted the Tenpō disturbances as evidence of how commercialization fueled social discontent. Writing in 1955, Ōtsuki Hiromu treated the "smashings" as an illustration of how domain policy and the increasing commercialization of the economy exacerbated class conflict within the village. While villages had presented a united front against the domain in the Hōreki era, in the Tenpō era the locus of conflict was within the village itself. Matsumoto Hiroshi, the prolific local historian, has linked the Tenpō disturbances with the process of proletarianization. The division of farm villages into a wealthy landlord class and landless laborers produced severe social tensions that were ignited by the privation of the Tenpō crisis.[86]

This emphasis on socioeconomic factors is not without merit, but the geography of the Tenpō disturbances suggests that other factors were also at work. Ironically, there were no major disturbances in the Yoshino river delta, the domain's most commercialized region and the area where wage labor was most common. The Tenpō "smashings" began in westernmost Tokushima and spread down the Yoshino river, as far east as Kagami village in Awa. The Tenpō rebellions were thus concentrated in the western mountain districts, some of the least commercialized districts of the domain.[87]

The distribution of the Tenpō disturbances was determined in large measure by the limits of domain power. Far from the castle town and near the domain border, the western districts had long been more rebellious and violent than the rest of the domain. Many of the most violent Tenpō disputes occurred in villages that had long histories of violent dissent. In Iyayama village, for example, the Tenpō protesters destroyed the houses of Kita Gennai and Asa Sabanosuke, rural samurai (*gōshi*). These protests resembled disputes in 1759 and 1780: all centered on the privileges the Kita and Asa held as *gōshi*. The farmers of Shigekiyo village who attacked their headman in 1842 had been short on village solidarity a century before as well. In 1758, led by the daughter of a local official (*goningumi*), they had protested the malfeasance of their headman directly to the domain elders in the castle town. Rough quantitative measures of rebellion show the west to have been far more contentious than the east. In the two western districts of Miyoshi and Mima, there are 25 recorded "incidents" (*ikki*) during the Tokugawa period, out of 49 for Tokushima as a whole. By contrast, in the four eastern districts, which specialized in indigo (Myōdō, Oe, Itano, and Awa), there are only 11 reported *ikki*, with 5 of these in Awa. If we allow for the larger population of the Yoshino lowlands, then Miyoshi and Mima were over four times as rebellious as the four eastern districts.[88]

Although uprisings did not occur in the more prosperous and commercialized districts, class tensions were heightened throughout the domain. Even in regions not affected by protest, local notables were gripped by paranoia. Both the Motoki family in Myōzai district and the Yoshida family in Mima district were convinced that Ōshio Heihachirō, leader of an abortive insurrection in Osaka, was from Tokushima and was planning to return and foment trouble. These fears were groundless: no genealogy of Ōshio traces him to Tokushima. But this misinformation reflects how the local elite interpreted Ōshio's insurrection as part of a broader systemic crisis. The Motoki's fear that a similar rebellion could erupt in Tokushima at any moment suggests a severe sense of vulnerability. The effects of a commercial economy on class tensions were arguably better reflected in the fears of the landlords than in the actions of tenants and laborers.[89]

## Millenarianism in Tokushima

Tokushima played a peripheral role in the political conflicts that unseated the shogunate. The domain's ambivalence toward both the restoration movement and the Tokugawa house were determined largely by the interests of the daimyo, Hachisuka Narihiro (1821–68). The penultimate daimyo of Tokushima, Narihiro was born the 22nd child of the shogun Tokugawa Ienari. Adopted by the Hachisuka house in 1827, he became daimyo of Tokushima in 1843. As the daimyo of a prominent domain, but a Tokugawa by birth, Narihiro was a natural advocate of political compromise. During the political conflicts of the 1850s and 1860s, he consistently favored settlements wherein the shogunate would recognize the importance of the imperial line and share authority with key daimyo. Given Narihiro's reputation as a "sensible advocate of Tokugawa supremacy," the shogunate repeatedly sought his support and advice in the 1850s and early 1860s. Narihiro, however, remained aloof.[90] When the shogunate requested support for the first Chōshū expedition, Tokushima responded that it could not send troops because of prior commitments to the defense of Yura and Iwaya, naval fortifications on Awaji. Pressed further, the domain agreed to follow shogunal orders, but it emphasized Chōshū's status as an "enemy of the court" and the need for the shogun to insure loyalty to the emperor throughout the realm. The domain similarly resisted requests for support during the second Chōshū expedition. The domain eventually dispatched troops, but the shogunate was defeated before they reached the front. During the final months of 1867, as troops poured into Kyoto and Osaka, Narihiro continued to advocate conciliation. After the victory of anti-shogunal forces at Toba-Fushimi, Tokushima sided with the new regime and dispatched forces to Tōhoku, but the domain's role in the Restoration struggle was minor.[91]

Irrespective of the ambivalence of the domain elite, the fall of the shogunate did not go unnoticed by Tokushima commoners. Beginning in late 1867, Tokushima was swept with a wave of religious fervor, a phenomenon known historically as *ee ja nai ka*. According to rumor, anyone who did not visit a temple or shrine would suffer a misfortune, and thousands left their villages to visit famous religious sites. Konpira shrine and Ise shrine were particularly popular, but the specific sect or religion does not seem to have mattered: thousands visited closer temples such as Yakuōji in Hiwasa and Hashikuraji in Ikeda. The pilgrimages rapidly acquired a millenarian tone: pilgrims stripped naked, cross-dressed, and danced wildly in the streets. Amulets (*omamori*) and religious stickers (*ofuda*), often those associated with the pilgrimages, began spreading throughout the domain. The mysterious appearance of the objects was declared supernatural, but they tended to concentrate in and around the homes of the wealthy, who were expected to celebrate the auspicious event by providing their neighbors with ample sake. As the celebrations grew wilder, revelers burst into wealthy homes, danced about in their wooden sandals (*geta*), and seized clothing and household goods.[92]

The name *ee jai nai ka*, or "ain't it great," comes from the doggerel chanted by the revelers. In Tokushima, as in much of Japan, *ee jai nai ka* were characterized in large measure by unfocused delirium: "If I get it, hey ain't it great! If he gives it, hey ain't it great! If I take it and leave, hey ain't it great! If I wear it or if I take it off, hey ain't it great!" Several verses, however, had a distinctly political edge. One verse lampooned the various forces struggling for political supremacy: "Aizu is pathetic, the Imperial Army [*kangun*] stinks, whichever is the coward, hey ain't it great." Given their open disgust with the various political contenders, the commoners turned to the supernatural for defense against foreign aggression: "Unto Japan [*Nipponkoku*], where the gods once descended, thereupon stones shall fall, smashing the homes of the foreigners, hey ain't it great."[93] The Tokushima *ee jai nai ka*, like the activities of the domain elite, were peripheral to the fall of the shogunate. Nonetheless, no observer viewing the revelries could doubt that the old regime had fallen.

# Conclusion

The Tokugawa "compound state" stood in contrast to the absolutist states of early modern Europe. Seventeenth- and eighteenth-century European political thought can be understood, with tolerable reduction, as the struggle between two absolute principles: the divine right of kings and the inalienable rights of the individual human being. Under the theory of divine right, kings held absolute and god-like authority over their dominion. In Alexander Pope's famous summary, a monarch possessed "the right divine of kings to govern wrong." This concept of monarchical absolutism was modified by Hobbes and Bodin, who both thought that a king's absolute authority was constrained by natural law. This did not, however, justify popular resistance to the king's power. Both Hobbes and Bodin saw the need to maintain civil order as a rationale for total obedience to absolute power. The theories of Locke and Rousseau can be seen as a dialectic response to absolutist thought. Instead of an absolute right to rule, Locke proposed absolute property rights and Rousseau, absolute rights to freedom and equality.

In the case of the Tokugawa "compound" state, this struggle between the rights of the individual and the powers of an absolute ruler was but one part of political discourse. The rhetoric of suzerain authority allowed for a supreme ruler responsible only to heaven.

Because lordship was understood as a "heavenly mandate," neo-Confucian monarchs, like Hobbes's and Bodin's absolute sovereigns, were bound only by "natural" constraints on their rule. Heaven's investiture was ultimately contingent upon the ruler's ability to bring peaceful (*ando*) and benevolent government (*jinsei*) to his people. Thus a recipient of "heaven's mandate" was not merely a superior noble but a sovereign with exclusive power over his dominion.

The discourse of patrimonial authority, by contrast, lacked such an explicit contest between the rights of the ruler and of the ruled. Instead, we find a concern with what Kasaya Kazuhiko calls the "autonomy of constituent members" (*seiin no jiritsusei*).[1] All members of a warrior band, for example, were entitled to traditional judicial and economic rights over their patrimony. Because the shogun and daimyo were themselves members of warrior houses, they were inclined to respect these traditions of the warrior estate. For the shogun, respect for patrimonial authority also meant recognizing daimyo autonomy in broad areas of civil affairs. For daimyo, it meant recognizing the perquisites of high-ranking retainers. This autonomy was, of course, partly sustained by the vassals themselves. As the Tokushima indigo dispute reveals, daimyo and their retainers tenaciously resisted shogunal intrusions into local politics and economic affairs. But the shogunate itself was ambivalent about excessive constraints on patrimonial authority. As a government that described its own decrees as "house laws" (*gotōke reijō*), the shogunate was itself dependent on the logic of patrimonial authority.

Feudal authority was predicated on a personal, rather than institutional, bond between lord and vassal. In each generation, vassals renewed this tie with vows of loyalty to their lord. By the mid-Tokugawa era, however, because most samurai could assume the heritability of their patrimony, lord-vassal relations had become depersonalized and feudal authority less important. For charismatic daimyo, however, feudal authority was still a powerful tool. Because feudal authority turned personal devotion into an abstract virtue, reformers like Uesugi Harunori of Yonezawa and Hachisuka Shigeyoshi of Tokushima could challenge entrenched interests by reminding their vassals that samurai lived to serve their lord.

Because of these multiple sources of political legitimacy, the compound state had multiple, overlapping spheres of political authority. The shogunate was a powerful force, but in broad areas of politics both its power and authority were remarkably slight. In the political culture of the great domains, the goal of statecraft was to secure the prosperity of the "state." By this, domain statesmen meant the financial health of their domain and the prosperity of their subject populace. This was not inherently contrary to shogunal authority. Daimyo were loath to confront the shogunate and sought to emphasize the coincidence of their duties as lords of their people and vassals of the shogun. When shogunal edicts impeded attempts to promote a domain's "national" welfare, however, daimyo justified the evasion of shogunal edicts with language from the discourse of suzerain authority. The shogunate thus lacked the ideological or political hegemony of a national sovereign. Although some of the shogunate's seventeenth-century edicts suggest the growth of a nation-state, the shogunate never abandoned its simultaneous identities as an imperial servant, the leader of a warlord federation, and an autonomous warlord house. These multiple identities complicate any estimation of shogunal "strength." Since, for example, the shogunate effected national defense by ordering daimyo to mobilize their samurai, wealthy, powerful domains were in the interests of the shogunate as a warlord commander. These same strong domains, however, were arguably an impediment to the expansion of the shogunate as a national sovereign.

It is tempting to view this tension as inherently paralyzing or destructive: trapped by its conflicting roles, the shogunate could not withstand the onslaught of the imperialist powers in the 1850s. But such an approach overlooks how the tension between the multiple identities of both the shogun and the daimyo served to define the Tokugawa order. Indeed, it was the lack of a modern sense of sovereignty that distinguished Tokugawa politics. The early modern order was resolutely rooted in the premodern concepts of feudal and patrimonial authority. Its coherence and legitimacy stemmed from a concatenation of multiple sovereignties, rather than a single exclusive sovereignty. It was thus, to borrow Benecké's description of the old Reich, "a vigorous entanglement of component parts."[2]

"Country" domains held a unique position within the compound state. Although patrimonial authority gave all landed retainers some autonomy from shogunal intervention, "country" domains functioned as independent regimes in broad areas of civil law. Under a shogunate that claimed sole authority over diplomacy and external affairs, the great domains were largely autonomous in their own finances and economic development. Their political landscapes were dominated by the struggle between two conflicting forces: the demand of retainers for revenue and the resistance of commoners to taxation. Domain administrators sought endlessly to find the most politically feasible combination of taxes and retainer stipends. Two phenomena affected the intensity and volatility of this struggle: demography and protoindustrialization.

Demography shaped domain politics because it determined how many commoners supported each retainer. This, in turn, affected how heavily the domain needed to tax and how generously it could reward. Demography affected domain finances in a predictable pattern: the fewer commoners available to support each samurai household, the more heavily they were taxed. The most striking aspect of demographic pressure was how it catalyzed the need for government reforms. In both Hirosaki and Yonezawa, demographic crises led statesmen to confront underlying population trends. Faced with shortages of commoners, both domains sought to get more: Hirosaki encouraged immigration, disguised as "repatriation," in order to increase its farm population. Yonezawa sought to reverse population trends with subsidies for marriage, childbirth, and large families.

In both Hirosaki and Yonezawa the burden of a large samurai class forced a reassessment of the duties and perquisites of the samurai estate. Yonezawa aimed to reduce the cost of its retainers through samurai weaving. Since it could not provide adequate stipends for its retainers, it sought to help them provide for themselves. The domain organized a putting-out system, whereby retainer families received thread and looms from government-authorized merchants and sold back silk cloth. Retainer income from weaving eased the poverty caused by Yonezawa's repeated reductions in stipends. This transformation of retainers from warriors to weavers ran contrary to much of early modern thought and tradition. In promoting this transformation, the domain relied on the daimyo's patrimonial and suzerain authority. As a patrimonial lord, the daimyo could demand service to his house, and as a suzerain lord he was obliged to serve in the interests of his people. Since the daimyo needed exports rather than warriors, weaving was not contrary to a samurai's station, but merely a different manner in which he might repay his obligation to his lord. The disgrace, according to government edicts, lay not in weaving, but in weaving badly and thereby sullying the state's reputation for quality.

In Hirosaki demographic pressure led to an abortive effort to promote samurai farming. To increase the farming population and decrease the cost of stipends, the domain attempted to resettle its retainers in the countryside where they could support themselves. Like samurai weaving in Yonezawa, the resettlement program was justified by invoking patrimonial and suzerain authority. Mōnai Ariemon, the original advocate of resettlement, envisioned his plan as a means of achieving a "rich country and strong army." Implicit in Mōnai's approach was the assumption that Hirosaki could, in the name of state interests, independently redefine the role of its samurai. In Hirosaki, however, such notions were far more muted than in Yonezawa. While the domain initially promoted resettlement in the name of "national interests" (*kokueki*), its later edicts appeared without any formal rationale. This failure to invoke the lord's suzerain and patrimonial authority reflected the fact that the Tsugaru never attained "country-holding" daimyo status. By the eighteenth century, Hirosaki was as large as Yonezawa, but seventeenth-century politics still shaped domain policy. Statesmen in Yonezawa continued to act as servants of a one-million *koku* "country." Retainers in Hirosaki were still the vassals of a wily but undistinguished warlord.

Protoindustrialization affected domain politics by changing the underlying economic order. Because wealthier commoners were both willing and able to pay higher taxes, all domains were concerned with increasing economic output per capita. Protoindustrialization complicated this goal. In a consumer economy, domains could no longer rely on the conceptions of a "natural" agrarian economy that had guided earlier reforms. In Tokushima, for example, the expansion of indigo cultivation mandated new forms of economic intervention. Because indigo was vulnerable to monopsony, Tokushima indigo producers fell under the control of the Osaka cartels in the mid-1700s. When this cartel used its influence to force down the price of indigo, Tokushima was driven to respond in order to maintain its "national" welfare. In the 1760s the domain instituted a trust-busting auction system, designed to force Osaka merchants to bid against each other for indigo. When the shogunate blocked this maneuver, the domain sponsored a system of supplier cartels to offset the power of the purchasing cartels in Osaka. Significantly, the Tokushima indigo market of 1766 and the indigo cartels of the 1800s were conceptually opposite policies. The Tokushima indigo market was based on the assumption that open bidding for indigo would raise the price, whereas the indigo cartels were designed to raise the price of indigo through price fixing. These two approaches were, however, both products of Tokushima's exercise of patrimonial and suzerain authority. Despite shogunal intervention, Tokushima officials thought that securing export markets and fair prices for indigo were primary goals of statecraft. As Hachisuka Haruaki explained to the shogunate in 1813, insuring the purity of Tokushima indigo was part of bringing "peace to the nation" (*kokumin mo ando*).[3] Haruaki thus treated indigo exports like a military campaign and linked his efforts to secure the reputation of Tokushima indigo to his legitimacy as daimyo.

In grappling with the challenges of demographic and economic change, great domains acted with broad autonomy and formidable authority. But early modern domains were not states in the modern sense. Early modern politics was relentlessly syncretic, and its most skilled practitioners were comfortable not with absolutism but with the concatenation of multiple ideologies. The art of daimyo governance lay neither in ruling as a national sovereign nor as a feudal chieftain but in simultaneously laying claim to both sources of authority. By modern standards, domain politics and the politics of the compound state were both fraught with contradictions. These contradictions mark the gulf between the compound state and modern politics.

The Meiji government systematically destroyed the Tokugawa compound state and replaced it with a modern system of absolute sovereignty. The new government dissolved the domains of the daimyo and replaced them with prefectures administered by centrally appointed governors. The samurai were stripped of their swords and stipends. The new national bureaucracy and armed forces were opened to all classes, abolishing the traditional samurai monopoly on military and government service. Despite this open assault on the old regime, the compound state found few defenders. Although tens of thousands of samurai rose in armed resistance to the new government, their rebellions were scattered and ineffective. Why did the compound state die with a whimper rather than a bang?

The foreign crisis of the nineteenth century systematically undermined the multiple sovereignties of the compound state. The appearance of foreign warships challenged Japan as a whole and thus transcended domain boundaries. But it was not the West that transformed Japanese politics in the 1850s and 1860s: the appearance of Russian warships in the 1770s had caused political conflict but no parallel widespread reevaluation of the bases of sovereignty. What Commodore Perry and subsequent British and French expeditions brought to Japan was not the West but the modern nation-state in its most corrosive form. This new political animal, an unprecedented fusion of popular mobilization and advanced technology, required an unprecedented response.

Presenting foreign intervention as a galvanizing force in Japanese history raises the specter of Orientalism, or a Western-impact paradigm in which a dynamic West awakes a slumbering East. But while the destruction of the Tokugawa order cannot be separated from the broader currents of imperialism, and hence from "Western impact," we misunderstand the impact of foreign powers if we view it entirely in an Asian or "Oriental" context. The Tokugawa political order fell to the very forces of modern nationalism that had transformed early modern Europe. Having cut its teeth on the Holy Roman Empire and the Hapsburgs, modern nationalism destroyed the multiple, coterminous sovereignties of Tokugawa Japan. The processes that led Japanese statesmen to destroy the subnational governments of Tokugawa Japan were simultaneously at work in Germany and Italy, creating nation-states out of "geographical expressions." The autonomy of Hirosaki, Tokushima, and Yonezawa fared as well as the autonomy of Mecklenburg, Württemberg, Tuscany, or Parma. What made the "Western impact" decisive was not its origin but its character. It is hard to imagine even a sustained military assault by a Parma or a Mecklenburg driving Japanese retainers to question the legitimacy of their domains.

The imperialist powers that besieged Japan in the 1860s, however, were not the "states" of Parma and Mecklenburg. Rather, the Japanese compound state was confronted by the centralized authority of the modern nation-state, which was able to mobilize both human and technological resources with a confidence and efficiency unknown in the Tokugawa world. The United States, Britain, and France could not only manufacture weapons of unprecedented destructiveness but also entrust these weapons to their "commoners." The Tokugawa order lacked not only the technological prowess but also the ideological "technology" of nationalism. It was only the Meiji state's program of modernization and indoctrination that turned Japanese peasants into Japanese nationals.

The fragmented authority of the compound state, by contrast, was unequal to the challenge. The shogunate found itself responsible for defending Japan against modern armies with advanced weapons, but lacked the authority or ideology to begin nationwide taxation or military centralization. The domains retained the authority to tax commoners and raise armies but had no precedent for independent defense against foreign forces. The more clearly observers understood the capacities of the modern state, the more acutely they sensed the need for a redistribution of power. In this way, the crisis, by undermining the shogunate, undermined all the components of the "compound state." While domains might have bristled at the shogunate's arrogance, they had assumed its international competence.

A response to the imperialist powers required, at the very least, that domains increase their level of military coordination. In 1859, for example, the Tokushima nativist scholar Ikebe Mahari questioned the efficacy of independent domain action: "The invasion of barbarians concerns not one country or one district, but is a matter of great concern to the entire realm." Any effective response would thus require "negotiations between countries." Ikebe further argued that domains should share military technology and techniques to meet this grave threat, which, he noted, had already ravaged China.[4]

As the foreign crisis dramatized the need for political action transcending the domain, it gave new meaning to imperial loyalism. Little in nativist thought (*kokugaku*) was inherently threatening to domain autonomy. Into the 1860s, most imperial loyalists saw the imperial institution as means of innervating domain reform. Loyalty to the emperor would unite both ruler and ruled in common purpose and ethical action, thereby restoring rather than effacing daimyo authority. But while nativism suggested how the existing polity could be given renewed vitality and purpose, it also provided a basis for political action beyond the domain. In Tokushima, loyalists opposed to Hachisuka Narihiro's support of the shogunate began to envision a polity that encompassed all Japan. In 1864 the loyalist activist Ogata Chōei argued that with a sound foundation for political action, Japan could both expel the barbarians and maintain foreign trade. This required three things: a gathering of loyalist samurai (*shi*), a unification of the domains (*han*), and a revival of imperial authority. "If the *han* are unified, the national essence [*kokutai*] will be exalted and the establishment of the national weal insured." This would in turn insure proper actions regarding foreign powers.[5]

It would be misleading, however, to treat imperial loyalism as a mass movement. In Tokushima, radical imperial loyalism was confined largely to the semi-autonomous investiture of the Inada, whose vassals, including Ogata, fought as partisans in the Boshin War. In Yonezawa samurai were unswayed by imperial loyalism and fought doggedly to defend their domain against the self-appointed imperial army. In Hirosaki, a majority of high retainers favored similar resistance. Only the recognition that the resistance movement could not prevail kept Hirosaki from fighting alongside Yonezawa.

By the late 1860s "country" domains were paradoxical institutions. Although manifestly unable to meet the foreign threat, they continued to exercise their domestic functions without serious challenge. The Tokushima *ee ja nai ka* protests point to this schism. The participants voiced deep anxieties that the political order could not survive: only the stones falling from heaven, they chanted, could defend Japan against the foreign threat. But this was a protest over what the domain could not do, not what it was doing. The *ee ja nai ka* never led to a widespread challenge to the domain's domestic policies. The participants reveled in inverting the social order: crashing into the houses of their creditors and dancing wildly with the wives and daughters of their social superiors. Once the carnivalesque furor subsided, however, commoners again obeyed domain laws and paid traditional taxes. Ironically, the Meiji government's new policies such as conscription and tax reform drew furious opposition from Tokushima commoners.

This sense that the domains, although still viable within their traditional ambit, were doomed by new challenges, was shared by the domain elite. This produced a curious alliance: the most astute and capable of the daimyo were among the most eager proponents of dissolving the domains. A prime example is the Hachisuka house of Tokushima. Hachisuka Narihiro had been a dedicated proponent of a confederation of daimyo that with imperial sanction would rule Japan in concert with a diminished shogunate. After his death in 1868, Narihiro was succeeded by his son, Mochiaki. Born in 1846, Mochiaki had never known a world in which the threat of foreign invasion was not a paramount political concern. When representatives of the British legation visited Tokushima in 1867/8, Mochiaki, then heir apparent, confessed to Ernest Satow a secret intention to abdicate and visit England. After the Restoration Mochiaki served as Tokushima *han* governor and worked on domain reform, establishing a school for foreign and medical studies.[6] In 1871 he petitioned the new government to dissolve the domains. Only a new government, superior to the domains, he argued, could achieve the goals of stipend reform, balancing the budget, and "completing the great task of unifying the country, so that we may stand as the equals of the foreign countries."[7]

Mochiaki thus argued that only a new government, with new bases of sovereignty, could address the most tendentious issues facing Japan. But Mochiaki's political beliefs were also shaped by his personal situation. The government reforms of 1869 had fixed daimyo income at 10 percent of their former domain revenue, irrespective of whether they continued to serve as governors. The daimyo were also granted lofty status in the new social hierarchy. The peerage reforms of 1869/6 created four elite classes: lower samurai (*sotsu*), full samurai (*shi*), nobles (*kazoku*), and the imperial family. Daimyo and court nobles formed this new *kazoku* class, second only to the imperial family in prestige. Daimyo were thus guaranteed both wealth and status whether or not their domains survived. The new order thus presented Mochiaki with great opportunities: when he was replaced as governor, he was able to leave for England to pursue his studies without sacrificing his wealth or status. He later held a series of prestigious government positions, including special envoy to France, governor of Tokyo, chairman of the House of Peers, and minister of education. For Mochiaki the transformation of Tokushima from a domain to a prefecture was hardly an unfortunate turn of events. It relieved him of onerous political obligations while allowing him great wealth, enormous prestige, and unprecedented opportunity.[8] Mochiaki was particularly well suited to the new order, but all daimyo were given the "golden parachutes" of wealth and peerage. This strategy neutralized the daimyo as a focus for samurai reaction.

Because the new order proved amenable to so many daimyo, the Meiji oligarchy could rely on their cooperation in the dissolution of the compound state. The Meiji settlement was far less generous to lower samurai, who unlike their lords, were stripped of status, income, perquisites, and purpose. Central to the success of the new regime was the staggered character of its assault on traditional privileges. The Meiji government dissolved the domains, eliminated the daimyo, and abolished the rights of the warrior estate. At no time, however, were these reforms announced in a coherent blueprint, which might have proven a focus for reaction. The autonomy of Japan's subnational countries was destroyed by attrition. By the time its defenders realized the implications of the dissolution of the domains, the institutional framework for resistance had been lost.

Little in the early actions of the new regime suggested the scope of the changes in progress. In disposing of Tokugawa lands, the new government invested its allies and created new daimyo, much as the Tokugawa had done two-and-a-half centuries before. As late as 1870, the government was still creating new investitures such as Asahiyama *han* and Matsuyama *han*. In toto the new government created over 25 new *han* by either moving or increasing investitures. The fear that Satsuma and Chōshū were conspiring to form a new shogunate was thus more widespread than any suspicion that the new government would dissolve the domains.

The Charter Oath of 1868/3, the government's first statement of principles, was pointedly conciliatory. References to "deliberative assemblies" and "public discussion" suggested that great daimyo would be consulted on matters of national importance. In this context the movement to return daimyo investitures to the imperial court was scarcely threatening. Rather than resist, many daimyo vied to follow the precedent of Chōshū, Satsuma, Tosa, and Saga on the assumption that the emperor would reinvest the daimyo and thereby strengthen rather than dilute daimyo legitimacy by granting it imperial sanction. Indeed, the emperor's formal acceptance of the investitures in 1869/6 resulted in no immediate diminution of daimyo authority: the vast majority of daimyo were reappointed as *han* governors.[9]

The political question of 1870 was not how to dissolve the domains but how to salvage them. The most pressing problem for most domains was crushing debt. The warfare of the Restoration and postwar inflation had severely undermined the finances of most domains. Over the years 1868–71 the spending of the domains outpaced their total revenue by some 15 percent per annum. Roughly 35 percent of all domains and one-quarter of domains over 100,000 *koku* had deficits approaching one year's income. In mid-1869 the government proposed guidelines for *han* reform (*hansei*). The cornerstone of the proposals was budgetary reform: no more than 72 percent of a domain's budget was to be spent on stipends, while 10 percent was to be directed toward retiring debt and 18 percent for armaments programs. The proposals were submitted for review to the *Shūgiin*, a deliberative body of daimyo. The assembly, while cognizant of the need for reform, was still reluctant to cede authority on so critical an issue. The *Shūgiin* deleted the provision for debt repayment and cut the recommendation for armaments by half to 9 percent. Guidelines for stipends were raised to 82 percent of spending. Most important, the final decree, issued on 1870/9/10, explicitly recognized the continued authority of the domains over their vassals:

The *hansei* [reform act] does not place restriction on the reform of the stipend system; thus the absolute authority of the *han* governor over the reform of upper and lower samurai stipends is no different than from before the enforcement of the *hansei*.[10]

Although many domains were similarly active in reform, the Meiji government's announcement in 1871/7 that domains would be replaced by prefectures met with little resistance. Yielding control of their domains relieved daimyo of an onerous burden. In the new international environment, maintaining autonomy required massing sufficient military force to hold off the Western powers, a seemingly hopeless task for the domains. Even as individual members of a defensive coalition, the domains needed expensive new arms and new forms of military organization. Modern warfare required that daimyo demand more of their commoners while, simultaneously, challenging traditional perquisites of rank in order to rationalize and streamline the military. This was a challenge few could relish, for it raised the prospect of both peasant rebellion and samurai resistance. Although the daimyo saw little reason to resist, the government was careful not to confront simultaneously the privileges of their vassals. When the central government began to pursue stipend reform in 1873, it had already eliminated one of the major institutions of local autonomy, the domain.

Samurai did resist the move to cut their stipends and convert stipends payments into bonds, but elimination of the domains severely hampered their struggle. Retainers could not resist in the name of their "countries," since those countries no longer existed. Nor could the samurai unite across regional lines, since stipends were, by nature, local rights. Samurai resistance was reduced to a dozen small insurrections, none of which commanded broad enough support to challenge the new government. Thus the rebellion of the Shinpūren in Kumamoto, Maebara Issei's rebellion in Hagi, and the samurai insurrection in Akizuki were all summarily suppressed by the central government. The rebellions, although close in space, time, and motivation, were separated by the divide of political allegiance.

The most telling example is the case of Saigō Takamori, military hero of the Restoration and a failed opponent of its outcome. Saigō split with his colleagues in 1873 over foreign policy. He had favored provoking a war with Korea as a means of demonstrating imperial honor and samurai valor. He was overruled by those who feared such a war would provoke Western intervention. Defeated, Saigō left the government and returned to his native Satsuma where his private academy became a center for dissident samurai. Since the governor of Satsuma was a close ally of Saigō, the prefecture remained strikingly independent of Tokyo and resisted the central government's attempt to demilitarize the samurai estate.[11]

Saigō welcomed the samurai rebellions of 1876. "The past few days have brought strikingly good news," he wrote in November 1876; "it seems Osaka may soon be in [their] hands." Yet Saigō declined to help unify the Kumamoto, Hagi, and Akizuki rebellions. His reasoning remains largely unknown, but Saigō was concerned foremost with the political legitimacy of resistance. The propriety of opposition was closely tied to imperial authority, but since the physical emperor was beyond his reach, Saigō sought symbolic imperial assent. The Shinpūren uprising, he reasoned, had been planned to correspond with the emperor's birthday on December 3 but had broken out prematurely. This supposed miscalculation was, for Saigō, devastating: had the rebellion occurred on schedule, the legitimacy of the project would have drawn support even in Tokyo. Instead, the rebellions seemed to lack any higher sanction.

Saigō was forced into action in February 1877 when his supporters mobilized in response to rumors that the government was planning his assassination. The rebellion quickly garnered support from samurai in neighboring domains and the allied forces moved north to seize Kumamoto castle. The ensuing conflict, which engaged roughly 100,000 troops, was decided in early March, when government forces broke Saigō's siege of the castle. Fighting continued into September, however, as Saigō's forces, despite casualities exceeding 90 percent, denied government forces a decisive victory. The rebellion was brought to a close on September 14, when Saigō and 300 remaining followers died in suicidal resistance to 50,000 government troops. The Satsuma Rebellion, or "War of the Southwest," as it is known in Japanese, engaged the full military might of the new government, but the defeat of Saigō brought an end to military resistance. The overwhelming power of the nation-state was now obvious to all.

The great challenge to interpreting the "War of the Southwest" is that the rebellion was fought without a manifesto. The focus of resistance was Saigō himself. This absence of a statement of purpose can be placed within a broader context of activist samurai thought, which valued action as text over text as action. Yet the lack of a unifying political project reflects the dilemma of samurai resistance. Had the "War of the Southwest" and the rebellions of 1876 been coordinated they might have crippled the Meiji government in its first decade, but the opposition could not unite because their goal was antithetical to a unitary state. The samurai opposition wanted a restoration of samurai privileges, but since stipends were based on local ties of vassalage, this failed as a unifying issue. A united defense of the compound state, like centralized feudalism or coordinated anarchy, was an oxymoron. By 1877 even the language in which such a project might be expressed had been overwhelmed: "country" and "state" could no longer invoke the desired local referents. The domains and their overlords had gradually been reformed into extensions of the new regime. Saigō himself, however, represented what could no longer be articulated. His loyalty to both the emperor and his daimyo unquestionable, Saigō represented a world in which dual loyalties were not divided loyalties. If Saigō's actions were the text of the rebellion, then his death—surrounded, outnumbered, and outgunned—might serve as metaphor for the demise of local autonomy and the triumph of the nation-state.

In his seminal 1944 essay, Maruyama Masao argued that modern Japanese nationalism was a natural outcome of its cultural development. Drawing on Meinecke, Maruyama described Tokugawa Japan as a "cultural nation," wherein people were aware of a "cultural unity, founded on a common language, religion, custom, habits, and other cultural heritages, but lack[ed] any political consciousness as a nation." In Japan, as in Italy and Germany, a sense of a common culture had preceded the nation-state. In such cases, the critical factor in transforming a "cultural nation" into a "political nation" was an external threat such as foreign intervention. "When such a cultural nation is forced to defend its cultural unity, its existence is immediately raised to the political level, and it is faced with the necessity of forming a common state unit."[12] Maruyama thus cited Tokutomi Iichirō's account of Meiji nationalism as simplistic but essentially correct.

A threat from abroad immediately directs the nation's thoughts outwards. This leads immediately to the rise of a spirit of nationalism. This directly induces national unification. . . . The concept "foreign nations" brought forth the concept "Japanese nation." The day when the concept "Japanese nation" arose was the day when the concept "*han*" vanished.[13]

Maruyama's account of Japanese nationalism hinges on the Hegelian underpinnings of his thought. For Maruyama, history was largely the story of the self-realization of nations. The political practices of Tokugawa Japan were thus "vegetative," since they divided the nation both spatially, into domains, and horizontally, into estates. Maruyama's attribution of nationalism to the defense of cultural unity also stems from nineteenth-century German historiography: cultural unity was not a product of nationalism or statecraft but a cause of nationalism and a justification for a powerful state. Maruyama's concern with the pathology of modern Japanese nationalism did not undermine his understanding of nationalism itself as inevitable.

My project has been to show how Tokugawa politics was not "vegetative" but dynamic and vital. This study thus implicitly problematizes the inevitability of the nation-state. Political action in the "country" domains of Tokugawa Japan was conducted with little regard for "national" interests in the modern sense. Aspects of Japanese culture, such as the emperor, that later historians identified as the foundations of an unawakened nationalism, were peripheral to much of political practice. The transformation of these elements into symbols of national unity was a process determined by specific historical conditions and state actions, not a simple reaction to a foreign threat. Hideyoshi, we might note, undertook the conquest of the "world" with a state less centralized or nationalist than the Tokugawa order. It was not foreign or Western powers that "awakened" Japanese nationalism, but a collision with the nation-state.

What Maruyama and Tokutomi have described as a response to foreigners might more fruitfully be described as a response to nationalism. The ability of Western nationalism to induce Japanese nationalism stemmed, of course, from its ability to destroy nonnational cultures: in a world of nation-states there are only nation-states and colonies. Thus the "victory" of Satsuma and Chōshū over the shogunate resulted not in regionalism but in centralization. The subnational political identities of early modern Japan were saved from domination by foreign nations but sacrificed and subordinated to the Japanese nation. These institutions were thus destroyed by imperialism, but by imperialism as an internal process. The "countries" of Hirosaki, Tokushima, and Yonezawa are gone and no amount of summoning can bring them back, nor should we indulge in the romantic effort to do so. But we must avoid effacing subnational political identities in order to emplot Japanese history in a metanarrative with the nation as subject, an "etatist *Bildungsroman*."[14] The nation dominated politics only after politics produced the nation.

Reference Matter

# Appendix

The domain-level data used in this study (see Figures 1 through 4, pp. 50–51, and Table A1) were compiled from early Meiji statistical abstracts. Data on *han* income (*gendaka*), revenue base (*kusadaka*), and commoner population were taken from two articles in *Tōkei shūshi*, a periodical of government statistics.[1] Although the source of the data is not cited, the statistics were apparently taken from an 1869 survey of *han* governments. In 1869/6/25 the Gyōseikan ordered that daimyo report population statistics and five-year averages (1864–68) for key financial statistics, such as the yield of lands under their control (*shihai sōdaka*) and income (*gendaka*) from these lands.[2] These data were presented in *Tōkei shūshi*, and parts were later revised and published in book form as *Hansei ichiran*. The figures in *Tōkei shūshi* and *Hansei ichiran* are similar, but in cases of harvest shortfall or suspiciously low revenue figures, the government requested additional data, presented only in *Hansei ichiran*.

*Tōkei shūshi* gives a breakdown of population into nine categories: *kazoku* (nobles of daimyo rank), *shizoku* (upper samurai), *sotsu* (lower samurai), *shinshoku* (Shinto priests), *zōni* (Buddhist monks), *heimin* (commoners), *eta* (untouchables), *hinin* (outcastes), and *shokei* (criminals under death sentence).[3] I defined per capita taxation as *gendaka* per *heimin* and per capita output as *kusadaka* per *heimin*.

Although *Tōkei shūshi* and *Hansei ichiran* give population figures for samurai (*kazoku*, *shizoku*, and *sotsu*), these figures included dependents. Data on the number of stipends are not included. Data on retainer stipends and stipend recipients were taken from a survey conducted in 1871. The government requested that *han* report only stipends paid to *shizoku* or *sotsu* lasting at least one generation. Special awards, benefices paid to commoners, and the stipends of *han* governors were to be excluded from calculations. The government converted *jikata chigyō* (landed fiefs) into stipend equivalents, although the exact procedure is unclear.[4] These data were used for calculating the number of retainers receiving stipends and the average stipend. The stipend data specify the form of payment: gold, silver, copper, rice, or other grain. These various payments were converted into *koku* or rice using the exchange rates in *Hansei ichiran*: 1 *koku* = 8 gold *ryō* = 480 silver *me*. Copper was converted at 1 gold *ryō* = 9 copper *kan*.[5]

In compiling the composite *han* data set, I used the *Tōkei shūshi* figures except where transcription errors produced spurious data (i.e., state revenue [*gendaka*] larger than revenue base [*kusadaka*]), or where harvest shortfalls deflated revenue. Where *Hansei ichiran* offered plausible alternative figures these numbers were used; otherwise the *han* was deleted from the data set. *Tōkei shūshi* gives data for 265 domains. I disregarded the 24 domains created or moved during or after the Restoration. I disregarded 4 tiny domains whose location and origin I could not determine. This left a base sample of 237 *han*. Some regressions, calculations, and tables have fewer observations because of outliers or partial data.

For the domain-level data (Figures 1 through 4 and Tables A1 and A4) I defined taxation per capita as *gendaka* per capita and output per capita as *kusadaka* per commoner. Because *gendaka* included income from non-tax sources such as domain monopolies, taxation per capita includes the burden of these forms of revenue extraction. *Kusadaka* per capita measures commoner output known to the domain, and this raises a potential estimation problem. As noted in the text, early modern land surveys varied widely in accuracy and were often decades out of date. Because domains tended to revise their surveys in order to raise revenue, measurement errors in output are probably correlated with taxation (*gendaka*). As an example, Tokushima had a lower *kusadaka* per capita than Hirosaki, a figure that contradicts most qualitative assessments. These correlated errors would tend to inflate regression coefficients.

As a check on this sort of error, I have compiled estimates of output based on *Fuken bussan*, an 1874 government survey (see Table A2).[6] This survey was nationally standardized and thus avoids the potential problem of correlated measurement error. These data, however, were compiled along prefectural, rather than domain, boundaries. These data are thus not strictly comparable with the domain-level tax data. Because the prefectural data were compiled on prefectural boundaries, this data set aggregates over 250 domains into 63 prefectures. The process of aggregation is known to generate unreliable statistics, and these distortions generally increase with the level of aggregation. Further, many prefectures were created by amalgamating shogunal and domain lands, further distorting the data. Fortunately, "country" domains were least affected by the new political divisions. Some domains, like Yonezawa, were merely renamed; others were combined with smaller, neighboring territories. For domains with low levels of aggregation, the degree of aggregation bias is probably small. Thus Yonezawa is reasonably well represented by the province of Okitama, Hirosaki by the province of Aomori, and Tokushima by the province of Myōtō. Of the 63 prefectures for which reliable production figures exist, 16 met my selection criteria for low aggregation bias. These prefectures included no former shogunal territories and comprised five or fewer former domains. I aggregated the data using the scheme in Table A3.

Regression analyses based on these prefectural data give results substantively identical to the domain-level regressions (compare Tables A4 and A5). The only substantive difference lies in the two multiple regressions, where the partial regression coefficient of output is negative when estimated using prefectural-level data. This curious result is not statistically significant and seems to stem largely from the small size of the sample and multicollinearity. The correlation coefficient for output per capita and the population ratio is 0.75, as high as the correlation coefficient between output and taxation. The regression models in Tables A4 and A5 are minimally specified, but the parameter values are not sensitive to the addition of controlling variables. Models that control for size of holdings, transfers (tenpō), and domain debt do not give substantively different results.

TABLE A1

*Data for Domains, 1869–71*

| Domain | Variant names | Assessed output (*kusadaka*) per commoner in *koku* | Retainers per 100 commoners | Tax burden (*gendaka*) per commoner in *koku* |
|---|---|---|---|---|
| Akashi | | 1.38 | 2.03 | 0.666 |
| Akita | | 0.88 | 1.81 | 0.049 |
| Akizuki | | 1.86 | 2.12 | 0.675 |
| Akō | | 0.60 | 1.05 | 0.310 |
| Amagasaki | | 1.20 | 1.83 | 0.645 |
| Annaka | | 1.32 | 0.99 | 0.306 |
| Anshi | | 1.11 | 1.50 | 0.550 |
| Asada | | 1.15 | 1.05 | 0.533 |
| Asao | | 1.63 | 1.45 | 0.652 |
| Ashikaga | | 0.62 | 0.70 | 0.152 |
| Ashimori | | 1.94 | 2.00 | 0.638 |
| Asō | | 1.37 | 1.26 | 0.549 |
| Ayabe | | 1.27 | 1.15 | 0.401 |
| Chōfu | Toyara, Chūfu | 1.51 | 2.81 | 0.447 |
| Chōshū | Hagi, Yamaguchi | 1.36 | 1.99 | 0.481 |
| Daishōji | | 1.91 | 3.59 | 0.609 |
| Fuchū | Ishioka (Hitachi province) | 1.74 | 1.46 | 0.329 |
| Fukiage | | 2.26 | 2.44 | 0.582 |
| Fukuchiyama | | 1.19 | 1.49 | 0.503 |
| Fukui | Kitanoshō | 1.25 | 1.31 | 0.414 |
| Fukuoka | | 1.87 | 2.30 | 0.765 |
| Fukuyama | | 0.67 | 1.33 | 0.324 |
| Funai | | 0.88 | 1.47 | 0.522 |
| Gotō | Fukue | 0.57 | 1.17 | 0.189 |
| Hachiman | Gujō | 0.96 | 0.93 | 0.307 |
| Hachinohe | | 0.63 | 0.88 | 0.149 |
| Hakata | | 1.41 | 1.43 | 0.599 |
| Hasunoike | | 2.32 | 3.96 | 0.794 |
| Hiji | | 1.50 | 3.05 | 0.512 |
| Hikone | | 1.17 | 2.73 | 0.540 |
| Himeji | | 1.06 | 1.42 | 0.447 |
| Hirado | | 0.96 | 2.67 | 0.404 |
| Hirosaki | | 1.20 | 1.89 | 0.620 |
| Hirose | | 1.38 | 1.55 | 0.542 |
| Hiroshima | | 0.57 | 0.95 | 0.304 |
| Hisai | | 1.78 | 0.94 | 0.745 |
| Hitoyoshi | | 1.86 | 1.85 | 0.718 |
| Honjō | | 0.76 | 2.86 | 0.579 |
| Ichinomiya | | 1.18 | 0.86 | 0.400 |
| Ichinoseki | | 1.31 | 2.65 | 0.470 |
| Iida | | 0.76 | 1.18 | 0.359 |
| Iino | | 0.99 | 1.25 | 0.352 |
| Iiyama | | 1.16 | 0.69 | 0.381 |
| Imabari | | 0.66 | 1.03 | 0.345 |
| Imao | | 1.19 | 2.21 | 0.463 |

Table A1, *continued*

| Domain | Variant names | Assessed output (*kusadaka*) per commoner in *koku* | Retainers per 100 commoners | Tax burden (*gendaka*) per commoner in *koku* |
|---|---|---|---|---|
| Inuyama | | 0.85 | 1.03 | 0.269 |
| Isezaki | | 1.28 | 1.16 | 0.276 |
| Itoigawa | Kiyosaki | 0.61 | 0.50 | 0.227 |
| Iwamura | | 0.99 | 0.99 | 0.378 |
| Iwamurata | | 1.39 | 1.49 | 0.385 |
| Iwasaki | Akita shinden | 1.15 | 1.61 | 0.622 |
| Iwatsuki | | 0.85 | 0.71 | 0.246 |
| Izumi | | 2.09 | 2.13 | 0.486 |
| Izushi | | 1.01 | 2.06 | 0.424 |
| Kaga | Kanazawa | 1.33 | 1.48 | 0.635 |
| Kaibara | | 1.25 | 1.26 | 0.572 |
| Kameda | | 0.97 | 2.83 | 0.594 |
| Kameyama | Ise province | 1.85 | 2.21 | 0.602 |
| Kameyama | Kameoka (Tanba province) | 1.26 | 1.49 | 0.619 |
| Kaminoyama | | 0.96 | 0.95 | 0.355 |
| Kamogata | Okayama shinden | 0.98 | 1.12 | 0.348 |
| Kanbe | | 1.73 | 1.64 | 0.758 |
| Kanō | | 1.33 | 1.29 | 0.471 |
| Karatsu | | 1.15 | 1.74 | 0.478 |
| Kasama | | 1.96 | 1.70 | 0.452 |
| Kashima | | 2.00 | 7.84 | 1.012 |
| Katsuyama | | 1.23 | 1.48 | 0.421 |
| Katsuyama | Kachiyama | 0.87 | 0.86 | 0.287 |
| Katsuyama | Mashima | 1.32 | 1.51 | 0.509 |
| Kawagoe | | 1.42 | 1.72 | 0.373 |
| Kishiwada | | 1.00 | 1.65 | 0.554 |
| Kitsuki | | 1.18 | 1.46 | 0.660 |
| Kiyosue | Chōfu shinden | 1.42 | 4.70 | 0.751 |
| Koga | | 1.35 | 1.31 | 0.390 |
| Koizumi | | 1.64 | 2.41 | 0.817 |
| Kokura | Toyotsu, Kawara | 1.77 | 3.88 | 0.852 |
| Kokura shinden | Chizuka | 2.07 | 5.51 | 0.979 |
| Komatsu | | 0.96 | 1.40 | 0.347 |
| Komono | | 1.33 | 1.35 | 0.613 |
| Komoro | | 1.01 | 0.99 | 0.371 |
| Kōriyama | | 1.66 | 2.09 | 0.648 |
| Koromo | | 1.24 | 1.23 | 0.356 |
| Kumamoto | | 1.30 | 1.61 | 0.627 |
| Kurobane | | 1.70 | 1.88 | 0.777 |
| Kuroishi | | 0.95 | 1.96 | 0.577 |
| Kurokawa | | 1.31 | 1.57 | 0.548 |
| Kurume | | 1.67 | 1.47 | 0.577 |
| Kururi | | 1.57 | 1.39 | 0.527 |
| Kushira | Shinjō | 3.11 | 4.05 | 1.335 |
| Kuwana | | 1.05 | 2.29 | 0.488 |
| Maebashi | Umabayashi | 1.34 | 1.53 | 0.335 |
| Marugame | | 0.67 | 1.41 | 0.267 |

*Table A1, continued*

| Domain | Variant names | Assessed output (kusadaka) per commoner in koku | Retainers per 100 commoners | Tax burden (gendaka) per commoner in koku |
|---|---|---|---|---|
| Maruoka | | 2.45 | 3.32 | 0.858 |
| Matsue | | 0.91 | 1.15 | 0.461 |
| Matsumae | Tate | 0.60 | 2.47 | 0.344 |
| Matsumoto | | 0.84 | 0.88 | 0.319 |
| Matsushiro | | 0.92 | 1.58 | 0.377 |
| Matsuyama | (Iyo province) | 0.81 | 2.02 | 0.597 |
| Matsuyama | Matsumine (Dewa province) | 1.30 | 2.34 | 0.504 |
| Matsuyama | Takahashi (Bitchū province) | 0.72 | 2.75 | 0.329 |
| Mibu | | 2.06 | 1.62 | 0.403 |
| Miharu | | 1.85 | 1.25 | 0.377 |
| Mikazuki | Noino | 0.92 | 1.87 | 0.496 |
| Mikusa | | 1.18 | 1.59 | 0.550 |
| Minakuchi | | 1.36 | 1.83 | 0.600 |
| Mineoka | | 1.36 | 1.13 | 0.402 |
| Mineyama | | 1.20 | 1.84 | 0.627 |
| Mito | | 1.16 | 2.10 | 0.227 |
| Mitsukaichi | | 1.36 | 1.40 | 0.641 |
| Miyagawa | | 1.98 | 1.65 | 0.725 |
| Miyazu | | 1.06 | 1.27 | 0.407 |
| Mori | | 1.13 | 2.32 | 0.435 |
| Murakami | | 1.04 | 0.99 | 0.429 |
| Muramatsu | Yasuda | 1.20 | 2.55 | 0.634 |
| Mutsuura | Kanazawa | 1.39 | 0.74 | 0.189 |
| Naegi | | 0.60 | 0.25 | 0.198 |
| Nagashima | | 1.15 | 1.88 | 0.522 |
| Nakatsu | | 1.35 | 1.80 | 0.554 |
| Nanokaichi | | 1.74 | 1.80 | 0.554 |
| Nariwa | | 0.79 | 0.92 | 0.248 |
| Nihonmatsu | | 1.52 | 2.68 | 0.392 |
| Niimi | | 1.20 | 2.21 | 0.431 |
| Niiya | | 0.78 | 1.28 | 0.391 |
| Nishihata | | 1.15 | 0.70 | 0.269 |
| Nishio | | 1.22 | 1.36 | 0.465 |
| Nishiōhira | | 1.54 | 1.08 | 0.481 |
| Nishōji | Nishiōji | 2.17 | 2.65 | 0.873 |
| Niwase | | 1.04 | 1.25 | 0.531 |
| Nobeoka | | 0.70 | 0.79 | 0.251 |
| Numata | | 1.13 | 1.19 | 0.425 |
| Obama | | 1.03 | 1.52 | 0.533 |
| Obata | | 1.74 | 1.55 | 0.314 |
| Obi | | 1.75 | 2.89 | 0.689 |
| Odawara | | 0.89 | 1.44 | 0.256 |
| Ōgaki | | 1.87 | 2.20 | 0.829 |
| Ogi | | 3.22 | 5.28 | 1.030 |
| Oimi | | 1.10 | 1.10 | 0.412 |
| Oka | | 1.33 | 1.80 | 0.356 |
| Okada | Kawabe | 1.04 | 1.93 | 0.520 |

*Table A1, continued*

| Domain | Variant names | Assessed output (kusadaka) per commoner in koku | Retainers per 100 commoners | Tax burden (gendaka) per commoner in koku |
|---|---|---|---|---|
| Okayama | | 1.41 | 1.68 | 0.540 |
| Okazaki | | 1.25 | 1.62 | 0.442 |
| Omigawa | | 1.34 | 1.11 | 0.301 |
| Ōmizo | | 1.75 | 1.15 | 0.584 |
| Ōmura | | 0.47 | 2.60 | 0.216 |
| Ono | | 1.50 | 2.23 | 0.714 |
| Ōno | | 1.36 | 1.88 | 0.516 |
| Oshi | | 1.35 | 1.30 | 0.374 |
| Ōsu | | 0.59 | 1.07 | 0.244 |
| Ōtaki | | 1.27 | 0.89 | 0.339 |
| Ōtawara | | 1.00 | 1.60 | 0.218 |
| Owari | Nagoya | 1.04 | 0.92 | 0.390 |
| Sabae | | 1.70 | 2.24 | 0.552 |
| Saijō | | 0.75 | 1.36 | 0.316 |
| Saiki | | 0.34 | 0.76 | 0.189 |
| Sakura | | 1.20 | 1.34 | 0.453 |
| Sanda | | 2.00 | 0.89 | 0.809 |
| Sano | | 1.46 | 1.09 | 0.449 |
| Sanuki | | 0.96 | 0.71 | 0.259 |
| Sasayama | | 1.30 | 1.36 | 0.694 |
| Satsuma | Kagoshima | 1.59 | 8.56 | 0.546 |
| Sekiyado | | 1.47 | 1.01 | 0.437 |
| Sendai | | 1.45 | 3.79 | 0.331 |
| Shibamura | Kaijū | 1.57 | 2.35 | 0.818 |
| Shibata | | 0.78 | 1.47 | 0.396 |
| Shichinohe | Morioka shinden | 0.78 | 0.49 | 0.121 |
| Shiiya | | 0.95 | 1.05 | 0.433 |
| Shimabara | | 0.45 | 0.80 | 0.272 |
| Shimodate | | 2.00 | 2.61 | 0.715 |
| Shimotsuma | | 1.54 | 1.28 | 0.271 |
| Shinjō | | 1.77 | 2.70 | 0.531 |
| Shishido | | 1.77 | 1.59 | 0.273 |
| Shōnai | Tsuruoka, Ōizumi | 1.55 | 5.46 | 0.893 |
| Sōma | Nakamura | 1.46 | 5.39 | 0.639 |
| Sonobe | | 1.17 | 1.33 | 0.460 |
| Suwa | Takashima | 0.77 | 1.45 | 0.269 |
| Suzaka | | 1.21 | 2.09 | 0.417 |
| Tahara | | 0.90 | 0.90 | 0.270 |
| Taira | Iwakitaira | 2.33 | 3.96 | 0.602 |
| Takada | | 0.99 | 1.21 | 0.275 |
| Takamatsu | | 0.75 | 1.47 | 0.282 |
| Takanabe | | 1.85 | 4.23 | 0.457 |
| Takaoka | | 1.53 | 1.22 | 0.433 |
| Takasaki | | 0.98 | 1.10 | 0.360 |
| Takatomi | Iwataki | 1.70 | 1.43 | 0.482 |
| Takatō | | 0.78 | 1.15 | 0.279 |
| Takatori | | 1.37 | 2.45 | 0.645 |

*Table A1, continued*

| Domain | Variant names | Assessed output (*kusadaka*) per commoner in *koku* | Retainers per 100 commoners | Tax burden (*gendaka*) per commoner in *koku* |
|---|---|---|---|---|
| Takatsuki | | 0.79 | 1.18 | 0.408 |
| Tako | | 1.96 | 1.56 | 0.380 |
| Tanakura | | 2.30 | 2.10 | 0.341 |
| Tannan | | 1.41 | 1.79 | 0.843 |
| Tanokuchi | Tatsuoka | 1.30 | 1.46 | 0.409 |
| Tateyama | | 0.53 | 0.42 | 0.150 |
| Tatsuno | | 1.15 | 1.19 | 0.613 |
| Tendō | | 1.76 | 2.26 | 0.544 |
| Toba | | 0.64 | 0.72 | 0.258 |
| Tokushima | | 0.65 | 1.06 | 0.304 |
| Tokuyama | Kudamatsu | 1.37 | 2.32 | 0.424 |
| Tosa | Kōchi | 1.11 | 2.29 | 0.556 |
| Tottori | Inshū | 1.30 | 2.02 | 0.479 |
| Toyama | | 1.64 | 3.64 | 0.681 |
| Toyooka | | 0.89 | 1.07 | 0.341 |
| Tsu | Anotsu | 1.34 | 0.73 | 0.574 |
| Tsuchiura | | 1.53 | 1.33 | 0.369 |
| Tsurumaki | | 1.02 | 0.75 | 0.369 |
| Tsuruta | | 1.30 | 3.32 | 0.430 |
| Tsuwano | | 1.18 | 2.42 | 0.441 |
| Tsuyama | | 1.08 | 1.71 | 0.447 |
| Ueda | | 1.05 | 1.39 | 0.394 |
| Ushiku | | 1.41 | 1.30 | 0.437 |
| Usuki | | 0.71 | 1.78 | 0.499 |
| Utsunomiya | | 1.66 | 1.70 | 0.334 |
| Uwajima | | 0.64 | 0.92 | 0.336 |
| Wakayama | Kii, Kishū | 1.14 | 2.25 | 0.592 |
| Yagyū | | 1.72 | 3.03 | 0.994 |
| Yamaga | | 1.62 | 0.98 | 0.407 |
| Yamagami | | 1.46 | 1.24 | 0.526 |
| Yamazaki | | 1.22 | 2.43 | 0.803 |
| Yanagawa | | 1.42 | 2.29 | 0.641 |
| Yanagimoto | | 1.69 | 2.68 | 1.110 |
| Yodo | | 1.70 | 1.70 | 0.655 |
| Yoita | | 1.03 | 1.44 | 0.343 |
| Yonezawa | | 3.23 | 6.77 | 0.970 |
| Yoshida | | 0.60 | 1.47 | 0.275 |
| Yoshida | Toyohashi | 1.27 | 1.35 | 0.369 |
| Yunagaya | | 2.13 | 1.63 | 0.444 |
| Yūki | | 1.55 | 1.28 | 0.280 |
| Zeze | | 1.67 | 0.53 | 0.739 |

NOTE: Domain names follow Kodama and Kitajima, eds., *Hanshi sōran*. Where a name is used by more than one domain, I have also listed the province.

TABLE A2

*Data for Prefectures, 1869–74*

| Prefecture | Commoners | Stipended retainers | Population ratio | Taxation percommoner in *koku* | Output per capita in *yen* |
|---|---|---|---|---|---|
| Akita | 454,339 | 8,529 | 1.88 | 0.13 | 11.45 |
| Aomori | 256,371 | 4,789 | 1.87 | 0.59 | 12.26 |
| Fukuoka | 333,883 | 7,623 | 2.28 | 0.76 | 17.14 |
| Hiroshima | 850,193 | 8,065 | 0.95 | 0.30 | 9.76 |
| Hōjō | 147,806 | 2,927 | 1.98 | 0.45 | 18.47 |
| Ishikawa | 1,047,359 | 16,425 | 1.57 | 0.63 | 6.35 |
| Kōchi | 445,353 | 10,180 | 2.29 | 0.56 | 12.78 |
| Kokura | 187,206 | 5,494 | 2.93 | 0.71 | 16.07 |
| Mizuma | 336,561 | 5,899 | 1.75 | 0.59 | 11.35 |
| Myōtō | 1,071,300 | 12,870 | 1.20 | 0.29 | 12.67 |
| Okitama | 88,127 | 5,963 | 6.77 | 0.97 | 25.25 |
| Sakata | 98,213 | 4,718 | 4.80 | 0.81 | 21.71 |
| Shirakawa | 637,379 | 10,372 | 1.63 | 0.63 | 10.92 |
| Tottori | 329,620 | 6,666 | 2.02 | 0.48 | 9.09 |
| Wakayama | 585,406 | 12,013 | 2.05 | 0.53 | 8.40 |
| Yamaguchi | 729,289 | 15,757 | 2.16 | 0.47 | 21.45 |

NOTE: Taxation refers to all government income other than gifts or loans, and thus includes revenue from government enterprises. Taxation is measured in *koku* per capita, and the population ratio is stipends per 100 commoners. Output is production per capita in *koku* converted at 8 *yen* = 1 *koku*. Revenue and commoner population figures are based on 1864–68 five-year averages. Stipends are for 1871. Production figures are from 1874. Domains are aggregated into prefectures based on the format in Table A3. For data sources, see pp. 213–15.

TABLE A3
*Domain to Prefecture Aggregation Scheme*

| Prefecture | Han |
|---|---|
| Akita | Kubota, Akita shinden, Honjoμ, Yajima, and Kameda |
| Aomori | Hirosaki, Shichinoe, Hachinoe, Kuroishi, and Tonami |
| Fukuoka | Fukuoka and Akizuki |
| Hiroshima | Hiroshima |
| Hōjō | Tsuyama, Hamada, and Katsuyama |
| Ishikawa | Kanazawa and Daijōji |
| Kōchi | Kōchi |
| Kokura | Nakatsu, Kokura, and Kokura shinden |
| Mizuma | Yanagawa, Kurume, and Shimote |
| Myōtō | Tokushima, Takamatsu, and Marugame |
| Okitama | Yonezawa |
| Sakata | Shōnai and Matsumine |
| Shirakawa | Kumamoto and Hitokichi |
| Tottori | Tottori |
| Wakayama | Wakayama, Tanabe, and Niimiya |
| Yamaguchi | Tokuyama, Yamaguchi, Iwakuni, Kiyomatsu, and Toyoura |

NOTE: Based on Takayanagi and Takeuchi, eds., *Kadokawa Nihonshi jiten*, pp. 1271–78, and Nihonshi yōgō jiten henshū iinkai, ed., *Nihonshi yōgō jiten*, pp. 847–78.

TABLE A4
*Regression Parameters for Domains*

The dependent variable is the natural logarithm of taxation for all models.

| | | | Regression coefficients ($\beta$) | | |
|---|---|---|---|---|---|
| Adjusted $R^2$ | F | N | ln (output) | ln (population ratio) | Intercept |
| 44.2% | 182 | 230 | 0.73<br>$t = 13.52$ | | -0.95<br>$t = -42.01$ |
| 38.9% | 145 | 227 | | 0.50<br>$t = 12.03$ | -1.03<br>$t = -36.39$ |
| 54.5% | 136 | 227 | 0.51<br>$t = 8.84$ | 0.30<br>$t = 7.15$ | -1.04<br>$t = -42.59$ |

NOTE: Taxation refers to all government income other than gifts or loans, and thus includes revenue from government enterprises. Taxation is measured in *koku* per capita, population ratio is stipends per 100 commoners, and output is assessed output (*kusadaka*) per capita in *koku*. Revenue, output, and commoner population figures are based on 1864–68 five-year averages. Stipends are for 1871. For data sources and details, see pp. 213–15.

## TABLE A5
### Regression Parameters for Prefectures

The dependent variable is the natural logarithm of taxation for all models.

| Adjusted $R^2$ | F | N | ln (output) | ln (population ratio) | Intercept |
|---|---|---|---|---|---|
| 3.7% | 1.58 | 16 | 0.40<br>$t = 1.26$ | | -0.87<br>$t = -4.42$ |
| 30.3% | 7.52 | 16 | | 0.60<br>$t = 2.74$ | -1.12<br>$t = -5.85$ |
| 36.4% | 3.72 | 16 | -0.21<br>$t = -0.54$ | 0.71<br>$t = -2.32$ | -1.10<br>$t = -5.54$ |

Regression coefficients ($\beta$)

NOTE: Taxation refers to all government income other than gifts or loans, and thus includes revenue from government enterprises. Taxation is measured in *koku* per capita, population ratio is stipends per 100 commoners, and output is assessed output (*kusadaka*) per capita in *koku*. Revenue, output, and commoner population figures are based on 1864–68 five-year averages. Stipends are for 1871. For data sources and details, see pp. 213–15.

# Glossary

| | | |
|---|---|---|
| aiba yakusho | 藍場役所 | Indigo office. |
| aidama yokomeyaku | 藍玉横目役 | Indigo cube inspector. |
| aikata bugyō | 藍方奉行 | Indigo magistrate. |
| aikata daikansho | 藍方代官所 | Indigo intendant's office. |
| bakuhan | 幕藩 | The shogunate and the domains. |
| bakuhan kokka | 幕藩国家 | *Bakuhan* state. |
| bakuhan taisei | 幕藩体制 | *Bakuhan* order. |
| daikan | 代官 | Intendant. Commonly a samurai official who administered a rural district, usually by supervising village headmen. |
| daikōgi | 大公儀 | "Great public authority." A contemporary term for the shogunate. |
| dochaku | 土着 | Resettlement of samurai in the countryside. A policy attempted in Hirosaki between 1784 and 1798. |
| fudai | 譜代 | Vassal. Used in the term *fudai daimyō* to designate the class of daimyo eligible for important shogunal offices. |
| fukugō kokka | 複合国家 | "Compound state." A term coined by Mizubayashi Takeshi to describe the multiple sites of power in the Tokugawa order. |

| | | |
|---|---|---|
| fushin bugyō | 普請奉行 | Magistrate of corvée or magistrate of construction. |
| gendaka | 現高 | Domain revenue. |
| genin | 下人 | A subservient agricultural tenure. |
| gōshi | 郷士 | Rural samurai. Such samurai were usually engaged in by-employments. |
| gundaisho | 郡代所 | Office of rural affairs. |
| han | 藩 | Daimyo domain. A term in common use only since the Meiji Restoration. |
| hankoku han'ei | 半石半永 | A system of "half rice, half copper" tax payments used in Yonezawa. |
| hatamoto | 旗本 | Liege vassal (lit., "bannerman"). Shogunal retainers with landed fiefs smaller than 10,000 koku. |
| hatamotoryō | 旗本領 | Liege vassal holding. |
| heinō bunri | 兵農分離 | The separation of samurai and farmer. A term used by historians to refer to the urbanization of the retainer population in the seventeenth century. |
| hōdaka | 封高 | Investiture; the official size of a daimyo's holdings, also known as *omotedaka*. Cf. *uchidaka* and *kusadaka*. |
| hōkō minarai | 奉公見習 | Apprentice page, a personal attendant to a daimyo. |
| hōkōnin | 奉公人 | A servant or vassal. |
| honbyakushō keiei | 本百姓経営 | Farming by small independent cultivators. |
| honkunimochi | 本国持 | "True country holders." A reference to the ten elite daimyo families. |
| hōroku | 俸禄 | A retainer salary. |
| hyōfu | 標符 | A rationing coupon used in Hirosaki in the 1750s. |
| inzūyakusho | 員数役所 | Survey office. |
| itomono oshimari ton'ya | 糸物御締問屋 | Cartel of silk cloth wholesalers. |

| | | |
|---|---|---|
| iutsurinin | 居移人 | "Migrants." A term used in Hirosaki to describe displaced farmers engaged in government-sponsored land reclamation. |
| jikata chigyō | 地方知行 | Landed fief. |
| jinsei | 仁政 | "Benevolent rule." |
| jōmen | 定免 | A system of fixed tax (*nengu*) assessments. |
| junkokushu | 准国主 | "Quasi-country lords." |
| kabunakama | 株仲間 | Guild or cartel. |
| kaihatsuyaku | 開発役 | Director of land development. |
| kamadome | 鎌留 | Lit., "stop the scythe." The practice of prohibiting the harvest until back taxes were paid. |
| kamon | 家門 | Collateral houses of the Tokugawa line. |
| kan'i | 官位 | Court rank. |
| kanjō bugyō | 勘定奉行 | Magistrate of the exchequer, a high-ranking position in domain politics. |
| kanjōyaku | 勘定役 | Office of the exchequer. |
| karō | 家老 | "House elder." Domain elder, a powerful senior position in the most domain administrations. |
| kemi | 検見 | A system of regular tax assessments designed to record fluctuations and increases in output. |
| kikokunin | 帰国人 | "Repatriates." A term used in Hirosaki to describe displaced farmers engaged in government-sponsored land reclamation. |
| kimoiri | 肝煎 | A village headman. More rarely, an inspector or investigator. |
| kinju | 近習 | Personal attendant to a noble. A term often used in titles such as *kinju ishi* (personal physician) and *kinju koshō* (personal secretary). |
| kirimai chigyō | 切米 | An alternative term for *kuramai chigyō*. |

| | | |
|---|---|---|
| kitte | 切手 | A coupon or promissory note. |
| kochigyō | 小知行 | Lit., "little fief." Fiefs granted by Hiro-saki domain in the early seventeenth century to encourage land development. The most common *kochigyō* holders were low-ranking, low-income retainers who lived on the land they reclaimed. Many were also working farmers. |
| kōgi | 公儀 | "Public authority." Used in the Toku-gawa era to refer to either the shogunate or a great domain. |
| kokka | 国家 | "State." In early modern Japan, a large political unit, such as a great domain. |
| koku | 国 | "Country." In early modern Japan, a term used to refer to domains, prefec-tures, and countries. |
| kokueki | 国益 | "National" prosperity or "national" interest. |
| kokuō | 国王 | "King." Used in the Tokugawa era to refer to the shogun. |
| kokuon | 国恩 | Debt or obligation to one's "country." |
| kokusan kaijo | 国産会所 | Domain commodity agency. |
| kokushu | 国主 | "Country lord," a great daimyo. |
| kokutai | 国体 | National polity, or, more literally, the "body politic." In the early modern era *kokutai* could refer to the polity of an individual domain. Since the late nine-teenth century, however, the term has re-ferred almost exclusively to the imperial body politic, or the emperor-centered Japanese state. |
| komononari | 小物成 | Taxes, generally used for levies other than *nengu*. |
| konando | 小納戸 | A lord's privy purse, a treasury used for personal expenses. |
| konandoyaku | 小納戸役 | Valet, a personal attendant to a daimyo. |
| kōri bugyō | 郡奉行 | District magistrate. |

| | | |
|---|---|---|
| koshō | 小姓 | Secretary, a personal attendant to a daimyo. |
| koshō gashira | 小姓頭 | Lead secretary. |
| kunimochi nami | 国持並 | "Country-holding quality." |
| kuramai | 蔵米 | Lit., "treasury rice." A samurai stipend, commonly paid in rice. |
| kuramai chigyō | 蔵米知行 | Stipended fief. Retainers with *kuramai chigyō* were paid out of the domain treasury, but their income was legally associated with a specific parcel. |
| kusadaka | 草高 | Investiture; the actual size of a daimyo's holdings, also known as *uchidaka*. Cf. *omotedaka* and *hōdaka*. |
| machi bugyō | 町奉行 | City magistrate. |
| mekiki | 目利 | Assessor. |
| mononari | 物成 | Taxes, commonly used to refer to *nengu*. Also known as *hondo mononari* 本途物成. |
| motoshi | 元司 | General overseer. |
| nago | 名子 | A subservient agricultural tenure. |
| nakagai | 仲買 | Jobber or broker, a middleman between producers and wholesalers. |
| narashimen | 平均免 | Lit., "Average rate." A system of adjusting tax rates on individual parcels of land to generate a specified rate for a larger fief or district. |
| nengu | 年貢 | Tribute, the primary tax of the early modern period. *Nengu* was assessed as a percentage of the annual harvest and was commonly measured in bushels of rice. But some domains allowed or demanded payment in other commodities, specie, or paper currency. |
| ōhiroma | 大広間 | "Great chamber." One of seven halls in which the shogun received daimyo. With rare exceptions, the most prestigious chamber for *tozama* daimyo. |

| | | |
|---|---|---|
| omemi | 御目見 | Lit., "honorable audience." A samurai rank including the privilege of an audience with the daimyo. |
| omotedaka | 表高 | Investiture; the official size of a daimyo's holdings, also known as *hōdaka*. Cf. *uchidaka* and *kusadaka*. |
| on no nushi | 恩の主 | "Lord of obligation." |
| osobayaku | 御側役 | Chamberlain. |
| rōjū | 老中 | Shogunal elder or council of elders. |
| rusuiyaku | 留守居役 | Chargé d'affaires. |
| ryō | 領 | Territory. |
| ryōbun | 領分 | Investiture or holding. |
| ryōchi | 領地 | Investiture or holding. |
| saiso bugyō | 裁訴奉行 | Magistrate of appeals. |
| sanbutsu kaijo | 産物会所 | Domain commodity agency. |
| sankin kōtai | 参勤交代 | System of alternate attendance. |
| sashigami | 指紙 | A form of fiat money used in Tokushima. |
| seinan yūhan | 西南雄藩 | The great southwestern domains: Satsuma, Chōshū, Tosa, and Hizen. |
| shihin | 四品 | Fourth court rank. |
| shinden bugyō | 新田奉行 | Magistrate of land development. |
| shinpan | 親藩 | A modern term for *kamon*. |
| shiokiyaku | 仕置役 | Domain executor. |
| shōnō keiei | 小農経営 | Farming by small landholders. Cf *honbyakushō keiei*. |
| shōya | 庄屋 | A village headman. |
| sōbaso | 相場苧 | "Market flax." |
| sukegō | 助郷 | Corvée and requisitions demanded along the national highway system. |
| taishin kunomichi | 大身国持 | "Great country holders." |
| tenbatsu | 天罰 | "Divine punishment." |
| tenryō | 天領 | Direct shogunal holding. |
| ton'ya or toiya | 問屋 | A whloesaler, usually based in Edo |

| | | |
|---|---|---|
| | | or Osaka. *Ton'ya* commonly operated within cartel-like associations that sought to limit competition among members and fix consumer and producer prices. In certain cases, wholesalers also participated in government-recognized merchant guilds, or *kabunakama*. |
| tozama | 外様 | "Outsider." Used in the term *tozama daimyō* to designate the class of daimyo excluded from shogunal office. |
| tsumugi ton'ya | 紬問屋 | Silk pongee wholesaler. |
| uchidaka | 内高 | Investiture; the actual size of a daimyo's holdings, also known as *kusadaka*. Cf. *omotedaka* and *hōdaka*. |
| udaijin | 右大臣 | Minister of the right. |
| uneso | 畝苧 | "Field flax." |
| unsōyaku | 運送役 | Distribution bureau. |
| yakuseki yakudaka | 役席役高 | Rank and stipend reforms of Hachisuka Shigeyoshi. |
| yanaginoma | 柳間 | "Hall of Willows." One of seven halls in which the shogun received daimyo. |
| yokomeyaku | 横目役 | Inspector. |
| yōnin | 用人 | Steward. |

# Notes

INTRODUCTION

1. Kasaya, *Shukun "oshikome,"* pp. 252–53.

2. Tahara, "Kinsei chūki no seiji shisō," pp. 303–4.

3. By "formal investiture" I refer to *omotedaka*. See Kasaya, *Kinsei buke shakai*, pp. 150–51, and the discussion to follow in the text.

4. Totman, *Early Modern Japan*, pp. 573–74.

5. Hall, *Government and Local Power in Japan*; McClain, "Failed Expectations"; McClain, *Kanazawa*.

6. Totman, *Politics in the Tokugawa Bakufu*; Bolitho, "*Han*," pp. 183–234.

7. Yoshikawa et al., *Ogyū Sorai*, in NST, 36: 299; see also McEwan, *Political Writings of Ogyū Sorai*, pp. 60–61.

8. My definition of political economy draws on Scruton, *Dictionary of Political Thought*, p. 359.

9. *Kokushi daijiten*, s.v. "Shinden kaihatsu." See also Kikuchi Toshio, *Shinden kaihatsu*, esp. pp. 223–25.

10. My definition of protoindustrialization is similar to Wigen's. See Wigen, *Making of a Japanese Periphery*, pp. 8–9.

11. For an overview of cartels, see Hauser, *Economic Institutional Change*, pp. 1–58.

12. For a discussion of the Keian proclamation, see Nakane and Ōishi, *Tokugawa Japan*, pp. 41–42. The original text may be found in Ishii Ryōsuke, *Tokugawa kinreikō*, 5: 242–48.

13. Bolitho, "*Han*," p. 215.

14. In this study I refer to sales outside the domain, as well as sales outside Japan, as "exports." Although nonstandard, this usage aptly reflects

the mercantilist attitude of many domain officials. It also reflects how sales across domain borders involved changes in currency, government regulation, and government authority.

15. Wigen, *Making of a Japanese Periphery*, pp. 1–21.

16. Curiously, the shogunate never produced a definitive list of "country holders." See Kodama, *Daimyō*, pp. 203–6.

17. For *gendaka* and *hōdaka* figures, see the Appendix.

18. Craig, *Chōshū in the Meiji Restoration*.

CHAPTER I

1. For the purposes of this study I define "modern state" as a political institution with exclusive sovereign power over its populace and effective means of exercising that power. In practice, the modern state is closely related to the nation-state. The modern state's extensive and exclusive control over its population is legitimized by the belief that the state is culturally linked to the nation and thus represents the intentions, desires, fate, or best interests of that nation. My approach here draws heavily on Tivey, "Introduction," and Gellner, *Nations and Nationalism*.

Modern federal systems, wherein government power is constrained by explicit systems of laws, fit this definition of a modern state. In the case of American federalism, for example, the federal government is constrained only by the Constitution. The ability of local states to contest federal power exists only within this totalizing and unitary constitutional system. Thus Texas challenges federal power under the federal constitution, not by asserting an independent claim to sovereign power. The premodern state is defined by the absence of such a coherent and totalizing framework for the division of power, not by the mere division of power. In the absence of a totalizing legal framework, the Tokugawa shoguns maintained multiple roles, serving, for example, not only as warlords but also as imperial servants.

2. *Koku* was a measure of volume, equal to 4.48 gallons or 180 liters. Because rice was used as a currency of account, investitures were also commonly measured in *koku*. A samurai with a fief of 40 *koku* held land with a putative yield of 40 *koku* of rice.

3. Waters, *Japan's Local Pragmatists*, pp. 40–43.

4. All daimyo, save a handful with special exemptions, spent alternate twelve-month periods in Edo and in their home territory. Because daimyo traveled in either the fourth or the eight month, they were in Edo every calendar year.

5. *Kamon* are sometimes referred to as *shinpan*, but this term was not used in the Tokugawa era. The *kamon* were subdivided into distinct groups based on their relationship to the Tokugawa line. For a discussion of the differences between *tozama*, *fudai*, and *kamon*, see Totman, *Politics in the*

*Tokugawa Bakufu,* pp. 110–30, 153–78; Kasaya, *Kinsei buke shakai,* pp. 139–50; and Bolitho, *Treasures Among Men,* esp. pp. 42–49.

6. For a useful overview of these issues, see Kasaya, "Bushi no mibun to kakushiki," pp. 179–224.

7. Shinmi, *Hatamoto,* pp. 1–3.

8. Kodama, *Daimyō,* pp. 203–6. See also Kikuchi Yamon, *Ryūei hikan,* 1: 427–30.

9. Katō Takashi, *Daimyō kakakusei,* pp. 118–20; Nakamura Takaya, "Daimyō no kenkyū," pp. 376–79.

10. Kodama, *Daimyō,* pp. 203–6; Kikuchi Yamon, *Ryūei hikan,* 1: 427–30.

11. Kasaya, *Kinsei buke shakai,* pp. 150–51.

12. Illustrations of different mansion gates can be found in Asao, *Nihon no kinsei 7,* p. 13. Alternate attendance processions are discussed in Kodama, *Daimyō,* p. 203.

13. For data on attainder and transfer, see Fujino, *Shintei bakuhan taiseishi,* appendixes 1 and 2. I define "large" domains as 100,000 *koku* or above.

14. Wigen, "Social and Spatial Divisons of Labor," p. 1.

15. Wigen, *Making of a Japanese Periphery,* pp. 9–10.

16. Yabuta, *Kokuso to hyakushō ikki no kenkyū,* pp. 11–32, 60–63.

17. Nishikawa and Ishibe, "Han senbaisei," pp. 268–70. These calculations use the 237 domains in the aggregate *han* data set described in the Appendix.

18. White, "State Growth and Popular Protest," pp. 1–25.

19. Toby, *State and Diplomacy,* 242 and introduction. Toby's emphasis on foreign policy is reminiscent of the *Primat der Außenpolitik* tradition of German historiography.

20. Schumpeter, "Crisis of the Tax State," pp. 5–38.

21. Tilly, "European State-making," pp. 3–83, esp. pp. 3–6, 70–71.

22. Migdal, *Strong Societies and Weak States,* pp. 3–5.

23. Ooms, *Tokugawa Ideology,* pp. 162–65.

24. Sasaki and Toby, "Changing Rationale of Daimyo Control," pp. 271–94.

25. See, for example, *GG,* 2: 80, 4: 130–31.

26. Berry, "Public Peace," pp. 237–71, quotation from p. 248.

27. Hall, *Government and Local Power in Japan,* p. 347.

28. Ooms, *Tokugawa Ideology,* pp. 162–93.

29. For an overview of the Japanese historiography and a discussion of the related terminology, see Sasaki, *Bakuhansei kokka ron,* 1: 1–95. A valuable recent discussion is Fukaya, "Bakuhansei kokka to wa dō iu kokka ka?" pp. 35–49.

30. Mizubayashi, *Hōkensei no saihen,* p. 279. Mizubayashi's strict division of daimyo as *fudai* or *tozama* is arguably unwise. This distinction had

its origins in late-sixteenth-century politics and had lost much of its importance by the mid-Tokugawa era. But *fudai* houses still held a monopoly on major shogunal offices; hence Mizubayashi's notion that *fudai* daimyo were part of the Tokugawa state.

31. Hall, "Ikeda House," pp. 79–80.

32. The Motoki diary is from "Kadoya nikki hikae," reproduced in Fukui Yoshiyuki, *Awa no rekishi chiri* 2, pp. 157–364. For the reference to Ōshio Heihachirō, see pp. 261–64.

33. "Kadoya nikki hikae," pp. 210, 356. Because the ancient province of Awa and the Hachisuka domain of Tokushima were largely coterminous, it is sometimes unclear to which the Motoki referred. The unambiguous use of *kuni* to mean "domain" can be found in diaries from domains such as Yonezawa and Hirosaki, whose boundaries did not correspond to *ritsu-ryō* provinces. See, for example, Aomori ken bunkazai hogo kyōkai, *Eiroku nikki.*

34. Kasaya, *Shukun "oshikome,"* pp. 249–50.

35. Aomori ken bunkazai hogo kyōkai, *Tsugaru han kyūki denrui*, pp. 233–34.

36. GG, 6: 75–76.

37. Roberts, "Merchant Origins of National Prosperity Thought."

38. It is worth noting the limits of who was included in this "family" of Yonezawa subjects. The four classes did not include untouchables such as *eta* or *hinin*.

39. Jakobson, "On Linguistic Aspects of Translation," p. 236.

40. Nakamichi, *Nyūi Mitsugi zenshū*, 2: 308. For an overview of Nyūi's thought, see Kojima, "Thought of Nyūi Mitsugi," and Kojima, "Jugaku no shakaika."

41. I have relied here on the 1663 English translation of Caron's *Rechte Beschryvinge Van het Machtigh Koninghrijck van Iappan.* See Caron and Schouten, *True Description.*

42. Sheehan, *German History*, pp. 11–41. For the Metternich quotation, see Wehler, *German Empire*, p. 20.

43. Sansom, *A History of Japan*, p. 46. See also Reischauer, "Japanese Feudalism," pp. 26–48.

44. Kitajima, *Edo jidai*, pp. 74–82. For a detailed discussion of these issues, see Ikegami, *Taming of the Samurai*, pp. 151–378.

45. *Kokushi daijiten*, s.v. "Daimyō seishi."

46. Abe, "Bushi no kōshi no seikatsu," pp. 111–12.

47. For a consideration of the personal nature of shogunal authority, see Berry, "Public Peace."

48. Takayanagi and Ishii, *Ofuregaki Kanpō shūsei*, pp. 1–2.

49. Philip Brown, *Central Authority*, p. 24; Fujino, *Shintei bakuhan taiseishi*, appendix.

50. For a discussion of the *ie*, see Nakane, *Kazoku no kōzō*, esp. pp. 101–5. Also valuable is Murakami's provocative essay "*Ie* Society as a Pattern of Civilization," esp. pp. 297–339. This is best read in tandem with the critiques in *Journal of Japanese Studies* 11, no. 1 (Summer 1985).

51. For Mizubayashi's summary of his own work, see Mizubayashi, *Hōkensei no saihen*, esp. pp. 272–307.

52. Mizubayashi, "Kinsei no hō to kokusei kenkyū josetsu 2," pp. 1–63.

53. Kasaya, "Nihon kinsei shakai," pp. 35–61.

54. Ibid., pp. 35–61; Kasaya, *Shukun "oshikome,"* esp. pp. 273–79. See also Mizubayashi, "Kinsei no hō to kokusei kenkyū josetsu 1," and "Kinsei no hō to kokusei kenkyū josetsu 2."

55. Shizuo and Colcutt, "Development of Sengoku Law," pp. 101–24.

56. For discussion of *jinsei*, see Harootunian, *Toward Restoration*, pp. 62–65; Scheiner, "Benevolent Lords and Honorable Peasants," pp. 46–47; and Fukaya, "Hyakushō ikki," pp. 206–27.

57. Tahara, "Kinsei chūki no seiji shisō," pp. 301–3.

58. Hall, *Government and Local Power in Japan*, p. 403; Sasaki and Toby, "Changing Rationale of Daimyo Control," pp. 284–86. For the original edicts, see *HP*, 1: 264–65 and 335.

59. Ooms, *Tokugawa Ideology*, p. 56.

60. *NST*, 27: 31–32.

61. Tahara, "Kinsei chūki no seiji shisō," pp. 301–2.

62. Tsuji, "Bakuhan taisei no henshitsu," pp. 203–14.

63. See, for example, *GG*, 1: 46 (1623/5/16); 1: 50 (1626/5/22); 1: 51 (1626/6/19); and 1: 103 (1662/4/28).

64. See *GG*, 1: 93 (1657/2/–).

65. See *GG*, 1: 160 (1695/10/23).

66. Ogi, "Chūki hansei kaikaku," p. 27.

67. Ibid., pp. 25–26.

68. Nagao, *Awa ai enkakushi*, vol. 2, part 2. For details, see Chapter 3.

69. The definitive study of forced retirements is Kasaya, *Shukun "oshikome."*

CHAPTER 2

1. Fukaya, "Hyakushō ikki."

2. See Chapter 3.

3. Takahashi, "Tokushima han no chūki hansei kaikaku," pp. 188–89.

4. Scott, *Weapons of the Weak*, pp. 28–41.

5. *HN*, pp. 438–39.

6. See Hanseishi kenkyūkai, *Hansei seiritsushi no sōgō kenkyū*, pp. 495–97; 754–60.

7. Yoshida, *Okitama*, pp. 196–208.

8. Tokushima ken bussan chinretsujō, *Awa han minsei shiryō*, pp. 549–59.

9. Thomas Smith, "Land Tax in the Tokugawa Period."

10. A good, brief summary of both systems can be found in Kimura, *Kinsei no mura*, pp. 55–67.

11. For a good overview, see Philip Brown, "Practical Constraints on Early Tokugawa Land Taxation," pp. 369–401, or Ōishi, *Kyōhō kaikaku no keizai seisaku*, pp. 132–45. A recent neoclassical perspective is Iwahashi, "Tokugawa keizai no seidoteki wakugumi," pp. 85–128. A representative Marxist argument based on Saga domain is Nagano Susumu, *Bakuhansei shakai no zaisei kōzō*.

12. Fukushi, *Tsugaru heiya kaitakushi*, pp. 184–85.

13. Kimura, *Kinsei no mura*, pp. 67–68; Fujino, *Daimyō to ryōgoku keiei*, pp. 166–69. See also Thomas Smith, "Land Tax in the Tokugawa Period."

14. *YKS*, 2: 410–12.

15. See, for example, Yamaguchi and Sasaki, *Taikei Nihon rekishi 4: Bakuhan taisei*, pp. 420–52.

16. Horie, *Hansei kaikaku no kenkyū*, pp. 2–7.

17. Tōyama, *Meiji Ishin*, pp. 24–29.

18. The major study of *kokusan kaijo* is Yoshinaga, *Kinsei no senbai seido*.

19. The seminal study of this phenomenon is Thomas Smith, *Agrarian Origins of Modern Japan*, esp. pp. 108–200.

20. On peasant rebellion, see Walthall, *Social Protest and Popular Culture*; Walthall, *Peasant Uprisings in Japan*; Vlastos, *Peasant Protests and Uprisings in Tokugawa Japan*; and Bix, *Peasant Protest in Japan*.

21. See Chapter 3 and Watanabe, *Yonezawa han no tokusangyō*, pp. 68–70.

22. Theoretically, *nengu* might have encouraged a flow of capital from agriculture to manufacturing and trade, activities that were comparatively lightly taxed. Land remained a principal store of wealth because, in the absence of a banking system and a formal commercial code, land was the safest form in which to hold assets. More broadly, land was a source of status and political power in village society, giving it a value that transcended its simple economic value.

23. See Chapter 3.

24. *YKSS*, 4: 753.

25. See Chapter 3.

26. For a discussion of *ton'ya* and *kabunakama*, see Miyamoto and Uemura, "Tokugawa keizai no junkan kōzō," pp. 307–11.

27. Nishikawa, *Nihon keizai no seichōshi*, pp. 66–69. An excellent sur-

vey of currency issues is Yamaguchi, "Hansatsu shi kenkyū josetsu," pp. 1–13.

28. It is important to note that the Mino merchants sued the Akita merchants who had guaranteed the convertibility of the currency rather than the state of Akita. See Ono Masao, "Bakuhansei," pp. 312–14; Yoshinaga, *Kinsei no senbai seido*, pp. 27–28.

29. Miki, "Awa hansatsu kangae, I," pp. 93–94.

30. Yamaguchi, "Hansatsu shi kenkyū josetsu," pp. 1–13.

31. David Brown, "From Tempō to Meiji," pp. 101–6.

32. Kelly, *Deference and Defiance*, pp. 26, 37–40.

33. See Chapter 3.

34. Ono Masao, "Bakuhansei," pp. 317–18.

35. Najita, *Visions of Virtue*, pp. 249–52.

36. Totman, *Early Modern Japan*, pp. 518–20.

37. For an example, see Kasaya, *Samurai no shisō*, pp. 75–78.

38. Actual stipend systems were far more complex, and many domains employed more than one system at a time. Some scholars treat *kuramai chigyō* and *hōroku* as two distinct types of investiture. Although holders of *kuramai chigyō* did not have extensive rights over their holdings, their income was associated with a specific parcel of land. *Hōroku*, by contrast, were simply salaries. *Kuramai chigyō* thus combined elements of *hōroku* and *jikata chigyō*. See Morisu [John Francis Morris], *Kinsei Nihon chigyōsei*, esp. pp. 3–4.

39. The thesis that the disappearance of *jikata chigyō* marks the beginning of Tokugawa feudalism originated with Itō Tasaburō. For a good overview of this historiography, see Morisu, *Kinsei Nihon chigyōsei*, pp. 1–20.

40. Vlastos, *Peasant Protests*, pp. 8–9.

41. For a concise *kōzaha* interpretation, see Yamaguchi and Sasaki, *Taikei Nihon rekishi 4: Bakuhan taisei*, pp. 420–52.

42. Kanai, *Hansei*, pp. 59–75; or see Kanai's edition of *Dokai kōshūki*.

43. Sasaki, *Daimyō to hyakushō*, pp. 325–26; Suzuki Hisashi, *Kinsei chigyōsei no kenkyū*, pp. 470–71, 567–600.

44. Miki, "Awa han kyūchisei no tokushitsu," pp. 221–39; Sasaki, *Daimyō to hyakushō*, pp. 93–94.

45. Miyoshi, "Tokushima han ni okeru Inada ke kashindan no sonzai keijō," pp. 209–25.

46. Watanabe, *Yonezawa han no seiji to nōson shakai*, pp. 74–85; YKS, 2: 403–10.

47. Nishikawa, "Grain Consumption: The Case of Chōshū," p. 434; Kimura, "Hagi han zaichi kashindan ni tsuite," pp. 27–50.

48. Totman, *Early Modern Japan*, pp. 108–11, 153.

49. Thomas Smith, "'Merit' as Ideology in the Tokugawa Period," pp. 156–72; Huber, *Revolutionary Origins of Modern Japan.*

CHAPTER 3

1. Kadokawa Nihon chimei daijiten hansan iinkai, *Kadokawa Nihon chimei daijiten*, 6: 20–21, 39–41; Trewartha, *Japan*, pp. 395–98.

2. *YKS*, 2: 113–15.

3. *YKS*, 2: 681–84; Enomoto, "Yonezawa han," pp. 366–68.

4. Yoshida, *Okitama*, p. 119.

5. For details on the data, see the Appendix. The Meiji government reduced Yonezawa by 40,000 *koku* in 1868, indirectly increasing the population ratio. Yonezawa, however, had grown by 30,000 *koku* and roughly 15,000 people in 1866, when the shogunate put the adjacent Yashiro region under Uesugi control. The data used here are thus a good reflection of Yonezawa prior to 1866.

6. *YKS*, 2: 113–15, 2: 683–86.

7. *GG*, 1: 176–78 (1702/8i).

8. *GG*, 1: 187–88 (1704/9), 2: 58 (1719/11/5), 2: 76–78 (1721/7i).

9. Yoshida, *Okitama*, pp. 125–29; *YKSS*, 4: 342–43. Some sources list the 1702 cuts as 50 percent for stipends over 80 *koku*. See Yonezawa shishi hensan iinkai, *Yonezawa nenpyō: chū-kinsei hen*, pp. 158, 178.

10. Yoshida, *Okitama*, pp. 126–29. The 1791 budget is reprinted in Amakasu, *Yōzan kō isekiroku*, pp. 222–26. For summary and analysis, see Yoshida, *Okitama*, pp. 171–75, and *YKS*, 3: 204–7.

11. *YKS*, 2: 410–11.

12. *YKSS*, 4: 353–54; Yoshida, *Okitama*, p. 156.

13. Yoshida, *Okitama*, p. 156.

14. *YKSS*, 4: 355.

15. Population data are from Yoshida, *Okitama*, pp. 112–18.

16. For a discussion of these demographic issues, see Hayami, "Kinsei Okubane chihō jinkō," and Hayami, "Population Changes," pp. 290–301.

17. According to a 1771 budget, the registered yield of the domain was 181,021 *koku*: 91,257 *koku* of treasury land (*kurairichi*) and 82,524 *koku* of *jikata chigyō*. At the statutory *nengu* rate of 48 percent, treasury revenues should thus have been roughly 21,900 *koku* in rice and an equivalent amount in cash. Rice revenue, however, was only 16,141 *koku*, a shortfall of 26 percent. See *YKS*, 3: 186–87.

18. The figure of 6.96 years uses the total outstanding debt of 310,000 *ryō*, but even allowing for 200,000 *ryō* in bad debts, Yonezawa's debt was equal to 2.47 years' revenue. In combining gold and rice income, I converted gold to rice at 2.05 *koku* per *ryō*, the rate used in the budget. See

Amakasu, *Yōzan kō isekiroku*, pp. 222–26; Yoshida, *Okitama*, pp. 171–75; and *YKS*, 3: 204–7.

19. Ikeda, *Yōzan kō seiki*, pp. 1043–45. See also Yonezawa shishi hensan iinkai, *Yonezawa nenpyō: chū-kinsei hen*, p. 238.

20. Watanabe, *Yonezawa han no tokusangyō*, pp. 88–89. The regulations are reprinted, in part, in *YKSS*, 4: 497–99.

21. Villages were grouped into three categories: good-quality village (*jōson*), medium-quality village (*chūson*), or poor-quality village (*geson*). The wax fruit tax also had a surcharge of 5 percent. The cup for lacquer sap collection measured 5 *sun* by 5 *sun* by 2.2 *sun*, for a capacity of about 1,500 cc. Five *gō* is approximately 0.9 liters, or roughly ninety cubic centimeters. The lacquer sap tax could also be paid in copper or silver equivalents. Watanabe, *Yonezawa han no tokusangyō*, pp. 89–91, 110.

22. *YKSS*, 4: 351.

23. Yoshida, *Okitama*, p. 120; Watanabe, *Yonezawa han no tokusangyō*, pp. 88, 110. These figures refer to *yakuki*, or taxable trees. Later reforms allowed for *muyakuki*, or tax-exempt trees. The trees planted as part of the An'ei reforms, known as "one million trees," are also excluded.

24. Izuta, "Aoso to Mogami benihana," in *NSST*, 3: 43–44.

25. Watanabe, *Yonezawa han no tokusangyō*, pp. 66–68.

26. The monopsony rates for a bundle (180 *me*) of "field flax" (*uneso*) were 1 silver *me* for top quality, 0.8 *me* for medium quality, and 0.6 *me* for low quality. For a bundle (170 *me*) of "market flax" (*sōbaso*) the rates were 1.2 *me* for top quality, 1 *me* for medium quality, 0.8 *me* for low quality, and 0.4 *me* for poor quality. By the 1780s the market price of a bundle of flax in the Etchū area had risen to 3.63 *me*. See Watanabe, *Yonezawa han no tokusangyō*, pp. 69–70, and Yokoyama, "Yonezawa han ni okeru aoso senbaisei," pp. 11–12.

27. According to Nozoki Yoshimasa, by the 1780s one-fifth of the land planted in flax in the 1650s lay fallow. See *Juchiku kengi narabi shūhyō* (Recommendations on tree farming and animal husbandry with public commentary), in *YKSS*, 4: 753. Documents from Kamiisazawa village for the same period suggest that roughly 10 percent of arable land had been abandoned. Yokoyama, "Yonezawa han ni okeru aoso senbaisei," p. 15.

28. *YKSS*, 4: 753–54.

29. Watanabe, *Yonezawa han no tokusangyō*, pp. 69–70; Izuta, "Aoso to Mogami benihana," in *NSST*, 3: 50.

30. Yokoyama, "Yonezawa han ni okeru aoso senbaisei," pp. 16–17; *YKS*, 3: 13–14; Izuta, "Aoso to Mogami benihana," in *NSST*, 3: 50–52; *YKSS*, 16: 982–85. For a discussion of the ideology of "continuing as farmers," see Vlastos, *Peasant Protests*, pp. 14–20.

31. Technically the stipend was 3 *koku* 2 *ninbuchi*.

32. *YKS*, 3: 14; Kashin jinmei jiten hensan iinkai, *Sanbyakuhan kashin*

*jinmei jiten*, 1: 456. I use "secretary" for *koshō* rather than the established term "page" to better reflect the power of the office. Although the main duties of the *koshō* were clerical, their intimate and constant contact with the daimyo gave them considerable power. See Totman, *Politics in the Tokugawa Bakufu*, pp. 100–103.

33. *YKS*, 3: 14–16; Yokoyama, *Uesugi*, pp. 28–30.

34. *YKS*, 3: 10–12. For the distribution of stipends, see Yoshida, *Okitama*, p. 144.

35. Yoshida, *Okitama*, pp. 134–36; *GG*, 3: 43 (1754/3/23).

36. Yoshida, *Okitama*, pp. 135–36.

37. Ibid., pp. 137–38.

38. *YKSS*, 4: 220–21; *YKS*, 3: 12–13; Yoshida, *Okitama*, p. 137.

39. Ogi, "Chūki hansei kaikaku," pp. 19–21.

40. *GG*, 3: 57–58 (1757/8/2).

41. Yoshida, *Okitama*, pp. 139–41; *GG*, 3: 65 (1758/9/4).

42. For the secret memorials opposing Mori, see *YKSS*, 16: 197–207; for a summary, see Yokoyama, *Uesugi*, pp. 30–33.

43. Ogi, "Chūki hansei kaikaku," pp. 20–22.

44. Yokoyama, *Uesugi*, pp. 1–2.

45. Ogi, "Chūki hansei kaikaku," pp. 21–24; Yokoyama, *Uesugi*, pp. 25–26.

46. *YKS*, 3: 183.

47. Yokoyama, *Uesugi*, pp. 71–76.

48. *YKS*, 3: 191–93.

49. Yokoyama, *Uesugi*, pp. 9–10, 121–33.

50. *YKSS*, 4: 688.

51. Maruyama Masao, *Studies in the Intellectual History of Tokugawa Japan*, p. 141.

52. Kinugasa, "Setchū gakuha," pp. 217–18.

53. Ibid., p. 219.

54. Yokoyama, *Uesugi*, pp. 10–11.

55. Ibid., pp. 37–38.

56. Kinugasa, "Setchū gakuha," pp. 218–19.

57. Yokoyama, *Uesugi*, preface, pp. 1–6.

58. Bellah, *Tokugawa Religion*, pp. 112–13.

59. Yokoyama, *Uesugi*, pp. 132–33.

60. Kinugasa, "Setchū gakuha," pp. 221–22.

61. *YKS*, 3: 193–95; Yoshida, *Okitama*, pp. 149–50.

62. Yoshida, *Okitama*, pp. 153–54; Yonezawa shishi hensan iinkai, *Koshikata monogatari, Itsushūhen, Dokuhen, Oyakobanashi*, pp. 126–30.

63. Farmers were to plant 640,000 trees at 30 per *kama*, or hearth. Another 265,000 were to be planted on fallow land. See Watanabe, *Yonezawa han no tokusangyō*, pp. 94, 108–12; Ikeda, *Yōzan kō seiki*, pp. 189–93;

*YKSS*, 4: 743–44. For differing estimates of the number of trees planted, see Yoshida, *Okitama*, p. 153, and Watanabe, *Yonezawa han no tokusangyō*, pp. 112–13.

64. Watanabe, *Yonezawa han no tokusangyō*, pp. 111–15, 162; Yoshida, *Okitama*, p. 156.

65. *GG*, 3: 185–86 (1779/5).

66. Watanabe, *Yonezawa han no tokusangyō*, p. 96.

67. Yokoyama and Yoshinaga, "Kokusan shōrei," pp. 87–88; Watanabe, *Yonezawa han no tokusangyō*, pp. 97–98.

68. Ono Takeo, *Kinsei chihō keizai shiryō*, 5: 179–80.

69. *YKSS*, 4: 740–41; Ikeda, *Yōzan kō seiki*, pp. 191–92.

70. Watanabe, *Yonezawa han no tokusangyō*, pp. 109–11; Ikeda, *Yōzan kō seiki*, pp. 190–93.

71. Yokoyama, *Uesugi*, pp. 147–51; Ikeda, *Yōzan kō seiki*, pp. 303–6.

72. Yokoyama, *Uesugi*, pp. 138–47. Population data are from Yoshida, *Okitama*, p. 115.

73. Yokoyama, *Uesugi*, pp. 161–71.

74. *YKS*, 3: 196, 203; Yokoyama, *Uesugi*, pp. 179–82.

75. Sugihara, *Nozoki Taika ō*, pp. 319–20.

76. Ibid., p. 315.

77. Ibid., p. 524. The title *Jujin kengi* involves subtle word play. In classical Chinese, *jujin* is an agricultural allusion to the cultivation of human faculties. Nozoki here uses it in the sense of "growing" more people.

78. *YKSS*, 4: 753.

79. *YKSS*, 4: 753–54, 759–60.

80. *YKSS*, 4: 752.

81. Sugihara, *Nozoki Taika ō*, p. 315.

82. *YKSS*, 4: 769; Yokoyama, "Yonezawa han ni okeru aoso senbaisei," pp. 21–22.

83. *GG*, 4: 116–17 (1791/6), 128–30 (1792/11/28); *YKS*, 3: 208–9; Ikeda, *Yōzan kō seiki*, pp. 531–33; Yoshida, *Okitama*, pp. 181–83.

84. *GG*, 4: 130–31 (1792/11/28).

85. Watanabe and Ozawa, *Yonezawa orimono shi*, pp. 88–90; Ikeda, *Yōzan kō seiki*, pp. 528–29; Imai, *Yonezawa orimono dōgyō kumiaishi*, pp. 36–38; and *GG*, 5: 87 (1806/2).

86. Yoshida, *Okitama*, pp. 185–86. For taxes on textiles, see Watanabe and Ozawa, *Yonezwa orimono shi*, pp. 177–78. By the 1830s and 1840s the taxes on silk thread were roughly 2.5 percent. For prices, see Watanabe, *Yonezawa no tokusangyō*, p. 203.

87. Yoshida, *Okitama*, pp. 187–89, 194–208; *GG*, 6: 41–42 (1829/5/27).

88. Yonezawa shishi hensan iinkai, *Yonezawa nenpyō: chū-kinsei hen*, p. 238.

89. *YKSS*, 4: 343–46.

90. Watanabe and Ozawa, *Yonezawa orimono shi*, pp. 99–101; Yoshida, "Yonezawa no orimono," pp. 296–98.

91. *GG*, 4: 130 (1792/11/28); Ikeda, *Yōzan kō seiki*, p. 533.

92. *GG*, 4: 189 (1797/3/2).

93. Watanabe and Ozawa, *Yonezawa orimono shi*, pp. 111–12.

94. *GG*, 4: 131 (1792/11/28).

95. See, for example, *GG*, 4: 189 (1797/3/2) and 4: 221–22 (1799/3/21).

96. *Yōsan tebiki*, no. 603, Shiritsu Yonezawa toshokan.

97. Watanabe and Ozawa, *Yonezawa orimono shi*, pp. 134.

98. Ibid., pp. 133–36.

99. Ibid., pp. 131–32.

100. Ibid., pp. 131, 140–41.

101. Watanabe, *Yonezawa no tokusangyō*, pp. 170–72; *GG*, 4: 138 (1793/11/3).

102. Watanabe and Ozawa, *Yonezawa orimono shi*, pp. 142–43; Yonezawa shishi hensan iinkai, *Yonezawa nenpyō: chū-kinsei hen*, p. 211.

103. *GG*, 6: 251–52 (1796/7/9).

104. Weavers were to sell only to brokers authorized by the cartel. The cartel was allowed to charge sellers a 2 percent service charge. *GG*, 5: 178 (1822/11i), 6: 35 (1824/11/24); 6: 49–50 (1827/12/15).

105. Watanabe and Ozawa, *Yonezawa orimono shi*, pp. 189–90.

106. *GG*, 4: 221–22 (1799/3/21).

107. *GG*, 6: 251–52 (1796/7/9).

108. *GG*, 5: 87 (1806/2).

109. *GG*, 5: 48–49 (1801/6).

110. *GG*, 5: 100 (1807/7).

111. Nagao, *Ushi no yogore*, 3: 58.

112. Gellner, *Nations and Nationalism*, pp. 56–57.

113. *GG*, 4: 131 (1792/11/28).

114. Watanabe, *Yonezawa no tokusangyō*, pp. 192–93. Minamoto was technically a subinfeudated vassal of the Honjō family who administered the Ayukai office.

115. Watanabe, *Yonezawa no tokusangyō*, pp. 194–204.

116. Ibid., pp. 198–200.

117. Gabe, *Chihō junsatsu shifuku meisho*, 1: 650.

118. Yoshida, "Yonezwa no orimono," pp. 305–7.

119. Gabe, *Chihō junsatsu shifuku meisho*, 1: 650.

120. *YKS*, 3: 508–9; Yoshida, "Yonezawa no orimono," pp. 301–2; Watanabe and Ozawa, *Yonezawa orimono shi*, pp. 108–10, 132, 160–61.

121. Kadokawa Nihon chimei daijiten hensan iinkai, *Kadokawa Nihon chimei daijiten*, 6: 45.

122. *GG*, 6: 97–98 (2834/8/23).

CHAPTER 4

1. Kadokawa Nihon chimei daijiten hensan iinkai, *Kadokawa Nihon chimei daijiten*, 2: 19–22, 47–49.

2. Kudō, "Hirosaki han," in *Monogatari hanshi*, 1: 113–17; Miyazaki, *Aomori ken no rekishi*, pp. 124–39.

3. The domain's main holdings in Hirosaki were 45,000 *koku*, but Ieyasu rewarded Tamenobu with a 6-village, 2,000 *koku* investiture in Seta county, Kōzuke province. In 1655 the Hirosaki Tsugaru gave these holdings to the branch domain of Kuroishi, but half was seized by the shogunate because of succession problems in the Kuroishi Tsugaru lineage. In 1698 the shogunate and the Tsugaru arranged an exchange of holdings, and the Tsugaru's "external" holdings were reduced to a single village in Date county, Mutsu province. For details, see Hirosaki daigaku kokushi kenkyūkai, *Tsugarushi jiten*, pp. 105–6. For a discussion of the hierarchy of daimyo, see Kasaya, *Kinsei buke shakai*, pp. 138–57.

4. Kokuritsu shiryōkan, *Tsugaruke osadamegaki*, pp. 141–42, 175–77.

5. Matsuki, "Tsugaru han no shitsuju saibai," p. 113.

6. "Tsugaru han zaisei hikae," MSS GK 342–9, Hirosaki shi shiritsu toshokan, Hirosaki.

7. Nakamura Satoru, *Meiji ishin no kiso kōzō*, pp. 125–27.

8. Matsuki, "Tsugaru han no shitsuju saibai," pp. 113–25.

9. Kikuchi Toshio, *Shinden kaihatsu*, pp. 201–3. The value of the initial investiture was based on a 1592 cadastral survey supervised by Maeda Toshiie. See Fukushi, *Tsugaru heiya kaitakushi*, pp. 16–17.

10. Kikuchi Toshio, *Shinden kaihatsu*, pp. 201–3. Several sources substantiate this remarkable growth. According to a report submitted to the *bakufu* in 1645, newly opened land totaled 57,468 *koku*. HSS, 1: 101.

11. Some details of land reclamation in early Tsugaru remain unclear and the meaning of certain terms are disputed. The difference between the two types of reclamation, *kochigyō hadachi* and *okura hadachi*, remains particularly opaque. For a detailed and critical study, see Namikawa, "Hansei kakuritsuki," pp. 1–23. See also Miyazaki, *Aomori ken no rekishi*, pp. 149–51; HSS, 1: 98–101; Kikuchi Toshio, *Shinden kaihatsu*, pp. 201–3; Hashimura, "Tsugaru han no gen'ya kaikon no taisei," pp. 1–6.

12. For a detailed discussion, see Namikawa, "Hansei kakuritsuki," pp. 1–10.

13. *AKS*, 1: 662.

14. Namikawa, "Hansei kakuritsuki," pp. 8–9. See also Kanagi kyōdo shi hensan iinkai, *Kanagi kyōdo shi*, pp. 314–16.

15. This assumes that stipends of 30 *hyō* were granted for 30 *koku* of *shinden*.

16. *AKS*, 1: 862; Namikawa, "Hansei kakuritsuki," p. 17.

17. Namikawa, "Hansei kakuritsuki," pp. 15–19.

18. HSS, 1: 248–49, 306.

19. HSS, 1: 737–38, and appendix, pp. 55–68; Hirosaki daigaku kokushi kenkyūkai, Tsugarushi jiten, p. 377. See also HN, pp. 268–72; Kudō, "Hiroskai han," in Shinpen monogatari hanshi, 1: 100–103; and Kojima, "Thought of Nyūi Mitsugi," pp. 45–46.

20. Kojima, "Thought of Nyūi Mitsugi," pp. 35–37.

21. Ibid., pp. 39–42.

22. Ibid., pp. 42–43. Kojima translates tenka as "society."

23. "Shōka ridō," in Nakamichi, Nyūi Mitsugi zenshū, 2: 303–5. "Shōka ridō" was not written until 1789, but it accurately summarizes Nyūi's economic thought.

24. Nakamichi, Nyūi Mitsugi zenshū, 2: 304–15.

25. Ibid., 2: 347–48.

26. Kojima, "Thought of Nyūi Mitsugi," pp. 46–47; AKS, 2: 277, 291–93; and Kudō, "Hirosaki han," in Shinpen monogatari hanshi, 1: 103–5.

27. HSS, 1: 730; Aomori ken bunkazai hogo kyōkai, Tsugaru rekidai kirui, 1: 209.

28. Kojima, "Thought of Nyūi Mitsugi," pp. 46–48; HSS, 1: 727–31; Kudō, "Hirosaki han," in Shinpen monogatari hanshi, 1: 104–6.

29. Katō Tetsusaburō, "Hōreki no kaikaku," p. 16.

30. Aomori ken bunkazai hogo kyōkai, Eiroku nikki, pp. 200–202; see also HSS, 1: 730–31, and Kudō, "Hirosaki han," in Shinpen monogatari hanshi, 1: 104–6.

31. HSS, 1: 730–31; AKS, 2: 313–14; HN, pp. 312–13.

32. Hirosaki daigaku kokushi kenkyūkai, Tsugarushi jiten, p. 398; HSS, 1: 483–84. HSS reports an eruption of Mt. Iwaki in 1783 as well.

33. AKS, 2: 420, 2: 425.

34. Tsugaru traditionally took a census every six years.

35. "Ikensho—Mōnai Giō zonjiyorigaki," MSS GK 304.1, Hirosaki shi shiritsu toshokan, Hirosaki.

36. Ibid.

37. Ibid.

38. Ibid.

39. Ogyū Sorai, in NST, 36: 299; see also McEwan, Political Writings of Ogyū Sorai, pp. 60–61.

40. HSS, 1: 484; Imanaka, Sorai-gaku no kisoteki kenkyū, pp. 269–70.

41. AKS, 2: 445–46; Takimoto, "Kansei kaikaku," pp. 346–47.

42. AKS, 2: 484, 2: 495.

43. HSS, 1: 487–90; AKS, 2: 499–505.

44. Asakura, "Tsugaru han hanshi 'zaitaku' seisaku ni tsuite," pp. 179–80. The proposal is "Zonjiyorigaki," MSS GK 304-5, Hirosaki shi shiritsu toshokan, Hirosaki.

45. *AKS*, 2: 540–41.

46. *AKS*, 2: 556.

47. The "group of seven" had probably been stymied by high-level intransigence. The openly coercive policy began three days after Makino Sajirō was appointed *karō*. See *AKS*, 2: 557–58. See also Aomori ken bunkazai hogo kyōkai, *Tsugaru han kyūki denrui*, p. 253.

48. *HN*, pp. 510–11.

49. *AKS*, 2: 559.

50. In 1792/10, for example, the domain exempted *zaitaku* retainers from service in Hirosaki, but this is contradicted by a 1793/9 edict stating that no orders regarding service from *zaitaku* retainers had been issued, and retainers were therefore uneasy. For a discussion of such inconsistencies, see Asakura, "Tsugaru han hanshi 'zaitaku' seisaku ni tsuite," pp. 180–81.

51. *AKS*, 2: 561.

52. *AKS*, 2: 588. One *ninbuchi* was five *gō* per day or 1.8 *koku* per year; 40 *hyō* 3 *ninbuchi* was thus 21.5 *koku*.

53. Asakura, "Tsugaru han hanshi 'zaitaku' seisaku ni tsuite," pp. 173–79; Takimoto, "Kansei kaikaku," pp. 349–70; *AKS*, 2: 536–43. According to a 1792/8/22 edict, *kirimaitori* retainers who resettled to reclaim land continued to receive one-fourth of their stipends until their land was recognized as *chigyō*. Asakura argues that this payment and the right to receive reclaimed land as *chigyō* were special privileges allowed only *kirimaitori* retainers. Edicts issued on 1792/10/3 and 1792/12/3, however, extended this payment to *chigyōtori* retainers as well. See *AKS*, 2: 538, 542, 551–52.

54. *AKS*, 2: 536–37, 2: 566–67. See also Takimoto, "Kansei kaikaku," pp. 367–70.

55. Aomori ken bunkazai hogo kyōkai, *Tsugaru han kyūki denrui*, p. 253.

56. *AKS*, 2: 561.

57. *HN*, p. 512.

58. *HN*, pp. 512–13.

59. *HN*, p. 513.

60. *HN*, p. 496. The entry can be dated to 1792/9. See also p. 516.

61. Takimoto, "Kansei kaikaku," p. 374.

62. *AKS*, 2: 614–16.

63. *AKS*, 2: 670.

64. *AKS*, 2: 669.

65. *HN*, pp. 552–53. Akaishi Konojirō was allowed a stipend of 5 *ryō* and 3 *ninbuchi*, worth about ten *koku*. His father's stipend as *yōnin* had been 300 *koku*. The hereditary stipends of Kikuchi, Sasamori, and Yoshikawa were reduced in similar fashion.

66. *AKS*, 2: 735. See also Asakura, "Tsugaru han hanshi 'zaitaku' seisaku ni tsuite," pp. 186–87.

67. Hirasawa's plans are detailed in *AKS*, 2: 721–24.

68. *Hirosaki han shōshi*, cited in Fukushi, *Tsugaru heiya kaitakushi*, p. 88.

69. *HN*, pp. 487–88.

70. *HN*, p. 501. Although the exact date of the entry is unclear, it was written in 1793, prior to 1793/3/11.

71. *HN*, pp. 515–16.

72. *HN*, pp. 541–42.

73. *AKS*, 2: 721–24; Aomori ken bunkazai hogo kyōkai, *Tsugaru han kyūki denrui*, pp. 272–75; Mikami, "Hirasawa Sanemon," pp. 30–35.

74. Takimoto, "Kansei kaikaku," p. 372.

75. "Kaihatsu denbata toshi no mashidaka taito shirabe," Tsugaruke monjō, MSS 22B 199, Kokubungaku kenkyū shiryōkan shiryōkan, Tokyo.

76. "Tsugaru han zaisei hikae," MSS GK 342-9, Hirosaki shi shiritsu toshokan, Hirosaki. The budget calculates gold and rice separately. In my calculations, however, I combined both accounts converting at 1.2 *ryō* = one *koku*.

77. "Okonando jōnō kaneshirabe," Tsugaruke monjō, MSS 22B 1718, Kokubungaku kenkyū shiryōkan shiryōkan, Tokyo.

78. *AKS*, 2: 731–33. The Hirayama diary records a similar effort in Ubayachi, an area near the Hirayama's home village of Minato but some 65 miles from Tsukari. There settlers were given a three-year exemption from *nengu* and a five-year exemption from other additional levies. The reclamation allowance was eight *to* per *tan*, rather than six as in Tsukari. Corvée was also required and paid at one copper *me* per day. See *HN*, pp. 605–6.

79. Between the 1790s and the 1830s the price of rice varied between 20 and 30 silver *me* per *hyō* or 50 to 75 *me* per *koku*. One *koku* was thus worth between 58.65 and 87.98 silver *me*. Over the same period, 1,000 *mon* (1 *kan*) of copper was worth about 9 silver *me*. See Hirosaki daigaku kokushi kenkyūkai, *Tsugarushi jiten*, pp. 155–56, and Shinpo, *Kinsei no bukka*, pp. 171–73.

80. *AKS*, 2: 715–22.

81. *AKS*, 2: 798–99. The magistrate's animosity toward Hirasawa may also have been motivated by political rivalry. Revenue from Hirasawa's development efforts flowed directly into the daimyo's purse, circumventing the authority of the magistrate. Although this appears to have had little effect on the end use of the funds, it was obviously a political challenge to the magistrate. See *AKS*, 2: 721–22.

82. *AKS*, 2: 798–99; Mikami, "Hirasawa Sanemon," pp. 31–35.

83. "Tsugaru han zaisei hikae." The figure of one-half of revenue is an average of two estimates. The first estimate includes only the itemized debt of 46,000 *ryō* converted at 1.2 *koku* per *ryō*. The second assumes a larger debt of 71,000 *ryō* and a 1.52 *koku* per *ryō* conversion rate. The rate of

1.52 *koku* per *ryō* is the standard used in this budget, while 1.2 *koku* per *ryō* allows for the cost of shipping the rice to Edo for sale. The debt of 71,000 *ryō* takes into account interest payments for which no outstanding balance is specified in the budget. Annual revenue was 151,070 *koku*.

84. The budget also notes that expenditure on certain items was cut in light of a budget shortfall, but it does not itemize these cuts. I therefore used the original expenditure figures, which neglect these reductions.

85. *AKS*, 3: 15–16.

86. *AKS*, 3: 78.

87. Kudō, "Tsugaru sōdō," pp. 301–12. These debt figures seem exaggerated.

88. Ibid., pp. 307–8.

89. Ibid., pp. 313–20. Kasahara Hachirobei remained under house arrest until 1834 and died months after his release.

90. Kudō, "Tsugaru sōdō," pp. 316–32.

91. Ibid., pp. 320–25.

92. Ibid., pp. 325–33.

93. Aomori ken bunkazai hogo kyōkai, *Tsugaru rekidai kirui*, 2: 109.

94. Tsugaru Yukitsugu (1800–65), the eleventh daimyo of Tsugaru, was born the third son of Matsudaira Nobuakira, the daimyo of Yoshida domain and a member of the shogunal council of elders. In 1825 Yukitsugu was adopted into the Tsugaru house and became daimyo of the branch domain of Kuroishi.

95. "Oshōraku kakitsukedome," MSS *ko* 11 618, Hirosaki shi shiritsu toshokan, Hirosaki.

96. Aomori ken bunkazai hogo kyōkai, *Tsugaru rekidai kirui*, 2: 120–21.

97. *AKS*, 3: 92. The term *jitō* usually refers to a position in the Heian or Kamakura military hierarchy. Here, however, it is used to mean a retainer with *jikata chigyō*. See *Nihon kokugo daijiten*, s.v. "jitō."

98. For an overview, see *HSS*, 1: 790–810.

99. Miyazaki, *Aomori ken no rekishi*, pp. 213–14; *HSS*, 1: 822–31.

100. Aomori ken bunkazai hogo kyōkai, *Tsugaru rekidai kirui*, 2: 240.

CHAPTER 5

1. For an overview, see Kadokawa Nihon chimei daijiten hensan iinkai, *Kadokawa Nihon chimei daijiten*, 36: 19–23.

2. For tax and stipend data, see the Appendix.

3. Sekiyama, *Kinsei Nihon no jinkō kōzō*, pp. 136–40.

4. Murakoshi, "Daimyō kashin no jinkōgakuteki tokuchō," pp. 1–27.

5. Ōtsuki, "Awa ni okeru hansei kaikaku," pp. 128–29.

6. Amano, *Awa ai keizaishi kenkyū*, pp. 13–14.

7. Bandō, "Yoshinogawa karyūchi ni okeru aisaku no tenkai," p. 180.

8. Yasuzawa, "Kansei-ki Tokushima han no nōgyō to suisangyō," pp. 10–11.

9. Ibid.

10. Nakamura Satoru, Meiji ishin no kiso kōzō, pp. 125–27.

11. For a technical description of indigo production, see Gotō, "Awa ai."

12. For the 1770s the data are 552 silver kan in indigo revenue and 13,070 kan total income. See Yasuzawa, "An'ei-ki Tokushima han no zaisei shūshi kōzō," pp. 102–5, and Miki, "Hōken kenryoku no shōhin tōsei (jō): Awa ai no baai," pp. 93–94. The bakumatsu figures are based on an indigo office (aikata) budget for 1861 presented in Nishino, Awa ai enkakushi, pp. 336–44. Nishino estimates annual receipts as some 8,000 kan but the basis for his calculations is unclear: he seems to have confused total assets and annual revenue. The total revenue figure (206,359 koku) comes from the aggregate han data set; exchange rates are from Shinbo, Kinsei no bukka, p. 338.

13. HP, 3: 482 (no. 1447, 1709/3/1), 3: 659–61 (no. 1846, 1681/11/1); Miki, "Awa hansatsu kangae, I," pp. 89–99.

14. For the original regulation, see HP, 3: 647–48 (no. 1826, 1798/10/6). See also Ōtsuki, "Awa ni okeru hansei kaikaku," pp. 164–65; Yamada, Iinuma and Oka, Nihon nōsho zenshū, 30: 382–83.

15. Ōtsuki, "Awa ni okeru hansei kaikaku," pp. 132–33; Nishino, Awa ai enkakushi, pp. 15–18.

16. Nishino, Awa ai enkakushi, pp. 23–25. Earth could be used only if allowed by the buyer.

17. Hasegawa Akira, "Awa ai senbai," pp. 140–41. Cf. HP, 3: 446–47 (no. 1353, 1711/4/28).

18. Nishino, Awa ai enkakushi, pp. 27–37.

19. Nagao, Awa ai enkakushi, vol. 1, part 2; HP, 3: 631–35 (nos. 1793, 1795, 1796, 1797, 1700, 1800); Nishino, Awa ai enkakushi, pp. 30–37, appendix, pp. 5–6.

20. HP, 3: 631 (nos. 1793 and 1795); Nishino, Awa ai enkakushi, pp. 27–32, appendix, p. 4; Ōtsuki, "Awa ni okeru hansei kaikaku," p. 134.

21. Nagao, Awa ai enkakushi, vol. 1, part 2.

22. The sales-tax rate is a topic of some debate, since the term four bu can mean either 4 percent or 40 percent. In his influential 1955 study, Ōtsuki argued that the tax was 40 percent, but Miki and Amano treat the rate as 4 percent. Although many details of the pre-Meiwa tax system remain unclear, the surviving records favor Miki and Amano. See, for example, "Aisaku shishū ryakugaki," in Yamada, Iinuma, and Oka, Nihon nōsho zenshū, 30: 343–89. See also HP, 3: 634–35 (no. 1801, 1733/6/7; no. 1802, 1734/2/3); Miki, "Hōken kenryoku no shōhin tōsei (jō): Awa ai no baai,"

pp. 90–92; Amano, *Awa ai keizaishi kenkyū*, pp. 14–15; Ōtsuki, "Awa ni okeru hansei kaikaku," p. 135. The mandatory exchange of silver involved a fee of about 2 percent. See Hasegawa Akira, "Awa ai senbai," pp. 141–42.

23. *HP*, 3: 635–36 (no. 1803, 1735/4/3); Hasegawa Akira, "Awa ai senbai," pp. 140–43.

24. *HP*, 3: 635–36 (no. 1803, 1735/4/3; no. 1805, 1739/3/18); Nishino, *Awa ai enkakushi*, pp. 43–44.

25. The following account is based on *Myōzai gun Takahara mura hyakushō sōdō jitsuroku*, reprinted in Miyoshi, *Awa no hyakushō ikki*, pp. 68–82.

26. Miyoshi, *Awa no hyakushō ikki*, pp. 68–69. The *tsukubō* was a barbed, T-shaped spear, originally used by police to seize suspected criminals. By the late Edo era, the weapon was used more to intimidate and subjugate victims than to impale them.

27. Nishino, *Awa ai enkakushi*, p. 52.

28. *HP*, 3: 636 (no. 1807, 1758/5/4).

29. *HP*, 3: 637–38 (no. 1808, 1760/8/7); Amano, *Awa ai keizaishi kenkyū*, pp. 15–16; Hasegawa Akira, "Awa ai senbai," pp. 144–47.

30. *HP*, 3: 637–38 (no. 1808, 1760/8/7).

31. This and the following quotations are from Ogawa's proposal as reproduced in Nishino, *Awa ai enkakushi*, pp. 58–67.

32. Nishino, *Awa ai enkakushi*, pp. 61–67; Hasegawa Akira, "Awa ai senbai," pp. 146–47.

33. Nishino, *Awa ai enkakushi*, pp. 68–69.

34. *HP*, 3: 639–40 (no. 1811, 1766/7/6); Tokushima ken, *Gotaiten kinen Awa han minsei shiryō*, 2: 1854–55, 2: 1868. See also Hasegawa Akira, "Awa ai senbai," pp. 147.

35. Nishino, *Awa ai enkakushi*, p. 82.

36. Technically Magaributchi, lord of Kai (*Magaributchi Kai no kami*).

37. Nishino, *Awa ai enkakushi*, pp. 82–83.

38. Technically Udono, lord of Izumo (*Udono Izumo no kami*).

39. Nishino, *Awa ai enkakushi*, pp. 84–85.

40. Ibid., pp. 86–89.

41. Ibid., pp. 89–90.

42. Such a split was suspected by Tokushima officials. See Nagao, *Awa ai enkakushi*, vol. 2, chap. 6.

43. Hall, *Tanuma Okitsugu*, pp. 45–47, 154 n.73.

44. Hasegawa Akira, "Awa ai senbai," p. 148; Amano, *Awa ai keizaishi kenkyū*, p. 26; Nishino, *Awa ai enkakushi*, pp. 90–91.

45. The original *buke shohatto* of 1615 required that the shogunate be informed of "innovations" and marriages. Later revisions in 1617, 1635, 1663, 1675, 1683, 1717, 1746, and 1787 banned "innovations" entirely.

See Takayanagi and Ishii, *Ofuregaki Kanpō shūsei*, pp. 1–13; Takayanagi and Ishii, *Ofuregaki Hōreki shūsei*, pp. 1–13; Takayanagi and Ishii, *Ofuregaki Tenmei shūsei*, pp. 1–2.

46. Nagao, *Awa ai enkakushi*, vol. 2, chap. 6; Nishino, *Awa ai enkakushi*, pp. 90–91.

47. Nagao, *Awa ai enkakushi*, vol. 2, chap. 6.

48. *HP*, 3: 641 (no. 1814, 1767/9/13); Tokushima ken, *Gotaiten kinen Awa han minsei shiryō*, 2: 1868; Miki, "Hōken kenryoku no shōhin tōsei (ge): Awa ai no baai," pp. 104–8; Amano, *Awa ai keizaishi kenkyū*, pp. 22–23; Nishino, *Awa ai enkakushi*, pp. 108–11.

49. Miki, "Hōken kenryoku no shōhin tōsei (ge): Awa ai no baai," pp. 107–10; Takahashi, "Awa ai no seisan to ryūtsū," pp. 70–71; Nishino, *Awa ai enkakushi*, pp. 178–80. See also Hasegawa Akira, "Awa ai senbai," pp. 106–8; Amano, *Awa ai keizaishi kenkyū*, pp. 26–27. Some details of Tokushima's response to the shogunal directives are unclear, probably because the domain was again trying to evade a shogunal ruling.

50. Nishino, *Awa ai enkakushi*, pp. 111–21, 178–80; Takahashi, "Awa ai no seisan to ryūtsū," p. 71.

51. Kasaya, *Shukun "oshikome,"* pp. 16–19, 25.

52. Ibid., pp. 14–20.      53. Ibid., pp. 19–20.

54. Ibid., pp. 21–22.      55. Ibid., pp. 22–24.

56. Kamikawa, *Awa kuni saikin bunmei shiryō*, pp. 32–36; Kasaya, *Shukun "oshikome,"* pp. 24–25.

57. Kamikawa, *Awa kuni saikin bunmei shiryō*, p. 33; Ōtsuki, "Awa ni okeru hansei kaikaku," p. 140; and Kasaya, *Shukun "oshikome,"* pp. 33–38.

58. Kasaya, *Shukun "oshikome,"* pp. 34–42; Amano, *Awa ai keizaishi kenkyū*, p. 27; Ōtsuki, "Awa ni okeru hansei kaikaku," pp. 142–43.

59. Takahashi, "Tokushima han no chūki hansei kaikaku," p. 186.

60. Ōtsuki, "Awa ni okeru hansei kaikaku," p. 142; Takahashi, "Tokushima han no chūki hansei kaikaku," pp. 186–88.

61. Takahashi, "Tokushima han no chūki hansei kaikaku," 186–88; Yasuzawa, "An'ei-ki Tokushima han no zaisei shūshi kōzō," p. 102.

62. Takahashi, "Awa ai no seisan to ryūtsū," pp. 70–71.

63. Ibid., p. 73; Hasegawa Akira, "Awa ai senbai," pp. 152–53.

64. Nishino, *Awa ai enkakushi*, appendix, p. 11.

65. Ibid., pp. 166–71; Takahashi, "Awa ai no seisan to ryūtsū," pp. 73–74; Hasegawa Akira, "Awa ai senbai," pp. 150–51.

66. Nishino, *Awa ai enkakushi*, pp. 168–74.

67. Ibid., pp. 174–77; Hasegawa Akira, "Awa ai senbai," pp. 151–55.

68. Nishino, *Awa ai enkakushi*, pp. 177–80.

69. Ibid., pp. 180–85.

70. Nagao, *Awa ai enkakushi*, vol. 4, chap. 6. The letter is in the daimyo's name but was probably written by written by the Edo chargé d'affaires.

71. Nishino, *Awa ai enkakushi*, pp. 192–97.

72. Takahashi, "Awa ai no seisan to ryūtsū," pp. 74–75; *HP*, 3: 656–58 (no. 1844, 1830/12/11).

73. Nishino, *Awa ai enkakushi*, pp. 212–13.

74. Ibid., pp. 203–5.

75. Ibid., pp. 219–21.

76. Ibid., pp. 222–26.

77. Hasegawa Akira, "Awa ai senbai," p. 154; Nishino, *Awa ai enkakushi*, pp. 253–61.

78. Miyoshi, *Awa no hyakushō ikki*, pp. 126–27.

79. The Motoki diary is from "Kadoya nikki hikae," reproduced in Fukui, *Awa no rekishi chiri* 2, pp. 157–364. See also Matsumoto, "Bakumatsu ishinki ni okeru Awa no minshū undō," pp. 158–61.

80. "Kadoya nikki hikae," in Fikui, *Awa no rekishi chiri* 2, p. 261.

81. 1837/2/26 entry in "Hyōsuke nikki," published in Hirata chōshi shuppan iinkai, *Hirata chōshi*, 3: 921, hereafter, "Hyōsuke nikki."

82. "Hyōsuke nikki," pp. 921–22.

83. See Miyoshi, *Awa no hyakushō ikki*, pp. 148–53.

84. Ibid., pp. 16–17, 152–62.

85. Ibid., pp. 16–17, 24, 164–82.

86. Ōtsuki, "Awa ni okeru hansei kaikaku," pp. 136–39; Matsumoto, *Meiji ishin to Awa no kiseki*, pp. 65–72.

87. For details, see Miyoshi, *Awa no hyakushō ikki*, pp. 15–20.

88. Ibid., pp. 8–24; Kadokawa Nihon chimei daijiten hansan iinkai, *Kadokawa Nihon chimei daijiten*, 36: 136–37, 216–17, 249–50, 360–63. Population figures are from Yasuzawa, "Kansei-ki Tokushima han ni okeru chihō shihai kaikaku no tokushitsu ni tsuite," p. 26.

89. Matsumoto, *Meiji ishin to Awa no kiseki*, pp. 39–42.

90. Totman, *Collapse of the Tokugawa Bakufu*, pp. 52–54.

91. Matsumoto, *Meiji ishin to Awa no kiseki*, pp. 218–54.

92. For the *ee ja nai ka* and their course, see Matsumoto, "Bakumatsu ishin-ki ni okeru Awa no minshū undō," pp. 151–95, and Matsumoto, *Meiji ishin to Awa no kiseki*, pp. 179–210. *Geta* were the basest form of footwear and were never worn indoors. The revelers were thus defiling the homes in which they danced.

93. Matsumoto, *Meiji ishin to Awa no kiseki*, pp. 182–95.

CONCLUSION

1. Kasaya, "Nihon kinsei shakai," p. 58; Kasaya, *Kinsei buke shakai*, pp. 435–39.

2. Benecké, *State and Politics in Germany*, p. 161.

3. Nagao, *Awa ai enkakushi*, vol. 4, chap. 6.

4. Ōsaka, "Bakumatsu sōmō no kenkyū," pp. 120–21.

5. Ibid., pp. 135–36.

6. For the Satow meeting, see Satow, *A Diplomat in Japan*, pp. 261–64.

7. Matsuo, "Haihan chiken no seijiteki chōryū," pp. 9, 12 nn. 1–2.

8. For biographical information on Mochiaki, see Fraser, "Hachisuka Mochiaki," and Tokushima ken kōtō gakkō kyōiku kenkyūkai chireki gakkai, *Tokushima ken kyōdo jiten.*

9. Umegaki, *After the Restoration*, pp. 52–65. For data on new domains, see a reference such as Kodama and Kitajima, *Hanshi sōran.*

10. Niwa, *Meiji ishin no tochi henkaku*, pp. 14–18.

11. Ikai, *Saigō Takamori*, esp. pp. 180–216.

12. Maruyama, *Studies in the Intellectual History of Tokugawa Japan*, pp. 323–26.

13. Ibid., pp. 342–43. The original citation is from Tokutomi Iichirō, *Yoshida Shōin* (Tokyo, 1908), p. 87.

14. Geyer, "Historical Fictions of Autonomy," pp. 321–22. For the concept of imperialism as an internal process, see Eugen Weber, *Peasants into Frenchmen*, pp. 485–96.

APPENDIX

1. *Tōkei shūshi* no. 5 (January 1882): 9–22; no. 8 (April 1882): 96–107.

2. Nihon shiseki kyōkai, *Hansei ichiran*, 2: 473–77. Income figures (*gendaka*) included revenue from monopolies and monopsonies as well as direct taxes.

3. Although *eta* and *hinin* paid taxes and could thus arguably be grouped with commoners, I defined the commoner population as the *heimin* population. The inclusion or omission of *eta* and *hinin*, however, has no substantive effect on the quantitative conclusions.

4. Ōuchi and Tsuchiya, eds., *Meiji zenki zaisei keizai shiryō shūsei*, 8: 212–54. The government made allowances for *jikata chigyō* in the *han*, noting that "there are [retainers] who receive their benefice [*kyūroku*] from their *han* as land, and those who receive it as rice, gold and copper, or grain." See p. 283.

5. The copper conversion rate is an approximation using the 1867 prices in Shinbo, *Kinsei no bukka*, p. 173. Less than 0.2 percent of stipends were paid in copper.

6. The survey is reproduced in Fujiwara, ed., *Meiji zenki sangyō hattatsushi shiryō*, vol. 1.

# Bibliography

ARCHIVAL SOURCES

Hirosaki, Hirosaki shi shiritsu toshokan:
　Kudō Kōichi, "Hodai jijitsu hien" (K 215-14).
　Mōnai Giō, "Ikensho—Mōnai Giō zonjiyorigaki." (GK 304.1).
　"Okuni nikki" (TK 215-1).
　"Oshōraku kakitsukedome" (ko 11 618).
　"Tsugaru han zaisei hikae" (GK 342-9).
　"Zonjiyorigaki" (GK 304-5).
Tokushima, Tokushima kenritsu toshokan:
　Nagao Satoru. Awa ai enkakushi. 15 vols. 1908.
Tokyo, Kokubungaku kenkyū shiryōkan shiryōkan:
　"Kaihatsu denbata toshi no mashidaka taito shirabe." Tsugaruke monjō
　　(22B 199).
　"Okonando jōnō kaneshirabe." Tsugaruke monjō (22B 1718).
Yonezawa, Shiritsu Yonezawa toshokan:
　Yōsan tebiki (603).

PUBLISHED WORKS

Abe Yoshio. "Bushi no kōshi no seikatsu." In Shinji Yoshimoto, Edo jidai
　bushi no seikatsu, pp. 103–24.
Amakasu Tsugushige, ed. Yōzan kō isekiroku. Yonezawa, 1934.
Amano Masatoshi. Awa ai keizaishi kenkyū. Tokyo: Yoshikawa kōbunkan,
　1986.
Aoki Michio and Hosaka Satoru, eds. Sōten Nihon no rekishi: 5 Kinsei hen.
　Vol. 5. Tokyo: Shin jinbutsu ōraisha, 1991.

Aomori ken bunkazai hogo kyōkai, ed. *Eiroku nikki*. Michinoko sōsho, vol. 1. Repr. Tokyo: Kokusho kankōkai, 1983. Orig. publ. Aomori: Aomori ken bunkazai hogo kyōkai, 1955 (Michinoko sōsho, vol. 1).

——. *Tsugaru han kyūki denrui*. Michinoko sōsho, vol. 3. Repr. Tokyo: Kokusho kankōkai, 1982. Orig. publ. Aomori: Aomori ken bunkazai hogo kyōkai, 1958 (Michinoko sōsho, vol. 5).

——. *Tsugaru rekidai kirui*. 2 vols. Michinoko sōsho, vols. 4 and 5. Repr. Tokyo: Kokusho kankōkai, 1982. Orig. publ. Aomori: Aomori ken bunkazai hogo kyōkai, 1959 (Michinoko sōsho, vols. 7 and 8).

Asakura Yūko. "Tsugaru han hanshi 'zaitaku' seisaku ni tsuite." In Hasegawa Seiichi, *Hokuō chiikishi no kenkyū*, pp. 171–89.

Asao Naohiro, ed. *Nihon no kinsei 7: mibun to kakushiki*. Tokyo: Chūō kōronsha, 1992.

Bandō Toshihiko. "Yoshinogawa karyūchi ni okeru aisaku no tenkai." In Miyoshi Shōichirō, *Tokushima han no shiteki kōzō*, pp. 175–86.

Beasley, W. G. "Feudal Revenue in Japan at the Time of the Meiji Restoration." *Journal of Asian Studies* 19, no. 3 (May 1960): 255–72.

——. *The Meiji Restoration*. Stanford, Calif.: Stanford University Press, 1972.

Bellah, Robert Neelly. *Tokugawa Religion: The Values of Pre-Industrial Japan*. Glencoe, Ill.: Free Press, 1957.

Benecké, Gerhard. *Society and Politics in Germany, 1500–1750*. London: Routledge & Kegan Paul, 1974.

Berry, Mary Elizabeth. *Hideyoshi*. Cambridge, Mass.: Harvard University Press, 1982.

——. "Public Peace and Private Attachment: The Goals and Conduct of Power in Early Modern Japan." *Journal of Japanese Studies* 12, no. 2 (Summer 1986): 237–71.

Bix, Herbert P. *Peasant Protest in Japan, 1590–1884*. New Haven, Conn.: Yale University Press, 1986.

Bolitho, Harold. "The Bakuhan System." In John Whitney Hall, *The Cambridge History of Japan*, vol. 4: *Early Modern Japan*, pp. 128–82.

——. "The *Han*." In John Whitney Hall, *The Cambridge History of Japan*, vol. 4: *Early Modern Japan*, pp. 183–234.

——. "The Tempō Crisis." In Marius B. Jansen, *The Cambridge History of Japan*, vol. 5: *The Nineteenth Century*, pp. 116–67.

——. *Treasures Among Men: The Fudai Daimyo in Tokugawa Japan*. New Haven, Conn.: Yale University Press, 1974.

Borton, Hugh. *Peasant Uprisings in Japan of the Tokugawa Period*. Transactions of the Asiatic Society of Japan, vol. 16, ser. 2, 1939. Reprint. New York: Paragon, 1968.

Braun, Rudolf. "Taxation, Sociopolitical Structure, and State-building:

Great Britain and Brandenburg-Prussia." In Charles Tilly and Gabriel Ardant, *The Formation of National States in Western Europe*, pp. 243–347.

Brower, Reuben A., ed. *On Translation*. Cambridge, Mass.: Harvard University Press, 1959.

Brown, David Douglas. "From Tempō to Meiji: Fukuoka Han in Late Tokugawa Japan" Ph.D. diss., University of Hawaii, 1981.

Brown, Philip C. *Central Authority and Local Autonomy in the Formation of Early Modern Japan: The Case of Kaga Domain*. Stanford, Calif.: Stanford University Press, 1993.

———. "Practical Constraints on Early Tokugawa Land Taxation: Annual Versus Fixed Assessments in Kaga Domain." *Journal of Japanese Studies* 14, no. 2 (Summer 1988): 369–401.

Brunner, Otto. *Land and Lordship: Structures of Governance in Medieval Austria*. Translated from the 4th revised edition by Howard Kaminsky and James van Horn Melton. Philadelphia: University of Pennsylvania Press, 1992.

Caron, François, and Joost Schouten. *A True Description of the Mighty Kingdoms of Japan and Siam*. 1663. Reprint. London: The Argonaut Press, 1935.

Chihōshi kenkyū kyōgikai, ed. *Nihon sangyōshi taikei*. 8 vols. Tokyo: Tōkyō daigaku shuppankai, 1960–61.

Cooper, Michael, ed. *They Came to Japan: An Anthology of European Reports on Japan, 1543–1640*. Berkeley: University of California Press, 1965.

Craig, Albert. *Chōshū in the Meiji Restoration*. Cambridge, Mass.: Harvard University Press, 1961.

Crawcour, E. Sidney. "The Tokugawa Heritage." In William W. Lockwood, *The State and Economic Enterprise in Japan*, pp. 31–32.

Enomoto Sōji. "Yonezawa han." In Kodama Kōta and Kitajima Masamoto, *Shinpen monogatari hanshi*, 1: 357–94.

Fischer, Stanley. "Seigniorage and the Case for a National Money." *Journal of Political Economy* 90 (April 1982): 295–307.

Fraser, Andrew. "Hachisuka Mochiaki (1846–1918): From Feudal Lord to Businessman." *Papers on Far Eastern History* (Australian National University) 37 (March 1988): 93–104.

———. "Local Administration: The Example of Awa-Tokushima." In Marius B. Jansen and Gilbert Rozman, *Japan in Transition*, pp. 111–30.

Fujino Tamotsu. *Daimyō to ryōgoku keiei*. Tokyo: Shinjin ōraisha, 1978.

———. *Shintei bakuhan taiseishi no kenkyū*. Tokyo: Yoshikawa kōbunkan, 1975.

Fujita Teiichirō. *Kinsei keizai shinsō no kenkyū*. Tokyo: Yoshikawa kōbunkan, 1966.

Fujiwara Masato, ed. *Meiji zenki sangyō hattatsushi shiryō.* Vol. 1. Tokyo Meiji bunken shiryō kankōkai, 1959.

Fukaya Katsumi. "Bakuhansei kokka to wa dō iu kokka ka?" In Aoki Michio and Hosaka Satoru, eds., *Sōten Nihon no rekishi: 5 Kinsei hen,* pp. 35–49. Tokyo: Shin jinbutsu ōraisha, 1991.

———. "Hyakushō ikki no shisō." *Shisō* 584 (February 1972): 206–27.

Fukui Toshitaka. "Tsugaru han ni okeru shihai kikō no ichi kōsatsu." In Hasegawa Seiichi, *Hokuō chiikishi no kenkyū,* pp. 43–82.

Fukui Yoshiyuki. *Awa no rekishi chiri* 2. Naruto, Tokushima: Tokushima ken kyōikukai insatsubu, 1968.

Fukushi Teizō, ed. *Tsugaru heiya kaitakushi.* Goshogawara, Aomori: Goshogawara kōminkan, 1951.

Furushima Toshio. "Shosangyō hatten no chiikisei." In *NSST,* 1: 273–338, 366–77.

Gabe Masao, ed. *Chihō junsatsu shifuku meisho: Meiji jūgo-nen Meiji jūroku-nen.* 2 vols. Tokyo: San-ichi shobō, 1980.

Gellner, Ernst. *Nations and Nationalism.* Ithaca, N.Y.: Cornell University Press, 1983.

Geyer, Michael. "Historical Fictions of Autonomy and the Europeanization of National History." *Central European History* 22, no. 3/4 (September/December 1989): 316–42.

Gluck, Carol. *Japan's Modern Myths.* Princeton, N.J.: Princeton University Press, 1985.

Gotō Shō'ichi. "Awa ai." In *NSST,* 7: 61–93.

Grunfeld, Yehuda, and Zvi Griliches. "Is Aggregation Necessarily Bad?" *Review of Economics and Statistics* 42, no. 1 (February 1960): 1–13.

Hall, John Whitney. *Government and Local Power in Japan, 500–1700: A Study Based on Bizen Province.* Princeton, N.J.: Princeton University Press, 1966.

———. "The Ikeda House and Its Retainers in Bizen." In John Whitney Hall and Marius B. Jansen, *Studies in the Institutional History of Early Modern Japan,* pp. 79–88.

———. "Introduction." In John Whitney Hall, *The Cambridge History of Japan,* vol. 4: *Early Modern Japan,* pp. 1–39.

———. *Tanuma Okitsugu, 1719–1788: Forerunner of Modern Japan.* Cambridge, Mass.: Harvard University Press, 1955.

———, ed. *The Cambridge History of Japan,* vol. 4: *Early Modern Japan.* Cambridge, Eng.: Cambridge University Press, 1991.

Hall, John Whitney, and Marius Jansen, eds. *Studies in the Institutional History of Early Modern Japan.* Princeton, N.J.: Princeton University Press, 1968.

Hall, John Whitney, Nagahara Keiji, and Kozo Yamamura, eds. *Japan Be-*

*fore Tokugawa: Political Consolidation and Economic Growth, 1500 to 1650*. Princeton, N.J.: Princeton University Press, 1981.

Hanley, Susan, and Kozo Yamamura. *Economic and Demographic Change in Preindustrial Japan, 1600–1868*. Princeton, N.J.: Princeton University Press, 1977.

Hanseishi kenkyūkai, ed. *Hansei seiritsushi no sōgō kenkyū: Yonezawa han*. Tokyo: Yoshikawa kōbunkan, 1963.

Harootunian, H. D. "Late Tokugawa Thought and Culture." In Marius Jansen, *The Cambridge History of Japan*, vol. 5: *The Nineteenth Century*, pp. 168–258. Cambridge, Eng.: Cambridge University Press, 1989.

———. *Toward Restoration: The Growth of Political Consciousness in Tokugawa Japan*. Berkeley: University of California Press, 1970.

Hasegawa Akira. "Awa ai senbai shihō o meguru bakuhan tairitsu: Ōsaka shijō o chūshin ni shite." In Miyoshi Shōichirō, *Tokushima han no shiteki kōzō*, pp. 138–55.

Hasegawa Seiichi, ed. *Hokuō chiikishi no kenkyū*. Tokyo: Meicho shuppan, 1988.

———. *Tsugaruhan no kisoteki kenkyū*. Tokyo: Kokusho kankōkai, 1984.

Hashimura Hiroshi. "Tsugaru han no gen'ya kaikon no taisei." *Rekishi chiri* 35, no. 6 (June 1920): 1–14.

Hauser, William B. *Economic and Institutional Change in Tokugawa Japan: Ōsaka and the Kinai Cotton Trade*. Cambridge, Eng.: Cambridge University Press, 1974.

Hayami Akira. "Kinsei Okubane chihō jinkō no shiteki kenkyū joron." *Mita gakkai zasshi* 75, no. 3 (June 1982): 70–92.

———. "Population Changes." In Marius B. Jansen and Gilbert Rozman, *Japan in Transition*, pp. 280–317.

Hayami Akira, and Miyamoto Matarō, eds. *Nihon keizaishi 1: keizai shakai no seiritsu*. Tokyo: Iwanami shoten, 1988.

Henderson, Dan Fenno. "The Evolution of Tokugawa Law." In John Whitney Hall and Marius Jansen, *Studies in the Institutional History of Early Modern Japan*, pp. 203–29.

Hirata chōshi shuppan iinkai, ed. *Hirata chōshi*. 3 vols. (*jo, ge, bekkan*). Tokushima: Hirata chōshi shuppan iinkai, 1978.

Hirosaki daigaku kokushi kenkyūkai, ed. *Tsugaru shi jiten*. Tokyo: Meicho shuppan, 1977.

Horie Hideichi, ed. *Hansei kaikaku no kenkyū*. Tokyo: Ochanomizu shobō, 1955.

Huber, Thomas M. *The Revolutionary Origins of Modern Japan*. Stanford, Calif.: Stanford University Press, 1981.

Ikai Takaaki. *Saigō Takamori: Seinan sensō e no michi*. Tokyo: Iwanami shinso, 1992.

Ikeda Nariaki, ed. *Yōzan kō seiki.* Tokyo: Yoshikawa kōbunkan, 1906.

Ikegami, Eiko. *The Taming of the Samurai.* Cambridge, Mass.: Harvard University Press, 1995.

Imai Kiyoaki. *Yonezawa orimono dōgyō kumiaishi.* Yonezwa: Yonezawa orimono dōgyō kumiai, 1940.

Imanaka Kanshi. *Sorai-gaku no kisoteki kenkyū.* Tokyo: Yoshikawa kōbunkan, 1966.

Ishii Ryōsuke, ed. *Tokugawa kinreikō.* 11 vols. Tokyo: Sōbunsha, 1959–60.

Ishiodori Tanehiro and Takahashi Hajime, eds. *Tokushima no kenkyū 4: kinsei hen II.* Osaka: Seibundō, 1982.

———. *Tokushima no kenkyū 5: kinsei kindai hen.* Osaka: Seibundō, 1983.

Iwahashi Masaru. "Tokugawa keizai no seidoteki wakugumi." In Hayami Akira and Miyamoto Matarō, *Nihon keizaishi 1,* pp. 85–128.

Izuta Tadanobu, "Aoso to Mogami benihana." In *NSST,* 3: 43–72.

Jakobson, Roman. "On Linguistic Aspects of Translation." In Reuben A. Brower, *On Translation,* pp. 232–39.

Jansen, Marius B. *Sakamoto Ryōma and the Meiji Restoration.* Princeton, N.J.: Princeton University Press, 1961.

———, ed. *The Cambridge History of Japan,* vol. 5: *The Nineteenth Century.* Cambridge, Eng.: Cambridge University Press, 1989.

Jansen, Marius B., and Gilbert Rozman, eds. *Japan in Transition: From Tokugawa to Meiji.* Princeton, N.J.: Princeton University Press, 1986.

Judt, Tony. "A Clown in Regal Purple." *History Workshop 7* (Spring 1979): 66–94.

Kadokawa Nihon chimei daijiten hensan iinkai, ed. *Kadokawa Nihon chimei daijiten.* 49 vols. Tokyo: Kadokawa shoten, 1978– .

Kamikawa Yasuzō, ed. *Awa kuni saikin bunmei shiryō.* Tokyo: Kamikawa Yasuzō, 1915.

Kanagi kyōdo shi hensan iinkai, ed. *Kanagi kyōdo shi.* Kanagi, Aomori: Kanagi chōyakusho, 1976.

Kanai Madoka. *Hansei.* Tokyo: Shibundō, 1962.

———, ed. *Dokai kōshūki.* Tokyo: Jinbutsu ōraisha, 1967.

Kasaya Kazuhiko. "Bushi no mibun to kakushiki." In Asao Naohiro, *Nihon no kinsei 7,* pp. 179–224.

———. "Daimyō rusuikumiai no seido shiteki kōsatsu." *Shirin* 65, no. 5 (September 1982): 80–119.

———. *Kinsei buke shakai no seiji kōzō.* Tokyo: Yoshikawa kōbunkan, 1993.

———. "Nihon kinsei shakai no atarashii rekishizō o motomete." *Nihonshi kenkyū,* no. 333 (May 1990): 35–61.

———. *Samurai no shisō.* Tokyo: Nihon keizai shinbunsha, 1993.

———. *Shukun "oshikome" no kōzō: kinsei daimyō to kashindan.* Tokyo: Heibonsha, 1988.

Kashin jinmei jiten hensan iinkai, ed. *Sanbyakuhan kashin jinmei jiten.* 6 vols. Tokyo: Shinjinbutsu ōraisha, 1987.

Katō Takashi. *Daimyō kakakusei no kenkyū.* Tokyo: Kinsei Nihon jōkaku kenkyūjo, 1969.

Katō Testusaburō. "Hōreki no kaikaku to aru gōshō no shuki." *Mutsu shidan* 18 (April 1951): 7–14.

Kelly, William W. *Deference and Defiance in Nineteenth-Century Japan.* Princeton, N.J.: Princeton University Press, 1985.

Kennedy, Peter. *A Guide to Econometrics.* 2d ed. Cambridge, Mass.: MIT Press, 1985.

Kikuchi Toshio. *Shinden kaihatsu.* Tokyo: Shibundō, 1963.

Kikuchi Yamon. *Ryūei hikan.* 2 vols. Naikaku bunko shozō shiseki sōkan, vols. 5 and 6. Tokyo: Shiseki kenkyūkai, kyūko shoin, 1981.

Kimura Motoi. "Hagi han zaichi kashindan ni tsuite." *Shigaku zasshi* 62, no. 8 (August 1953): 27–50.

———. *Kinsei no mura.* Tokyo: Kyōikusha, 1980.

Kinugasa Yasuki. "Setchū gakuha to kyōgaku tōsei." In *IKNR* (*Kinsei 4,* 1963), 12: 199–232.

Kitajima Masamoto. *Edo jidai.* Tokyo: Iwanami shoten, 1993.

———, ed. *Oie sōdō.* Tokyo: Jinbutsu ōraisha, 1965.

Kodama Kōta. *Daimyō.* Tokyo: Shōgakkan, 1975.

Kodama Kōta and Kitajima Masamoto, eds. *Hanshi sōran.* Tokyo: Shinjinbutsu ōraisha, 1977.

———. *Monogatari hanshi.* 8 vols. Tokyo: Shinjinbutsu ōraisha, 1964–65.

———. *Shinpen monogatari hanshi.* 12 vols. Tokyo: Shinjinbutsu ōraisha, 1975–77.

Kojima Yasunori. "Jugaku no shakaika." In Kiichi Rai, ed., *Jugaku, kokugaku, yōgaku,* pp. 123–74. *Nihon no kinsei,* vol. 13. Tokyo: Chūō kōron sha, 1993.

———. "The Thought of Nyūi Mitsugi: Practicality and Reform in Tsugaru Domain." *Asian Cultural Studies* 19 (March 1993): 35–51.

Kokuritsu shiryōkan, ed. *Tsugaruke osadamegaki.* Tokyo: Tōkyō daigaku shuppankai, 1981.

*Kokushi daijiten.* 14 vols. Tokyo: Yoshikawa kōbunkan, 1979–93.

Krugman, Paul R., and Maurice Obstfeld. *International Economics: Theory and Policy.* Glenview, Ill.: Scott, Foresman, 1988.

Kudō Mutsuo. "Hirosaki han." In Kodama Kōta and Kitajima Masamoto, *Monogatari hanshi,* 1: 107–201.

———. "Hirosaki han." In Kodama Kōta and Kitajima Masamoto, *Shinpen monogatari hanshi,* 1: 85–127.

———. "Tsugaru sōdō." In Kitajima Masamoto, *Oie sōdō,* pp. 291–336.

Lockwood, William W., ed. *The State and Economic Enterprise in Japan.* Princeton, N.J.: Princeton University Press, 1965.

Maruyama, Masao. *Studies in the Intellectual History of Tokugawa Japan.* Translated by Mikiso Hane. Princeton, N.J.: Princeton University Press, 1974.

Matsuki Naoshi. "Tsugaru han no shitsuju saibai." *Shakai keizai shigaku* 22, no. 3 (February 1956): 113–24.

Matsumoto Hiroshi. "Bakumatsu ishin-ki ni okeru Awa no minshū undō." In Ishiodori Tanehiro and Takahashi Hajime, *Tokushima no kenkyū 4,* pp. 151–95.

———. *Meiji ishin to Awa no kiseki.* Tokushima: Kyōiku shuppan sentā, 1977.

Matsuo Masahito. "Haihan chiken no seijiteki chōryū: haihanron no keisei to tenkai." *Rekishigaku kenkyū* 596 (August 1989): 1–17, 27.

McClain, James L. "Failed Expectations: Kaga on the Eve of the Meiji Restoration." *Journal of Japanese Studies* 14, no. 2 (Summer 1988): 403–47.

———. *Kanazawa: A Seventeenth-Century Japanese Castle Town.* New Haven, Conn.: Yale University Press, 1982.

McEwan, J. R. *The Political Writings of Ogyū Sorai.* Cambridge, Eng.: Cambridge University Press, 1962.

Migdal, Joel S. *Strong Societies and Weak States.* Princeton, N.J.: Princeton University Press, 1988.

Mikami Zenzaburō. "Hirasawa Sanemon." In Hirosaki shiritsu toshokan, ed., *Kyōdo no senjin o kataru 8,* pp. 7–45. Hirosaki: Hirosaki shiritsu toshokan, 1971.

Miki Yūsuke, "Awa han kyūchisei no tokushitsu." *Shigaku (Mita shi gakkai)* 43, no. 1–2 (1970): 221–39.

———. "Awa hansatsu kangae, I." *Shigaku* 37, no. 3 (1964): 79–99.

———. "Awa hansatsu kangae, II." *Shigaku* 38, no. 1 (1965): 126–42.

———. "Awa hansatsu kangae, III." *Shigaku* 38, no. 2 (1965): 73–95.

———. "Hōken kenryoku no shōhin tōsei (ge): Awa ai no baai." *Shigaku* 40, no. 1 (1967): 87–111.

———. "Hōken kenryoku no shōhin tōsei (jō): Awa ai no baai." *Shigaku* 39, no. 4 (1967): 89–113.

Miyamoto Matarō and Uemura Masahiro. "Tokugawa keizai no junkan kōzō." In Hayami Akira and Miyamoto Matarō, *Nihon keizaishi 1,* pp. 271–324.

Miyazaki Michio. *Aomori ken no rekishi.* Tokyo: Yamakawa shuppansha, 1970.

Miyoshi Shōichirō. "Tokushima han ni okeru Inada ke kashindan no sonzai keijō." In Miyoshi Shōichirō, *Tokushima han no shiteki kōzō,* pp. 209–25.

———. "Tokushima han ni okeru kinsei nōson no seiritsu ni tsuite." *Chihōshi kenkyū* 18, no. 1 (Feburary 1969): 32–47.

———, ed. *Awa no hyakushō ikki.* Tokushima: Shuppan, 1970.

———, ed. *Tokushima han no shiteki kōzō*. Tokyo: Meicho shuppan, 1975.

Mizubayashi Takeshi. *Hōkensei no saihen to Nihonteki shakai no kakuritsu*. Tokyo: Yamakawa shuppan, 1987.

———. "Kinsei no hō to kokusei kenkyū josetsu 1." *Kokka gakkai zasshi* 90 (January 1977): 1–61.

———. "Kinsei no hō to kokusei kenkyū josetsu 2." *Kokka gakkai zasshi* 90 (May 1977): 1–63.

———. Kinsei no hō to kokusei kenkyū josetsu 3." *Kokka gakkai zasshi* 91 (May 1978): 73–110.

———. Kinsei no hō to kokusei kenkyū josetsu 4." *Kokka gakkai zasshi* 92 (November 1979): 52–122.

———. Kinsei no hō to kokusei kenkyū josetsu 5." *Kokka gakkai zasshi* 94 (September 1981): 57–105.

———. Kinsei no hō to kokusei kenkyū josetsu 6." *Kokka gakkai zasshi* 95 (February 1982): 59–92.

Morisu, Jon [John Francis Morris]. *Kinsei Nihon chigyōsei no kenkyū*. Tokyo: Seibundō, 1988.

Murakami Yasusuke. "*Ie* Society as a Pattern of Civilization." *Journal of Japanese Studies* 10, no. 2 (Winter 1984): 281–363.

Murakoshi Kazunori. "Daimyō kashin no jinkōgakuteki tokuchō: keizaiteki konkyū kasetsu no kentō, Tokushima han chigyōtori no baai." *Shakai keizai shigaku* 57, no. 3 (August 1991): 1–27.

Nagano Susumu. *Bakuhansei shakai no zaisei kōzō*. Tokyo: Ōhara shinseisha, 1980.

Nagao Ushio. *Ushi no yogore*. 17 vols. Nishiokitama, Yamagata: Nishiokitama gun shakaikai kenkyūkai, 1954.

Najita, Tetsuo. "Introduction: A Synchronous Approach to the Study of Conflict in Modern Japanese History." In Tetsuo Najita and J. Victor Koschmann, *Conflict in Modern Japanese History*, pp. 3–21.

———. *Visions of Virtue in Tokugawa Japan: The Kaitokudō Merchant Academy of Osaka*. Chicago: University of Chicago Press, 1987.

Najita, Tetsuo, and J. Victor Koschmann, eds. *Conflict in Modern Japanese History: The Neglected Tradition*. Princeton, N.J.: Princeton University Press, 1982.

Najita, Tetsuo, and Irwin Scheiner, eds. *Japanese Thought in the Tokugawa Period, 1600–1868: Methods and Metaphors*. Chicago: University of Chicago, 1978.

Nakamichi Hitoshi, ed. *Nyūi Mitsugi zenshū*. 4 vols. Tokyo: Nyūi Mitsugi kenshōkai, 1935–37.

Nakamura Satoru. *Meiji ishin no kiso kōzō*. Tokyo: Miraisha, 1968.

Nakamura Takaya. "Daimyō no kenkyū." In Ōtsuka bungaku gakkai, ed., *Miyake hakase koki shukuga kinen ronbunshū*, pp. 329–85. Okashoin, 1929.

Nakane Chie. *Kazoku no kōzō.* Tokyo: University of Tokyo Press, 1970.

Nakane Chie and Ōishi Shinzaburō. *Tokugawa Japan.* Translation edited by Conrad Toman. Tokyo: University of Tokyo Press, 1990.

Namikawa Kenji. "Hansei kakuritsuki ni okeru shinden kaihatsu no tenkai." *Hirosaki daigaku kokushi kenkyū* 67 (1978): 1–23.

*Nihon kokugo daijiten.* 10 vols. Tokyo: Shōgakkan, 1976.

Nihon shiseki kyōkai, ed. *Hansei ichiran.* 2 vols. Tokyo: Tōkyō daigaku shuppankai, 1928–29. Reprint. Tokyo: Tōkyō daigaku shuppan, 1967.

Nihonshi yōgō jiten henshū iinkai, ed. *Nihonshi yōgō jiten.* Tokyo: Kashiwa shobō, 1979.

Nishikawa Shunsaku. "Grain Consumption: The Case of Chōshū." In Marius B. Jansen and Gilbert Rozman, *Japan in Transition,* pp. 421–46.

———. *Nihon keizai no seichōshi.* Tokyo: Tōyō keizai shinpōsha, 1985.

Nishikawa Shunsaku and Ishibe Yoshiko. "Han senbaisei no fukyū ni tsuite." *Keizai kenkyū* 36, no. 3 (July 1985): 268–73.

Nishino Kaeomon. *Awa ai enkakushi.* Komatsujima, Tokushima: Nishino Kaeomon, 1940.

Niwa Kunio. *Meiji ishin no tochi henkaku.* Tokyo: Ochanomizu shobō, 1962.

Ogi Seiichirō. "Chūki hansei kaikaku to han 'kokka' ron no keisei." *Rekishi* 52 (1978): 13–33.

Ōishi Seizaburō. *Kyōhō kaikaku no keizai seisaku.* Tokyo: Ochanomizu shobō, 1961.

Okamoto Yukisaburō, ed. *Zōjūgoi Shima Riuemon.* Tokushima: Okamoto Yukisaburō, 1916.

Ono Masao. "Bakuhansei seiji kaikakuron." In Rekishigaku kenkyūkai and Nihonshi kenkyūkai, *Kōza Nihon rekishi,* 6: 309–39.

Ono Takeo, ed. *Kinsei chihō keizai shiryō.* 10 vols. Tokyo: Yoshikawa kōbunkan, 1958.

Ooms, Herman. *Charismatic Bureaucrat: A Political Biography of Matsudaira Sadanobu.* Chicago: University of Chicago Press, 1975.

———. "Neo-Confucianism and the Formation of Early Tokugawa Ideology: Contours of a Problem." In Peter Nosco, ed., *Confucianism and Tokugawa Culture,* pp. 27–61. Princeton, N.J.: Princeton University Press, 1984.

———. *Tokugawa Ideology.* Princeton, N.J.: Princeton University Press, 1985.

Ōsaka Toshio. "Bakumatsu sōmō no kenkyū." In Ishiodori Tanehiro and Takahashi Hajime, *Tokushima no kenkyū* 4, pp. 99–150.

Ōtsuki Hiromu. "Awa ni okeru hansei kaikaku." In Horie Hideichi, *Hansei kaikaku no kenkyū,* pp. 119–82.

Ōuchi Hyōe and Tsuchiya Takao, eds. *Meiji zenki zaisei keizai shiryō shūsei.* Vol. 8. Tokyo: Meiji bunken shiryō kankōkai, 1933.

Parsons, Talcott, ed. *Max Weber: The Theory of Social and Economic Organization*. New York: The Free Press, 1947.

Pindyck, Robert S., and Daniel L. Rubinfeld. *Econometric Models and Economic Forecasts*. 2d ed. New York: McGraw-Hill, 1981.

Reischauer, Edwin O. *Japan: The Story of a Nation*. New York: Alfred A. Knopf, 1970.

———. "Japanese Feudalism." In Rushton Coulborn, ed., *Feudalism in History*, pp. 26–48. Princeton, N.J., New Jersey: Princeton University Press, 1956.

Rekishigaku kenkyūkai and Nihonshi kenkyūkai, eds. *Kōza Nihon rekishi*. 13 vols. Tokyo: Tōkyō daigaku shuppankai, 1984–85.

Roberts, Luke Shepherd. "The Merchant Origins of National Prosperity Thought in Eighteenth-Century Tosa." Ph.D. diss., Princeton University, 1991.

Sagara Eisuke. "Tokushima han ni okeru engyō seisaku no tenkai." In Ishiodori Tanehiro and Takahashi Hajime, *Tokushima no kenkyū 5*, pp. 87–131.

Sansom, George. *A History of Japan, 1615–1867*. Stanford, Calif.: Stanford University Press, 1963.

Sasaki Junnosuke. *Bakuhansei kokka ron*. 2 vols. Tokyo: Tōkyō daigaku shuppankai, 1984.

———. *Bakumatsu shakairon*. Tokyo: Hanawa shobō, 1969.

———. *Daimyō to hyakushō*. Tokyo: Chūō kōronsha, 1984.

Sasaki Junnosuke and Ronald P. Toby. "The Changing Rationale of Daimyo Control in the Emergence of the Bakuhan State." In John Whitney Hall, Nagahara Keiji, and Kozo Yamamura, *Japan Before Tokugawa*, pp. 271–94.

Satow, Ernest. *A Diplomat in Japan*. London: Oxford University Press, 1968.

Scheiner, Irwin. "Benevolent Lords and Honorable Peasants: Rebellion and Peasant Consciousness in Tokugawa Japan." In Tetsuo Najita and Irwin Scheiner, *Japanese Thought in the Tokugawa Period, 1600–1868*, pp. 39–62.

Schumpeter, Joseph. "The Crisis of the Tax State." In Alan T. Peacock, Ralph Turvey, Wolfgang F. Stolper et al., eds., *International Economic Papers: Translations Prepared for the International Economic Association*, 4: 5–38. New York: Macmillan, 1954.

Scott, James C. *Weapons of the Weak*. New Haven, Conn.: Yale University Press, 1985.

Scruton, Roger. *A Dictionary of Political Thought*. New York: Hill & Wang, 1982.

Sekiyama Naotarō. *Kinsei Nihon no jinkō kōzō*. Tokyo: Yoshikawa kōbunkan, 1985.

Sheehan, James J. *German History, 1700–1866.* Oxford: Oxford University Press, 1989.

———. "What Is German History? Reflections on the Role of the *Nation* in German History and Historiography." *Journal of Modern History* 53, no. 1 (March 1981): 1–23.

Shinbo Hiroshi. *Kinsei no bukka to keizai hatten.* Tokyo: Tōyō keizai shinpōsha, 1978.

Shinji Yoshimoto, ed. *Edo jidai bushi no seikatsu.* Tokyo: Yūzankaku, 1984.

Shinmi Kichiji. *Hatamoto.* Tokyo: Yoshikawa kōbunkan, 1967.

*Shintei Kansei chōshu shokafu.* 26 vols. Tokyo: Zoku gunsho ruiji kanseikai, 1964–69.

Shizuo Katsumata and Marin Colcutt. "The Development of Sengoku Law." In John Whitney Hall, Nagahara Keiji, and Kozo Yamamura, *Japan Before Tokugawa,* pp. 271–94.

Shōji Kichinosuke. "Aizu no urushi to rō." In *NSST,* 3: 160–76.

Shōji Kichinosuke and Matsuki Tadashi. "Tsugaru nuri to Aizu nuri." In *NSST,* 3: 285–95.

Smith, Mack. *Italy.* Ann Arbor: University of Michigan Press, 1959.

Smith, Thomas C. *The Agrarian Origins of Modern Japan.* Stanford, Calif.: Stanford University Press, 1959.

———. "Farm Family By-employments." *Journal of Economic History* 29, no. 4 (December 1969): 687–715.

———. "The Land Tax in the Tokugawa Period." *Journal of Asian Studies* 18, no. 1 (November 1958): 3–19.

———. "'Merit' as Ideology in the Tokugawa Period." In *Native Sources of Japanese Industrialization, 1750–1920,* pp. 156–72. Berkeley: University of California Press, 1988. Reprinted from Ronald P. Dore, ed., *Aspects of Social Change in Modern Japan* (Princeton, N.J.: Princeton University Press, 1967).

———. *Native Sources of Japanese Industrialization, 1750–1920.* Berkeley: University of California Press, 1988.

Suda Mizuho, ed. *Ginin Fujita Tamijirō den.* Hirosaki: Hirosaki chūō kōminkan, 1963.

Sugihara Ken, ed. *Nozoki Taika ō.* Tokyo: Sugihara Ken, 1898.

Sugimoto Kōichi. "Yonezawa han aoso tenpō to Echigo chijimi sanchi no dōkō." In Yamada Hideo sensei taikan kinenkai, eds., *Seiji shakaishi ronsō,* pp. 243–59. Tokyo: Kondō shuppansha, 1986.

Suzuki Hisashi. *Kinsei chigyōsei no kenkyū.* Tokyo: Nihon gakujutsu shinkōkai, 1971.

Suzuki Masayuki. "Shuken kokka, kokumin kokka, Nihon kindai kokka." In Suzuki Masayuki, Mizubayashi Takeshi, Watanabe Shin'ichirō, and Kojita Yasunao, *Hikaku kokuseishi kenkyū josetsu,* pp. 190–253.

Suzuki Masayuki, Mizubayashi Takeshi, Watanabe Shin'ichirō, and Kojita

Yasunao, eds. *Hikaku kokuseishi kenkyū josetsu.* Tokyo: Kashiwa shobō, 1992.

Tahara Tsuguo. "Kinsei chūki no seiji shisō to kokka ishiki." In *IKNR* 11 (1976): 297–329.

Tahara Tsuguo and Morimoto Junichirō, eds. *Yamaga Sokō.* In *NST*, vol. 32. Tokyo: Iwanami shoten, 1970.

Takahashi Hajime. "Awa ai no seisan to ryūtsū." In Ishiodori Tanehiro and Takahashi Hajime, *Tokushima no kenkyū 5*, pp. 49–85.

———. "Tokushima han no chūki hansei kaikaku ni tsuite." In Gotō Yōichi, ed., *Setonaikai chiiki no shiteki tenkai*, pp. 174–200. Tokyo: Fukutake shoten, 1978.

———. "Tokushima han sankan kōshin chiiki ni okeru sonraku keitai." *Chihōshi kenkyū* 18, no. 1 (Feburary 1969): 48–60.

Takayanagi Mitsutoshi, Okayama Taiji, Saiki Kazuma, Hotta Masaatsu, and Hayashi Jutsusai, eds. *Kansei choshu shokafu.* Rev. ed. 26 vols. Tokyo: Zoku Gunsho Ruiji Kanseikai, 1964–67.

Takayanagi Mitsutoshi and Takeuchi Rizō, eds. *Kadokawa Nihonshi jiten.* 2d ed. Tokyo: Kadokawa shoten, 1974.

Takayanagi Shinzō and Ishii Ryōsuke, eds. *Ofuregaki Hōreki shūsei.* Tokyo: Iwanami shoten, 1935.

———. *Ofuregaki Kanpō shūsei.* Tokyo: Iwanami shoten, 1934.

———. *Ofuregaki Tenmei shūsei.* Tokyo: Iwanami shoten, 1936.

———. *Ofuregaki Tenpō shūsei.* 2 vols. Tokyo: Iwanami shoten, 1939.

Takimoto Hisafumi. "Kansei kaikaku to hanshi dochaku seisaku." In Hasegawa Seiichi, *Tsugaruhan no kisoteki kenkyū*, pp. 331–94.

Takizawa Takeo. "Tsugaru han no hyōfu ni tsuite." *Shikan* 36 (1951): 100–120.

Tawney, R. H. *Land and Labor in China.* London: Allen & Unwin, 1937.

Tilly, Charles. "On the History of European State-making." In Charles Tilley and Gabriel Ardant, *The Formation of National States in Western Europe*, pp. 3–83.

Tilly, Charles, and Gabriel Ardant, eds. *The Formation of National States in Western Europe.* Princeton, N.J.: Princeton University Press, 1975.

Tivey, Leonard. "Introduction." In Leonard Tivey, *The Nation-State*, pp. 1–12.

———, ed. *The Nation-State: The Formation of Modern Politics.* New York: St. Martin's, 1981.

Toby, Ronald P. *State and Diplomacy in Early Modern Japan.* Princeton, N.J.: Princeton University Press, 1984.

Tokushima ken, ed. *Gotaiten kinen Awa han minsei shiryō.* 2 vols. Tokushima: Tokushima ken, 1916.

Tokushima ken bussan chinretsujō, ed. *Awa han minsei shiryō.* Tokushima: Tokushima ken bussan chinretsujō, 1914.

Tokushima ken kōtō gakkō kyōiku kenkyūkai chireki gakkai, eds. *Tokushima ken kyōdo jiten*. Tokushima: Tokushima ken, 1974.

Tokushima shi gakkai, ed. *Shin Tokushima hansei shi*. Tokushima: Tokushima shi gakkai, 1966.

Totman, Conrad. *The Collapse of the Tokugawa Bakufu, 1862–1868*. Honolulu: University Press of Hawaii, 1980.

————. *Early Modern Japan*. Berkeley: University of California Press, 1993.

————. *The Green Archipelago*. Berkeley: University of California Press, 1989.

————. *Politics in the Tokugawa Bakufu, 1600–1843*. Cambridge, Mass.: Harvard University Press, 1967.

Tōyama Shigeki. *Meiji ishin*. Tokyo: Iwanami shoten, 1951.

Trewartha, Glenn T. *Japan: A Geography*. Madison: University of Wisconsin Press, 1965.

Tsugaru Tsuguakira kō den kankōkai, ed. *Tsugaru Tsuguakira kō den*. Tokyo: Rekishi toshosha, 1976.

Tsuji Tatsuya. "Bakuhan taisei no henshitsu to chōbaku kankei." In Tsuji Tatsuya, ed., *Nihon no kinsei 2: Tennō to shōgun*, pp. 203–50. Tokyo: Chūō kōronsha, 1991.

Umegaki, Michio. *After the Restoration*. New York: New York University Press, 1988.

Vlastos, Stephen. *Peasant Protests and Uprisings in Tokugawa Japan*. Berkeley: University of California Press, 1986.

Walthall, Anne. *Peasant Uprisings in Japan: A Critical Anthology of Peasant Histories*. Chicago: University of Chicago Press, 1991.

————. *Social Protest and Popular Culture in Eighteenth-Century Japan*. Tuscon: University of Arizona Press, 1986.

Watanabe Fumio. *Yonezawa han no seiji to nōson shakai*. Yonezawa, Yamagata: Fubō shuppan, 1980.

————. *Yonezawa han no tokusangyō to senbaisei*. Yonezawa, Yamagata: Fubō shuppan, 1976.

Watanabe Satokichi and Ozawa Shizuo, eds. *Yonezawa orimono shi*. Yonezawa, Yamagata: Yonezawa orimono kyōdō kumiai rengōkai, 1970.

Waters, Neil L. *Japan's Local Pragmatists: The Transition from Bakumatsu to Meiji in the Kawasaki Region*. Cambridge, Mass.: Harvard University Press, 1983.

Weber, Eugen. *Peasants into Frenchmen*. Stanford, Calif.: Stanford University Press, 1976.

Wehler, Hans-Ulrich. *The German Empire*. Translated by Kim Traynor. Dover, N.H.: Berg Publishers, 1985.

White, James W. "State Growth and Popular Protest in Tokugawa Japan." *Journal of Japanese Studies* 14, no. 1 (Winter 1988): 1–25.

Wigen, Kären. "The Geographic Imagination in Early Modern Japanese History: Retrospect and Prospect." *Journal of Asian Studies* 51, no. 1 (February 1992): 3–29.

———. *The Making of a Japanese Periphery.* Berkeley: University of California Press, 1995.

———. "Social and Spatial Divisions of Labor in Nineteenth-Century Shinano: Mapping the Contested Terrain of Paper Craft Production." Paper presented at the 43d meeting of the Association for Asian Studies, New Orleans, La., 1991.

Yabuta Yutaka. *Kokuso to hyakushō ikki no kenkyū.* Tokyo: Azekura shobō, 1992.

Yamada Tatsuo, Iinuma Jirō, and Oka Mitsuo, eds. *Nihon nōsho zenshū.* 35 vols. Tokyo: Nōzangyoson bunka kyōkai, 1977–83.

Yamaguchi Kazuo. "Hansatsu shi kenkyū josetsu." *Keizaigaku ronshū* 31, no. 4 (January 1966): 1–13.

Yamaguchi Keiji and Sasaki Junnosuke. *Taikei Nihon rekishi 4: Bakuhan taisei.* Tokyo: Nihon hyōronsha, 1971.

Yamazaki Ryūzō. *Kinsei bukkashi kenkyū.* Tokyo: Hanawa shobō, 1983.

Yasuzawa Shūichi. "An'ei-ki Tokushima han no zaisei shūshi kōzo." In Miyoshi Shōichirō, *Tokushima han no shiteki kōzō,* pp. 101–17.

———. "Kansei-ki Tokushima han ni okeru chihō shihai kaikaku no tokushitsu ni tsuite," *Chihōshi kenkyū,* vol. 18, no. 2 (April 1968): 14–28.

———. "Kansei-ki Tokushima han no nōgyō to suisangyō." In Ishiodori Tanehiro and Takahashi Hajime, *Tokushima no kenkyū 4,* pp. 1–68.

Yokoyama Akio. *Uesugi Yōzan.* Tokyo: Yoshikawa kōbunkan, 1968.

———. "Yonezawa han ni okeru aoso senbaisei no tenkai katei." *Rekishigaku kenkyū* 250 (February 1961): 9–24.

Yokoyama Akio and Yoshinaga Akira. "Kokusan shōrei to hansei kaikaku." In *IKNR (Kinsei 3,* 1976), 11: 35–100.

Yonezawa shishi hensan iinkai, ed. *Koshikata monogatari, Itsushūhen, Dokuhen, Oyakobanashi.* Yonezawa shishi henshū shiryō no. 21. Yonezawa: Yonezawa shishi hensan iinkai, 1982.

———. *Yonezawa nenpyō: chū-kinsei hen.* Yonezawa shishi henshū shiryō no. 9. Yonezawa: Yonezawa shishi hensan iinkai, 1982.

Yoshida Yoshinobu. *Okitama minshū seikatsu shi.* Yonezawa, Yamagata: Yamagata higashi okitama shakaika kyōiku kenkyūkai, 1956.

———. "Yonezwa no orimono." In *NSST,* 3: 296–308.

Yoshikawa Kōjirō, Maruyama Masao, Nishida Taichirō, and Tsuji Tatsuya, eds. *Ogyū Sorai.* In *NST,* vol. 36. Tokyo: Iwanami shoten, 1973.

Yoshinaga Akira. *Kinsei no senbai seido.* Tokyo: Yoshikawa kōbunkan, 1973.

# Index

In this index an "f" after a number indicates a separate reference on the next page, and an "ff" indicates separate references on the next two pages. A continuous discussion over two or more pages is indicated by a span of page numbers. *Passim* is used for a cluster of references in close but not consecutive sequence.

abandoned land, 77, 80, 82, 120, 129, 133, 136, 144, 151, 181
adoption, 17, 37, 43, 68–69, 73, 87, 143, 147, 150, 176–78, 192
Akaishi Yasuemon, 134, 136f, 139–40
Akita domain 19, 59–60, 176
Akizuki Tanemi, 87
alternate attendance (*sankin kōtai*) system, 17, 21, 55, 67, 88, 122, 145, 148, 152
Arai Hakuseki, 25, 42
Arato, 72f, 111
Arima house, 19
Asano house, 19
Ashibane family, 127–28
*ashigaru*, 121, 130
Ashikaga shogunate, 25
attainder, 21, 36f, 73
authority: feudal, 34–40, 43–45, 46, 48, 74, 173, 179–80, 195–96; patrimonial, 34, 37–40, 43–45, 46, 48, 62, 67, 74, 87, 91, 133, 141, 177–80, 195–99; suzerain, 40–45, 46, 67, 91, 109, 118, 140, 146, 175, 179–80, 194–99

Awa district, 154–55, 157–58, 182–85, 190f
Awaji, 65, 154–55, 171, 192

*bakufu, see* shogunate
Bellah, Robert, 92
Berry, Mary Elizabeth, 26
Bolitho, Harold, 4, 9, 14
branch domain, 149–50
Brown, Philip, 37
Buddhism, 26–27, 40–41
*buke shohatto* ("Laws Governing the Military Houses"), 12, 36, 173, 251n45

Caron, François, 32, 33
cartels, 7–8, 10–11, 59, 107–8, 112, 158–62 *passim*, 168–71, 175, 181–86, 198–99
chamberlain (*jijū*), 117, 148
chargé d'affaires, 172–73, 182
*chigyō. See* fiefs
Chisaka Tsushima, 87
Chōshū domain, 4, 14, 17, 19, 56, 61, 64, 66, 152, 192, 201, 204ff
Chu Hsi, 32, 123

Chuang-tzu, 32, 123
class separation (*heinō bunri*), 63–64
commerce. *See* merchants
concubines, 68, 149
corvée, 55, 64, 75, 121, 139, 143ff, 167, 180
cotton 9, 75, 76, 88, 92, 99–100, 101, 125, 155, 180, 187
country. *See kuni*
court rank (*kan'i*) 12, 18–21, 117, 148
Craig, Albert, 4, 14

daikan. *See* intendants
daimyo: legitimacy of, 1–4, 21–28, 195–96, 199–206 *passim, see also* authority; autonomy of, 1–2, 5, 11–12, 15, 17, 20, 42, 72–73, 109–10, 117–18, 179–80; shogunal power over, 1–3, 5, 17–21, 23–28, 34–45, 73, 85, 117–18, 171–76, 179–84; status distinctions, 3, 13–22 *passim*, 27–28, 36, 117–18, 234–35n5, 235–36n30; "country holders" or "country lords," 2–3, 12–15, 19–23, 27, 28, 36, 117–18, 196–98, 202–3, 209; personal expenses of, 6, 67–69, 87–88, 147–50, 179; adoption of, 17, 37, 43, 68–69, 73, 87, 143, 147–50, 176–78, 192; attainder of holdings, 21, 36f, 73, 245n3; oaths, 35–36, 91; forced retirement of, 45, 88, 148–50, 176–80; austerity policies of, 67–69, 88–89, 150–51; transfer of daimyo, 21, 36–37. *See also individual domains and daimyo by name*
Date house, 17, 19, 20
Dazai Shundai, 123
demography, 5–7, 9–11, 52, 76–80, 118, 142, 155, 197–98. *See also* depopulation, population growth, population ratio, *and individual domains by name*
depopulation: in Hirosaki, 79–80, 118, 128–30, 145, 151; in Yonezawa, 76–80, 86, 97, 101
domain commodity agencies (*koku-*

san kaijo or *sanbutsu kaijo*), 22, 56, 106–7. *See also* guilds; cartels
domain elders, 48, 87–88. *See also individuals by name, including* Makino Sajirō, Kasahara Ōmi, Kasahara Hachirobei, Hasegawa Ōmi, Yamada Oribe
domains 11–12, 49–69. *See also* daimyo *and individual domains by name*

Eclectic school (*Setchūgakuha*), 90
economic thought, 8–9, 55–57, 98–101, 123–25, 162–63, 167–68
Edo, 7, 10, 17, 42, 61, 64, 67, 73, 85f, 90, 106, 122, 147, 158–63, 182–85
Edo city magistrate (*Edo machi bugyō*), 162, 175
Edo senior counselor, 172
*ee ja nai ka*, 192–93, 202
emperor. *See* imperial house

fallow land. *See* abandoned land
famine: in Yonezawa, 79–80, 85, 96–97, 103, 114; in Hirosaki, 118–20, 122, 125, 128–30, 147–49, 151–52, 187. *See also* Tenmei crisis, Tenpō crisis
fertilizer, 6f, 158, 174, 181
feudalism, 34–37, 62–63, 200, *see also* authority, feudal
fiat money, 59–60, 86–87, 125–28, 160, 163, 189
fiefs: landed (*jikata chigyō*), 62–67, 85–87, 121–22, 134–35, 136, 239n38; stipended (*kuramai chigyō*), 62–67, 134–36, 239n38. *See also individual domains by name*
flax, 47, 57, 59, 76–80 *passim*, 100–101, 111
Forbidden Gate Incident, 21
foreign policy, 2, 17–18, 23, 25, 198
Fuchū domain, 17, 19
Fujiwara house, 116
Fukui domain, 19–20
Fukuoka domain, 19, 30, 59ff, 64
Fukushima domain, 153
gambling, 85

Gellner, Ernest, 109
*genin*, 56
Germany, 200, 208. *See also* länder
Gosha rebellion, 164–68
*gōshi*, 66, 120, 136–37, 191
guilds, 56, 59, 158, 184

Hachisuka Haruaki, 175–81, 199
Hachisuka house, 11–12, 19, 65, 154, 176, 179, 203
Hachisuka Mitsutaka, 181
Hachisuka Mochiaki, 203–4
Hachisuka Narihiro, 192, 202f
Hachisuka Shigetaka, 178
Hachisuka Shigeyoshi, 68, 171, 176–81, 195
Hachisuka Tadateru, 181
Hachisuka Tsunenori, 178
Hachisuka Yoshihisa, 176
Hachisuka Yoshishige, 154, 181
Hall, John Whitney, 4
*han*, as term for domain; 13–14, 27f, 33, 202–205 *passim*, 209
Hara Shoemon, 137–39
Hara Shōhachi, 137–38
harvest shortfalls, 48; in Yonezawa, 80, 85–86, 96–97; in Hirosaki, 48, 125, 128–29, 151–52. *See also* famine, Tenmei crisis, Tenpō crisis
Hasegawa house, 176
Hasegawa Ōmi, 173–74, 176–81
*hatamoto* (liege vassals), 16f, 18–19, 23, 27–28, 33
heavenly mandate, 41–42
*heinō bunri*, 63–64
Herrschaft, 38
Himeiji domain, 59
Hirasawa San'emon, 141–47, 151
Hirayama family, 137–39, 141–42
*Hirayama nikki*, 137–39, 141–42
Hirosaki domain, 9–15 *passim*, 20–23, 32, 35, 70, 155, 167, 197–202 *passim*; and samurai resettlement, 9–10, 52, 118, 120, 130–41, 151–52, 198; and relations with shogunate, 14–15, 69, 118, 131, 140, 148–50, 152–53, 245n3; and harvest failures, 48, 118, 120, 123, 125–26, 129, 146, 147–49; and tax policy, 54–55, 118–22, 128–

30, 135–36, 139, 141–45, 151; and retainers' fiefs or stipends, 64, 66–67, 120–23, 125, 129–30, 136, 148, 150; and famine, 118–20, 122, 125–26, 128–30, 147–52 *passim*, 187; and land development, 118–22, 130–47 *passim*, 141–47, 151–52; and population policy, 79–80, 118, 141–47; finances of, 118–122, 125–28, 134, 143, 146–47, 161
Hiroshima domain, 19
Hizen domain, 14
Hokkaidō, 20, 117, 145, 152
Honma family, 60–61
Horie Hideichi, 56
Hosoi Heishū, 89–93, 95–96, 98–99, 100
Hosokawa house, 19
Hōjō region, 47, 83
*hyōfu*, 126–28

*ie* system, 37–40. *See also* authority, patrimonial
Igarashi house, 85
Ikebe Mahari, 201
Ikeda house, 19, 176
Ikeda Mitsumasa, 41
Ikeda Namie, 181
Ikeda Noboru, 178
Imogawa Masanori, 87, 89
imperial authority, 3, 15, 25–29
imperial house, 2, 16, 25, 42, 152–53, 192–93, 202, 207
imperial loyalism, 28, 63, 152–53, 192, 201–202
imperialism, 25, 196–210
Inada family, 65, 176, 202
Inada Kurobei, 176, 178
indigo, 7–11 *passim*, 22, 44–45; and cartels or guilds, 10–11, 158–175, 180–85; quality of, 8, 11, 159–62, 172, 174, 182, 184; government promotion and protection of, 58, 93, 154, 155–176, 167–176, 181–86; cubes (*aidama*), 155–60, 161, 167–76, 181–84; dyers, 158, 161, 169f, 172f, 175, 182f; prices of, 158f, 162f, 168–71, 175, 181–85
infanticide, 46, 75, 79, 102, 103

inflation, 58, 127, 205
Inoue Kinga, 90
intendants (*daikan*), 48, 66, 84, 174f,
  182
Irobe Tsuneyoshi, 87
Italy, 200, 208
Itano district, 157, 165, 191
Itō Tasaburō, 27
*iutsurinin* ("migrants"), 144

Jansen, Marius, 4
jobbers, 161, 169–72

*kabunakama*, 56, 59, 158, 184
Kaga domain, 4, 18f, 64
Kaiho Seiryō, 123
Kanai Madoka, 64
*Kangendan*, 76, 81, 104
Kasahara Hachirobei, 147–48
Kasahara Ōmi, 148–49
Kasaya Kazuhiko, 39–40, 195
Kashima Bizen, 177
Kashima house, 176
Kashima Kazusa, 177–78
Katayama Kenzan, 90
Keian proclamation, 9
*kikokunin* ("repatriates"), 142, 144
Kikuchi Kanji, 134, 136f, 139
Kitajima Masamoto, 35
*kochigyō*, 121–22, 130
Kojima Yasunori, 126
*kokka*: as term for domain, 1, 13–14,
  29–33, 38, 40, 109, 118, 173;
  translation of, 13, 32–34; as term
  for Japan, 29–33
*kokueki* ("national prosperity"), 100,
  105, 107, 109, 140, 198
*kokumin*: as term for domain subjects, 30–31, 33, 40, 109, 118,
  179, 184; as term for nation, 30,
  33, 199
*kokutai*, 89, 103
Konoe house, 153
Korea, 23, 206
*kōgi* ("public authority"), 25–26, 35,
  40, 44–45, 84
Kōnoike Zen'emon, 61
Kōriyama domain, 19–20
Kudō Genpachi, 137–39
Kuji house, 117

Kumamoto domain, 19, 61, 64,
  206–7
*kuni* ("country"): problems of translation, 13, 31–34; as term for domain, 28–34 *passim*, 38, 41–42,
  84, 117–19, 140–41, 153, 169,
  171, 173, 179, 187; as term for
  province, 29–34 *passim*, 117–19;
  as term for foreign country, 29, 31;
  as term for Japan, 33, 34, 153
Kuroda house, 19
Kuroda Nagamasa, 41
Kuroishi Tsugaru house, 143, 149
Kurume domain, 19

lacquer, 76, 100, 102, 104, 119,
  161, 189; monopsony on, 57–58,
  101; taxation of, 57–58, 80–81,
  93–96
land development, 7, 66, 79–80, 89,
  120–21, 130, 134–36, 139,
  141–47, 151–52, 161
land tax. See taxes, *nengu*
länder, 33, 38
Lao-tzu, 123
"Laws Governing the Military
  Houses" (*buke shohatto*), 12, 36,
  251n45
legitimacy: of domains, 2–4, 23–28,
  34–45 *passim*, 194–95, 198–204
  *passim*; of shogunate, 23–28,
  34–45 *passim*, 171–76, 179–80,
  196; of compound state, 27–28,
  34–45 *passim*, 196. See also
  authority
loans: to indigo growers, 58, 159,
  168–74, 181; to domains, 61, 77,
  85, 123, 126–28, 146–47; debt
  moratorium, 61, 101, 126–27; repayment problems, 61, 75, 85–86;
  domain financed, 101–103, 170,
  181
Machida Hachinosuke, 112–13
Machida Toyokatsu, 113
Machida Toyomasa, 113
Maeda house, 19
Magaribuchi Kai, 172
Makino Sajirō, 139
Makino Tadakiyo, 183

market economy, 49–59 *passim*, 107, 123–24, 168–75
markets, 7, 52, 56–57, 106–108, 167–75, 198–99; control over, 8–9, 158–59, 161–63, 169–72, 181–86. *See also under* prices
Maruyama Masao, 90, 208–209
Masue, 149f
Matsudaira Sadanobu, 25
Matsudaira Takemoto, 171–73
Matsue domain, 19–20
Matsumoto Hiroshi, 190
McClain, James, 4
Meiji government, 49, 55, 110, 112; and disssolution of the domains, 15, 33, 55, 70, 153, 199–210 *passim*
Meiji Restoration, 14, 15, 28, 30, 34, 114, 152–53, 192
Mencius, 1–2, 13, 32, 96, 104
merchants, 49, 56, 59–60, 83–85, 86, 88, 107, 111–13, 124–28, 189; in economic thought, 32, 104, 124–25, 162–64; and loans to domains, 60–61, 75, 84–85, 123, 127–28, 149, 180–81; purchase of status by, 60, 84–85, 97; and domain policies, 59, 84–86, 105–106, 162–76 *passim*, 181–86, 197, 199. *See also under* loans
Migdal, Joel, 24–25
millenarianism, 193
Mima district, 187, 190f
Minamoto Toshinaru, 110–11
Mitani house, 85
Mitani Sankurō, 106–107
Mito, 17
Miyoshi district, 189ff
Mizubayashi Takeshi, 27, 37–38
Mogami river, 71–72, 83
monopoly, 8, 11, 59, 158–59, 175, 182–86
monopsony, 10, 11, 57–59, 60, 76, 81–82, 94, 100, 102, 106, 107, 158, 198
Mori Heiemon, 61, 83, 84–87
Morioka domain, 20, 153
Mōnai Ariemon, 125–26, 130, 198
Mōnai Giō, 115, 130–34, 140
Mōri house. *See* Chōshū domain

Murdoch, 92
Myōdō district, 157, 165, 191
Myōzai district, 164, 187, 191

Nabeshima house, 19
Nagao Ushio, 109
*nago*, 56
Naka district, 158
*nakagai. See* jobbers
Nakamura Kichiji, 27
Nanbu house, 20, 116–17
nationalism, 14, 109–110, 118, 200–201, 208–209
*nengu. See* taxes, *nengu*
Neo-Confucianism, 26–27, 40, 90, 98, 195. *See also* Chu Hsi
Nihonmatsu domain, 20
Nikkō, 26
Nishimura Kyūzaemon, 59, 83
Nozoki Masamochi, 101
Nozoki Yoshimasa, 58, 71, 78, 88–89, 97–106, 109, 133
Numata domain, 17
Nyūi Mitsugi, 32, 123–28, 130

Obama domain, 41
Oe district, 157, 165, 191
Ogasawara Ryōhachi, 148–49
Ogata Chōei, 202
Ogata house, 202
Ogawa Yasozaemon, 168–71, 174
Ogyū Sorai, 5, 6, 16, 47, 90, 123, 131–33
Okayama domain, 4, 19, 41
oligopoly, 8, 159
oligopsony, 158–59, 163–64, 168, 182–86
Osaka, 7, 17, 61–64 *passim*, 75, 115, 125, 155, 191f, 207; and the indigo trade, 10–11, 158–62, 168–75, 182–87, 198–99
Osaka city magistrate, 172–73, 175, 182–84
Owari domain, 88
*Ōsaka machi bugyō*, 172–73, 175, 182–84
Ōshio Heihachirō, 191
Ōtsuki Hiromu, 190
*Ōuetsu reppan dōmei*, 114, 153
Ōura house, 117

Ōura Tamenori, 116

population growth, 7, 78–79, 101,
    103, 142, 155
population ratio, 73, 103, 118
prices, 7–8, 57–59, 82–83, 97, 100,
    108–113 *passim*, 124, 130, 172,
    174, 182ff, 189; of rice, 7–8, 29,
    86, 97, 130, 158, 187ff; deter-
    mined by cartels or guilds, 7–8,
    155f, 158ff, 164–72, 181–86,
    198–99; of indigo, 155f, 159f,
    164–72, 181–86, 198–99. *See also
    under individual commodities*
prostitution, 101, 148
protoindustrialization, 6–11 *passim*,
    21, 110, 155, 197–98

quality control, 8, 11, 106–110,
    159–60, 198

relief granaries, 85, 97, 114, 126,
    181
resettlement of samurai, 10, 52, 67,
    104–105, 118, 120–22, 130–42,
    151–52, 198
retainers, 34–40, 48–49, 61–67, 195,
    206, 213–14; by-employments of,
    10, 52, 75, 104–105, 109, 110–
    13, 140, 197–98; obligations to
    daimyo, 43–44, 61–62, 91–92,
    109, 136–37, 152; in countryside,
    50, 66, 118–22, 130–42, 152, 191;
    hierarchy among, 62, 89, 135–36,
    176–80; *See also under* fiefs *and
    individual domains by name*
Roberts, Luke, 31
*ryōbun* or *ryōchi*, 12–14, 28–29, 173
Ryukyus, 23

Saga domain, 14, 19, 205
Saigō Takamori, 206–208
Sakai Tadayuki, 41
salt farming, 154, 158, 181
sand, 11, 160
*sankin kōtai* ("alternate attendance")
    system, 17, 21, 55, 67, 88, 122,
    145, 148, 152
Sansom, George, 34
Sasaki Junnosuke, 56

*sashigami*, 189
Satake house, 19
Satake Yoshimichi, 176
Satow, Ernest, 203
Satsuma domain, 14, 17, 19, 56, 61,
    64, 66, 152, 204–209 *passim*
Satsuma rebellion, 206–208
Schumpeter, Joseph, 24
Scott, James, 48
*Seidan*, 131–32
*Seigasha*, 88–89
Sendai domain, 19, 20, 61, 66, 153
sericulture, 57, 79, 92, 96, 101–113
    *passim*, 158–59, 189–90
*Setchūgakuha* (Eclectic School), 90
Shibahashi territory, 114
Shiga Sukeyoshi, 88, 96–97
Shimaya Sajiro, 107
Shimazu house. *See* Satsuma domain
Shimonagai region, 81–82
Shintoism, 26–27, 35
shogunate, 2–15, 23–25, 73, 75,
    85, 114, 191–92 199, 201–210
    *passim*; control over daimyo, 12,
    17–20 *passim*, 44–45, 73, 85, 118,
    152, 171–76, 179–80, 196,
    245n3; sources of authority, 23–28
    *passim*, 31–45 *passim*, 173, 175,
    179–80, 201–202. *See also indi-
    vidual domains*
Shōnai domain, 60–61, 112, 114
silk, 57, 79, 92, 96, 101–113 *passim*,
    158–59, 189–90
Smith, T. C., 69
Sō house, 19
state: definitions of, 23–31 *passim*,
    234n1; "compound state," 27–28,
    38, 70, 194–204 *passim*, 208. *See
    also kokka*
status, 60–61, 84–85, 89, 97,
    135–37, 176ff; distinctions among
    daimyo, 2–3, 11, 13–15, 19–20,
    22, 27–28, 36, 117–18; purchase
    of, 60–61, 84–85, 97
Stephen Vlastos, 63
Suda Mitsutake, 89

Takakura Sagami, 148
Takanabe domain, 87
Takasaki domain, 35

Takenomata Masatsuna, 44, 87–89, 93–96, 97, 98, 100, 104
Takeuchi Jinsaemon, 143
Tanuma Okitsugu, 173
Tayasu Kanehime, 148
taxes, 5–6, 15, 24, 48–58, 65, 69–70, 86, 93, 197–98; *nengu*, 6, 53–55, 57–58, 75, 79, 82, 84, 102–103, 121, 132, 135, 139, 151, 160, 163, 169, 174, 175, 197, 201, 238n22; collection of, 54–55, 70, 76, 84, 138, 189; corvée, 55, 75–76, 121, 139, 143–44, 167, 180; evasion by commoners, 57–58, 80–81, 94–95, 142, 164; inability to remit, 76–77, 79, 81, 101, 129, 130, 139, 165ff; relief, 78, 101, 104–105, 129, 161, 174; on commodities, 81–84, 94, 96, 102, 161, 163–64, 167–68, 174; poll tax, 85; exemptions, 94, 101–102, 121–22, 135–36, 142–44. *See also individual domains by name*
temples, 17, 38, 69
Tenmei crisis, 67, 80, 96–97, 118, 120, 128–30, 147, 152, 181
Tenpō crisis 67, 79, 103, 113–14, 118, 147–52, 185–86, 187–91
Terashima house, 85, 88
textiles, 8, 11, 22, 93, 99, 102–110 *passim*, 155, 187; as samurai by-employment, 10, 75, 104–110, 112–13, 197–98; control by cartels, 106–108, 112, 158, 161–62, 169ff, 181f; indigo dyed, 155–58, 161–62, 169ff, 181f, 187
tobacco, 158, 180–81, 189
Toby, Ronald, 23
Tokugawa house, 12, 17f, 25, 29, 33, 41, 72–73, 88
Tokugawa Ienari, 148, 192
Tokugawa Ieyasu, 18, 26–27, 42, 72–73, 117
Tokugawa Yoshimune, 131
Tokushima domain, 7–14 *passim*, 19, 22, 70, 118, 195, 198–204; and indigo, 7–8, 10–11, 22, 52, 58–59, 155–76 *passim*, 181–86, 195, 198–99; and conflict with

shogunate, 44–45, 171–176, 179–83, 195; and commoner unrest, 47, 164–68, 187–93; tax policy, 53, 155–68, 174f, 180–81, 189, 199; finances of, 58, 60, 155, 161–64, 170ff, 181ff, 250–51n22; and re-tainers' fiefs, 64–65, 178–79
Tokutomi Iichirō, 208–209
*ton'ya. See* wholesalers
Tosa, 4, 14, 19, 66, 190, 205
Totman, Conrad, 4
Tottori domain, 19
Toyotomi Hideyori, 154
Toyotomi Hideyoshi, 117, 154, 209
Tōdō house, 19
Tōdō Takatora, 42
Tōyama Shigeki, 56
Tsu domain, 19, 42
Tsugaru Chikataru, 143
Tsugaru house, 12, 20, 22–23, 115–18, 153, 198
Tsugaru Mondo, 123, 125
Tsugaru Nobuaki, 35
Tsugaru Nobuharu, 130, 143
Tsugaru Nobumasa, 130
Tsugaru Nobuyasu, 130
Tsugaru Nobuyuki, 12, 147–50
Tsugaru Tamenobu, 116–17
Tsugaru Tsuguakira, 153
Tsugaru Yasuchika, 117, 143, 145–46, 147–50
Tsugaru Yukinori. *See* Tsugaru Yukitsugu
Tsugaru Yukitsugu, 68, 147, 149–51, 153
Tsushima domain, 19–20
Tsuyama domain, 20

Udono Izumo, 172
Uesugi Harunori (Yōzan), 1–4, 13–14, 30, 43–45, 68, 87–92, 105, 114, 150–51, 195
Uesugi house, 1–4, 12–13, 19, 21, 72–73, 81
Uesugi Kagekatsu, 72
Uesugi Kenshin, 96
Uesugi Narinori, 114
Uesugi Norihiro, 1, 43
Uesugi Shigesada, 45, 84, 87–89, 91
Uesugi Tsunakatsu, 73

Uesugi Tsunanori, 73, 87
Utsunomiya domain, 17
Uwajima domain, 20
Uzami Shinsui, 132

Vlastos, Stephen, 63

wage labor, 55ff, 106, 111, 129–30,
  159, 190. See also retainers,
  by-employments of
Wakayama domain, 66
Warashina Ritsutada, 104
Warashina Shōhaku, 88–89
wax, 60, 76, 80, 94–96, 101, 106
weaving. See textiles
Weber, Max, 23
wheat, 7, 187
White, James, 23–25
wholesalers (ton'ya), 106–108, 112;
  and cartels, 106–108, 112,
  158–63, 168–75, 181–86
Wigen, Kären, 21
women, 78–79, 100, 103–105
  passim

yakuseki yakudaka (rank and stipend
  reforms), 177–78
Yamada house, 176–77
Yamada Oribe, 177–78
Yamada Oribe Masatsune, 177

Yamaga Sokō, 123
Yamaguchi Keiji, 56
Yanagawa domain, 20
Yonezawa domain, 1–4, 8–14 passim,
  19–23 passim, 31, 45, 52, 66, 70,
  118, 133, 150–51, 155, 187,
  195–202; relations with shogunate,
  2–4, 42, 69, 72–73,
  85; samurai by-employments, 10,
  50, 75, 104–114, 140; peasant
  protest, 47, 83, 86; demography,
  50, 73–74, 76–80, 101–103, 114;
  tax policy, 52–57 passim, 75–84
  passim, 93–94, 96, 101–103, 113–
  14; flax policy, 59, 76, 81–83, 100–
  101; lacquer policy, 57–58, 76, 80–
  81, 93–96, 100–101, 104; sericulture policy, 58, 79, 96, 101–103,
  105–114; finances of, 61, 71, 73–
  79, 85, 94, 102–103; retainers' fiefs
  and stipends, 64–66, 73–75, 84–
  85, 86–87, 97, 103–104, 111–13;
  retrenchment and austerity programs, 74–75, 88–89, 97, 114
Yoshikawa Jinzaemon, 140
Yoshimune, 131
Yoshino river, 11, 154–55, 160–65
Yōsan tebiki, 102, 105

Zanshū ryūei hikan, 19–20

Library of Congress Cataloging-in-Publication Data

Ravina, Mark.
    Land and lordship in early modern Japan / Mark Ravina.
        p.        cm.
    Includes bibliographical references and index.
    ISBN 0-8047-2898-4 (cloth : alk. paper)
        1. Japan—Politics and government—1600–1868.
    2. Yonezawa-han—Politics and government.
    3. Tokushima-han—Politics and government.
    4. Hirosaki-han—Politics and government.   I. Title.
    DS871.R38   1998
    952'.025—dc21                                                    97-51268

(∞) This book is printed on acid-free, recycled paper.

Original printing 1999
Last figure below indicates year of this printing:
08   07   06   05   04   03   02   01   00   99


Designed by Eleanor Mennick
Typeset by James P. Brommer in 10/12.5 Sabon